Mediterranean Diet Cookbook for Beginners 2022

1000 Easy and Affordable Recipes for Healthy Living, 4-Week Meal Plan to Boost Energy and Live Healthily

By Mary N. Wilson

Table of Contents

Chapter 3 Vegetable 41

Chapter 4 Fish and Seafood

Chapter 5 Beans 91

Chapter 6 Grain and Rice 104

Chapter 7 Poultry 117

Chapter 11 Salads 167

Chapter 12 Breads, Flatbreads, Pizzas, and More 185

Chapter 13 Snacks 196

Chapter 14 Desserts 210

Chapter 15 Sauce, Spices and Salad Dressing 226

INTRODUCTION

I have always loved traveling to the countries surrounding the Mediterranean Sea. I fell in love with the Mediterranean and its stunning cuisine in my early childhood because I've spent my school holidays in a small Montenegro coastal town for many years. I will carry those precious memories with me as long as I live. Not only that, but I can smell aromas and the taste today... A sunny day at the beach with a basket full of watermelons and peaches, a sweet aroma of ripe figs in my mouth, grilled corn on the cob on the Mediterranean narrow streets crowded with tourists, a strong smell of barbecue fills the air in our backyard, my window is open, and heady aroma of jasmine and roses fill the night air, coming into my room.

My grandma used to make the best Mediterranean dishes ever! From succulent Bolognese pasta and fish stew to dolmas and baklava, she tended to use fresh Mediterranean veggies and fruits, extra-virgin olive oil, domestic sheep cheeses, and fresh seafood from fish markets. In my mind's eye, I can picture my grandma in her big, spacious kitchen where she cooks hearty, juicy moussaka with eggplants and flavor-packed filling. She used high-quality extra-virgin olive oil to make the best homemade aioli I've ever eaten. As kids, we've also enjoyed homemade sour cream, she used to make it from domestic goat's milk that was purchased from our neighbor. I have a vivid memory of the special smell of grandma's garden, where rosemary grows all year long and oranges and lemons bloom in the springtime. Oh my, I feel nostalgic for those times!

If you're still struggling to lose weight and improve your health, if you're searching for the best diet to achieve your wellness goals, you are not alone. I've been almost obsessed with healthy diets and eating for the last ten years. In keeping with the healthiest eating patterns and the latest culinary trends, I put my focus on diversity, creativity, and nutrient density. However, there are numerous diets, it seemed that every other year some new dietary regimen appears on the stage. With so many diet programs to choose from, I was overwhelmed and confused by the information out there. I thought "Dieting is hard" until I figured it out – I am supposed to listen to my grandma! She is a 90 years old lady with incredibly cooking experience, and best of all, she keeps in good health as she ages. I will whisper her biggest cooking secret in your ear – Everything is made with love. Shhh! When it all boils down to my love of cooking, it should come as no surprise that the Mediterranean diet does the right thing for my health and well-being. My burning desire to simplify my diet and my passion for Mediterranean food sparked the idea for this cookbook. With this collection, you can bring the Mediterranean to your kitchen all year long, whenever you are on a jam-packed schedule but still crave something healthy and flavorful. As I wrote this cookbook, I was so inspired by some of the world's most iconic recipes such as Greek moussaka, Italian pasta, and Spanish paella.

Unlike typical Western-style diets, the Mediterranean diet emphasizes the importance of the "real" food, family meals, socializing, staying calm at mealtimes, and regular physical activity. Mediterranean people are often health-conscious, the mental state while you eat can have a profound effect on your overall health. From Greece and Italy to Morocco and Tunisia, the Mediterranean region presents a wide spectrum of cuisines. Mediterranean people, with their respect for the bounty and beauty of the sea, prepare seafood in numerous ways, bringing out a range of tastes and producing flavorful traditional dishes. Mediterranean meals possess character, they keep you coming back for more. From glistening fresh fish and fine, delicate shellfish in the markets, pungent dairy products on rural farms, large and fertile vineyards, and blooming fields of herbs in Mediterranean islands, this region is blessed with a wide variety of ingredients. They have a long growing season thanks to the mild climate as well as good soil, air, and water. With an incredible bounty of wholesome and fresh ingredients, each country that borders the Mediterranean has its specific flavors, depending on aromatics and the way of cooking. They are very proud of their diversity and uniqueness.

With this in mind, I decided to put together this recipe collection, so I believe everyone will benefit. Through this cookbook, you'll find old-fashioned and innovative ethnic-inspired meals, and learn how to prepare them with confidence and ease. I'm bursting to show you my culinary masterpieces, but I have to tell you everything I know about the Mediterranean diet first. Now let's get it started!

Chapter 1 The Beginner's Guide to the Mediterranean Diet

Now, the questions are, "Whom is this cookbook for? Who will benefit most from possessing this cookbook?" If you are overweight, struggling to find a realistic diet plan, the Mediterranean diet might be your first choice. This is not just another of weight-loss diets, this is a way of life. Aim to find a diet program that will work for you, a diet plan that you will love, and your heart and soul will sing and rejoice! Your happiness is the top priority, so keep this in mind when making your diet and exercise plan. Further, if you're suffering from conditions such as high blood pressure, diabetes, hypertension cognitive disease, or cardiovascular disease, this diet might be for you. The Mediterranean diet is rich in omega 3 fatty acids, and they are known for their pain-reducing effects, hence, it may help you reduce headaches, too. If you just want to boost your metabolism, protect your immune system, and improve your fitness level, the Mediterranean diet could offer multiple benefits.

To clarify even further, if you follow a vegan, vegetarian, or pescatarian diet, you can still adapt to the Mediterranean way of eating, just skip the food group you don't eat or find them adequate replacement. For instance, if you are a vegan, you can still consume whole grains, legumes, fruits, veggies, seeds, nuts, and healthy fats. Dairy alternatives include plant-based milk, yogurt, and cheese, while good substitute for plant-based protein includes tofu, quinoa, and legumes. Long story short, everyone can adapt and enjoy this diet! It is important to set realistic goals and stick to your plan. This gives grounds for optimism for many people with health problems.

The Mediterranean Diet Pyramid

This is a general food pyramid guideline that is developed based on the communal eating habits of the Mediterranean people. In addition to eating habits, it implies an active lifestyle and food socialization that means the practice of eating together in a social group such as family, friends, or colleagues. A general guideline to bear in mind is that you should base every meal around vegetables, fruits, whole grains, legumes, and healthy fats, consume seafood twice a week, consume moderate portions of dairy, eggs, poultry, and red wine, limit saturated fats, red meat, and sweets as much as you can.

Base every meal around:

Vegetables – Eat seasonal and local products as much as possible, whether you live on the Mediterranean coast or not. No veggies are off-limits on this dietary regimen, you can eat them fresh or frozen, baked or roasted, sautéed or boiled. Avoid deep-fried vegetables because frying in lots of oil can add a lot of calories to your meal, causing the loss of valuable nutrients. The best Mediterranean vegetable options include zucchini, tomato, cucumbers, bell peppers, mushrooms, broccoli, eggplant, okra, leafy greens, cabbage, and lettuce. As a general rule, experts recommend regular consumption of greens on the Mediterranean diet for optimal health. Hence, throw chicory, amaranth, dandelion, and spinach into your favorite Mediterranean salad and enjoy!

Fruits – People in the Mediterranean region consume more citrus fruits than the rest of the world. Although there are several traditional Mediterranean fruits (cantaloupe, apricots, figs, grapes, and plums), mandarins, oranges, and lemon rank high on every healthy diet list, due to their rich levels of antioxidants. Plus, citrus fruits are rich in vitamins, minerals, soluble fiber, and flavonoids. People from countries bordering the Mediterranean Sea follow a simple rule – choose fresh, locally grown products, as close to your living place as possible, or grow your own food.

Whole grains – Mediterranean cooking focuses on whole grains paired with traditional veggies, legumes, aromatics. A typical Mediterranean plate always consists of some kind of this nutritional powerhouse such as couscous, bulgur, barley, buckwheat, or farro. Good sources of healthy carbohydrates include whole-grain bread or pasta made from whole grains.

Beans and Pulses – Beans, chickpea, and lentils are a typical source of protein and fiber on the Mediterranean diet. As a valuable and affordable staple of the Mediterranean diet, they make a healthy and delicious complement to the seafood and vegetables in many Mediterranean recipes.

Nuts and Seeds – Almonds, walnuts, pumpkin seeds, sunflower seeds are also staple foods, so we can't imagine Mediterranean cooking without them. They are an excellent source of healthy fats and plant protein. Tahini (sesame paste) is widely used in the Mediterranean cuisines, while seed oils can be used to treat many conditions.

Healthy fats – Olive oil, avocado, and fatty fish, with their numerous health benefits, contribute to the popularity of the Mediterranean diet. Olive trees are endlessly generous to the people in the Mediterranean region. In every Mediterranean kitchen, olive oil is an absolute must, from fried foods and salads to sauces and snacks, olive oil can be used in so many ways. When dining at many Mediterranean restaurants, instead of using butter, people like to dip whole-grain bread or cornbread in a mix of olive oil and fresh herbs. Olive oil is not only rich in phytonutrients but is also loaded with powerful antioxidants that have certain anti-cancer properties.

Fish and Seafood – Seafood is a primary protein source on a typical Mediterranean menu. Fatty fish, also called oily fish, makes an excellent source of Omega-3 fatty acids. Since they are considered good fats, they can be beneficial to your heart, arteries, circulation, and lungs. Furthermore, recent studies have suggested that a healthy heart is linked to better brain health. Experts recommend 8 ounces (ca. 302g) or two servings of omega-3-rich fish per week for adults.

Herbs and Spices – Spice up your Mediterranean diet with basil, oregano, oregano, mint, cinnamon, allspice, dill, cilantro, parsley, rosemary, and other herbs. Besides being fragrant and delicious, herbs and spices have endless health benefits.

Beverages – Drink fresh water and herbal teas every day, enjoy red wine in moderation, make smoothies and lemonade, pay attention to added sugar.

Foods you should consume in low to moderate amounts:

Dairy products and Eggs – Eat cheese and yogurt in moderation. Cut back on dairy and eggs in meals. Instead of having your favorite beverage with regular milk, try coffee with almond milk. Pile your plate with vegetables and whole grains, add 1-2 hard-boiled eggs and a few drizzles of extra-virgin olive oil, to garnish, add a few sprinkles of your favorite Mediterranean herbs to enhance flavors and awaken all your senses!

Food that should be eaten very rarely:

Meat and Poultry – Opt for lean cuts such as chicken breasts or lean ground beef. Replace meat with plant protein and fish.

Foods to avoid on a healthy Mediterranean diet:

Avoid hydrogenated oil such as highly-processed palm oil, trans fats such as margarine, saturated fats, deep-fried foods, junk food high in sodium and sugar, refined grains, and processed meat. Avoid sweets, soft drinks, sweetened tea and coffee, and energy drinks.

And last but not least ¬– A healthy lifestyle isn't just dieting and calorie counting. Physical activity is extremely important for good mental and physical health.

Scientific Health Benefits of the Mediterranean Diet

What does "healthy eating" actually mean? There is so much conflicting information on the Internet, but every diet expert must agree that a healthy eating plan is designed to provide your body with the essential nutrients. It excludes junk food, highly-processed foods, and artificial ingredients. In fact, your eating plan should decrease your risk of health conditions as well as premature death. According to the study in JAMA Internal Medicine, which tracked eating habits in more than 44,000 French men and women over eight years, eating instant foods and deep-fried foods could significantly shorten our life. They state that "In this cohort study of 44 551 French adults 45 years or older, a 10% increase in the proportion of ultra-processed food consumption was statistically significantly associated with a 14% higher risk of all-cause mortality." [1]

Hence, it has been scientifically proven that healthy eating patterns are key factors that contribute to our overall well-being. Many health benefits come from an eating pattern that promotes a variety of wholesome and real ingredients. As you probably already know, healthy food choices implicate a quality lifestyle that is free of mental and physical illness. In other words, you can significantly improve the quality of your life on the Mediterranean diet. It can help in reducing the risk of serious diseases and treating certain conditions such as stroke, hyperglycemia, diabetes, and cancer. It can also boost your immune system and metabolism naturally. Remember, what you put on your table can affect every aspect of your health, from ideal weight to blood pressure and inflammation.

- **Heart-healthy diet**

When we say "Mediterranean food", the first things that come to mind are Italian pizza, Greek gyros, and Turkish baklava. A real Mediterranean diet is a heart-healthy and weight loss diet based on local veggies and fruits, as well as nuts, seafood, olive oil, and domestic wine. If you are not highly motivated to dietary changes, keep in mind that the world's healthiest populations live on the Mediterranean cost. That is not a coincidence. Their rates of cardiovascular and other chronic disease are among the lowest in the world. That's why this eating pattern has been recommended by medical experts for years due to its distinctiveness and numerous health benefits.

The Mediterranean diet is one of the best heart-healthy diets, and we all know that heart disease is the leading cause of death, the number one killer disease at the global level. The Centers for Disease Control and Prevention, the national public health agency of the United States, states that "heart disease is the leading cause of death for women in the United States, killing 301,280 women in 2019 – or about 1 in every 5 female deaths." [2]

Experts are warning of obesity, which is one of the most common risk factors for stroke. As a general rule, obesity can significantly increase bad cholesterol and triglyceride levels, moreover, it can lower good HDL cholesterol (high-density lipoproteins). In this way, overweight and obesity can notably contribute to heart disease. Obesity goes hand in hand with high blood pressure and hypertension. Fortunately, our food is the best medicine, so you just have to find out what works best for you. Eating a well-balanced diet such as a Mediterranean diet is a good way to maintain ideal weight. Every pound that you lose can help you keep your heart healthy and strong. The best heart-healthy foods include whole grains, beans, tomatoes, almonds, leafy greens, fish, and olive oil. And the Mediterranean diet promotes those super foods!

- **Diabetes prevention**

Numerous studies tend to show that individuals with unhealthy eating patterns, sedentary lifestyle, and obesity, have a higher risk of developing type 2 diabetes type. [3]

Unfortunately, this is a short list of risks, in reality, lots of factors can contribute to someone being at risk of developing this condition. One thing is for sure, though: good eating habits and a healthy lifestyle could help prevent and control type 2 diabetes.

- **Immune system booster**

Simple health habits can go a long way in improving your body's natural defense. You should eat more whole plant foods, healthy fats (such as avocado and nuts), omega-3 fatty acids (such as olive oil and seeds). One of the greatest rules of a healthy diet such as a Mediterranean diet are: eat smart, drink smart, enjoy every meal.

- **Losing weight naturally**

Highly refined carbs and processed foods that are loaded with sugars may remarkably contribute to overweight. Excess weight may likewise increase your risk of chronic health conditions such as atherosclerosis, metabolic syndrome, sleep disorders, high blood pressure, and certain cancers. The higher the amount of fat cells in your body, the greater the risk of serious disease. Unhealthy eating patterns such as eating too much saturated and trans fats, lack of physical activity, and streets are key factors to overweight and obesity. Moreover, being overweight can trigger hormone changes and cause serious complications. The Mediterranean diet can help you shed extra pounds and burn body fat naturally. Add an extra serving of high protein food to your diet each day, good protein-rich foods on the Mediterranean diet include lean poultry, seafood, dairy products, and legumes. Then, decrease your intake of refined carbs such as pasta, white bread, pastry, and instant cereal, consume refined carbs in moderation and replace them with brown rice and whole grains such as quinoa, buckwheat, and barley as much as you can. Further, increase your intake of high-fiber foods such as fresh fruits and vegetables, beans, whole grains, and nuts. And last but not least, choose natural, healthy and nutritious fats that are less processed and lower in sugar. Opt for avocado, fatty fish, chia seeds, and extra-virgin olive oil. High-quality olive oil is an essential component and the star of the Mediterranean diet, which has been proven to possess enormous health benefits regarding weight management.

- **Reduced risk of mental and cognitive problems**

What we eat doesn't just affect our physical body: it can have a profound impact on our mental health. Eating well can also improve your mood and your cognitive functions. There are factors that can negatively affect neurogenesis such as sugar, saturated fats, alcohol, overeating, under-eating, and so forth. Consume plenty of fruits and vegetables, whole grains, beans and pulses, nuts, olive oil, low-to-moderate amounts of fish and eggs, and low amounts of high-quality red wine.

Quick Start to a Mediterranean Diet:

The easiest way to make the change to a Mediterranean diet is to start small and grow big. Although you may have tried Mediterranean dishes before, you probably associate them with special cooking skills and techniques. Nothing could be further from the truth! For instance, these recipes call for food that you most likely already have in your kitchen! Do you have pasta, rice, a can of tomatoes, and a pinch of oregano in your pantry? I think it is a good start. The next question: Do you know how to cook pasta? If you know some basic steps such as water to pasta ratio or cooking time, it is a good

start as well. You will learn how to make the perfect pasta by browsing through this cookbook. Learning how to choose and prepare Mediterranean foods will help you make the most delicious, well-balanced Mediterranean meals for you and your family.

As you get more comfortable with the Mediterranean diet, you will be able to fit your eating habits into your new lifestyle. It won't be too difficult to achieve, since the Mediterranean diet is more about good eating habits rather than sacrificing pleasure and following a rigid plan. Although there is not a rigid plan, you should follow three simple rules. Rule number one: base every meal around fresh and clean foods, or foods in minimally-processed forms. In order to get the most health benefits from your food, choose healthier cooking methods such as baking, roasting, grilling, or boiling. Rule two, keep your pantry stocked with staples and your meal will practically make itself. These staples include canned beans, olives, canned tomatoes, sun-dried tomatoes, canned fish, nuts, hard cheese, and tahini. Rule three, "Eating the rainbow" is one of the best approaches to dieting, and the same goes for the Mediterranean diet. Go ahead, define your wellness goals and eat more staple foods than you normally do. So easy!

5 Tips from Top Nutritionists and Professional Chefs

- **Well-balanced meals**

Remember – balance is the key to the best Mediterranean dishes. Balance sea salt with sweet and earthy flavors, for example, salty fish goes well with sweet potatoes and acidic ingredients. Balance smoke and heat with aromatic herbs and garlic. Spicy foods can be balanced with something sweet, while sweet foods pair well with smoke, acid, and aromatics. Add a splash of vinegar or lemon juice to cooked meat or fish at the last minute to "lock" the flavor. Here's an extra tip from a longtime chef: In addition to focusing on perfect cooking, make sure you make it fun!

- **Stock your Mediterranean pantry**

In addition to staples such as legumes, grains, canned food, and fresh products, there are ingredients that can enhance the meal's flavor and improve its quality. Do not forget Mediterranean herbs and aromatics. Mediterranean spice blends can save your time and nerves, especially if you are new to Mediterranean cooking. A considerable number of classic, old-fashioned Mediterranean dishes are made with a few simple ingredients, but aromatics will give the simplest meal that extra sparkle. Do not underestimate the power of good-quality olive oil, garlic, leafy greens, dried fruits, seeds, and nuts!

- **Macronutrients on a Mediterranean diet**

"Calculate your macros." Did you hear that advice? It may sound cliché, but dieting isn't just about how much you eat, but what to eat. When it comes to your caloric intake, your body needs fundamental nutrients to keep your energy levels high and burn body fat. Macronutrients are building blocks that help your body to perform these tasks, hence, finding your macronutrient balance ensures that you will feel good in your skin without feeling deprived. There are 3 macronutrients: carbohydrates, proteins, and fats. The general rule of thumb is – carbohydrates should make up 35% of your total energy intake, 25% to 35% of calories should come from protein (with a heavy emphasis on lean protein), and 25%- 35% fat (focusing on healthy and natural unsaturated fats).

- **Meal Prep**

Wouldn't it be nice if you were like some of the foodies and nutritionists who eat well all week? Even on workdays? Their secrets don't require too much time. It is meal prepping! In other words, they prefer cooking shortcuts, and meal preparing is one of their favorites. Nutritionists and chefs usually cook big batches of grains, protein, and sauces and then, they store prepared food in airtight containers or Ziplock bags in the refrigerator or freezer. Be sure to label your food for the freezer. Consequently, they can combine these prepared items for lunch or dinner throughout the week. Meal prep is the key to controlling your healthy diet and staying fit forever! Isn't it easy?

- **Small swaps, big health benefits**

There are easy Mediterranean diet swaps you can make right now. When it comes to protein-rich foods, instead of red meat, you can eat seafood or beans. Try whole-grain bread or pasta instead of white bread and pasta that are made from refined flour. Brown rice makes a great substitute for white rice, while sugar and sweets can be replaced with fresh or dried fruits. Further, a health swap for animal-based fat is a plant-based fat. When you're eating out, swap part of your meal for extra vegetables or a salad. Order a soup or a salad before your main course, this little trick can significantly reduce your total calorie intake, making you feel full.

Myths and Facts about the Mediterranean Diet

Myth 1: It can be hard to stick to a Mediterranean diet

If you are sick and tired of dieting, give this diet a try. This is more than just a diet, this is a healthy lifestyle that can help you improve your relationship with food, tackle overeating and find a diet that you can sustain for a lifetime.

Myth 2: Weight-loss Med diet is all about restricted portions and boring foods

Nothing could be further from the truth! This dietary pattern is characterized by high consumption of various and palatable foods, preventing malnutrition and under-eating. The Mediterranean diet has been studied for decades, and research repeatedly proves that this eating pattern can help you lose weight naturally and safely.

Myth 3: Fats are unhealthy

When all is said and done, we know that not all fat is the same. The Mediterranean diet emphasizes the difference between good fats and bad fats. Besides being extremely healthy, eating good fats in moderation can contribute to healthy skin, provide your body with energy, and fight viruses and bacteria.

Myth 4: Grains make you gain weight

In their attempts to lose weight, people often try to limit carbs. In reality, eating a moderate amount of healthy carbs such as whole grains can help you lose weight and maintain ideal weight rather than practicing a short-term solution with limited and unhealthy options. A balanced mix of good carbs, protein, and healthy fats has been associated with a reduced risk of obesity and other conditions.

What is so fascinating about this Mediterranean Recipe Collection?

Do you want healthy and delicious homemade food on your table? Do you think that cooking homemade food from scratch is time-consuming and difficult, so you simply do not have nerves and hours to spend in the kitchen? If so, this recipe collection might help. With today's busy lifestyles, most of us do not want to spend all day in the kitchen, cooking, serving, and cleaning. After all, our diet should improve our lives, not consume them! These recipes do use natural, easy-to-find ingredients, emphasizing real food without additives or preservatives. All the recipes have easy-to-follow instructions. Regardless of the complexity of this cuisine, I like to keep it simple for everyone, from enthusiastic beginners to skilled home cooks. These recipes are timeless and perfectly adapted to any lifestyle, promoting a wide variety of dishes, making cooking a cinch.

Once you give these recipes a try, you and your cookbook are sure to become inseparable in the kitchen! I hope it will help you start your culinary adventure. Good luck and bon appétit!

FAQs of the Mediterranean Diet

At this stage of this book, you must have read a lot about the Mediterranean diet. I have taken you through what the Mediterranean diet is, its history, the meals that make up the diet, and the health benefits of maintaining this diet. You have read a lot about it, and you have questions lingering on your mind. In this chapter, I will answer questions that are frequently asked about the Mediterranean diet and clear any doubts you may have about this diet.

1. **The Mediterranean diet uses mainly olive oil and also includes nuts. Aren't these high in fats?**

The fats contained in olive oil and nuts are healthy unsaturated fats, compared to the fat that is contained in butter, margarine, or other cooking fats. Olive oil and nuts are a good fat substitute for your meals.

2. **What are some tips for beginners on the Mediterranean diet?**

If you are just starting your journey on the Mediterranean diet, these are the basic things you should know:

* Eat fruits and vegetables daily

* Cook with olive oil, and avoid using butter, margarine, or another form of solid fats in your cooking

* Eat fish at least twice a week

* Avoid eating processed or canned food

* Consume whole-grain

* Eat nuts and food rich in fiber

* Avoid regular consumption of red meat and sweets

* Drink wine in moderation

* Savor and enjoy each meal with friends and family.

3. **Why is it called the Mediterranean Diet?**

It is called a Mediterranean diet because it is particular to countries that are around the Mediterranean Sea.

4. **Will I always feel hungry once I start following the Mediterranean Diet?**

The Mediterranean diet isn't really a "diet" that controls how and when you should eat. It is more of a lifestyle of healthy living. You don't have to starve or stay hungry to be on the Mediterranean diet. When you are hungry, you can eat nuts or drink a vegetable smoothie or any meal at all that falls under this diet. The main thing is to eat fresh, healthy meals that fall under this diet.

5. **Is it easy to follow the Mediterranean Diet correctly?**

It is easy to follow the Mediterranean diet correctly, as long as you know the right meals to eat. The Mediterranean diet doesn't have a strict way of eating or a rule you have to follow. I follow the diet, and it has been easy for me. The meals are not difficult to find or prepare.

6. Why should I abide by the Mediterranean Diet?

The Mediterranean diet has many health benefits that will help improve your health. People who follow this way of eating have a lower risk of suffering coronary or cardiovascular disease, stroke, and heart diseases. This means that you have a higher chance of living longer if you follow this diet rather than sticking to an unhealthy eating lifestyle. It is also a good way to lose weight and enjoy delicious meals all at once.

7. Is it true that the Mediterranean diet is just another fad diet?

This is not true. The Mediterranean diet has been in existence for decades and will continue to be for a long time. It is a long-term diet you can adopt to live a long healthy life. From the history part I wrote in this book, you should know it has been existing way longer than you can imagine. It is a lifestyle for those living in the Mediterranean Sea area.

8. Is it true that the Mediterranean Diet is a fairly new way of eating?

It is not a fairly new way of eating. It has been existing among countries surrounding the Mediterranean Sea for a long time.

9. Will the Mediterranean Diet involve foods that are foreign and hard to access?

The Mediterranean diet doesn't involve foods that are foreign and hard to access. You can get many of the meal ingredients in stores around you. It is not a complicated way of eating, and you can get it easily. I get my ingredients from stores around me. I don't travel to the Mediterranean areas to get my ingredients.

10. Am I allowed to consume sweets or meats if I follow the Mediterranean Diet?

You are allowed to eat meat and/or sweets when you are on this diet, but they should only be consumed and in small quantity, maybe once a month. What I do is replace my sweets with fruits and nuts, and I eat fish more than I eat meat.

11. Is it true that I will lose weight if I follow the Mediterranean Diet?

The Mediterranean diet isn't really a weight loss diet. It is more of a healthy eating lifestyle, but you can also lose weight while you're on this diet. I have been able to maintain a healthy weight since I started this diet.

12. Can I eat whatever I want on the Mediterranean diet?

No, you cannot. You shouldn't eat sweets, processed or canned meals, saturated and solid fats while on this diet. You can only eat sweets and red meat, but not as regular meals while you're on this diet.

4-Week Meal Plan

Below is a tabular representation of what a Mediterranean diet meal plan should look like:

Week One

Week-1	Breakfast	Lunch	Dinner	Snack
Mon	Tomato and Goat Cheese Frittata (page 22)	Toasted Barley and Almond Pilaf (page 109)	Sea Scallops with White Bean Purée (page 72)	Hummus Dip (page 200)
Tues	Breakfast Berry Smoothie (page 33)	Almond-Crusted Salmon Steaks (page 72)	American Baked Ziti (page 138)	Orange-Marinated Olives (page 207)
Wed	Prosciutto, Avocado, and Veggie Sandwiches (page 18)	Baked Za'atar Pizza (page 186)	Balsamic Asparagus Salad (page 175)	Honey-Glazed Rosemary Almonds (page 207)
Thurs	Peach Smoothie (page 39)	Whole-Wheat Couscous with Apricots (page 135)	Hazelnut and Leek Soup (page 144)	An apple
Fri	Chickpea and Hummus Patties in Pitas (page 17)	Cod Gratin with Olives and Leeks (page 74)	Asparagus and Grape Tomato Pasta (page 137)	Plain Greek yogurt
Sat	Cheesy Green Bites (page 20)	Brown Rice and Lentils (page 110)	North African Veggie and Bean Stew (page 97)	Sage-Basil White Beans (page 207)
Sun	Dilled Tuna and Avocado Salad Sandwich (page 33)	Buckwheat Groats with Root Vegetables (page 104)	Sautéed Sole Fillet (page 83)	Paprika Chickpeas (page 205)

Week Two

Week-2	Breakfast	Lunch	Dinner	Snack
Mon	Garlicky Mushrooms (page 30)	Spaghetti with Mussels and White Wine (page 134)	Moroccan Tomato and Pepper Salad (page 169)	Turkish Spiced Mixed-Nuts (page 206)
Tues	Morning Creamy Iced Coffee (page 38)	Veggie and Double Cheese Pizza (page 186)	Shrimp and Leek Soup (page 147)	Light Pesto Cucumber Boats (page 197)
Wed	Greek Feta Cheese Pie (page 22)	Pan-Roasted Sea Bass Fillet (page 83)	Rice Salad with Asparagus and Parsley (page 113)	Hot Spiced Roasted Cashews (page 208)
Thurs	Healthy Green Smoothie (page 32)	Barley Pilaf with Mushrooms (page 114)	Za'atar Bread Slices (page 187)	A banana
Fri	Honey Spinach Muffins (page 37)	Whole-Wheat Fusilli with Chickpea Sauce (page 139)	Turmeric-Spiced Organic Chickpeas (page 50)	Savory Mediterranean Spiced Popcorn (page 204)
Sat	Parmesan Spinach Pie (page 29)	Provençal Hake Fillet (page 86)	Bow Ties with Zucchini (page 138)	Plain Greek yogurt
Sun	Avocado Toast with Tomato (page 21)	Rice with Oranges, Green Olives, and Almonds (page 112)	White Bean, Kale, and Tomato Soup (page 147)	Healthy Trail Mix (page 202)

Week Three

Week-3	Breakfast	Lunch	Dinner	Snack
Mon	Tangy Almond-Pistachio Smoothie (page 21)	Moroccan Chicken Thighs and Vegetable Tagine (page 120)	Grilled Lemony Squid (page 76)	A peach
Tues	Pumpkin Layers with Honey Granola (page 34)	Penne with Cherry Tomato and Arugula (page 139)	Beans and Kale Fagioli (page 149)	Orange-Marinated Olives (page 207)
Wed	Ricotta Strawberry and Basil Toast (page 31)	Veggie and Double Cheese Pizza (page 186)	Jumbo Shrimp with Fresh Parsley (page 78)	Hummus Dip (page 200)
Thurs	Blueberry and Chia Seeds Smoothie (page 34)	Mediterranean Lentils and Brown Rice (page 115)	Avocado and Tomato Gazpacho (page 151)	Plain Greek yogurt
Fri	Whole Wheat Applesauce Blueberry Muffins (page 23)	Pesto and Roasted Red Pepper Pizza (page 187)	Sea Bass with Orange-Olive Salad (page 71)	Light Pesto Cucumber Boats (page 197)
Sat	Baby Spinach, Tomato, and Egg Wraps (page 31)	Warm Farro with Mushrooms and Shallot (page 107)	Citrus Fennel and Pecan Salad (page 171)	An apple
Sun	Parmesan Green Oatmeal (page 23)	Panko-Crusted Fish Sticks (page 76)	Warm Couscous (page 136)	Healthy Trail Mix (page 202)

Week Four

Week-4	Breakfast	Lunch	Dinner	Snack
Mon	Lemony Breakfast Cakes with Berry Syrup (page 26)	Vegetable Kebabs (page 61)	Salmon Fillets with Dill (page 88)	Curried Roasted Walnuts (page 202)
Tues	Avocado Toast with Tomato (page 21)	Roasted White Beans with Herb (page 99)	Chicken Thigh with Roasted Artichokes (page 123)	A banana
Wed	Parmesan Spinach Pie (page 29)	Healthy Vegetable Broth (page 51)	Tilapia Fillet with Onion and Avocado (page 84)	Apple Pockets Bake (page 223)
Thurs	Peach Smoothie (page 39)	Oregano Wheat Berries with Veggie (page 110)	Moroccan Lamb Chops and Lentil Soup (page 157)	A pear
Fri	Maple Cherry and Almond Oatmeal (page 27)	Chickpeas with Coriander and Sage (page 95)	Provençal Hake Fillet (page 86)	Cool Vanilla Apple Tart (page 218)
Sat	Baklava Hot Porridge with Walnut (page 22)	Balsamic-Honey Collard Greens (page 56)	Lemon-Herb Spatchcock Chicken (page 121)	Citrus-Thyme Chickpeas (page 199)
Sun	Egg in a Hole with Avocado (page 28)	Turkish Green Lentil Soup (page 148)	Panko-Crusted Fish Sticks (page 76)	Baklava with Syrup (page 211)

About This Cookbook

I hope you enjoyed reading this book and you are ready to start your own diet. I will do a quick recap of what I said in this book, so you can go right shopping and start preparing your meals.

The Mediterranean diet isn't just a dieting plan that you have to strictly follow, it is more of a healthy lifestyle. The history of this diet is traced to countries that surround the Mediterranean Sea. To be on the Mediterranean diet, you have to consume unsaturated fats, vegetables, fruits, nuts, fish, eggs, wine, and meals rich in fiber and protein. You can also eat meat and sweets while on this diet but in small quantities and rarely. This diet also involves enjoying each meal with friends and family.

This diet has many benefits, including reduced risks of cancer, cardiovascular and coronary diseases, blood sugar level, stroke, etc. There is nothing really spectacular about this diet because they are meals you can easily access. You also get to lose weight while on this diet.

In this book, I have explained the Mediterranean diet, its benefits, and the right way to follow the diet, and I have answered possible questions you may have about the diet. You also have access to a meal plan and the Mediterranean diet pyramid to guide you through this diet. You are more likely to live a disease-free, healthy, and long life if you adopt this healthy lifestyle of eating.

Now, let's take this cookbook to your kitchen, and try the delicious and easy recipes, you will see a new you a few days. Happy dieting!

Chapter 2 Breakfast

Chickpea and Hummus Patties in Pitas

Prep time: 15 minutes | Cook time: 13 minutes | Serves: 4

1 (15-ounce / 425-g) can chickpeas, drained and rinsed
½ cup lemony garlic hummus or ½ cup prepared hummus
½ cup whole-wheat panko bread crumbs
1 large egg
2 teaspoons dried oregano
¼ teaspoon freshly ground black pepper
1 tablespoon extra-virgin olive oil
1 cucumber, unpeeled (or peeled if desired), cut in half lengthwise
1 (6-ounce / 170-g) container 2% plain Greek yogurt
1 garlic clove, minced
2 whole-wheat pita breads, cut in half
1 medium tomato, cut into 4 thick slices

1. In a large bowl, mash the chickpeas with a potato masher or fork until coarsely smashed (they should still be somewhat chunky). Add the hummus, bread crumbs, egg, oregano, and pepper. Stir well to combine. With your hands, form the mixture into 4 (½-cup-size) patties. Press each patty flat to about ¾ inch thick and put on a plate.
2. In a large skillet over medium-high heat, heat the oil until very hot, about 3 minutes. Cook the patties for 5 minutes, then flip with a spatula. Cook for an additional 5 minutes.
3. While the patties are cooking, shred half of the cucumber with a box grater or finely chop with a knife. In a small bowl, stir together the shredded cucumber, yogurt, and garlic to make the tzatziki sauce. Slice the remaining half of the cucumber into ¼-inch-thick slices and set aside.
4. Toast the pita breads. To assemble the sandwiches, lay the pita halves on a work surface. Into each pita, place a few slices of cucumber, a chickpea patty, and a tomato slice, then drizzle the sandwich with the tzatziki sauce and serve.

PER SERVING
Calories: 308, Fat: 8.2g, Total Carbohydrates: 45.1g, Protein: 14.9g, Fiber: 7.8g, Sodium: 321mg

Greek-Style Raspberry Yogurt

Prep time: 5 minutes | Cook time: 8 hours | Serves: 12

1 pound (454 g) hulled and halved raspberries
1 cup maple syrup
3 tablespoons gelatin
1 tablespoon fresh
orange juice
8 cups low-fat milk
¼ cup Greek yogurt containing active cultures

1. In a bowl, mash raspberries with a potato masher. Add maple syrup and stir well to dissolve, let soak for 30 minutes at room temperature. Add in lemon juice and gelatin and mix well until dissolved.
2. Remove the mixture and place in a sealable container, close, and allow to sit for 12 hours to 24 hours at room temperature before placing in a refrigerator. Refrigerate for a maximum of 2 weeks.
3. Into the cooker, add milk and close the lid. The steam vent should be set to Venting then to Sealing.
4. Select Yogurt until "Boil" is displayed on the readings. When complete there will be a display of "Yogurt" on the screen. Open the lid and using a food thermometer ensure the milk temperature is at least 185° F.
5. Transfer the steel pot to a wire rack and allow cool for 30 minutes until milk has reached 110ºF (43ºC).
6. In a bowl, mix ½ cup warm milk and yogurt. Transfer the mixture into the remaining warm milk and stir without having to scrape the steel pot's bottom.
7. Take the pot back to the base of the pot and seal the lid. Select Yogurt mode and cook for 8 hours.
8. Allow the yogurt to chill in a refrigerator for 1 to 2 hours.
9. Transfer the chilled yogurt to a large bowl and stir in fresh raspberry jam.

PER SERVING
Calories: 175, Fat: 3.5g, Carbohydrates: 30.8g, Protein: 6.25g, Sugar: 26.56g, Fiber: 2.5g, Sodium: 84mg

Cumin Scrambled Eggs

Prep time: 10 minutes | Cook time: 25 minutes | Serves: 4

2 tablespoons olive oil
1 small red onion, chopped
1 medium green pepper, cored, seeded, and finely chopped
1 red Fresno or jalapeño chili pepper, seeded and cut into thin strips
3 medium tomatoes, chopped
Sea salt and freshly ground pepper, to taste
1 tablespoon ground cumin
1 teaspoon ground coriander
4 large eggs, lightly beaten

1. Heat the olive oil in a large, heavy skillet over medium heat.
2. Add the onion and cook until soft and translucent, 6 to 7 minutes.
3. Add the peppers and continue to cook until soft, another 4 to 5 minutes. Add in the tomatoes and season to taste.
4. Stir in the cumin and coriander.
5. Simmer for 10 minutes over medium-low heat.
6. Add the eggs, stirring them into the mixture to distribute.
7. Cover the skillet and cook until the eggs are set but still fluffy and tender, about 5 to 6 minutes more.
8. Divide between 4 plates and serve immediately.

PER SERVING
Calories: 154, Fat: 11.89g, Carbohydrates: 8.92g, Protein: 4.46g, Sugar: 4.47g, Fiber: 2g, Sodium: 18mg

Prosciutto, Avocado, and Veggie Sandwiches

Prep time: 10 minutes | Cook time: 0 minutes | Serves: 4

8 slices whole-grain or whole-wheat bread
1 ripe avocado, halved and pitted
¼ teaspoon freshly ground black pepper
¼ teaspoon kosher or sea salt
4 romaine lettuce leaves, torn into 8 pieces total
1 large, ripe tomato, sliced into 8 rounds
2 ounces (57 g) prosciutto, cut into 8 thin slices

1. Toast the bread and place on a large platter.
2. Scoop the avocado flesh out of the skin into a small bowl. Add the pepper and salt. Using a fork or a whisk, gently mash the avocado until it resembles a creamy spread. Spread the avocado mash over all 8 pieces of toast.
3. To make one sandwich, take one slice of avocado toast, and top it with a lettuce leaf, tomato slice, and prosciutto slice. Top with another slice each of lettuce, tomato, and prosciutto, then cover with a second piece of avocado toast (avocado-side down on the prosciutto). Repeat with the remaining ingredients to make three more sandwiches and serve.

PER SERVING
Calories: 262, Fat: 12.2g, Total Carbohydrates: 35.1g, Protein: 7.9g, Fiber: 9.8g, Sodium: 162mg

Spanish Tuna Tortilla with Bell Peppers

Prep time: 10 minutes | Cook time: 17 minutes | Serves: 4

4 large eggs
¼ cup olive oil
2 small russet potatoes, diced
1 small onion, chopped
1 roasted red bell pepper, sliced
1 (7-ounce / 198-g) tuna, flaked
2 plum tomatoes, seeded and diced
1 teaspoon dried tarragon

1. Preheat the broiler on high.
2. Crack the eggs in a large bowl and whisk them together until just combined. Heat the olive oil in a large, oven-safe, nonstick or cast-iron skillet over medium-low heat.
3. Add the potatoes and cook until slightly soft, about 7 minutes. Add the onion and the peppers and cook until soft, 3 to 5 minutes.
4. Add the tuna, tomatoes, and tarragon to the skillet and stir to combine, then add the eggs.
5. Cook for 7 to 10 minutes until the eggs are bubbling from the bottom and the bottom is slightly brown.
6. Place the skillet into the oven on 1 of the first 2 racks, and cook until the middle is set and the top is slightly brown.
7. Slice into wedges and serve warm or at room temperature.

PER SERVING
Calories: 400, Fat: 18.59g, Carbohydrates: 39.91g, Protein: 19.89g, Sugar: 5.24g, Fiber: 3.6g, Sodium: 92mg

Cheddar Broccoli and Bell Pepper Frittata

Prep time: 15 minutes | Cook time: 15 minutes | Serves: 4

4 eggs	1 cup chopped broccoli, pre-cooked
8 ounces (227 g) spinach, finely chopped	4 tablespoons olive oil
½ cup Cheddar cheese	½ teaspoon salt
½ cup fresh ricotta cheese	¼ teaspoon freshly ground black pepper
3 cherry tomatoes, halved	¼ teaspoon dried oregano
¼ cup red bell pepper, chopped	½ cup fresh celery leaves, finely chopped

1. Heat olive oil on Sauté. Add spinach and cook for 5 minutes, stirring occasionally. Add tomatoes, peppers, and broccoli. Cook for more 3 to 4 minutes.
2. In a bowl, Whisk 2 eggs, Cheddar, and ricotta. Pour in the pot and cook for 2 more minutes. Then, crack the remaining 2 eggs and cook for another 5 minutes.
3. When done, press Cancel. Serve immediately with chopped celery leaves.

PER SERVING
Calories: 329, Fat: 27.73g, Carbohydrates: 5.88g, Protein: 15.03g, Sugar: 1.85g, Fiber: 2g, Sodium: 507mg

Shakshuka with Cilantro

Prep time: 15 minutes | Cook time: 18 minutes | Serves: 4

2 tablespoons extra-virgin olive oil	into small pieces
1 cup chopped shallots	¼ teaspoon turmeric
1 cup chopped red bell peppers	¼ teaspoon paprika
1 cup finely diced potato	¼ teaspoon ground cardamom
1 teaspoon garlic powder	4 large eggs
2 (400g) tomatoes, cut	¼ cup chopped fresh cilantro

1. Preheat the oven to 350ºF (180ºC).
2. In an oven-safe sauté pan or skillet, heat the olive oil over medium-high heat and sauté the shallots, stirring occasionally, for about 3 minutes, until fragrant. Add the bell peppers, potato, and garlic powder. Cook, uncovered, for 10 minutes, stirring every 2 minutes.

3. Add the tomatoes, turmeric, paprika, and cardamom to the skillet and mix well. Once bubbly, remove from heat and crack the eggs into the skillet so the yolks are facing up.
4. Put the skillet in the oven and cook for an additional 5 to 10 minutes, until eggs are cooked to your preference. Garnish with the cilantro and serve.

PER SERVING
Calories: 224, Fat: 12.2g, Total Carbohydrates: 20.1g, Protein: 8.9g, Fiber: 2.8g, Sodium: 278mg

Mediterranean Herb Frittata

Prep time: 10 minutes | Cook time: 7 minutes | Serves: 2

4 large eggs	1 cup fresh spinach, arugula, kale, or other leafy greens
2 tablespoons fresh chopped herbs, such as rosemary, thyme, oregano, basil or 1 teaspoon dried herbs	4 ounces (113 g) quartered artichoke hearts, rinsed, drained, and thoroughly dried
¼ teaspoon salt	8 cherry tomatoes, halved
Freshly ground black pepper, to taste	½ cup crumbled soft Goat cheese
4 tablespoons extra-virgin olive oil, divided	

1. Preheat the oven to broil on low.
2. In small bowl, combine the eggs, herbs, salt, and pepper and whisk well with a fork. Set aside.
3. In a 4- to 5-inch oven-safe skillet or omelet pan, heat 2 tablespoons olive oil over medium heat. Add the spinach, artichoke hearts, and cherry tomatoes and sauté until just wilted, 1 to 2 minutes.
4. Pour in the egg mixture and let it cook undisturbed over medium heat for 3 to 4 minutes, until the eggs begin to set on the bottom.
5. Sprinkle the Goat cheese across the top of the egg mixture and transfer the skillet to the oven.
6. Broil for 4 to 5 minutes, or until the frittata is firm in the center and golden brown on top.
7. Remove from the oven and run a rubber spatula around the edge to loosen the sides. Invert onto a large plate or cutting board and slice in half. Serve warm and drizzled with the remaining 2 tablespoons olive oil.

PER SERVING
Calories: 527, Fat: 47.2g, Total Carbohydrates: 10.1g, Protein: 20.9g, Fiber: 2.8g, Sodium: 626mg

Spanish-Style Horchata with Cinnamon

Prep time: 5 minutes | Cook time: 1 minute | Serves: 6

2 cups water
1 cup chufa seed, overnight soak
¼ stick cinnamon

Zest from 1 lemon
2 tablespoons honey
4 cups cold water

1. In the pot, combine cinnamon, chufa seed and 4 cups water. Seal the lid cook on High Pressure for 1 minute. Release Pressure naturally for 10 minutes, then release the remaining Pressure quickly.
2. In a blender, add chufa seed mixture, lemon zest and honey. Blend well to form a paste. Add 2 cups cold water into a large container. Strain the blended chufa mixture into the water. Mix well and place in the refrigerator until ready for serving. Add cinnamon stick for garnishing.

PER SERVING
Calories: 162, Fat: 12.03g, Carbohydrates: 11.77g, Protein: 4.95g, Sugar: 6.48g, Fiber: 2.9g, Sodium: 7mg

Cheesy Green Bites

Prep time: 15 minutes | Cook time: 15 minutes | Serves: 8

¼ cup frozen chopped kale
¼ cup finely chopped artichoke hearts
¼ cup ricotta cheese
2 tablespoons grated Parmesan cheese
¼ cup Goat cheese
1 large egg white

1 teaspoon dried basil
1 lemon, zested
½ teaspoon salt
½ teaspoon freshly ground black pepper
4 frozen filo dough, thawed
1 tablespoon extra-virgin olive oil

1. In a bowl, combine kale, artichoke, ricotta, Parmesan, Goat cheese, egg white, basil, lemon zest, salt, and pepper. Place a filo dough on a clean flat surface. Brush with olive oil.
2. Place a second filo sheet on the first and brush with more oil. Continue layering to form a pile of four oiled sheets. Working from the short side, cut the phyllo sheets into 8 strips and half them.
3. Spoon 1 tablespoon of filling onto one short end of every strip. Fold a corner to cover the filling and a triangle, continue folding over and over to the end of the strip, creating a triangle-shaped filo packet.
4. Repeat the process with the other filo bites. Place a trivet into the pot. Pour in 1 cup of water. Place the bites on top of the trivet. Seal the lid and cook on High Pressure for 15 minutes. Do a quick release.

PER SERVING
Calories: 110, Fat: 4.74g, Carbohydrates: 12.1g, Protein: 5.81g, Sugar: 0.5g, Fiber: 2g, Sodium: 229mg

Hearty Honey-Apricot Granola

Prep time: 15 minutes | Cook time: 30 minutes | Serves: 6

1 cup rolled oats
¼ cup dried apricots, diced
¼ cup almond slivers
¼ cup walnuts, chopped
¼ cup pumpkin seeds
¼ cup hemp hearts
¼ to ⅓ cup coconut sugar
1 tablespoon olive oil

1 teaspoon ground cinnamon
¼ teaspoon ground nutmeg
¼ teaspoon salt
2 tablespoons sugar-free dark chocolate chips (optional)
3 cups nonfat plain Greek yogurt

1. Preheat the air fryer to 260°F (127°C). Line the air fryer basket with parchment paper.
2. In a large bowl, combine the oats, apricots, almonds, walnuts, pumpkin seeds, hemp hearts, honey, olive oil, cinnamon, nutmeg, and salt, mixing so that the coconut sugar, oil, and spices are well distributed.
3. Pour the mixture onto the parchment paper and spread it into an even layer.
4. Bake for 10 minutes, then shake or stir and spread back out into an even layer. Continue baking for 10 minutes more, then repeat the process of shaking or stirring the mixture. Bake for an additional 10 minutes before removing from the air fryer.
5. Allow the granola to cool completely before stirring in the chocolate chips (if using) and pouring into an airtight container for storage.
6. For each serving, top ½ cup Greek yogurt with ⅓ cup granola and a drizzle of honey, if needed.

PER SERVING
Calories: 342, Fat: 16.2g, Total Carbohydrates: 31.1g, Protein: 19.9g, Fiber: 3.8g, Sodium: 162mg

Tangy Almond-Pistachio Smoothie

Prep time: 10 minutes | Cook time: 0 minutes | Serves: 1

½ cup plain low-fat milk Greek yogurt
½ cup unsweetened almond milk, plus more as needed
Zest and juice of 1 clementine or ½ orange
1 tablespoon extra-virgin olive oil or MCT oil
1 tablespoon shelled pistachios, coarsely chopped
1 to 2 teaspoons monk fruit extract or honey (optional)
¼ to ½ teaspoon ground allspice or unsweetened pumpkin pie spice
¼ teaspoon ground cinnamon
¼ teaspoon vanilla extract

1. In a blender or a large wide-mouth jar, if using an immersion blender, combine the yogurt, ½ cup almond milk, clementine zest and juice, olive oil, pistachios, monk fruit extract (if using), allspice, cinnamon, and vanilla and blend until smooth and creamy, adding more almond milk to achieve your desired consistency.

PER SERVING
Calories: 264, Fat: 22.2g, Total Carbohydrates: 12.1g, Protein: 5.9g, Fiber: 1.8g, Sodium: 127mg

Avocado Toast with Tomato

Prep time: 10 minutes | Cook time: 5 minutes | Serves: 2

2 tablespoons ground flaxseed
½ teaspoon baking powder
2 large eggs
½ teaspoon salt
½ teaspoon freshly ground black pepper, plus more for serving
½ teaspoon garlic
powder, sesame seed, caraway seed or other dried herbs (optional)
3 tablespoons extra-virgin olive oil, divided
1 medium ripe avocado, peeled, pitted, and sliced
2 tablespoons chopped ripe tomato or salsa

1. In a small bowl, combine the flaxseed and baking powder, breaking up any lumps in the baking powder. Add the eggs, salt, pepper, and garlic powder (if using) and whisk well. Let sit for 2 minutes.
2. In a small nonstick skillet, heat 1 tablespoon olive oil over medium heat. Pour the egg mixture into the skillet and let cook undisturbed until the egg begins to set on bottom, 2 to 3 minutes.
3. Using a rubber spatula, scrape down the sides to allow uncooked egg to reach the bottom. Cook another 2 to 3 minutes.
4. Once almost set, flip like a pancake and allow the top to fully cook, another 1 to 2 minutes.
5. Remove from the pan and allow to cool slightly. Slice into 2 pieces.
6. Top each "toast" with avocado slices, additional salt and pepper, chopped tomato, and drizzle with the remaining 2 tablespoons olive oil.

PER SERVING (1 toast)
Calories: 287, Total Fat: 25g, Total Carbs: 10g, Net Carbs: 3g, Fiber: 7g, Protein: 9g, Sodium: 790mg

Fresh Vegetable Frittata

Prep time: 10 minutes | Cook time: 8 minutes | Serves: 1

3 large eggs
1 teaspoon almond milk
1 tablespoon olive oil
1 handful baby spinach leaves
½ baby eggplant, peeled and diced
¼ small red bell pepper, chopped
Sea salt and freshly ground pepper, to taste
1 ounce (28 g) crumbled Goat cheese

1. Preheat the broiler.
2. Beat the eggs with the almond milk until just combined.
3. Heat a small nonstick, broiler-proof skillet over medium-high heat. Add the olive oil, followed by the eggs.
4. Spread the spinach on top of the egg mixture in an even layer and top with the rest of the veggies.
5. Reduce heat to medium and season with sea salt and freshly ground pepper to taste. Allow the eggs and vegetables to cook 3 to 5 minutes until the bottom half of the eggs are firm and vegetables are tender.
6. Top with the crumbled Goat cheese and place on middle rack under the broiler, and then cook another 3 to 5 minutes until the eggs are firm in the middle and the cheese has melted.
7. Slice into wedges and serve immediately.

PER SERVING
Calories: 517, Fat: 39.32g, Total Carbohydrates: 24.9g, Protein: 22.91g, Sugar: 11.87g, Fiber: 11.2g, Sodium: 233mg

Baklava Hot Porridge with Walnut

Prep time: 10 minutes | Cook time: 3 minutes | Serves: 2

2 cups riced cauliflower
¾ cup unsweetened almond, flax, or hemp milk
4 tablespoons extra-virgin olive oil, divided
2 teaspoons grated fresh orange peel
½ teaspoon ground cinnamon

½ teaspoon almond extract or vanilla extract
⅛ teaspoon salt
4 tablespoons chopped walnuts, divided
1 to 2 teaspoons liquid honey, monk fruit, or other sweetener of choice (optional)

1. In medium saucepan, combine the riced cauliflower, almond milk, 2 tablespoons olive oil, grated orange peel, cinnamon, almond extract, and salt. Stir to combine and bring just to a boil over medium-high heat, stirring constantly.
2. Remove from heat and stir in 2 tablespoons chopped walnuts and sweetener (if using). Stir to combine.
3. Divide into bowls, topping each with 1 tablespoon of chopped walnuts and 1 tablespoon of the remaining olive oil.

PER SERVING
Calories: 382, Total Fat: 38g, Total Carbs: 11g, Net Carbs: 7g, Fiber: 4g, Protein: 5g, Sodium: 229mg

Greek Feta Cheese Pie

Prep time: 10 minutes | Cook time: 35 minutes | Serves: 6

4 tablespoons extra-virgin olive oil, divided
1¼ cups crumbled traditional Greek Feta
½ cup whole-milk ricotta
2 tablespoons chopped fresh mint
1 tablespoon chopped

fresh dill
½ teaspoon lemon zest
¼ teaspoon freshly ground black pepper
2 large eggs
½ teaspoon baking powder

1. Preheat the oven to 350°F (180°C).
2. Pour 2 tablespoons olive oil into an 8-inch square baking dish and swirl to coat the bottom and about 1 inch up the sides of the dish.
3. In a medium bowl, combine the Feta and ricotta and blend well with a fork, crumbling the Feta into very small pieces.
4. Stir in the mint, dill, lemon zest, and pepper and mix well.
5. In a small bowl, beat together the eggs and baking powder. Add to the cheese mixture and blend well.
6. Pour into the prepared baking dish and drizzle the remaining 2 tablespoons olive oil over top.
7. Bake until lightly browned and set, 35 to 40 minutes.

PER SERVING
Calories: 182, Total Fat: 17g, Total Carbs: 2g, Net Carbs: 2g, Fiber: 0g, Protein: 7g, Sodium: 322mg

Tomato and Goat Cheese Frittata

Prep time: 10 minutes | Cook time: 16 minutes | Serves: 2

1 tablespoon olive oil
½ pint cherry or grape tomatoes
2 garlic cloves, minced
5 large eggs, beaten
3 tablespoons milk
½ teaspoon salt
Pinch freshly ground

black pepper
2 tablespoons minced fresh oregano
2 tablespoons minced fresh basil
2 ounces (57 g) crumbled Goat cheese

1. Heat the oil in a nonstick skillet over medium heat. Add the tomatoes. As they start to cook, pierce some of them so they give off some of their juice. Reduce the heat to medium-low, cover the pan, and let the tomatoes soften.
2. When the tomatoes are mostly softened and broken down, remove the lid, add the garlic and continue to sauté.
3. In a medium bowl, combine the eggs, milk, salt, pepper, and herbs and whisk well to combine.
4. Turn the heat up to medium-high. Add the egg mixture to the tomatoes and garlic, then sprinkle the Goat cheese over the eggs.
5. Cover the pan and let cook for about 7 minutes.
6. Uncover the pan and continue cooking for another 7 to 10 minutes, or until the eggs are set. Run a spatula around the edge of the pan to make sure they won't stick.
7. Let the frittata cool for about 5 minutes before serving. Cut it into wedges and serve.

PER SERVING
Calories: 350, Fat: 28.97g, Total Carbohydrates: 6.03g, Protein: 16.61g, Sugar: 2.34g, Fiber: 0.9g, Sodium: 733mg

Egg Baked in Avocado with Pesto

Prep time: 5 minutes | Cook time: 10 minutes | Serves: 2

1 ripe large avocado
2 large eggs
Salt, to taste
Freshly ground black pepper, to taste
4 tablespoons jarred

pesto, for serving
2 tablespoons chopped tomato, for serving
2 tablespoons crumbled Feta, for serving (optional)

1. Preheat the oven to 425°F (220°C).
2. Slice the avocado in half and remove the pit. Scoop out about 1 to 2 tablespoons from each half to create a hole large enough to fit an egg. Place the avocado halves on a baking sheet, cut-side up.
3. Crack 1 egg in each avocado half and season with salt and pepper.
4. Bake until the eggs are set and cooked to desired level of doneness, 10 to 15 minutes.
5. Remove from oven and top each avocado with 2 tablespoons pesto, 1 tablespoon chopped tomato, and 1 tablespoon crumbled Feta (if using).

PER SERVING
Calories: 302, Total Fat: 26g, Total Carbs: 10g, Net Carbs: 5g, Fiber: 5g, Protein: 8g, Sodium: 436mg

Parmesan Green Oatmeal

Prep time: 10 minutes | Cook time: 16 minutes | Serves: 2

1 tablespoon olive oil
¼ cup minced onion
1 ounce (28 g) prosciutto, minced
2 cups greens (arugula, baby spinach, chopped kale, or Swiss chard)
¾ cup gluten-free old-fashioned oats

1½ cups water, unsalted, or low-sodium chicken stock
2 tablespoons Parmesan cheese
Salt, to taste
Pinch freshly ground black pepper

1. Heat the olive oil in a saucepan over medium-high heat. Add the onion and prosciutto and sauté for 4 minutes, or until the prosciutto starts to crisp and the onion turns golden.
2. Add the greens and stir until they begin to wilt. Transfer this mixture to a bowl.
3. Add the oats to the pan and let them toast for about 2 minutes. Add the water or chicken stock and bring the oats to a boil. Reduce the heat to low, cover the pan, and let the oats cook for 10 minutes, or until the liquid is absorbed and the oats are tender.
4. Stir the Parmesan cheese into the oats, and add the onions, prosciutto, and greens back to the pan. Add additional water if needed, so the oats are creamy and not dry.
5. Stir well and add salt and freshly ground black pepper to taste.

PER SERVING
Calories: 258, Total Fat: 12g, Total Carbohydrates: 29g, Fiber: 6g, Sugar: 1g, Protein: 11g, Sodium: 260mg

Whole Wheat Applesauce Blueberry Muffins

Prep time: 10 minutes | Cook time: 12 minutes | Serves: 6

Olive oil cooking spray
½ cup unsweetened applesauce
¼ cup raw honey
½ cup nonfat plain Greek yogurt
1 teaspoon vanilla extract
1 large egg
1½ cups plus 1

tablespoon whole wheat flour, divided
½ teaspoon baking soda
½ teaspoon baking powder
½ teaspoon salt
½ cup blueberries, fressh or frozen

1. Preheat the air fryer to 360°F (182°C). Lightly coat the inside of six silicone muffin cups or a six-cup muffin tin with olive oil cooking spray.
2. In a large bowl, combine the applesauce, honey, yogurt, vanilla, and egg and mix until smooth.
3. Sift in 1½ cups of the flour, the baking soda, baking powder, and salt into the wet mixture, then stir until just combined.
4. In a small bowl, toss the blueberries with the remaining 1 tablespoon flour, then fold the mixture into the muffin batter.
5. Divide the mixture evenly among the prepared muffin cups and place into the basket of the air fryer. Bake for 12 to 15 minutes, or until golden brown on top and a toothpick inserted into the middle of one of the muffins comes out clean.
6. Allow to cool for 5 minutes before serving.

PER SERVING
Calories: 186, Total Fat: 2g, Saturated Fat: 0g, Protein: 7g, Total Carbohydrates: 38g, Fiber: 4g, Sugar: 16g

Mediterranean Fruity Bulgur Breakfast Bowl

Prep time: 10 minutes | Cook time: 11 minutes | Serves: 6

1½ cups uncooked bulgur
2 cups 2% milk
1 cup water
½ teaspoon ground cinnamon
2 cups frozen (or fresh, pitted) dark sweet cherries

8 dried (or fresh) figs, chopped
½ cup chopped almonds
¼ cup loosely packed fresh mint, chopped
Warm 2% milk, for serving (optional)

1. In a medium saucepan, combine the bulgur, milk, water, and cinnamon. Stir once, then bring just to a boil. Cover, reduce the heat to medium-low, and simmer for 10 minutes or until the liquid is absorbed.
2. Turn off the heat, but keep the pan on the stove, and stir in the frozen cherries (no need to thaw), figs, and almonds. Stir well, cover for 1 minute, and let the hot bulgur thaw the cherries and partially hydrate the figs. Stir in the mint.
3. Scoop into serving bowls. Serve with warm milk, if desired. You can also serve it chilled.

PER SERVING
Calories: 207g, Total Fat: 6g, Saturated Fat: 3g,Total Carbs: 32g, Fiber: 4g, Protein: 8g, Sugar: 21g, Sodium: 82mg

Feta Egg and Tomato Scramble

Prep time: 10 minutes | Cook time: 15 minutes | Serves: 4

¼ cup extra-virgin olive oil, divided
1½ cups chopped fresh tomatoes
¼ cup finely minced red onion
2 garlic cloves, minced
½ teaspoon dried oregano or 1 to 2 teaspoons chopped fresh oregano

½ teaspoon dried thyme or 1 to 2 teaspoons chopped fresh thyme
8 large eggs
½ teaspoon salt
¼ teaspoon freshly ground black pepper
¾ cup crumbled Feta cheese
¼ cup chopped fresh mint leaves

1. In large skillet, heat the olive oil over medium heat. Add the chopped tomatoes and red onion and sauté until tomatoes are cooked through and soft, 10 to 12 minutes.
2. Add the garlic, oregano, and thyme and sauté another 2 to 4 minutes, until fragrant and liquid has reduced.
3. In a medium bowl, whisk together the eggs, salt, and pepper until well combined.
4. Add the eggs to the skillet, reduce the heat to low, and scramble until set and creamy, using a spatula to move them constantly, 3 to 4 minutes. Remove the skillet from the heat, stir in the Feta and mint, and serve warm.

PER SERVING
Calories: 338, Total Fat: 28g, Total Carbs: 6g, Net Carbs: 5g, Fiber: 1g, Protein: 16g, Sodium: 570mg

Allergen Friendly Breakfast Cookies

Prep time: 10 minutes | Cook time: 12 minutes | Serves: 10 Cookies

3 very ripe bananas
2 tbsps. raw honey
½ cup almond butter
2 tsps. vanilla extract
1 tbsp. coconut oil, melted
1 tsp. ground cinnamon

1 tsp. baking powder
½ tsp. salt
2½ cups rolled oats
¾ cup dairy-free semi-sweet chocolate chips (optional)

1. Preheat the oven to 350°F(180°C).
2. Use parchment paper to line a large baking sheet.
3. Use a potato masher or a fork to mash the bananas in a large bowl.
4. Add the honey, almond butter, vanilla and coconut oil, stir until well mixed.
5. Sprinkle the banana mixture with the cinnamon, baking powder, and salt. Add the oats and chocolate chips (if using) in batches, stirring after each addition until all ingredients are incorporated.
6. On the prepared sheet, add heaping tablespoons of dough, leaving at least 1 inch between dough balls. Bake for 10 to 12 minutes.
7. Allow the cookies to rest in the pan for 5 minutes, and then transfer to a cooling rack. Place the cookies in a sealed container, and store in the refrigerator for several days.

PER SERVING
Calories: 306, Total Fat: 16g, Saturated Fat: 5g, Carbohydrates: 39g, Protein: 7g, Fiber: 5g

Tangy Cardamom Buckwheat Pancakes

Prep time: 10 minutes | Cook time: 10 minutes | Serves: 2

½ cup buckwheat flour
½ teaspoon cardamom
½ teaspoon baking powder
¼ teaspoon baking soda
½ cup milk
¼ cup plain Greek yogurt
1 egg
½ teaspoon orange extract

1. In a medium bowl, combine the buckwheat flour, cardamom, baking powder, and baking soda.
2. In another bowl, combine the milk, yogurt, egg, and orange extract and whisk well to combine.
3. Add the wet ingredients to the dry ingredients and stir until the batter is smooth.
4. Heat a nonstick skillet or a griddle over high heat. When the pan is hot, reduce the heat to medium.
5. Pour the batter into the pan to make four 6-inch pancakes. Depending on the size of your pan, you may need to do this in four batches.

PER SERVING
Calories: 196, Total Fat: 6g, Total Carbohydrates: 27g, Fiber: 3g, Sugar: 6g, Protein: 10g, Sodium: 242mg

Scrambled Eggs with Peppers and Goat Cheese

Prep time: 10 minutes | Cook time: 8 minutes | Serves: 4

1½ teaspoons extra-virgin olive oil
1 cup chopped bell peppers, any color
2 garlic cloves, minced
4 large eggs
¼ teaspoon kosher or
sea salt
2 tablespoons water
½ cup crumbled Goat cheese
2 tablespoons loosely packed chopped fresh mint

1. In a large skillet over medium-high heat, heat the oil. Add the peppers and cook for 5 minutes, stirring occasionally. Add the garlic and cook for 1 minute.
2. While the peppers are cooking, in a medium bowl, whisk together the eggs, salt, and water.
3. Turn the heat down to medium-low. Pour the egg mixture over the peppers. Let the eggs cook undisturbed for 1 to 2 minutes, until they begin to set on the bottom. Sprinkle with the Goat cheese.
4. Cook the eggs for about 1 to 2 more minutes, stirring slowly, until the eggs are soft-set and custardy. (They will continue to cook off the stove from the residual heat in the pan.)
5. Top with the fresh mint and serve.

PER SERVING
Calories: 259g, Total Fat: 16g, Saturated Fat: 5g, Total Carbs: 2g, Fiber: 1g, Protein: 29g, Sugar: 1g, Sodium: 176mg

Marinara Eggs with Parsley and Bread

Prep time: 10 minutes | Cook time: 14 minutes | Serves: 6

1 tablespoon extra-virgin olive oil
1 cup chopped onion
2 garlic cloves, minced
2 (14½-ounce / 411-g) cans Italian diced tomatoes, undrained, no salt added
6 large eggs
½ cup chopped fresh flat-leaf (Italian) parsley
Crusty Italian bread and grated Parmesan or Romano cheese, for serving (optional)

1. In a large skillet over medium-high heat, heat the oil. Add the onion and cook for 5 minutes, stirring occasionally. Add the garlic and cook for 1 minute.
2. Pour the tomatoes with their juices over the onion mixture and cook until bubbling, 2 to 3 minutes. While waiting for the tomato mixture to bubble, crack one egg into a small custard cup or coffee mug.
3. When the tomato mixture bubbles, lower the heat to medium. Then use a large spoon to make six indentations in the tomato mixture. Gently pour the first cracked egg into one indentation and repeat, cracking the remaining eggs, one at a time, into the custard cup and pouring one into each indentation. Cover the skillet and cook for 6 to 7 minutes, or until the eggs are done to your liking (about 6 minutes for soft-cooked, 7 minutes for harder cooked).
4. Top with the parsley, and serve with the bread and grated cheese, if desired.

PER SERVING
Calories: 89g, Total Fat: 6g, Saturated Fat: 2g, Total Carbs: 4g, Fiber: 1g, Protein: 4g, Sugar: 2g, Sodium: 77mg

Moroccan Dried Fruit Oatmeal

Prep time: 5 minutes | Cook time: 3 hours | Serves: 4

3 cups low-fat milk
1 cup steel-cut oats
½ teaspoon sea salt
1 teaspoon ground cinnamon

½ cup any combination of diced dried apricots, dates, figs, and raisins (raisins can be whole)

1. Combine the milk and the oats in the slow cooker. Sprinkle in the salt and cinnamon.
2. Add the dried fruit to the mixture. Cover and cook on low heat for 3 hours. Do not open and/ or stir until the cooking time has elapsed and the oats are cooked.
3. Serve hot.

PER SERVING
With low-fat milk: Calories: 177, Fat: 2.36g, Carbohydrates: 38.91g, Protein: 10.25g, Sugar: 21.29g, Fiber: 5.6g, Sodium: 488mg

Lemony Breakfast Cakes with Berry Syrup

Prep time: 5 minutes | Cook time: 10 minutes | Serves: 4

For the Pancakes
6 tbsp. extra-virgin olive oil, divided
2 large eggs
1 cup almond flour
1 tsp. baking powder
¼ tsp. salt
Zest and juice of 1 lemon

½ tsp. almond or vanilla extract
For the Berry Sauce
1 cup frozen mixed berries
½ tsp. vanilla extract
1 tbsp. water or lemon juice

To Make the Pancakes
1. In a large bowl, mix the baking powder, almond flour, and salt and whisk to break up any clumps.
2. Add 4 tablespoons olive oil, lemon zest and juice, eggs, and almond extract and mix well.
3. In a large skillet, heat 1 tablespoon olive oil and spoon about 2 tablespoons batter for each pancake. Cook 4 to 5 minutes, until bubbles begin to form, and flip. Cook another 2 to 3 minutes on second side. Repeat with remaining olive oil and batter.
To Make the Berry Sauce
1. In a small saucepan, heat the water, frozen berries, and vanilla extract over medium-high for 3 to 4 minutes, until bubbly, adding more water if mixture is too thick. Using the back of a spoon or fork to mash the berries and whisk until smooth.

PER SERVING
Calories: 275, Total Carbohydrates: 8g, Protein: 4g, Total Fat: 26g, Net Carbs: 6g, Fiber: 2g, Sodium: 271mg

Polenta with Arugula, Figs, and Blue Cheese

Prep time: 10 minutes | Cook time: 40 minutes | Serves: 4

1 cup coarse-ground cornmeal
½ cup oil-packed sun-dried tomatoes, chopped
1 teaspoon minced fresh thyme or ¼ teaspoon dried
½ teaspoon table salt
¼ teaspoon pepper
3 tablespoons extra-virgin olive oil, divided

2 ounces (57 g) baby arugula
4 figs, cut into ½-inch-thick wedges
1 tablespoon balsamic vinegar
2 ounces (57 g) blue cheese, crumbled
2 tablespoons pine nuts, toasted

1. Arrange trivet included with Instant Pot in base of insert and add 1 cup water. Fold sheet of aluminum foil into 16 by 6-inch sling, then rest 1½-quart round soufflé dish in center of sling. Whisk 4 cups water, cornmeal, tomatoes, thyme, salt, and pepper together in bowl, then transfer mixture to soufflé dish. Using sling, lower soufflé dish into pot and onto trivet, allow narrow edges of sling to rest along sides of insert.
2. Lock lid in place and close pressure release valve. Select high pressure cook function and cook for 40 minutes. Turn off Instant Pot and quick-release pressure. Carefully remove lid, allowing steam to escape away from you.
3. Using sling, transfer soufflé dish to wire rack. Whisk 1 tablespoon oil into polenta, smoothing out any lumps. Let sit until thickened slightly, about 10 minutes. Season with salt and pepper to taste.
4. Toss arugula and figs with vinegar and remaining 2 tablespoons oil in bowl, and season with salt and pepper to taste. Divide polenta among individual serving plates and top with arugula mixture, blue cheese, and pine nuts. Serve.

PER SERVING
Calories: 360, Fat: 21.2g, Total Carbohydrates: 38.1g, Protein: 6.9g, Fiber: 7.8g, Sodium: 510mg

Mediterranean Tomato Pizza

Prep time: 5 minutes | Cook time: 4 minutes | Serves: 2

2 (6- to 8-inch-long) pieces of whole-wheat naan bread	pesto
	1 medium tomato, sliced
	2 large eggs
2 tablespoons prepared	

1. Heat a large nonstick skillet over medium-high heat. Place the naan bread in the skillet and let it warm for about 2 minutes on each side. The bread should be softened and just starting to turn golden.
2. Spread 1 tablespoon of the pesto on one side of each slice. Top the pesto with tomato slices to cover. Remove the pizzas from the pan and place each one on its own plate.
3. Crack the eggs into the pan, keeping them separated, and cook until the whites are no longer translucent and the yolk is cooked to desired doneness.
4. With a spatula, spoon one egg onto each pizza.

PER SERVING
Calories: 427, Total Fat: 17g, Total Carbohydrates: 10g, Fiber: 5g, Sugar: 4g, Protein: 17g, Sodium: 279mg

Maple Cherry and Almond Oatmeal

Prep time: 10 minutes | Cook time: 35 minutes | Serves: 2

½ cup gluten-free old-fashioned oats	1 egg, beaten
2 tablespoons sliced almonds	2 tablespoons maple syrup
Pinch salt	1 cup frozen cherries, thawed
¾ cup milk	Ricotta cheese (optional, for topping)
½ teaspoon almond extract	Greek yogurt (optional, for topping)
½ teaspoon vanilla	

1. Preheat the oven to 350ºF (180ºC) and set the rack to the middle position. Oil two 8-ounce ramekins and place them on a baking sheet.
2. In a medium bowl, combine all of the ingredients and mix well.
3. Spoon half of the mixture into each ramekin.
4. Bake for 35 to 45 minutes, or until the oats are set and a knife inserted into the middle comes out clean. They will be soft but should not be runny.
5. Let the baked oats cool for 5 to 10 minutes. Top with ricotta cheese or plain Greek yogurt, if desired.

PER SERVING
Calories: 287, Total Fat: 9g, Total Carbohydrates: 43g, Fiber: 4g, Sugar: 24g, Protein: 11g, Sodium: 155mg

Egg and Potato in Tomato Sauce

Prep time: 10 minutes | Cook time: 25 minutes | Serves: 2

3 medium tomatoes, seeded and coarsely chopped	olive oil, divided
	Sea salt and freshly ground pepper, to taste
2 tablespoons fresh chopped basil	3 large russet potatoes
1 garlic clove, minced	4 large eggs
2 tablespoons plus ½ cup	1 teaspoon fresh oregano, chopped

1. Put tomatoes in a food processor and puree them, skins and all.
2. Add the basil, garlic, 2 tablespoons olive oil, sea salt, and freshly ground pepper, and pulse to combine.
3. Put the mixture in a large skillet over low heat and cook, covered, for 20 to 25 minutes, or until the sauce has thickened and is bubbly.
4. Meanwhile, dice the potatoes into small cubes. Put ½ cup olive oil in a nonstick skillet over medium-low heat.
5. Fry the potatoes for 5 minutes until crisp and browned on the outside, then cover and reduce heat to low. Steam potatoes until done.
6. Carefully crack the eggs into the tomato sauce. Cook over low heat until the eggs are set in the sauce, about 6 minutes.
7. Remove the potatoes from the pan and drain them on paper towels, then place them in a bowl.
8. Sprinkle with sea salt and freshly ground pepper to taste and top with the oregano.
9. Carefully remove the eggs with a slotted spoon and place them on a plate with the potatoes. Spoon sauce over the top and serve.

PER SERVING
Calories: 1184, Fat: 77.42g, Total Carbohydrates: 110.06g, Protein: 19.2g, Sugar: 8.53g, Fiber: 10g, Sodium: 55mg

Rosemary Sweet Potato Hash

Prep time: 10 minutes | Cook time: 18 minutes | Serves: 6

2 medium sweet potatoes, peeled and cut into 1-inch cubes	bella mushrooms, diced
	2 tablespoons olive oil
½ green bell pepper, diced	1 garlic clove, minced
	½ teaspoon salt
½ red onion, diced	½ teaspoon black pepper
4 ounces (113 g) baby	½ tablespoon chopped fresh rosemary

1. Preheat the air fryer to 380°F (193°C).
2. In a large bowl, toss all ingredients together until the vegetables are well coated and seasonings distributed.
3. Pour the vegetables into the air fryer basket, making sure they are in a single even layer. (If using a smaller air fryer, you may need to do this in two batches.)
4. Cook for 9 minutes, then toss or flip the vegetables. Cook for 9 minutes more.
5. Transfer to a serving bowl or individual plates and enjoy.

PER SERVING
Calories: 91, Total Fat: 5g, Saturated Fat: 1g, Protein: 2g, Total Carbohydrates: 12g, Fiber: 2g, Sugar: 3g

Egg in a Hole with Avocado

Prep time: 15 minutes | Cook time: 5minutes | Serves: 4

4 bell peppers, any color	¾ tsp. kosher salt, divided
1 tbsp. extra-virgin olive oil	¼ tsp. freshly ground black pepper, divided
8 large eggs	
¼ cup red onion, diced	1 avocado, peeled, pitted, and diced
¼ cup fresh basil,chopped	Juice of ½ lime

1. Remove stem and seeds in the bell peppers. Cut 2 rings from each pepper. Chop the remaining bell pepper into small dice, and set aside.
2. Heat the olive oil in a large skillet over medium heat. Add 4 bell pepper rings, then crack 1 egg in the middle of each ring. Season with a dash of the salt and black pepper. Cook 2 to 3 minutes until the egg whites are mostly set but the yolks are still runny. Gently flip and cook 1 additional minute. Move the egg–bell pepper rings to a platter or onto plates, and repeat with

the remaining 4 bell pepper rings.
3. Combine the avocado, basil, onion, lime juice, reserved diced bell pepper, the remaining kosher salt, and the remaining black pepper in a medium bowl. Divide among the 4 plates.

PER SERVING
Calories: 270, Total fat: 19g, Saturated fat: 4g, Total Carbohydrates: 12g, Protein: 15g, Sodium: 360mg, Fiber: 5g, Sugar: 6g

Breakfast Pancake with Berry Sauce

Prep time: 10 minutes | Cook time: 10 minutes | Serves: 4

For the Pancakes:	vanilla extract
1 cup almond flour	For the Berry Sauce:
1 teaspoon baking powder	1 cup frozen mixed berries
¼ teaspoon salt	1 tablespoon water or lemon juice, plus more if needed
6 tablespoon extra-virgin olive oil, divided	
2 large eggs	½ teaspoon vanilla extract
Zest and juice of 1 lemon	
½ teaspoon almond or	

Make the Pancakes
1. In a large bowl, combine the almond flour, baking powder, and salt and whisk to break up any clumps.
2. Add the 4 tablespoons olive oil, eggs, lemon zest and juice, and almond extract and whisk to combine well.
3. In a large skillet, heat 1 tablespoon of olive oil and spoon about 2 tablespoons of batter for each of 4 pancakes. Cook until bubbles begin to form, 4 to 5 minutes, and flip. Cook another 2 to 3 minutes on second side. Repeat with remaining 1 tablespoon olive oil and batter.
Make the Berry Sauce
1. In a small saucepan, heat the frozen berries, water, and vanilla extract over medium-high for 3 to 4 minutes, until bubbly, adding more water if mixture is too thick. Using the back of a spoon or fork, mash the berries and whisk until smooth.

PER SERVING (2 pancakes with ¼ cup berry syrup)
Calories: 275, Total Fat: 26g, Total Carbs: 8g, Net Carbs: 6g, Fiber: 2g, Protein: 4g, Sodium: 271mg

Homemade Pistachio Basil Pesto

Prep time: 10 minutes | Cook time: 0 |
Serves: 4 cups

½ cup extra-virgin olive oil, divided
1 cup raw pistachios
2 cups tightly packed fresh basil leaves
2 tsps. freshly squeezed lemon juice

½ cup shredded raw Parmesan cheese
½ tsp. garlic powder
¼ tsp. salt
Freshly ground black pepper

1. Add the ¼ cup of olive oil, pistachios and basil into a food processor or blender, blend for 15 seconds.
2. Then place the lemon juice, cheese, garlic powder, and salt in the processor or blender, season with pepper.
3. Add the remaining ¼ cup of olive oil slowly with the processor or blender running, until all ingredients are well combined.
4. Serve immediately, cover and keep in the refrigerator for up to 5 days, or freeze for 3 to 4 months.

PER SERVING
Calories: 229, Total Fat: 22.3g, Saturated Fat: 3.6g, Carbohydrates: 3.8g, Protein: 5.5g, Fiber: 1.7g

Harissa Shakshuka with Bell Peppers

Prep time: 10minutes | Cook time: 20minutes | Serves: 4

½ onion, diced
4 large eggs
1 (28-ounce, 794 g) can no-salt-added diced tomatoes
1 bell pepper, seeded

and diced
3 garlic cloves, minced
½ tsp. kosher salt
2 to 3 tbsps. fresh basil, chopped or cut into ribbons

1. Preheat the oven to 375°F (190°C).
2. Heat the olive oil in a 12-inch ovenproof skillet over medium heat. Add the harissa, onion, tomato paste, and bell pepper, sauté for 3 to 4 minutes. Put in the garlic and cook about 30 seconds until fragrant. Add the diced tomatoes and salt and simmer for about 10 minutes.
3. Make 4 wells in the sauce and gently break 1 egg into each. Transfer to the oven and bake 10 to 12 minutes until the whites are cooked and the yolks are set.

4. Cool down for 3 to 5 minutes, and carefully spoon onto plates. Garnish with the basil.

PER SERVING
Calories: 190, Total fat: 10g, Saturated fat: 2g, Total Carbohydrates: 15g, Protein: 9g, Sodium: 255mg, Fiber: 4g, Sugar: 9g

Parmesan Spinach Pie

Prep time: 10 minutes | Cook time: 20 minutes | Serves: 8

Nonstick cooking spray
2 tablespoons extra-virgin olive oil
1 onion, chopped
1 pound (454 g) frozen spinach, thawed
¼ teaspoon garlic salt
¼ teaspoon freshly ground black pepper
¼ teaspoon ground

nutmeg
4 large eggs, divided
1 cup grated Parmesan cheese, divided
2 puff pastry doughs, (organic, if available), at room temperature
4 hard-boiled eggs, halved

1. Preheat the oven to 350°F (180°C). Spray a baking sheet with nonstick cooking spray and set aside.
2. Heat a large sauté pan or skillet over medium-high heat. Put in the oil and onion and cook for about 5 minutes, until translucent.
3. Squeeze the excess water from the spinach, then add to the pan and cook, uncovered, so that any excess water from the spinach can evaporate. Add the garlic salt, pepper, and nutmeg. Remove from heat and set aside to cool.
4. In a small bowl, crack 3 eggs and mix well. Add the eggs and ½ cup Parmesan cheese to the cooled spinach mix.
5. On the prepared baking sheet, roll out the pastry dough. Layer the spinach mix on top of dough, leaving 2 inches around each edge.
6. Once the spinach is spread onto the pastry dough, place hard-boiled egg halves evenly throughout the pie, then cover with the second pastry dough. Pinch the edges closed.
7. Crack the remaining egg in a small bowl and mix well. Brush the egg wash over the pastry dough.
8. Bake for 15 to 20 minutes, until golden brown and warmed through.

PER SERVING
Calories: 417, Fat: 28.2g, Total Carbohydrates: 25.1g, Protein: 16.9g, Fiber: 2.8g, Sodium: 490mg

Bell Pepper and Garlic Frittata

Prep time: 5 minutes | Cook time: 5 minutes | Serves: 2

2 red bell peppers, chopped
4 eggs
2 tablespoons olive oil
2 garlic cloves, crushed
1 teaspoon Italian Seasoning mix

1. Grease the pot with oil. Stir-fry the peppers for 2 to 3 minutes, or until lightly charred. Set aside. Add garlic and stir-fry for 1 minute, until soft.
2. Whisk the eggs and season with Italian seasoning. Pour the mixture into the pot and cook for 2 to 3 minutes, or until set. Using a spatula, loosen the edges and gently slide onto a plate. Add charred peppers and fold over. Serve hot.

PER SERVING
Calories: 405, Fat: 32.99g, Carbohydrates: 7.83g, Protein: 19.03g, Sugar: 3.87g, Fiber: 0.9g, Sodium: 314mg

Lemony Olives and Feta Cheese Medley

Prep time: 10 minutes | Cook time: 5 minutes | Serves: 8

½ (½-pound / 272-g) block of Greek Feta cheese
3 cups mixed olives (Kalamata and green), drained from brine, pitted preferred
¼ cup extra-virgin olive oil
3 tablespoons lemon juice
1 teaspoon grated lemon zest
1 teaspoon dried oregano
Pita bread, for serving

1. Cut the Feta cheese into ½-inch squares and put them into a large bowl.
2. Add the olives to the Feta and set aside.
3. In a small bowl, whisk together the olive oil, lemon juice, lemon zest, and oregano.
4. Pour the dressing over the Feta cheese and olives and gently toss together to evenly coat everything.
5. Serve with pita bread.

PER SERVING
Calories: 406, Fat: 38.2g, Total Carbohydrates: 8.1g, Protein: 7.9g, Fiber: 0g, Sodium: 660mg

Garlicky Mushrooms

Prep time: 5 minutes | Cook time: 10 minutes | Serves: 4 to 6

2 pounds (907 g) cremini mushrooms, cleaned
3 tablespoons unsalted butter
2 tablespoons garlic, minced
½ teaspoon salt
½ teaspoon freshly ground black pepper

1. Cut each mushroom in half, stem to top, and put them into a bowl.
2. Preheat a large sauté pan or skillet over medium heat.
3. Cook the butter and garlic in the pan for 2 minutes, stirring occasionally.
4. Add the mushrooms and salt to the pan and toss together with the garlic butter mixture. Cook for 7 to 8 minutes, stirring every 2 minutes.
5. Remove the mushrooms from the pan and pour into a serving dish. Top with black pepper.

PER SERVING
Calories: 183, Fat: 9.2g, Total Carbohydrates: 10.1g, Protein: 8.9g, Fiber: 2.8g, Sodium: 334mg

Italian Ricotta Cheese and Tomato Omelet

Prep time: 10 minutes | Cook time: 18 minutes | Serves: 4

1 pound (454 g) tomatoes, peeled, roughly diced
1 tablespoon tomato paste
1 teaspoon coconut sugar
1 cup ricotta cheese
4 eggs
3 tablespoons olive oil
1 tablespoon Italian seasoning mix
¼ cup fresh parsley, chopped
¼ teaspoon salt

1. Grease the inner pot with oil. Press Sauté and add tomatoes, coconut sugar, Italian seasoning, parsley, and salt. Give it a good stir and cook for 15 minutes or until the tomatoes soften. Stir occasionally.
2. Meanwhile, whisk eggs and cheese. Pour the mixture into the pot stir well. Cook for 3 more minutes. Serve immediately.

PER SERVING
Calories: 359, Fat: 28.08g, Carbohydrates: 9.37g, Protein: 17.64g, Sugar: 2.18g, Fiber: 1.6g, Sodium: 507mg

Ricotta Strawberry and Basil Toast

Prep time: 5 minutes | Cook time: 10 minutes | Serves: 2

4 slices of whole-grain bread	Sea salt, to taste
½ cup ricotta cheese (whole milk or low-fat)	1 cup fresh strawberries, sliced
1 tablespoon honey	4 large fresh basil leaves, sliced into thin shreds

1. Toast the bread.
2. In a small bowl, combine the ricotta, honey, and a pinch or two of sea salt. Taste and add additional honey or salt if desired.
3. Spread the mixture evenly over each slice of bread (about 2 tablespoons per slice).
4. Top each piece with sliced strawberries and a few pieces of shredded basil.

PER SERVING
Calories: 275, Total Fat: 8g, Total Carbohydrates: 41g, Fiber: 5g, Sugar: 16g, Protein: 15g, Sodium: 323mg

Vegetable Baked Egg Casseroles

Prep time: 10 minutes | Cook time: 30 minutes | Serves: 2

1 slice whole-grain bread	black pepper
2 large eggs, beaten	¾ cup chopped vegetables (any kind you like—e.g., cherry tomatoes, mushrooms, scallions, spinach, broccoli, etc.)
3 tablespoons milk	
¼ teaspoon salt	
½ teaspoon onion powder	
¼ teaspoon garlic powder	
Pinch freshly ground	

1. Heat the oven to 375ºF (190ºC) and set the rack to the middle position. Oil two 8-ounce ramekins and place them on a baking sheet.
2. Tear the bread into pieces and line each ramekin with ½ of a slice.
3. Mix the eggs, milk, salt, onion powder, garlic powder, pepper, and vegetables in a medium bowl.
4. Pour half of the egg mixture into each ramekin.
5. Bake for 30 minutes, or until the eggs are set.

PER SERVING
Calories: 163, Total Fat: 12g, Total Carbohydrates: 20g, Fiber: 3g, Sugar: 10g, Protein: 7g, Sodium: 387mg

Peach and Avocado Smoothie Bowl

Prep time: 10 minutes | Cook time: 0 minutes | Serves: 2

2 cups packed partially thawed frozen peaches	2 tablespoons flax meal
½ cup plain or vanilla Greek yogurt	1 teaspoon vanilla extract
½ ripe avocado	1 teaspoon orange extract

1. Combine all of the ingredients in a blender and blend until smooth.
2. Pour the mixture into two bowls, and, if desired, sprinkle with additional toppings.

PER SERVING
Calories: 213, Total Fat: 13g, Total Carbohydrates: 23g, Fiber: 7g, Sugar: 15g, Protein: 6g, Sodium: 41mg

Baby Spinach, Tomato, and Egg Wraps

Prep time: 10 minutes | Cook time: 4 minutes | Serves: 2

1 tablespoon olive oil	1½ cups packed baby spinach
¼ cup minced onion	1 ounce (28 g) crumbled Feta cheese
3 to 4 tablespoons minced sun-dried tomatoes in olive oil and herbs	Salt, to taste
3 large eggs, beaten	2 (8-inch) whole-wheat tortillas

1. In a large skillet, heat the olive oil over medium-high heat. Add the onion and tomatoes and sauté for about 3 minutes.
2. Turn the heat down to medium. Add the beaten eggs and stir to scramble them.
3. Add the spinach and stir to combine. Sprinkle the Feta cheese over the eggs. Add salt to taste.
4. Warm the tortillas in the microwave for about 20 seconds each.
5. Fill each tortilla with half of the egg mixture. Fold in half or roll them up and serve.

PER SERVING
Calories: 435, Total Fat: 28g, Total Carbohydrates: 31g, Fiber: 6g, Sugar: 6g, Protein: 17g, Sodium: 552mg

Chia Seed Pudding with Berries on Top

Prep time: 10 minutes | Cook time: 15 minutes | Serves: 4

½ cup chia seeds
2 cups almond milk
1 tsp. vanilla extract
¼ cup maple syrup or raw honey
1 cup frozen no-added-

sugar pitted cherries, thawed, juice reserved, divided
½ cup chopped cashews, divided

1. Add the chia seeds, almond milk, vanilla, and maple syrup to a quart jar with a tight-fitting lid. Shake well and set aside for at least 15 minutes, or refrigerate overnight.
2. Evenly divide the pudding among four bowls, and top ¼ cup of cherries and 2 tablespoons of cashews on each bowl. Serve.

PER SERVING
Calories: 272, Total Fat: 14g, Total Carbohydrates: 38g, Sugar: 25g, Fiber: 6g, Protein: 7g, Sodium: 84mg

Easy Sweet Potato Hash

Prep time: 15 minutes | Cook time: 15 minutes | Serves: 4

2 large sweet potatoes, cooked and cut into ½-inch cubes
2 tbsps. coconut oil
1 cup sliced mushrooms
1 garlic clove, sliced thin
½ onion, sliced thin
1 cup finely chopped Swiss chard

½ cup (120 ml) vegetable broth
1 tbsp. chopped fresh thyme
1 tbsp. chopped fresh sage
1 tsp. salt
¼ tsp. freshly ground pepper

1. Melt the coconut oil in a large skillet over high heat.
2. Add the mushrooms, onion, and garlic. Sauté for about 8 minutes until the mushrooms and onions are tender.
3. Add the Swiss chard, sweet potatoes, and vegetable broth. Cook for 5 minutes.
4. Stir in the salt, thyme, pepper, and sage.

PER SERVING
Calories: 212, Total Carbohydrates: 35g, Protein: 30g, Total Fat: 7g, Sugar: 2g, Fiber: 6g, Sodium: 708mg

Healthy Green Smoothie

Prep time: 10 minutes | Cook time: 0 minutes | Serves: 1

1 small very ripe avocado, peeled and pitted
1 cup unsweetened almond milk or water, plus more as needed
1 cup tender baby spinach leaves, stems removed

½ medium cucumber, peeled and seeded
1 tablespoon extra-virgin olive oil or avocado oil
8 to 10 fresh mint leaves, stems removed
1 to 2 tablespoons juice of 1 lime

1. In a blender or a large wide-mouth jar, if using an immersion blender, combine the avocado, almond milk, spinach, cucumber, olive oil, mint, and lime juice and blend until smooth and creamy, adding more almond milk or water to achieve your desired consistency.

PER SERVING
Calories: 330, Fat: 30.2g, Total Carbohydrates: 19.1g, Protein: 3.9g, Fiber: 8.8g, Sodium: 36mg

Mediterranean Scramble with Cherry Tomatoes

Prep time: 5 minutes | Cook time: 10 minutes | Serves: 2

½ garlic clove, sliced
½ avocado, sliced
4 eggs
2 tsps. chopped fresh oregano

1 cup cherry tomatoes, halved
1 tbsp. extra-virgin olive oil

1. Beat the eggs in a medium bowl until well combined, mix in the oregano.
2. Put a large skillet over medium heat. Add the olive oil when the pan is hot.
3. Pour the eggs into the skillet and use a wooden spoon to scramble the eggs. Transfer the eggs to a serving dish.
4. Add the cherry tomatoes and garlic to the pan and sauté for about 2 minutes. Spoon the tomatoes over the eggs and top with avocado slices.

PER SERVING
Calories: 310, Total Carbohydrates: 10g, Protein: 13g, Total Fat: 26g, Sugar: 3g, Fiber: 5g, Sodium: 131mg

Breakfast Berry Smoothie

Prep time: 5 minutes | Cook time: 0 minutes | Serves: 1

½ cup vanilla low-fat Greek yogurt	frozen blueberries or strawberries (or a combination)
¼ cup low-fat milk	
½ cup fresh or	6 to 8 ice cubes

1. Place the Greek yogurt, milk, and berries in a blender and blend until the berries are liquefied. Add the ice cubes and blend on high until thick and smooth. Serve immediately.

PER SERVING
Calories: 230, Fat: 8.88g, Carbohydrates: 22.67g, Protein: 15.83g, Sugar: 20.61g, Fiber: 1.4g, Sodium: 339mg

Crustless Greek Feta Pie

Prep time: 10 minutes | Cook time: 40 minutes | Serves: 6

2 large eggs	milk ricotta
½ tsp. baking powder	2 tbsps. chopped fresh mint
4 tbsps. extra-virgin olive oil, divided	1 tbsp. chopped fresh dill
1¼ cups crumbled traditional Greek feta	½ tsp. lemon zest
½ cup (120 ml) whole-	¼ tsp. freshly ground black pepper

1. Preheat the oven to 350°F (180°C).
2. Pour 2 tablespoons olive oil into an 8-inch square baking dish and swirl to coat the bottom.
3. In a medium bowl, put in feta and ricotta and blend well with a fork, crumbling the feta into very small pieces.
4. Stir in the mint, lemon zest, dill, and pepper and mix well.
5. In a small bowl, whisk together the eggs and baking powder. Add to the cheese mixture and mix well.
6. Pour into the prepared baking dish and drizzle the remaining olive oil over top.
7. Bake 35 to 40 minutes until lightly browned and set.

PER SERVING
Calories: 182, Total Carbohydrates: 2g, Protein: 7g, Total Fat: 17g, Net Carbs: 2g, Fiber: 0g, Sodium: 322mg

Traditional Tzatziki

Prep time: 5 minutes | Cook time: 0 minutes | Serves: 6

2 Persian cucumbers	½ teaspoon salt
3 cups Greek yogurt	1 teaspoon dried dill or mint
2 medium garlic cloves, minced	

1. Cut off both tips of the cucumber. Using a vegetable grater, grate the cucumber onto a paper towel. Alternatively, finely chop the cucumbers.
2. Wrap the towel around the cucumbers and squeeze out the excess liquid.
3. Put the prepared cucumbers into a large bowl and add the Greek yogurt, garlic, and salt. Stir until well combined.
4. Add the mint or dill and stir.

PER SERVING
Calories: 127, Fat: 6.2g, Total Carbohydrates: 7.1g, Protein: 10.9g, Fiber: 0.8g, Sodium: 237mg

Dilled Tuna and Avocado Salad Sandwich

Prep time: 10 minutes | Cook time: 2 minutes | Serves: 4

4 versatile sandwich rounds	and/or zest
2 (4-ounce/ 113-g) cans tuna, packed in olive oil	1 very ripe avocado, peeled, pitted, and mashed
2 tablespoons roasted garlic aioli, or avocado oil low fat yogurt with 1 to 2 teaspoons freshly squeezed lemon juice	1 tablespoon chopped fresh capers (optional)
	1 teaspoon chopped fresh dill or ½ teaspoon dried dill

1. Make sandwich rounds according to recipe. Cut each round in half and set aside.
2. In a medium bowl, place the tuna and the oil from cans. Add the aioli, avocado, capers (if using), and dill and blend well with a fork.
3. Toast sandwich rounds and fill each with one-quarter of the tuna salad, about ⅓ cup.

PER SERVING (1 sandwich)
Calories: 436, Fat: 36.2g, Total Carbohydrates: 5.1g, Protein: 22.9g, Fiber: 2.8g, Sodium: 124mg

Homemade Versatile Sandwich Round

Prep time: 5 minutes | Cook time: 2 minutes | Serves: 1

3 tablespoons almond flour
1 tablespoon extra-virgin olive oil
1 large egg
½ teaspoon dried

rosemary, oregano, basil, thyme, or garlic powder (optional)
¼ teaspoon baking powder
⅛ teaspoon salt

1. In a microwave-safe ramekin, combine the almond flour, olive oil, egg, rosemary (if using), baking powder, and salt. Mix well with a fork.
2. Microwave for 90 seconds on high.
3. Slide a knife around the edges of ramekin and flip to remove the bread.
4. Slice in half with a serrated knife if you want to use it to make a sandwich.

PER SERVING
Calories: 232, Fat: 22.2g, Total Carbohydrates: 1.1g, Protein: 7.9g, Fiber: 0g, Sodium: 450mg

Blueberry and Chia Seeds Smoothie

Prep time: 10 minutes | Cook time: 0 minutes | Serves: 1

1 cup unsweetened almond milk, plus more as needed
¼ cup frozen blueberries
2 tablespoons unsweetened almond butter
1 tablespoon ground flaxseed or chia seeds

1 tablespoon extra-virgin olive oil or avocado oil
1 to 2 teaspoons honey or monk fruit extract (optional)
½ teaspoon vanilla extract
¼ teaspoon ground cinnamon

1. In a blender or a large wide-mouth jar, if using an immersion blender, combine the almond milk, blueberries, almond butter, flaxseed, olive oil, honey (if using), vanilla, and cinnamon and blend until smooth and creamy, adding more almond milk to achieve your desired consistency.

PER SERVING
Calories: 460, Fat: 40.2g, Total Carbohydrates: 20.1g, Protein: 8.9g, Fiber: 9.8g, Sodium: 147mg

Pumpkin Layers with Honey Granola

Prep time: 5 minutes | Cook time: 0 minutes | Serves: 4

1 (15-ounce / 425-g) can pure pumpkin puree
4 teaspoons honey
1 teaspoon pumpkin pie spice
¼ teaspoon ground

cinnamon
2 cups plain, unsweetened, full-fat Greek yogurt
1 cup honey granola

1. In a large bowl, mix the pumpkin puree, honey, pumpkin pie spice, and cinnamon. Cover and refrigerate for at least 2 hours.
2. To make the parfaits, in each cup, pour ¼ cup pumpkin mix, ¼ cup yogurt and ¼ cup granola. Repeat Greek yogurt and pumpkin layers and top with honey granola.

PER SERVING
Calories: 264, Fat: 9.2g, Total Carbohydrates: 35.1g, Protein: 14.9g, Fiber: 5.8g, Sodium: 90mg

Breakfast Parmesan Pita

Prep time: 10 minutes | Cook time: 6 minutes | Serves: 2

1 whole wheat pita
2 teaspoons olive oil
½ shallot, diced
¼ teaspoon garlic, minced
1 large egg

¼ teaspoon dried oregano
¼ teaspoon dried thyme
⅛ teaspoon salt
2 tablespoons shredded Parmesan cheese

1. Preheat the air fryer to 380ºF (193ºC).
2. Brush the top of the pita with olive oil, then spread the diced shallot and minced garlic over the pita.
3. Crack the egg into a small bowl or ramekin, and season it with oregano, thyme, and salt.
4. Place the pita into the air fryer basket, and gently pour the egg onto the top of the pita. Sprinkle with cheese over the top.
5. Bake for 6 minutes.
6. Allow to cool for 5 minutes before cutting into pieces for serving.

PER SERVING
Calories: 191, Total Fat: 10g, Saturated Fat: 3g, Protein: 8g, Total Carbohydrates: 19g, Fiber: 3g, Sugar: 1g

Baked Oatmeal with Berries

Prep time: 10minutes | Cook time: 45-50minutes | Serves: 8

2 cups gluten-free rolled oats
2 cups (10-ounce bag, 283 g) frozen mixed berries (blueberries and raspberries work best)
¼ cup (60 ml) maple syrup
2 cups (480 ml) plain, unsweetened almond milk
1 cup (240 ml) plain Greek yogurt
2 tbsps. extra-virgin olive oil
2 tsps. ground cinnamon
1 tsp. baking powder
1 tsp. vanilla extract
½ tsp. kosher salt
¼ tsp. ground nutmeg
⅛ tsp. ground cloves

1. Preheat the oven to 375°F (190ºC).
2. In a large bowl, mix all the ingredients together. Pour into a 9-by-13-inch baking dish. Bake for 45 to 50 minutes until golden brown.

PER SERVING
Calories: 180, Total fat: 6g, Saturated fat: 1g, Total Carbohydrates: 28g, Protein: 6g, Sodium: 180mg, Fiber: 4g, Sugar: 11g

Parmesan Kale Frittata

Prep time: 10 minutes | Cook time: 10 minutes | Serves: 6

6 large eggs
2 tablespoons low-fat cream
½ teaspoon freshly grated nutmeg
Salt and ground black
pepper, to taste
1½ cups kale, chopped
¼ cup grated Parmesan Cheese
Cooking spray
1 cup water

1. In a bowl, beat eggs, nutmeg, pepper, salt, and cream until smooth. Stir in Parmesan Cheese and kale.
2. Apply a cooking spray to a cake pan. Wrap aluminum foil around outside of the pan to cover completely.
3. Place egg mixture into the prepared pan. Pour in water, set a steamer rack over the water. Gently lay the pan onto the rack. Seal the lid and cook for 10 minutes on High Pressure. Release the pressure quickly.

PER SERVING
Calories: 93, Fat: 7.3g, Carbohydrates: 2.28g, Protein: 4.49g, Sugar: 0.49g, Fiber: 0.3g, Sodium: 104mg

Greek Yogurt Parfait with Nuts

Prep time: 10 minutes | Cook time: 0 minutes | Serves: 1

½ cup plain low-fat Greek yogurt
2 tablespoons cream
¼ cup frozen berries, thawed with juices
½ teaspoon vanilla or almond extract (optional)
¼ teaspoon ground cinnamon (optional)
1 tablespoon ground flaxseed
2 tablespoons chopped nuts (walnuts or pecans)

1. In a small bowl or glass, combine the yogurt, cream, thawed berries in their juice, vanilla or almond extract (if using), cinnamon (if using), and flaxseed and stir well until smooth. Top with chopped nuts and enjoy.

PER SERVING
Calories: 267, Total Fat: 19g, Total Carbs: 12g, Net Carbs: 8g, Fiber: 4g, Protein: 12g, Sodium: 63mg

Chile Rellenos Egg Souffle

Prep time: 15 minutes | Cook time: 45 minutes | Serves: 8

2 cans (4 oz. each, 113 g) chopped green chilies
¼ cup finely chopped onion
¼ cup sliced ripe olives
2 cups sharp shredded cheddar cheese
1 ½ cups biscuit/baking
mix
4 large eggs
2 cups 2% milk
¼ tsp. pepper
1 cup 4% small-curd cottage cheese
Salsa and sour cream, optional

1. Preheat oven to 350°F(180°C). In a greased 11x7-in. baking dish, spread with green chilies, sprinkle with the onion, olives, and cheese. Add biscuit mix, whisk eggs, milk and pepper into a large bowl, whisk them until blended. Add the cottage cheese and stir well, pour mixture over top.
2. Uncovered and bake for 45 to 50 minutes, until golden brown, puffed and a knife inserted in the center comes out clean. Allow it to stand for 5 to 10 minutes before serving. Serve with salsa and sour cream if desired.

PER SERVING
Calories: 305, Fat: 17g, Carbohydrates: 23g, Protein: 16g, Sugar: 5g, Fiber: 1g, Sodium: 708mg

Greek Yogurt Parfait with Berries

Prep time: 5 minutes | Cook time: 0 |
Serves: 1

½ cup (120 ml) plain whole-milk Greek yogurt
2 tbsps. heavy whipping cream
1 tbsp. ground flaxseed
2 tbsps. chopped nuts

¼ cup frozen berries, thawed with juices
½ tsp. vanilla or almond extract (optional)
¼ tsp. ground cinnamon (optional)

1. In a small bowl, mix the yogurt, thawed berries in their juice, heavy whipping cream, vanilla or almond extract, cinnamon, and flaxseed and stir well until smooth.
2. Top with chopped nuts and serve.

PER SERVING
Calories: 267, Total Carbohydrates: 12g, Protein: 12g, Total Fat: 19g, Net Carbs: 8g, Fiber: 4g, Sodium: 63mg

Fruity Pancakes with Berry-Honey Compote

Prep time: 10 minutes | Cook time: 4 minutes | Serves: 4

1 cup almond flour
1 cup plus 2 tablespoons skim milk
2 large eggs, beaten
⅓ cup coconut sugar
1 teaspoon baking soda
¼ teaspoon salt

2 tablespoons extra-virgin olive oil
1 sliced banana or 1 cup sliced strawberries, divided
2 tablespoons berry and honey compote

1. In a bowl, mix together the almond flour, milk, eggs, coconut sugar, baking soda, and salt.
2. In a large sauté pan or skillet, heat the olive oil over medium-high heat and pour ⅓ cup pancake batter into the pan. Cook for 2 to 3 minutes. Right before pancake is ready to flip, add half of the fresh fruit and flip to cook for 2 to 3 minutes on the other side, until cooked through.
3. Top with the remaining fruit, drizzle with berry and honey compote and serve.

PER SERVING
Calories: 415, Fat: 24.2g, Total Carbohydrates: 46.1g, Protein: 11.9g, Fiber: 3.8g, Sodium: 526mg

Cardamom-Cinnamon Overnight Oats

Prep time: 10 minutes | Cook time: 0 minutes | Serves: 2

½ cup vanilla, unsweetened almond milk (not Silk brand)
½ cup rolled oats
2 tablespoons sliced almonds
2 tablespoons simple

sugar liquid sweetener
1 teaspoon chia seeds
¼ teaspoon ground cardamom
¼ teaspoon ground cinnamon

1. In a mason jar, combine the almond milk, oats, almonds, liquid sweetener, chia seeds, cardamom, and cinnamon and shake well. Store in the refrigerator for 8 to 24 hours, then serve cold or heated.

PER SERVING
Calories: 131, Fat: 6.2g, Total Carbohydrates: 17.1g, Protein: 4.9g, Fiber: 3.8g, Sodium: 45mg

Garlicky Pea Fried Rice Breakfast

Prep time: 10 minutes | Cook time: 15 minutes | Serves: 2

1 tbsp. avocado oil
2 garlic cloves, minced
½ white onion, diced
¼ cup peas
¼ cup non-GMO organic sweet corn kernels
¼ cup shredded carrots

1 tbsp. sesame oil
2 cups cooked rice
2 eggs, whisked
¼ tsp. salt
Dash red pepper flakes
Freshly ground black pepper

1. Add the avocado oil, garlic and onion to a medium skillet, sauté over medium heat for 5 minutes, until translucent.
2. Add the peas, corn, and carrots, stir well and cook for another 5 minutes, stirring occasionally.
3. Stir in the sesame oil and rice, using a spoon to break the rice up. As the rice begins to soften, add the eggs. Cook for 5 minutes, until thoroughly cooked, stirring occasionally.
4. Sprinkle with the salt and red pepper flakes, season with pepper. Serve hot.

PER SERVING
Calories: 453, Total Fat: 19g, Saturated Fat: 43, Carbohydrates: 59g, Protein: 13g, Fiber: 3g

Fig and Ricotta Toast with Walnuts

Prep time: 5 minutes | Cook time: 5 minutes | Serves: 2

¼ cup ricotta cheese
2 pieces whole-wheat bread, toasted
4 figs, halved
2 tbsps. walnuts, chopped
1 tsp. honey

1. Spread 2 tablespoons of ricotta cheese on each piece of toast. Add 4 fig halves to each one, pressing firmly to keep the figs in the ricotta.
2. Sprinkle walnuts and drizzle half teaspoon of honey on each piece of toast.

PER SERVING
Calories: 215, Total fat: 10g, Saturated fat: 3g, Total Carbohydrates: 26g, Protein: 7g, Sodium: 125mg, Fiber: 3g, Sugar: 9g

Honey Spinach Muffins

Prep time: 15 minutes | Cook time: 15 minutes | Serves: 12

2 cups packed spinach
Cooking spray
2 eggs
¼ cup (60 ml) raw honey
3 tbsps. extra-virgin olive oil
1 tsp. vanilla extract
1 cup almond flour
1 cup oat flour
1 tsp. baking soda
2 tsps. baking powder
½ tsp. salt
Pinch freshly ground black pepper

1. Preheat the oven to 350°F (180°C).
2. Grease 12 muffin cups with cooking spray.
3. Combine the eggs, spinach, olive oil, honey, and vanilla in a food processor. Process until smooth.
4. Whisk together the almond flour, oat flour, baking soda, baking powder, salt, and pepper in a medium bowl. Transfer the spinach mixture to the bowl and mix well.
5. Fill each muffin cup 2/3 full. Put the muffins in the preheated oven and bake for about 15 minutes until lightly browned and the centers touched firm.
6. Transfer the pan to a cooling rack, and cool down for 10 minutes before removing the muffins from the tin.

PER SERVING
Calories: 108, Total Carbohydrates: 12g, Protein: 3g, Total Fat: 6g, Sugar: 6g, Fiber: 1g, Sodium: 217mg

Soft-Boiled Eggs with Sage

Prep time: 5 minutes | Cook time: 3 minutes | Serves: 4

4 large eggs
1 cups water
Salt and ground black
pepper, to taste
1 tablespoon sage

1. To the pressure cooker, add water and place a wire rack. Carefully place eggs on it. Seal the lid, press Steam and cook for 3 minutes on High Pressure. Do a quick release.
2. Allow to cool completely in an ice bath. Peel the eggs, in half lengthwise and season with sage, salt, and pepper before serving.

PER SERVING
Calories: 58, Fat: 4.59g, Carbohydrates: 1.28g, Protein: 2.81g, Sugar: 0.11g, Fiber: 0.3g, Sodium: 10mg

Pears with Ricotta Topping

Prep time: 10 minutes | Cook time: 32 minutes | Serves: 4

Nonstick cooking spray
1 (16-ounce / 454-g) container whole-milk ricotta cheese
2 large eggs
¼ cup white whole-wheat flour or whole-wheat pastry flour
1 tablespoon coconut sugar
1 teaspoon vanilla extract
¼ teaspoon ground nutmeg
1 pear, cored and diced
2 tablespoons water
1 tablespoon honey

1. Preheat the oven to 400°F (205°C). Spray four 6-ounce ramekins with nonstick cooking spray.
2. In a large bowl, beat together the ricotta, eggs, flour, sugar, vanilla, and nutmeg. Spoon into the ramekins. Bake for 22 to 25 minutes, or until the ricotta is just about set. Remove from the oven and cool slightly on racks.
3. While the ricotta is baking, in a small saucepan over medium heat, simmer the pear in the water for 10 minutes, until slightly softened. Remove from the heat, and stir in the honey.
4. Serve the ricotta ramekins topped with the warmed pear.

PER SERVING:
Calories: 329g, Total Fat: 19g, Saturated Fat: 11g, Total Carbs: 23g, Fiber: 3g, Protein: 17g, Sugar: 12g, Sodium: 109mg

Pomegranate Muesli

Prep time: 10 minutes | Cook time: 0 minutes | Serves: 2

½ cup gluten-free old-fashioned oats
¼ cup shelled pistachios
3 tablespoons pumpkin seeds
2 tablespoons chia seeds

¾ cup milk
½ cup plain Greek yogurt
2 to 3 teaspoons honey (optional)
½ cup pomegranate arils

1. In a medium bowl, mix together the oats, pistachios, pumpkin seeds, chia seeds, milk, yogurt, and honey, if using.
2. Divide the mixture between two 12-ounce mason jars or another type of container with a lid.
3. Top each with ¼ cup of pomegranate arils.
4. Cover each jar or container and store in the refrigerator overnight or up to 4 days.
5. Serve cold, with additional milk if desired.

PER SERVING
Calories: 502, Total Fat: 24g, Total Carbohydrates: 60g, Fiber: 10g, Sugar: 33g, Protein: 17g, Sodium: 171mg

Easy Turkey Sausage

Prep time: 15 minutes | Cook time: 15 minutes | Serves: 4

1½ pounds (680 g) ground turkey
½ cup dried blueberries
1 tsp. salt
½ tsp. freshly ground black pepper

½ tsp. ground nutmeg
1 tbsp. chopped fresh sage
2 scallions, sliced
Extra-virgin olive oil, for brushing

1. Preheat the oven to 400°F (205°C).
2. Brush a rimmed baking sheet with olive oil.
3. Mix together the salt, turkey, nutmeg, pepper, scallions, sage, and blueberries in a medium bowl, do this with your hands.
4. Scoop the mixture onto the prepared baking sheet with a small ice cream scoop. Gently flatten the mounds into a patty shape with your fingers or the back of a spatula.
5. Put the sheet in the preheated oven and bake for 10 to 15 minutes until touches firm.

PER SERVING
Calories: 348, Total Carbohydrates: 4g, Protein: 47g, Total Fat: 19g, Sugar: 2g, Fiber: 1g, Sodium: 765mg

Morning Creamy Iced Coffee

Prep time: 5 minutes | Cook time: 0 minutes | Serves: 1

1 cup freshly brewed strong black coffee, cooled slightly
1 tablespoon extra-virgin olive oil
1 teaspoon MCT oil

(optional)
⅛ teaspoon almond extract
⅛ teaspoon ground cinnamon

1. Pour the slightly cooled coffee into a blender or large glass (if using an immersion blender).
2. Add the olive oil, MCT oil (if using), almond extract, and cinnamon.
3. Blend well until smooth and creamy. Drink warm and enjoy.

PER SERVING
Calories: 128, Fat: 14.2g, Total Carbohydrates: 0g, Protein: 0g, Fiber: 0g, Sodium: 5mg

Baklava Porridge

Prep time: 5 minutes | Cook time: 5 minutes | Serves: 2

4 tbsps. extra-virgin olive oil, divided
2 tsps. grated fresh orange peel (from ½ orange)
2 cups Riced Cauliflower
¾ cup (180 ml) unsweetened almond, flax, or hemp milk
½ tsp. ground cinnamon

½ tsp. almond extract or vanilla extract
⅛ tsp. salt
4 tbsps. chopped walnuts, divided
1 to 2 tsps. liquid stevia, monk fruit, or other sweetener of choice (optional)

1. In medium saucepan, mix the riced cauliflower, cinnamon, 2 tablespoons olive oil, almond milk, grated orange peel, almond extract, and salt. Stir to combine and bring to a boil over medium-high heat, stirring constantly.
2. Remove from heat and stir in 2 tablespoons chopped walnuts and sweetener. Stir to combine.
3. Divide into bowls, topping each with chopped walnuts and the remaining olive oil.

PER SERVING
Calories: 382, Total Carbohydrates: 11g, Protein: 5g, Total Fat: 38g, Net Carbs: 7g, Fiber: 4g, Sodium: 229mg

Avocado Smoothie

Prep time: 5 minutes | Cook time: 5 minutes | Serves: 2

1 large avocado
1 1/2 cups (360 ml) milk
of your choice
2 tbsps. honey

1. Put all ingredients in your blender and mix until smooth and creamy. Serve immediately.

PER SERVING
Calories: 316, Fat: 18.36g, Carbohydrates: 34.66g, Protein: 8.11g, Sodium: 94mg, Fiber: 6.8g

Peach Smoothie

Prep time: 5 minutes | Cook time: 0 minutes | Serves: 1

1 large unpeeled peach, pitted and sliced
6 ounces (170 g) vanilla or peach low-fat Greek
yogurt
2 tablespoons low-fat milk
6 to 8 ice cubes

1. Combine all ingredients in a blender and blend until thick and creamy. Serve immediately.

PER SERVING
Calories: 228, Fat: 3.17g, Carbohydrates: 41.63g, Protein: 10.98g, Sugar: 39.7g, Fiber: 2.6g, Sodium: 127mg

Vanilla Raspberry Overnight Oats

Prep time: 10 minutes | Cook time: 0 minutes | Serves: 2

⅔ cup vanilla, unsweetened almond milk (not Silk brand)
⅓ cup rolled oats
¼ cup raspberries
1 teaspoon honey
¼ teaspoon turmeric
⅛ teaspoon ground cinnamon
Pinch ground cloves

1. In a mason jar, combine the almond milk, oats, raspberries, honey, turmeric, cinnamon, and cloves and shake well. Store in the refrigerator for 8 to 24 hours, then serve cold or heated.

PER SERVING
Calories: 82, Fat: 2.2g, Total Carbohydrates: 14.1g, Protein: 1.9g, Fiber: 2.8g, Sodium: 98mg

Lemon Honey Cider Spritzer

Prep time: 5 minutes | Cook time: 0 | Serves: 1

Few drops raw honey
1 tbsp. apple cider vinegar
1 tbsp. freshly squeezed
lemon juice
8 ounces(227 g) sparkling water
Ice, for serving

1. Add the honey, vinegar, lemon juice and sparkling water into a tall glass, gently stir them together.
2. Drop the ice into the glass and serve immediately.

PER SERVING
Calories: 6, Total Fat: 0g, Saturated Fat: 0g, Carbohydrates: 1.8g, Protein: 0.1g, Fiber: 0g

Baked Egg and Avocado

Prep time: 5 minutes | Cook time: 15 minutes | Serves: 2

1 ripe large avocado
2 large eggs
4 tbsps. jarred pesto, for serving
2 tbsps. chopped tomato, for serving
2 tbsps. crumbled feta, for serving (optional)
Salt
Freshly ground black pepper

1. Preheat the oven to 425°F (220°C).
2. Cut the avocado in half and remove the pit. Scoop out 1 to 2 tablespoons from each half to create a hole large enough to fit an egg. Put the avocado halves on a baking sheet, cut-side up.
3. Crack 1 egg in each avocado half and season with salt and pepper.
4. Bake 10 to 15 minutes until the eggs are set and cooked to desired level of doneness.
5. Remove from oven and top each avocado with pesto, chopped tomato, and crumbled feta.

PER SERVING
Calories: 302, Total Carbohydrates: 10g, Protein: 8g, Total Fat: 26g, Net Carbs: 5g, Fiber: 5g, Sodium: 436mg

Chapter 3 Vegetable

Mediterranean Mixed Vegetables Platter

Prep time: 20 minutes | Cook time: 20 minutes | Serves: 8

1 tbsp. canola oil
1 head cauliflower, cut into 1-inch florets
1 bunch asparagus, woody ends trimmed
5 baby bell peppers, halved and seeded
1 tbsp. curry powder
Kosher salt and freshly ground black pepper, to taste

1 (5-ounce, 142 g) block feta cheese
5 pitas, quartered
1 (8-ounce, 227 g) can Greek dolmas (stuffed grape leaves)
1 (6-ounce, 170 g) jar olive tapenade
Chopped fresh parsley, for garnish

1. Add the cauliflower, asparagus, bell peppers, curry powder, canola oil, salt, and black pepper to a large bowl, combine well and toss to coat the vegetables. Arrange the mixture in the air fryer basket.
2. On the sheet pan, place the block of feta.
3. Install a wire rack on Level 1. Select AIR FRY, select 2 LEVEL, set the temperature to 400°F(204°C), and set the time to 20 minutes. Press START/STOP to begin preheating.
4. After the unit has finished preheating, place the sheet pan on the wire rack and insert the air fryer basket on Level 3.
5. Cook for 10 minutes, remove the sheet pan and add in the pita quarters. Remove the basket and move the wire rack to Level 3. Insert the air fryer basket on Level 1 and place the sheet pan on the wire rack. Close the oven door to continue cooking.
6. Cook until the feta turns brown and the inside soft and spreadable. Place the feta on a platter and top with the tapenade. Place the warm vegetables, dolmas, and pitas around it. Garnish the vegetables with parsley before serving.

PER SERVING
Calories: 189, Total Fat: 9g, Saturated Fat: 3g, Sodium: 473mg, Carbohydrates: 23g, Fiber: 7g, Protein: 8g

Mushrooms and Asparagus Farrotto

Prep time: 15 minutes | Cook time: 16 minutes | Serves: 2

½ ounce dried porcini mushrooms
1 cup hot water
3 cups low-sodium vegetable stock
2 tablespoons olive oil
½ large onion, minced
1 garlic clove
1 cup diced mushrooms

¾ cup farro
½ cup dry white wine
½ teaspoon dried thyme
4 ounces (113 g) asparagus, cut into ½-inch pieces
2 tablespoons grated Parmesan cheese
Salt, to taste

1. Soak the dried mushrooms in the hot water for about 15 minutes. When they're softened, drain the mushrooms, reserving the liquid. (I like to strain the liquid through a coffee filter in case there's any grit.) Mince the porcini mushrooms.
2. Add the mushroom liquid and vegetable stock to a medium saucepan and bring it to a boil. Reduce the heat to low just to keep it warm.
3. Heat the olive oil in a Dutch oven over high heat. Add the onion, garlic, and mushrooms, and sauté for 10 minutes.
4. Add the farro to the Dutch oven and sauté it for 3 minutes to toast.
5. Add the wine, thyme, and one ladleful of the hot mushroom and chicken stock. Bring it to a boil while stirring the farro. Do not cover the pot while the farro is cooking.
6. Reduce the heat to medium. When the liquid is absorbed, add another ladleful or two at a time to the pot, stirring occasionally, until the farro is cooked through. Keep an eye on the heat, to make sure it doesn't cook too quickly.
7. When the farro is al dente, add the asparagus and another ladleful of stock. Cook for another 3 to 5 minutes, or until the asparagus is softened.
8. Stir in Parmesan cheese and season with salt.

PER SERVING
Calories: 341, Total Fat: 16g, Total Carbohydrates: 26g, Fiber: 5g, Sugar: 4g, Protein: 13g, Sodium: 259mg

Roasted Artichokes with Lemony Vinaigrette

Prep time: 10 minutes | Cook time: 25 minutes | Serves: 4

3 lemons
4 artichokes (8- to 10 ounce / 227- to 283-g)
9 tablespoons extra-virgin olive oil
Salt and pepper

½ teaspoon garlic, minced to paste
½ teaspoon Dijon mustard
2 teaspoons chopped fresh parsley

1. Adjust oven rack to lower-middle position and heat oven to 475°F (245°C). Cut 1 lemon in half, squeeze halves into container filled with 2 quarts water, then add spent halves.
2. Working with 1 artichoke at a time, trim stem to about ¾ inch and cut off top quarter of artichoke. Break off bottom 3 or 4 rows of tough outer leaves by pulling them downward. Using paring knife, trim outer layer of stem and base, removing any dark green parts. Cut artichoke in half lengthwise, then remove fuzzy choke and any tiny inner purple-tinged leaves using small spoon. Submerge prepped artichokes in lemon water.
3. Coat bottom of 13 by 9-inch baking dish with 1 tablespoon oil. Remove artichokes from lemon water and shake off water, leaving some water still clinging to leaves. Toss artichokes with 2 tablespoons oil, ¾ teaspoon salt, and pinch pepper, gently rub oil and seasonings between leaves. Arrange artichokes cut side down in prepared dish. Trim ends off remaining 2 lemons, halve crosswise, and arrange cut side up next to artichokes. Cover tightly with aluminum foil and roast until cut sides of artichokes begin to brown and bases and leaves are tender when poked with tip of paring knife, 25 to 30 minutes.
4. Transfer artichokes to serving platter. Let lemons cool slightly, then squeeze into fine-mesh strainer set over bowl, extracting as much juice and pulp as possible, press firmly on solids to yield 1½ tablespoons juice. Whisk garlic, mustard, and ½ teaspoon salt into juice. Whisking constantly, slowly drizzle in remaining 6 tablespoons oil until emulsified. Whisk in parsley and season with salt and pepper to taste. Serve artichokes with dressing.

PER SERVING
Calories: 209, Fat: 13.88g, Carbohydrates: 20.17g, Protein: 5.69g, Sugar: 2.53g, Fiber: 9.1g, Sodium: 430mg

Zucchini Lasagna with Cheese

Prep time: 15 minutes | Cook time: 1 hour | Serves: 8

½ cup (120 ml) extra-virgin olive oil, divided
2 cups shredded fresh whole-milk mozzarella cheese
1¾ cups shredded Parmesan cheese
4 to 5 medium zucchini squash
1 tsp. salt
8 ounces (227 g) frozen spinach, thawed and well

drained (about 1 cup)
2 cups whole-milk ricotta cheese
¼ cup chopped fresh basil or 2 tsps. dried basil
1 tsp. garlic powder
½ tsp. freshly ground black pepper
½ (24-ounce, 680 g) jar low-sugar marinara sauce (less than 5g sugar)

1. Preheat the oven to 425°F (220°C).
2. Line two baking sheets with parchment paper and drizzle each with 2 tablespoons olive oil evenly.
3. Slice the zucchini lengthwise into ¼-inch-thick slices and place on the prepared baking sheet in a single layer. Sprinkle with ½ teaspoon salt each sheet. Bake until softened for 15 to 18 minutes. Remove from the oven and cool down slightly before assembling the lasagna.
4. Reduce the oven temperature to 375°F (190°C).
5. In a large bowl, combine the ricotta, spinach, garlic powder, basil, and pepper. In a small bowl, mix together the Parmesan and mozzarella cheeses. Combine the marinara sauce and remaining olive oil in a medium bowl, and stir to fully incorporate the oil into sauce.
6. To assemble the lasagna, spoon 1/3 of the marinara sauce mixture into the bottom of a 9 x13-inch glass baking dish and spread evenly. Put 1 layer of softened zucchini slices to fully cover the sauce, then add 1/3 of the ricotta-spinach mixture and spread evenly over the zucchini. Sprinkle 1/3 of the mozzarella-Parmesan mixture over the ricotta. Repeat with 2 more cycles of these layers: marinara, zucchini, ricotta-spinach, then cheese blend.
7. Bake for 30 to 35 minutes until the cheese is bubbly and melted. Turn the broiler to low and broil about 5 minutes until the top is golden brown. Remove from the oven and cool down slightly before slicing.

PER SERVING
Calories: 521, Total Fat: 41g, Total Carbohydrates: 13g, Net Carbs: 10g, Protein: 25g, Fiber: 3g, Sodium: 712mg

Tabbouleh Stuffed Tomatoes

Prep time: 15 minutes | Cook time: 10 minutes | Serves: 4

8 medium beefsteak or similar tomatoes
3 tablespoons extra-virgin olive oil, divided
½ cup water
½ cup uncooked regular or whole-wheat couscous
1½ cups minced fresh curly parsley
⅓ cup minced fresh mint
2 scallions, green and white parts, chopped
¼ teaspoon freshly ground black pepper
¼ teaspoon kosher or sea salt
1 medium lemon
4 teaspoons honey
⅓ cup chopped almonds

1. Preheat the oven to 400°F (205°C).
2. Slice the top off each tomato and set aside. Scoop out all the flesh inside, and put the tops, flesh, and seeds in a large mixing bowl.
3. Grease a baking dish with 1 tablespoon of oil. Place the carved-out tomatoes in the baking dish, and cover with aluminum foil. Roast for 10 minutes.
4. While the tomatoes are cooking, make the couscous by bringing the water to boil in a medium saucepan. Pour in the couscous, remove from the heat, and cover. Let sit for 5 minutes, then stir with a fork.
5. While the couscous is cooking, chop up the tomato flesh and tops. Drain off the excess tomato water using a colander. Measure out 1 cup of the chopped tomatoes (reserve any remaining chopped tomatoes for another use). Add the cup of tomatoes back into the mixing bowl. Mix in the parsley, mint, scallions, pepper, and salt.
6. Using a Microplane or citrus grater, zest the lemon into the mixing bowl. Halve the lemon, and squeeze the juice through a strainer (to catch the seeds) from both halves into the bowl with the tomato mixture. Mix well.
7. When the couscous is ready, add it to the tomato mixture and mix well.
8. With oven mitts, carefully remove the tomatoes from the oven. Divide the tabbouleh evenly among the tomatoes and stuff them, using a spoon to press the filling down so it all fits. Cover the pan with the foil and return it to the oven. Cook for another 8 to 10 minutes, or until the tomatoes are tender-firm. (If you prefer softer tomatoes, roast for an additional 10 minutes.) Before serving, top each tomato with a drizzle of ½ teaspoon of honey and about 2 teaspoons of almonds.

PER SERVING
Calories: 160g, Total Fat: 7g, Saturated Fat:1g, Total Carbs: 22g, Protein: 5g, Sugar: 13g, Fiber: 5g, Sodium: 351mg

Stewed Zucchini with Olive and Mint

Prep time: 10 minutes | Cook time: 1½ hours | Serves: 6 to 8

1 (28-ounce / 794-g) can whole peeled tomatoes
3 tablespoons extra-virgin olive oil
5 (8-ounce / 227-g) zucchini, trimmed, quartered lengthwise, seeded, and cut into 2-inch lengths
1 onion, chopped fine
Salt and pepper, to taste
3 garlic cloves, minced
1 teaspoon minced fresh oregano or ¼ teaspoon dried
¼ teaspoon red pepper flakes
2 tablespoons chopped pitted kalamata olives
2 tablespoons shredded fresh mint

1. Adjust oven rack to lower-middle position and heat oven to 325°F (163°C). Process tomatoes and their juice in food processor until completely smooth, about 1 minute, set aside.
2. Heat 2 teaspoons oil in Dutch oven over medium-high heat until just smoking. Brown one-third of zucchini, about 3 minutes per side, transfer to bowl. Repeat with 4 teaspoons oil and remaining zucchini in 2 batches.
3. Add remaining 1 tablespoon oil, onion, and ¾ teaspoon salt to now-empty pot and cook, stirring occasionally, over medium-low heat until onion is very soft and golden brown, 9 to 11 minutes. Stir in garlic, oregano, and pepper flakes and cook until fragrant, about 30 seconds. Stir in olives and tomatoes, bring to simmer, and cook, stirring occasionally, until sauce has thickened, about 30 minutes.
4. Stir in zucchini and any accumulated juice, cover, and transfer pot to oven. Bake until zucchini is very tender, 30 to 40 minutes. Stir in mint and adjust sauce consistency with hot water as needed. Season with salt and pepper to taste. Serve.

PER SERVING
Calories: 109, Fat: 7.52g, Carbohydrates: 10.54g, Protein: 2.03g, Sugar: 6.46g, Fiber: 3.6g, Sodium: 187mg

Caramelized Rosemary Acorn Squash

Prep time: 5 minutes | Cook time: 30 minutes | Serves: 4

1 acorn squash
2 tablespoons coconut sugar
2 tablespoons rosemary, finely chopped
2 tablespoons olive oil
Sea salt, to taste

1. Preheat oven to 400ºF (205ºC).
2. Cut squash in half, and clean out the seeds. Slice each half into 4 wedges.
3. Mix coconut sugar, rosemary, and olive oil.
4. Lay squash on baking sheet, and sprinkle each slice with a bit of the mixture and a touch of sea salt.
5. Turn over and sprinkle other side.
6. Bake for 30 minutes or so until squash is tender and slightly caramelized, turning each slice over halfway through.
7. Serve immediately.

PER SERVING
Calories: 119, Fat: 6.91g, Carbohydrates: 15.39g, Protein: 0.89g, Sugar: 3.91g, Fiber: 1.7g, Sodium: 585mg

Cheesy Cauliflower Cakes

Prep time: 15 minutes | Cook time: 35 minutes | Serves: 4

1 (2-pound / 907-g) head cauliflower, cored and cut into 1-inch florets
¼ cup extra-virgin olive oil
1 teaspoon ground turmeric
1 teaspoon ground coriander
1 teaspoon salt
½ teaspoon ground ginger
¼ teaspoon pepper
4 ounces (113 g) Goat cheese, softened
2 scallions, sliced thin
1 large egg, lightly beaten
2 garlic cloves, minced
1 teaspoon grated lemon zest, plus lemon wedges for serving
¼ cup all-purpose flour

1. Adjust oven rack to middle position and heat oven to 450ºF (235ºC). Toss cauliflower with 1 tablespoon oil, turmeric, coriander, salt, ginger, and pepper. Transfer to aluminum foil–lined rimmed baking sheet and spread into single layer. Roast until cauliflower is well browned and tender, about 25 minutes. Let cool slightly, then transfer to large bowl.
2. Line clean rimmed baking sheet with parchment paper. Mash cauliflower coarsely with potato masher. Stir in Goat cheese, scallions, egg, garlic, and lemon zest until well combined. Sprinkle flour over cauliflower mixture and stir to incorporate. Using wet hands, divide mixture into 4 equal portions, pack gently into ¾-inch-thick cakes, and place on prepared sheet. Refrigerate cakes until chilled and firm, about 30 minutes.
3. Line large plate with paper towels. Heat remaining 3 tablespoons oil in 12-inch nonstick skillet over medium heat until shimmering. Gently lay cakes in skillet and cook until deep golden brown and crisp, 5 to 7 minutes per side. Drain cakes briefly on prepared plate. Serve with lemon wedges.

PER SERVING
Calories: 317, Fat: 25.07g, Carbohydrates: 12.69g, Protein: 11.79g, Sugar: 2.45g, Fiber: 2g, Sodium: 726mg

Roasted Beets with Oranges and Onions

Prep time: 10 minutes | Cook time: 40 minutes | Serves: 6

4 medium beets, trimmed and scrubbed
Juice and zest of 2 oranges
1 red onion, thinly sliced
2 tablespoons olive oil
1 tablespoon red wine vinegar
Juice of 1 lemon
Sea salt and freshly ground pepper, to taste

1. Preheat oven to 400ºF (205ºC).
2. Wrap the beets in a foil pack and close tightly. Place them on a baking sheet and roast 40 minutes until tender enough to be pierced easily with a knife.
3. Cool until easy to handle.
4. Combine the beets with the orange juice and zest, red onion, olive oil, vinegar, and lemon juice.
5. Season with sea salt and freshly ground pepper to taste, and toss lightly. Allow to sit for about 15 minutes for the flavors to meld before serving.

PER SERVING
Calories: 80, Fat: 4.68g, Carbohydrates: 9.15g, Protein: 1.17g, Sugar: 6.37g, Fiber: 1.7g, Sodium: 43mg

Traditional Peanut Stew over Cauliflower Rice

Prep time: 20 minutes | Cook time: 25 minutes | Serves: 4

1 cup frozen corn
2 tablespoons extra-virgin olive oil
1 cup chopped onion
2 medium Yukon Gold potatoes, unpeeled, cut into ½-inch cubes
1 large sweet potato, unpeeled, cut into ½-inch cubes
3 garlic cloves, minced
1½ teaspoons ground cumin
1 teaspoon ground allspice
1 teaspoon freshly grated ginger root or ½ teaspoon ground ginger
½ teaspoon crushed red

pepper, or to taste
¼ teaspoon kosher or sea salt
½ cup water
1 (28-ounce / 794-g) can diced tomatoes, undrained
1 (12-ounce / 340-g) package frozen plain cauliflower rice
1 (15-ounce / 425-g) can lentils, undrained
⅓ cup creamy peanut butter
Pickled hot peppers, chopped roasted peanuts, chopped fresh cilantro, for serving (optional)

1. Put the corn on the counter to partially thaw while making the stew.
2. In a large stockpot over medium-high heat, heat the oil. Add the onion, potatoes, and sweet potatoes. Cook for 7 minutes, stirring occasionally, until some of the potatoes and onion get golden and crispy. Move the potatoes to the edges of the pot, and add the garlic, cumin, allspice, ginger, crushed red pepper, and salt. Cook for 1 minute, stirring constantly. Stir in the water and cook for 1 more minute, scraping up the crispy bits from the bottom of the pan.
3. Add the tomatoes with their juices to the stockpot. Cook for 15 minutes uncovered, stirring occasionally.
4. While the tomatoes are cooking, cook the cauliflower rice according to the package directions.
5. Into the tomato mixture, stir in the lentils, partially thawed corn, and peanut butter. Reduce the heat to medium and cook for 1 to 2 minutes, until all the ingredients are warmed, stirring constantly to blend in the peanut butter. Serve over the cauliflower rice with hot peppers, peanuts, and fresh cilantro, if desired.

PER SERVING
Calories: 1827g, Total Fat: 88g, Saturated Fat: 9g, Total Carbs: 250g, Protein: 33g, Sugar: 15g, Fiber: 33g, Sodium: 652mg

Lush Roasted Mixed Vegetables

Prep time: 15 minutes | Cook time: 50 minutes | Serves: 2

1 head garlic, cloves split apart, unpeeled
2 tablespoons olive oil, divided
2 medium carrots
¼ pound asparagus
6 Brussels sprouts
2 cups cauliflower florets
½ pint cherry or grape tomatoes

½ fresh lemon, sliced
Salt, to taste
Freshly ground black pepper, to taste
3 sprigs fresh thyme or ½ teaspoon dried thyme
Freshly squeezed lemon juice

1. Preheat oven to 375°F (190°C) and set the rack to the middle position. Line a sheet pan with parchment paper or foil.
2. Place the garlic cloves in a small piece of foil and wrap lightly to enclose them, but don't seal the package. Drizzle with 1 teaspoon of olive oil. Place the foil packet on the sheet pan and roast for 30 minutes while you prepare the remaining vegetables.
3. While garlic is roasting, clean, peel, and trim vegetables: Cut carrots into strips, ½-inch wide and 3 to 4 inches long, snap tough ends off asparagus, trim tough ends off the Brussels sprouts and cut in half if they are large, trim cauliflower into 2-inch florets, keep tomatoes whole. The vegetables should be cut into pieces of similar size for even roasting.
4. Place all vegetables and the lemon slices into a large mixing bowl. Drizzle with the remaining 5 teaspoons of olive oil and season generously with salt and pepper.
5. Increase the oven temperature to 400°F (205°C).
6. Arrange the vegetables on the sheet pan in a single layer, leaving the packet of garlic cloves on the pan. Roast for 20 minutes, turning occasionally, until tender.
7. When the vegetables are tender, remove from the oven and sprinkle with thyme leaves. Let the garlic cloves sit until cool enough to handle, and then remove the skins. Leave them whole, or gently mash.
8. Toss garlic with the vegetables and an additional squeeze of fresh lemon juice.

PER SERVING
Calories: 256, Total Fat: 15g, Total Carbohydrates: 31g, Fiber: 9g, Sugar: 12g, Protein: 7g, Sodium: 168mg

Sautéed Cherry Tomatoes

Prep time: 5 minutes | Cook time: 2 minutes | Serves: 4 to 6

1 tablespoon extra-virgin olive oil	taste
	Salt and pepper, to taste
1½ pounds (680 g) cherry tomatoes, halved	1 garlic clove, minced
2 teaspoons sugar, or to	2 tablespoons chopped fresh basil

1. Heat oil in 12-inch skillet over medium-high heat until shimmering. Toss tomatoes with sugar and ¼ teaspoon salt, then add to skillet and cook, stirring often, for 1 minute. Stir in garlic and cook until fragrant, about 30 seconds. Off heat, stir in basil and season with salt and pepper to taste. Serve.

PER SERVING

Calories: 68, Fat: 3.75g, Carbohydrates: 8.51g, Protein: 1.65g, Sugar: 5.71g, Fiber: 2.2g, Sodium: 9mg

Blistered Tomatoes

Prep time: 5 minutes | Cook time: 1½ hours | Serves: 4

3 pounds (1.4kg) large tomatoes, cored, bottom ⅛ inch trimmed, and sliced ¾ inch thick	¼ teaspoon dried oregano
	Kosher salt and pepper, to taste
2 garlic cloves, peeled and smashed	¾ cup extra-virgin olive oil

1. Adjust oven rack to middle position and heat oven to 425°F (220°C). Line rimmed baking sheet with aluminum foil. Arrange tomatoes in even layer in prepared sheet, with larger slices around edge and smaller slices in center. Place garlic cloves on tomatoes. Sprinkle with oregano and ¼ teaspoon salt and season with pepper to taste. Drizzle oil evenly over tomatoes.
2. Bake for 30 minutes, rotating sheet halfway through baking. Remove sheet from oven. Reduce oven temperature to 300°F (150°C) and prop open door with wooden spoon to cool oven. Using thin spatula, flip tomatoes.
3. Return tomatoes to oven, close oven door, and continue to cook until spotty brown, skins are blistered, and tomatoes have collapsed to ¼ to ½ inch thick, 1 to 2 hours. Remove from oven and let cool completely, about 30 minutes.

Discard garlic and transfer tomatoes and oil to airtight container. (Tomatoes can be refrigerated for up to 5 days or frozen for up to 2 months.)

PER SERVING

Calories: 423, Fat: 41.21g, Carbohydrates: 14.15g, Protein: 3.16g, Sugar: 8.97g, Fiber: 4.3g, Sodium: 18mg

Butternut Squash with Tahini and Feta

Prep time: 10 minutes | Cook time: 41 minutes | Serves: 6

3 pounds (1.4kg) butternut squash	1 teaspoon honey
	1 ounce (28 g) Feta cheese, crumbled
3 tablespoons extra-virgin olive oil	¼ cup shelled pistachios, toasted and chopped fine
Salt and pepper, to taste	
1 tablespoon tahini	2 tablespoons chopped fresh mint
1½ teaspoons lemon juice	

1. Adjust oven rack to lowest position and heat oven to 425°F (220°C). Using sharp vegetable peeler or chef's knife, remove squash skin and fibrous threads just below skin (squash should be completely orange with no white flesh). Halve squash lengthwise and scrape out seeds. Place squash cut side down on cutting board and slice crosswise into ½-inch-thick pieces.
2. Toss squash with 2 tablespoons oil, ½ teaspoon salt, and ½ teaspoon pepper and arrange in rimmed baking sheet in single layer. Roast squash until sides touching sheet toward back of oven are well browned, 25 to 30 minutes. Rotate sheet and continue to roast until sides touching sheet toward back of oven are well browned, 6 to 10 minutes.
3. Use metal spatula to flip each piece and continue to roast until squash is very tender and sides touching sheet are browned, 10 to 15 minutes.
4. Transfer squash to serving platter. Whisk tahini, lemon juice, honey, remaining 1 tablespoon oil, and pinch salt together in bowl. Drizzle squash with tahini dressing and sprinkle with Feta, pistachios, and mint. Serve.

PER SERVING

Calories: 212, Fat: 11.68g, Carbohydrates: 27.1g, Protein: 4.03g, Sugar: 1.61g, Fiber: 4.3g, Sodium: 53mg

Oven-Roasted Asparagus

Prep time: 5 minutes | Cook time: 8 minutes | Serves: 4 to 6

2 pounds (907 g) thick asparagus, trimmed
2 tablespoons plus 2 teaspoons extra-virgin

olive oil
½ teaspoon salt
¼ teaspoon pepper

1. Adjust oven rack to lowest position, place rimmed baking sheet on rack, and heat oven to 500°F (260°C). Peel bottom halves of asparagus spears until white flesh is exposed, then toss with 2 tablespoons oil, salt, and pepper.
2. Transfer asparagus to preheated sheet and spread into single layer. Roast, without moving asparagus, until undersides of spears are browned, tops are bright green, and tip of paring knife inserted at base of largest spear meets little resistance, 8 to 10 minutes. Transfer asparagus to serving platter and drizzle with remaining 2 teaspoons oil. Serve.

PER SERVING
Calories: 126, Fat: 9.29g, Carbohydrates: 9.07g, Protein: 5.03g, Sugar: 4.27g, Fiber: 4.9g, Sodium: 295mg

Braised Radishes, Asparagus, and Peas

Prep time: 15 minutes | Cook time: 8 minutes | Serves: 4 to 6

¼ cup extra-virgin olive oil
1 shallot, sliced into thin rounds
2 garlic cloves, sliced thin
3 fresh thyme sprigs
Pinch red pepper flakes
10 radishes, trimmed and quartered lengthwise
1¼ cups water
2 teaspoons grated

lemon zest
2 teaspoons grated orange zest
1 bay leaf
Salt and pepper, to taste
1 pound (454 g) asparagus, trimmed and cut into 2-inch lengths
2 cups frozen peas
4 teaspoons chopped fresh tarragon

1. Cook oil, shallot, garlic, thyme sprigs, and pepper flakes in Dutch oven over medium heat until shallot is just softened, about 2 minutes. Stir in radishes, water, lemon zest, orange zest, bay leaf, and 1 teaspoon salt and bring to simmer. Reduce heat to medium-low, cover, and cook until radishes can be easily pierced with tip

of paring knife, 3 to 5 minutes. Stir in asparagus, cover, and cook until tender, 3 to 5 minutes.
2. Off heat, stir in peas, cover, and let sit until heated through, about 5 minutes. Discard thyme sprigs and bay leaf. Stir in tarragon and season with salt and pepper to taste. Serve.

PER SERVING
Calories: 342, Fat: 14.96g, Carbohydrates: 48.3g, Protein: 10.37g, Sugar: 24g, Fiber: 19.4g, Sodium: 186mg

Asparagus with Tomato and Olive

Prep time: 10 minutes | Cook time: 16 minutes | Serves: 6

2 tablespoons extra-virgin olive oil
2 garlic cloves, minced
12 ounces (340 g) cherry tomatoes, halved
½ cup pitted kalamata olives, chopped coarse

2 pounds (907 g) thick asparagus, trimmed
2 tablespoons shredded fresh basil
¼ cup grated Parmesan cheese
Salt and pepper, to taste

1. Cook 1 tablespoon oil and garlic in 12-inch skillet over medium heat, stirring often, until garlic turns golden but not brown, about 3 minutes. Add tomatoes and olives and cook until tomatoes begin to break down, about 3 minutes, transfer to bowl.
2. Heat remaining 1 tablespoon oil in now-empty skillet over medium-high heat until shimmering. Add half of asparagus with tips pointed in 1 direction and remaining asparagus with tips pointed in opposite direction. Shake skillet gently to help distribute spears evenly (they will not quite fit in single layer). Add 1 teaspoon water, cover, and cook until asparagus is bright green and still crisp, about 5 minutes.
3. Uncover, increase heat to high, and cook, moving spears around with tongs as needed, until asparagus is well browned on 1 side and tip of paring knife inserted at base of largest spear meets little resistance, 5 to 7 minutes. Season with salt and pepper to taste. Transfer asparagus to serving platter, top with tomato mixture, and sprinkle with basil and Parmesan. Serve.

PER SERVING
Calories: 230, Fat: 7.17g, Carbohydrates: 9.95g, Protein: 5.23g, Sugar: 4.35g, Fiber: 4.3g, Sodium: 164mg

Artichoke with Low-fat Yogurt

Prep time: 5 minutes | Cook time: 14 minutes | Serves: 4

2 large artichokes	Salt and black pepper, to
2 cups water	taste
2 garlic cloves, smashed	Juice of 1 Lime
½ cup low fat yogurt	

1. Using a serrated knife, trim about 1 inch from the artichokes' top. Into the pot, add water and set trivet over. Lay the artichokes on the trivet. Seal lid and cook for 14 minutes on High Pressure.
2. Release the pressure quickly. Mix the low fat yogurt with garlic and lime juice. Season with salt and pepper. Serve artichokes in a platter with garlic mayo on the side.

PER SERVING
Calories: 64, Fat: 0.63g, Carbohydrates: 12.46g, Protein: 4.46g, Sugar: 3.16g, Fiber: 4.6g, Sodium: 101mg

Sweet Potato Medallions with Rosemary

Prep time: 5 minutes | Cook time: 16 minutes | Serves: 4

1 cup water	4 sweet potatoes
1 tablespoon fresh rosemary	2 tablespoons almond butter
1 teaspoon garlic powder	Salt, to taste

1. Add water and place steamer rack over the water. Use a fork to prick sweet potatoes all over and set onto steamer rack. Seal the lid and cook on High Pressure for 12 minutes. Release the pressure quickly.
2. Transfer sweet potatoes to a cutting board and slice into ½-inch medallions and ensure they are peeled.
3. Melt butter in the on Sauté mode. Add in the medallions and cook each side for 2 to 3 minutes until browned. Season with salt and garlic powder. Serve topped with fresh rosemary.

PER SERVING
Calories: 166, Fat: 5.85g, Carbohydrates: 26.81g, Protein: 2.24g, Sugar: 5.46g, Fiber: 4g, Sodium: 700mg

Speedy Colorful Vegetable Medley

Prep time: 5 minutes | Cook time: 3 minutes | Serves: 4

1 cup water	5 ounces (142 g) green
1 small head broccoli, broken into florets	beans
16 asparagus, trimmed	2 carrots, peeled and cut on bias
1 small head cauliflower, broken into florets	Salt, to taste

1. Add water and set trivet on top of water and place steamer basket on top. In an even layer, spread green beans, broccoli, cauliflower, asparagus, and carrots in a steamer basket. Seal the lid and cook on Steam for 3 minutes on High. Release the pressure quickly. Remove basket from the pot and season with salt.

PER SERVING
Calories: 66, Fat: 0.73g, Carbohydrates: 13.13g, Protein: 5.49g, Sugar: 3.54g, Fiber: 4g, Sodium: 638mg

Herb Potatoes

Prep time: 10 minutes | Cook time: 10 minutes | Serves: 4

1½ pounds (680 g) potatoes	½ teaspoon fresh thyme, chopped
3 tablespoons butter	½ teaspoon fresh parsley, chopped
3 cloves garlic, thinly chopped	¼ teaspoon ground black pepper
2 tablespoons fresh rosemary, chopped	½ cup vegetable broth

1. Use a small knife to pierce each potato to ensure there are no blowouts when placed under pressure. Melt butter on Sauté. Add in potatoes, rosemary, parsley, pepper, thyme, and garlic, and cook for 10 minutes until potatoes are browned and the mixture is aromatic.
2. In a bowl, mix miso paste and vegetable stock. Stir in to the mixture in the instant pot. Seal the lid and cook for 5 minutes on High Pressure. Release the pressure quickly.

PER SERVING
Calories: 214, Fat: 8.86g, Carbohydrates: 31.16g, Protein: 3.73g, Sugar: 1.61g, Fiber: 4g, Sodium: 148mg

Sautéed Swiss Chard with Garlic Cloves

Prep time: 5 minutes | Cook time: 10 minutes | Serves: 4

2 tablespoons extra-virgin olive oil
3 garlic cloves, sliced thin
1½ pounds (680 g) Swiss chard, stems sliced ¼ inch thick on bias, leaves sliced into ½-inch-wide strips
Salt and pepper, to taste
2 teaspoons lemon juice

1. Heat oil in 12-inch nonstick skillet over medium-high heat until just shimmering. Add garlic and cook, stirring constantly, until lightly browned, 30 to 60 seconds. Add chard stems and ⅛ teaspoon salt and cook, stirring occasionally, until spotty brown and crisp-tender, about 6 minutes.
2. Add two-thirds of chard leaves and cook, tossing with tongs, until just starting to wilt, 30 to 60 seconds. Add remaining chard leaves and continue to cook, stirring frequently, until leaves are tender, about 3 minutes. Off heat, stir in lemon juice and season with salt and pepper to taste. Serve.

PER SERVING
Calories: 97, Fat: 7.13g, Carbohydrates: 7.65g, Protein: 3.27g, Sugar: 1.96g, Fiber: 2.9g, Sodium: 363mg

Greek-Style Oregano Potatoes

Prep time: 10 minutes | Cook time: 21 minutes | Serves: 4 to 6

3 tablespoons extra-virgin olive oil
1½ pounds (680 g) Yukon Gold potatoes, peeled and cut lengthwise into ¾-inch-thick wedges
1½ tablespoons minced fresh oregano
3 garlic cloves, minced
2 teaspoons grated lemon zest plus 1½ tablespoons juice
Salt and pepper, to taste
1½ tablespoons minced fresh parsley

1. Heat 2 tablespoons oil in 12-inch nonstick skillet over medium-high heat until shimmering. Add potatoes cut side down in single layer and cook until golden brown on first side (skillet should sizzle but not smoke), about 6 minutes. Using tongs, flip potatoes onto second cut side and cook until golden brown, about 5 minutes.

Reduce heat to medium-low, cover, and cook until potatoes are tender, 8 to 12 minutes.
2. Meanwhile, whisk remaining 1 tablespoon oil, oregano, garlic, lemon zest and juice, ½ teaspoon salt, and ½ teaspoon pepper together in small bowl. When potatoes are tender, gently stir in garlic mixture and cook, uncovered, until fragrant, about 2 minutes. Off heat, gently stir in parsley and season with salt and pepper to taste. Serve.

PER SERVING
Calories: 234, Fat: 10.44g, Carbohydrates: 32.96g, Protein: 3.93g, Sugar: 1.54g, Fiber: 5.1g, Sodium: 12mg

Garlicky-Lemony Braised Kale

Prep time: 10 minutes | Cook time: 31 minutes | Serves: 8

6 tablespoons extra-virgin olive oil
1 large onion, chopped fine
10 garlic cloves, minced
¼ teaspoon red pepper flakes
2 cups chicken or vegetable broth
1 cup water
Salt and pepper, to taste
4 pounds (1.8 kg) kale, stemmed and cut into 3-inch pieces
1 tablespoon lemon juice, plus extra for seasoning

1. Heat 3 tablespoons oil in Dutch oven over medium heat until shimmering. Add onion and cook until softened and lightly browned, 5 to 7 minutes. Stir in garlic and pepper flakes and cook until fragrant, about 1 minute. Stir in broth, water, and ½ teaspoon salt and bring to simmer.
2. Add one-third of kale, cover, and cook, stirring occasionally, until wilted, 2 to 4 minutes. Repeat with remaining kale in 2 batches. Continue to cook, covered, until kale is tender, 13 to 15 minutes.
3. Remove lid and increase heat to medium-high. Cook, stirring occasionally, until most liquid has evaporated and greens begin to sizzle, 10 to 12 minutes. Off heat, stir in remaining 3 tablespoons oil and lemon juice. Season with salt, pepper, and extra lemon juice to taste. Serve.

PER SERVING
Calories: 244, Fat: 13.12g, Carbohydrates: 25.78g, Protein: 12.99g, Sugar: 6.87g, Fiber: 9.1g, Sodium: 251mg

Lightly Glazed Slow-Cooked Carrots

Prep time: 5 minutes | Cook time: 49 minutes | Serves: 4 to 6

1 tablespoon extra-virgin olive oil
½ teaspoon salt

1½ pounds (680 g) carrots, peeled

1. Cut parchment paper into 11-inch circle, then cut 1-inch hole in center, folding paper as needed.
2. Bring 3 cups water, oil, and salt to simmer in 12-inch skillet over high heat. Off heat, add carrots, top with parchment, cover skillet, and let sit for 20 minutes.
3. Uncover, leaving parchment in place, and bring to simmer over high heat. Reduce heat to medium-low and cook until most of water has evaporated and carrots are very tender, about 45 minutes.
4. Discard parchment, increase heat to medium-high, and cook carrots, shaking skillet often, until lightly glazed and no water remains, 2 to 4 minutes. Serve.

PER SERVING
Calories: 89, Fat: 3.68g, Carbohydrates: 13.98g, Protein: 1.29g, Sugar: 5.87g, Fiber: 5.1g, Sodium: 389mg

Mini Potatoes Bake

Prep time: 10 minutes | Cook time: 30 minutes | Serves: 2

10 ounces (283 g) golden mini potatoes, halved
4 tablespoons extra-virgin olive oil
2 teaspoons dried, minced garlic
1 teaspoon onion salt
½ teaspoon paprika
¼ teaspoon freshly ground black pepper
¼ teaspoon red pepper flakes
¼ teaspoon dried dill

1. Preheat the oven to 400°F (205°C).
2. Soak the potatoes and put in a bowl of ice water for 30 minutes. Change the water if you return and the water is milky.
3. Rinse and dry the potatoes, then put them on a baking sheet.
4. Drizzle the potatoes with oil and sprinkle with the garlic, onion salt, paprika, pepper, red pepper flakes, and dill. Using tongs or your hands, toss well to coat.
5. Lower the heat to 375°F (190°C), add potatoes to the oven, and bake for 20 minutes.
6. At 20 minutes, check and flip potatoes. Bake for another 10 minutes, or until the potatoes are fork-tender.

PER SERVING (½ cup servings)
Calories: 344, Total Fat: 28g, Saturated Fat: 4g, Total Carbohydrates: 24g, Protein: 3g, Sugar: 1g, Fiber: 4g, Sodium: 423mg

Turmeric-Spiced Organic Chickpeas

Prep time: 10 minutes | Cook time: 30 minutes | Serves: 4

2 (15-ounce / 425-g) cans organic chickpeas, drained and rinsed
3 tablespoons extra-virgin olive oil
2 teaspoons Turkish or smoked paprika
2 teaspoons turmeric
½ teaspoon dried oregano
½ teaspoon salt
¼ teaspoon ground ginger
⅛ teaspoon ground white pepper (optional)

1. Preheat the oven to 400°F (205°C). Line a baking sheet with parchment paper and set aside.
2. Completely dry the chickpeas. Lay the chickpeas out on a baking sheet, roll them around with paper towels, and allow them to air-dry. I usually let them dry for at least 2½ hours, but can also be left to dry overnight.
3. In a medium bowl, combine the olive oil, paprika, turmeric, oregano, salt, ginger, and white pepper (if using).
4. Add the dry chickpeas to the bowl and toss to combine.
5. Put the chickpeas on the prepared baking sheet and cook for 30 minutes, or until the chickpeas turn golden brown. At 15 minutes, move the chickpeas around on the baking sheet to avoid burning. Check every 10 minutes in case the chickpeas begin to crisp up before the full cooking time has elapsed.
6. Remove from the oven and set them aside to cool.

PER SERVING (½ cup)
Calories: 308, Total Fat: 13g, Saturated Fat: 2g, Total Carbohydrates: 40g, Protein: 11g, Sugar: <1g, Fiber: 11g, Sodium: 292mg

Freekeh Pilaf with Dates

Prep time: 15 minutes | Cook time: 20 minutes | Serves: 4 to 6

2 tbsps. extra-virgin olive oil, plus extra for drizzling
1 shallot, minced
1½ tsp. grated fresh ginger
½ tsp. table salt
¼ tsp. ground coriander
¼ tsp. ground cumin
¼ tsp. pepper
1¾ cups (420 ml) water

1½ cups cracked freekeh, rinsed
3 ounces (85 g) pitted dates, chopped (½ cup)
¼ cup shelled pistachios, toasted and coarsely chopped
1½ tbsps. lemon juice
¼ cup chopped fresh mint

1. In Instant Pot, use highest sauté function, heat oil until shimmering. Add cumin, shallot, salt, ginger, coriander, and pepper and cook about 2 minutes until shallot is softened. Stir in freekeh and water.
2. Lock lid and close pressure release valve. Choose high pressure cook function and cook for 4 minutes. Turn off and quick-release pressure. Carefully remove lid, letting steam escape away from you.
3. Add pistachios, dates, and lemon juice and gently fluff freekeh with fork to combine. Season with salt and pepper. Transfer to a dish, sprinkle with mint and drizzle with extra oil. Serve.

PER SERVING
Calories: 280; Total Fat: 8g; Sat Fat: 1g; Total Carbohydrates: 46g; Protein: 8g; Sugar: 10g; Fiber: 9g; Sodium: 200mg

Healthy Vegetable Broth

Prep time: 15 minutes | Cook time: 35 minutes | Serves: 3 quarts

1 tbsp. vegetable oil
2 carrots, peeled and chopped
2 celery ribs, chopped
3 onions, chopped
4 scallions, chopped
15 garlic cloves, smashed and peeled
12 cups (2880 ml) water, divided

½ head cauliflower (1 pound, 454 g), cored and cut into 1-inch pieces
1 tomato, cored and chopped
3 bay leaves
8 sprigs fresh thyme
1 tsp. peppercorns
½ tsp. table salt

1. In Instant Pot, use highest sauté function, heat oil until shimmering. Add scallions, onions, celery, carrots, and garlic and cook about 15 minutes until vegetables are softened and lightly browned. Add 1 cup water, scraping up any browned bits, then stir in remaining water, tomato, cauliflower, peppercorns, thyme sprigs, salt, and bay leaves.
2. Lock lid and close pressure release valve. Choose high pressure cook function and cook for 1 hour. Turn off and let pressure release naturally for 15 minutes. Quick-release any remaining pressure and carefully remove lid, letting steam escape away from you.
3. Strain broth through colander into large container, without pressing on solids, throw away solids. (Broth can be refrigerated for up to 4 days or frozen for 2 months.)

PER SERVING
Calories: 9, Total Fat: 0g, Sat Fat: 0g, Total Carbohydrates: 0g, Protein: 1g, Sugar: 0g, Fiber: 0g, Sodium: 95mg

Herb and Ricotta–Stuffed Mushrooms

Prep time: 10 minutes | Cook time: 30 minutes | Serves: 4

⅓ cup chopped fresh herbs (such as basil, parsley, rosemary, oregano, or thyme)
6 tbsps. extra-virgin olive oil, divided
2 garlic cloves, finely minced

4 portobello mushroom caps, cleaned and gills removed
1 cup whole-milk ricotta cheese
½ tsp. salt
¼ tsp. freshly ground black pepper

1. Preheat the oven to 400°F (205°C).
2. Line a baking sheet with parchment and drizzle with 2 tablespoons olive oil evenly. Put the mushroom caps on the baking sheet, gill-side up.
3. Mix together the herbs, ricotta, garlic, 2 tablespoons olive oil, salt, and pepper in a medium bowl. Stuff each mushroom cap with 1/4 of the cheese mixture, pressing down if needed. Drizzle with remaining olive oil and bake 30 to 35 minutes until golden brown and the mushrooms are soft.

PER SERVING
Calories: 285, Total Fat: 25g, Total Carbohydrates: 8g, Net Carbs: 6g, Protein: 7g, Fiber: 2g, Sodium: 325mg

Feta Cheese and Mushrooms Stuffed Potatoes

Prep time: 10 minutes | Cook time: 35 minutes | Serves: 3

6 potatoes, whole, rinsed, drained
¼ cup olive oil
3 garlic cloves, crushed
¼ cup Feta cheese
1 teaspoon fresh

rosemary, chopped
½ teaspoon dried thyme
2 ounces (57 g) button mushrooms, chopped
1 teaspoon salt

1. Rub the potatoes with salt and place them in the instant pot. Add enough water to cover and seal the lid. Cook on High Pressure for 30 minutes. Do a quick release and remove the potatoes. Let chill for a while.
2. Meanwhile, in the pot, mix olive oil, garlic, rosemary, thyme, and mushrooms. Sauté until the mushrooms soften, about 5 minutes, on Sauté. Remove from the cooker and stir in Feta. Cut the top of each potato and spoon out the middle. Fill with cheese mixture and serve immediately.

PER SERVING
Calories: 821, Fat: 21.54g, Carbohydrates: 144.76g, Protein: 18.78g, Sugar: 6.72g, Fiber: 18.5g, Sodium: 937mg

Mediterranean-Style Lentil Sloppy Joes

Prep time: 15 minutes | Cook time: 15 minutes | Serves: 4

1 tablespoon extra-virgin olive oil
1 cup chopped onion
1 cup chopped bell pepper, any color
2 garlic cloves, minced
1 (15-ounce / 425-g) can lentils, drained and rinsed
1 (14½-ounce / 411-g) can low-sodium or no-salt-added diced

tomatoes, undrained
1 teaspoon ground cumin
1 teaspoon dried thyme
¼ teaspoon kosher or sea salt
4 whole-wheat pita breads, split open
1½ cups chopped seedless cucumber
1 cup chopped romaine lettuce

1. In a medium saucepan over medium-high heat, heat the oil. Add the onion and bell pepper and cook for 4 minutes, stirring frequently. Add the garlic and cook for 1 minute, stirring frequently.

Add the lentils, tomatoes (with their liquid), cumin, thyme, and salt. Turn the heat to medium and cook, stirring occasionally, for 10 minutes, or until most of the liquid has evaporated.

2. Stuff the lentil mixture inside each pita. Lay the cucumbers and lettuce on top of the lentil mixture and serve.

PER SERVING
Calories: 241g, Total Fat: 3g, Saturated Fat:1g,Total Carbs: 43g, Protein: 13g, Sugar: 7g, Fiber: 13g, Sodium: 317mg

Spicy Chickpeas with Turnips and Parsley

Prep time: 15 minutes | Cook time: 31 minutes | Serves: 4 to 6

2 tablespoons extra-virgin olive oil
2 onions, chopped
2 red bell peppers, stemmed, seeded, and chopped
Salt and pepper, to taste
¼ cup tomato paste
1 jalapeño chile, stemmed, seeded, and minced
5 garlic cloves, minced
¾ teaspoon ground cumin

¼ teaspoon cayenne pepper
2 (15-ounce / 425-g) cans chickpeas
12 ounces (340 g) turnips, peeled and cut into ½-inch pieces
¾ cup water, plus extra as needed
¼ cup chopped fresh parsley
2 tablespoons lemon juice, plus extra for seasoning

1. Heat oil in Dutch oven over medium heat until shimmering. Add onions, bell peppers, ½ teaspoon salt, and ¼ teaspoon pepper and cook until softened and lightly browned, 5 to 7 minutes. Stir in tomato paste, jalapeño, garlic, cumin, and cayenne and cook until fragrant, about 30 seconds.
2. Stir in chickpeas and their liquid, turnips, and water. Bring to simmer and cook until turnips are tender and sauce has thickened, 25 to 35 minutes.
3. Stir in parsley and lemon juice. Season with salt, pepper, and extra lemon juice to taste. Adjust consistency with extra hot water as needed. Serve.

PER SERVING
Calories: 290, Fat: 7.27g, Carbohydrates: 45.71g, Protein: 13.78g, Sugar: 11.95g, Fiber: 13.2g, Sodium: 406mg

Caramelized Root Vegetables with Parsley

Prep time: 10 minutes | Cook time: 30 minutes | Serves: 6

2 medium carrots, peeled and cut into chunks
2 medium red or gold beets, cut into chunks
2 turnips, peeled and cut into chunks
2 tablespoons olive oil
1 teaspoon cumin
1 teaspoon sweet paprika
Sea salt and freshly ground pepper, to taste
Juice of 1 lemon
1 small bunch flat-leaf parsley, chopped

1. Preheat oven to 400°F (205°C).
2. Toss the vegetables with the olive oil and seasonings.
3. Lay in a single layer on a sheet pan, cover with lemon juice, and roast for 30 to 40 minutes, until veggies are slightly browned and crisp.
4. Serve warm, topped with the chopped parsley.

PER SERVING
Calories: 168, Fat: 7.31g, Carbohydrates: 13.45g, Protein: 2.21g, Sugar: 7.04g, Fiber: 4g, Sodium: 104mg

Wild Mushroom Farro

Prep time: 15 minutes | Cook time: 25 minutes | Serves: 4 to 6

1½ cups whole farro
3 tbsps. extra-virgin olive oil, divided, plus extra for drizzling
12 ounces (340 g) cremini or white mushrooms, trimmed and sliced thin
½ onion, chopped fine
½ tsp. table salt
¼ tsp. pepper
1 garlic clove, minced
¼ ounce (7 g) dried porcini mushrooms, rinsed and chopped fine
2 tsps. minced fresh
thyme or ½ teaspoon dried
¼ cup (60 ml) dry white wine
2½ cups (600 ml) chicken or vegetable broth, plus extra as needed
2 tsps. lemon juice
½ cup chopped fresh parsley
2 ounces (57 g) Parmesan cheese, grated (1 cup), plus extra for serving

1. Pulse farro in blender for about 6 pulses until about half of grains are broken into smaller pieces.
2. In Instant Pot, use highest sauté function, heat 2 tablespoons oil until shimmering. Add onion, cremini mushrooms, salt, and pepper, partially cover, and cook about 5 minutes until mushrooms are softened and have released their liquid. Stir in garlic, farro, porcini mushrooms, and thyme and cook about 1 minute until fragrant. Stir in wine and cook about 30 seconds until nearly evaporated. Stir in broth.
3. Lock lid and close pressure release valve. Choose high pressure cook function and cook for 12 minutes. Turn off and quick-release pressure. Carefully remove lid, letting steam escape away from you.
4. If necessary adjust consistency with extra hot broth. With highest sauté function, stirring frequently, until proper consistency is achieved. Add Parmesan and remaining oil and stir vigorously until creamy. Add lemon juice and season with salt and pepper. Sprinkle each portion with parsley and extra Parmesan, and drizzle with extra oil. Serve.

PER SERVING
Calories: 280, Total Fat: 10g, Sat Fat: 2.5g, Total Carbohydrates: 35g, Protein: 13g, Sugar: 2g, Sodium: 630mg, Fiber: 4g

Sauté Riced Cauliflower

Prep time: 5 minutes | Cook time: 5 minutes | Serves: 6 to 8

1 small head cauliflower, broken into florets
¼ cup extra-virgin olive oil
2 garlic cloves, finely
minced
1½ teaspoons salt
½ teaspoon freshly ground black pepper

1. Place the florets in a food processor and pulse several times, until the cauliflower is the consistency of rice or couscous.
2. In a large skillet, heat the olive oil over medium-high heat. Add the cauliflower, garlic, salt, and pepper and sauté for 5 minutes, just to take the crunch out but not enough to let the cauliflower become soggy.
3. Remove the cauliflower from the skillet and place in a bowl until ready to use. Toss with chopped herbs and additional olive oil for a simple side, top with sautéed veggies and protein, or use in your favorite recipe.

PER SERVING
Calories: 92, Total Fat: 9g, Total Carbs: 3g, Net Carbs: 2g, Protein: 1g, Fiber: 1g, Sodium: 595mg

Garlicky Herb Roasted Grape Tomatoes

Prep time: 5 minutes | Cook time: 45 minutes | Serves: 2

1 pint grape tomatoes
10 whole garlic cloves, skins removed
¼ cup olive oil
½ teaspoon salt
1 fresh rosemary sprig
1 fresh thyme sprig

1. Preheat oven to 350°F (180°C).
2. Toss tomatoes, garlic cloves, oil, salt, and herb sprigs in a baking dish.
3. Roast tomatoes until they are soft and begin to caramelize, about 45 minutes.
4. Remove herbs before serving.

PER SERVING
Calories: 271, Total Fat: 26g, Total Carbohydrates: 12g, Protein: 3g, Fiber: 3g, Sugar: 5g, Sodium: 593mg

Eggplant with Minty Yogurt Sauce

Prep time: 10 minutes | Cook time: 10 minutes | Serves: 4 to 6

6 tablespoons extra-virgin olive oil
5 garlic cloves, minced
⅛ teaspoon red pepper flakes
½ cup plain whole-milk yogurt
3 tablespoons chopped fresh mint
1 teaspoon grated lemon zest plus 2 teaspoons juice
1 teaspoon ground cumin
Salt and pepper, to taste
2 pounds (907 g) eggplant, sliced into ¼-inch-thick rounds

1. Combine oil, garlic, and pepper flakes in bowl. Microwave until garlic is golden brown and crisp, about 2 minutes. Strain garlic oil through fine-mesh strainer into small bowl. Reserve garlic oil and garlic separately.
2. Whisk 1 tablespoon garlic oil, yogurt, mint, lemon zest and juice, cumin, and ¼ teaspoon salt together in separate bowl, set aside for serving.
3. For a charcoal, grill Open bottom vent completely. Light large chimney starter filled with charcoal briquettes (6 quarts). When top coals are partially covered with ash, pour evenly over grill. Set cooking grate in place, cover, and open lid vent completely. Heat grill until hot, about 5 minutes.
4. For a gas grill, turn all burners to high, cover, and heat grill until hot, about 15 minutes. Turn all burners to medium-high.
5. Clean and oil cooking grate. Brush eggplant with remaining garlic oil and season with salt and pepper. Place half of eggplant on grill and cook (covered if using gas) until browned and tender, about 4 minutes per side, transfer to serving platter. Repeat with remaining eggplant, transfer to platter. Drizzle yogurt sauce over eggplant and sprinkle with garlic. Serve.

PER SERVING
Calories: 286, Fat: 21.85g, Carbohydrates: 16.84g, Protein: 3.77g, Sugar: 9.54g, Fiber: 7.2g, Sodium: 21mg

Stuffed Zucchini with Mushrooms

Prep time: 10 minutes | Cook time: 39 minutes | Serves: 2

2 tablespoons olive oil
2 cups button mushrooms, finely chopped
2 cloves garlic, finely chopped
2 tablespoons chicken broth
1 tablespoon flat-leaf parsley, finely chopped
1 tablespoon Italian seasoning
Sea salt and freshly ground pepper, to taste
2 medium zucchini, cut in half lengthwise

1. Preheat oven to 350°F (180°C).
2. Heat a large skillet over medium heat, and add the olive oil. Add the mushrooms and cook until tender, about 4 minutes. Add the garlic and cook for 2 more minutes.
3. Add the chicken broth and cook another 3–4 minutes.
4. Add the parsley and Italian seasoning, and season with sea salt and freshly ground pepper.
5. Stir and remove from heat.
6. Scoop out the insides of the halved zucchini and stuff with mushroom mixture.
7. Place zucchini in a casserole dish, and drizzle a tablespoon of water or broth in the bottom.
8. Cover with foil and bake for 30 to 40 minutes until zucchini are tender. Serve immediately.

PER SERVING
Calories: 219, Fat: 15.56g, Carbohydrates: 13.68g, Protein: 9.14g, Sugar: 7.32g, Fiber: 3.9g, Sodium: 394mg

Vegan Carrot and Tomato Gazpacho

Prep time: 10 minutes | Cook time: 20 minutes | Serves: 4

1 pound (454 g) trimmed carrots
1 pound (454 g) tomatoes, chopped
1 cucumber, peeled and chopped
¼ cup olive oil
2 tablespoons lemon juice
1 red onion, chopped
2 cloves garlic
2 tablespoons white wine vinegar
Salt and freshly ground black pepper, to taste

1. Add carrots, salt and enough water. Seal the lid and cook for 20 minutes on High Pressure. Do a quick release. Set the beets to a bowl and place in the refrigerator to cool. In a blender, add carrots, cucumber, red onion, pepper, garlic, oil, tomatoes, lemon juice, vinegar, and salt. Blend until very smooth. Place gazpacho to a serving bowl, chill while covered for 2 hours.

PER SERVING
Calories: 206, Fat: 14.07g, Carbohydrates: 19.64g, Protein: 3.15g, Sugar: 6.55g, Fiber: 5.5g, Sodium: 117mg

Radicchio on Fennel with Parmesan

Prep time: 10 minutes | Cook time: 30 minutes | Serves: 6

3 tablespoons extra-virgin olive oil
3 (12-ounce / 340-g) fennel bulbs, 2 tablespoons fronds minced, stalks discarded, bulbs cut vertically into ½-inch-thick slabs
½ teaspoon grated lemon zest plus 2 teaspoons juice
Salt and pepper, to taste
½ cup dry white wine
1 (10 ounce / 283-g) head radicchio, cored and sliced thin
¼ cup water
2 teaspoons honey
2 tablespoons pine nuts, toasted and chopped
Shaved Parmesan cheese

1. Heat oil in 12-inch skillet over medium heat until shimmering. Add fennel pieces, lemon zest, ½ teaspoon salt, and ¼ teaspoon pepper, then pour wine over fennel. (Skillet will be slightly crowded at first, but fennel will fit into single layer as it cooks.) Cover, reduce heat to medium-low, and cook until fennel is just tender, about 20 minutes.
2. Increase heat to medium, flip fennel pieces, and continue to cook, uncovered, until fennel is well browned on first side and liquid is almost completely evaporated, 5 to 8 minutes. Flip fennel pieces and continue to cook until well browned on second side, 2 to 4 minutes. Transfer fennel to serving platter and tent loosely with aluminum foil.
3. Add radicchio, water, honey, and pinch salt to now-empty skillet and cook over low heat, scraping up any browned bits, until wilted, 3 to 5 minutes. Off heat, stir in lemon juice and season with salt and pepper to taste. Arrange radicchio over fennel and sprinkle with pine nuts, minced fennel fronds, and shaved Parmesan. Serve.

PER SERVING
Calories: 192, Fat: 9.22g, Carbohydrates: 13.08g, Protein: 4.26g, Sugar: 6.87g, Fiber: 4.2g, Sodium: 224mg

Super Cheesy Eggplant Lasagna

Prep time: 10 minutes | Cook time: 4 minutes | Serves: 4

1 large eggplant, chopped
4 ounces (113 g) Mozzarella, chopped
3 ounces (85 g) Mascarpone cheese, at room temperature
2 tomatoes, chopped
¼ cup olive oil
1 teaspoon salt
½ teaspoon freshly ground black pepper
1 teaspoon oregano, dried

1. Grease a baking dish with olive oil. Slice the eggplant and make a layer in the dish. Cover with Mozzarella and tomato slices. Top with Mascarpone cheese.
2. Repeat the process until you run out of ingredients. Meanwhile, in a bowl, mix olive oil, salt, pepper, and dried oregano.
3. Pour the mixture over the lasagna, and add ½ cup of water. In your inner pot, Pour 1½ cups of water and insert a trivet.
4. Lower the baking dish on the trivet, Seal the lid and cook on High Pressure for 4 minutes. When ready, do a natural release, for 10 minutes.

PER SERVING
Calories: 268, Fat: 18.41g, Carbohydrates: 13.71g, Protein: 14.42g, Sugar: 8.44g, Fiber: 5.6g, Sodium: 1144mg

Light Sweet Potato Gratin

Prep time: 10 minutes | Cook time: 4 hours | Serves: 12

1 tablespoon butter, at room temperature
1 large sweet onion, such as vidalia, thinly sliced
2 pounds (907 g) sweet potatoes, peeled and thinly sliced
1 tablespoon all-purpose flour
1 teaspoon chopped fresh thyme
½ teaspoon sea salt
½ teaspoon black pepper
2 ounces (57 g) grated fresh Parmesan cheese
Nonstick cooking oil spray
½ cup vegetable stock

1. Melt the butter in a medium nonstick skillet over medium heat. Add the onion and sauté 5 minutes, or until lightly browned. Remove to a large bowl.
2. Add the sweet potatoes, flour, thyme, salt, pepper, and one-half of the grated Parmesan cheese in the large bowl. Toss gently to coat the sweet potato slices with the flour mixture.
3. Coat the slow cooker with cooking oil spray. Transfer the sweet potato mixture to the slow cooker.
4. Pour the stock over the mixture. Sprinkle with the remaining Parmesan. Cover and cook on low for 4 hours or until the potatoes are tender. Serve hot.

PER SERVING
Calories: 102, Fat: 2.48g, Carbohydrates: 17.15g, Protein: 3.36g, Sugar: 2.13g, Fiber: 2.1g, Sodium: 220mg

Balsamic-Honey Collard Greens

Prep time: 10 minutes | Cook time: 4 minutes | Serves: 5

3 bacon slices
1 cup chopped sweet onion
1 pound (454 g) fresh collard greens, rinsed, stemmed, and chopped
¼ teaspoon sea salt
2 garlic cloves, minced
1 bay leaf
2 cups vegetable or chicken stock
3 tablespoons balsamic vinegar
1 tablespoon honey

1. Cook bacon in a medium skillet over medium heat until crisp, about 6 minutes. Remove the bacon to a paper towel–lined plate to cool. Crumble the bacon.
2. Add the onion to bacon drippings and cook for 5 minutes, or until tender.
3. Add the collard greens and cook 2 to 3 minutes or until the greens begin to wilt, stirring occasionally.
4. Place the collard greens, salt, garlic, bay leaf, and stock in the slow cooker. Cover and cook on low for 3½ to 4 hours.
5. Combine the balsamic vinegar and honey in a small bowl. Stir the vinegar mixture into the collard greens just before serving. Serve hot, sprinkled with the crumbled bacon.

PER SERVING
Calories: 173, Fat: 7.56g, Carbohydrates: 21.47g, Protein: 7.07g, Sugar: 10.16g, Fiber: 5.4g, Sodium: 439mg

Spanish-Style Vegetable Stew

Prep time: 15 minutes | Cook time: 6 hours | Serves: 4

2 tablespoons olive oil
3 shallots, chopped
1 large carrot, sliced
2 garlic cloves, minced
1 pound (454 g) red potatoes, quartered
1 red bell pepper, chopped
1 (9-ounce / 255-g) package quartered artichoke hearts
1 (15-ounce / 425-g) can diced tomatoes with the juice
1½ cups cooked chickpeas
⅓ cup dry white wine
1½ cups vegetable stock
1 teaspoon minced fresh thyme leaves (or ½ teaspoon dried)
1 teaspoon minced fresh oregano leaves (or ½ teaspoon dried)
1 large bay leaf
Sea salt and black pepper, to taste

1. Heat the oil in a large skillet over medium heat. Add the shallots, carrot, and garlic, and cook, stirring often, until the vegetables are soft, about 8 minutes. Put the vegetables in the slow cooker.
2. Add the potatoes, bell pepper, artichoke hearts, tomatoes, chickpeas, wine, and stock to the slow cooker.
3. Sprinkle in the thyme, oregano, and bay leaf, and season with salt and pepper. Cover and cook on low for 6 to 8 hours. Serve hot.

PER SERVING
Calories: 395, Fat: 15.48g, Carbohydrates: 50.59g, Protein: 17.51g, Sugar: 8.94g, Fiber: 11.7g, Sodium: 781mg

Vegan Lemon Hummus Burgers

Prep time: 10 minutes | Cook time: 30 minutes | Serves: 4

1 tbsp. extra-virgin olive oil, plus additional for brushing	¼ cup tahini
	2 garlic cloves, minced
	4 scallions, minced
2 (15-ounce, 425 g) cans garbanzo beans, drained and rinsed	1 tbsp. freshly squeezed lemon juice
	2 tsps. lemon zest
2 tbsps. chickpea flour	1 tsp. salt

1. Preheat the oven to 375°F(190°C).
2. Use olive oil to brush a baking sheet.
3. Add the garbanzo beans, tahini, lemon juice, lemon zest, garlic, and the remaining 1 tablespoon of olive oil into a food processor. Process until smooth. Then mix in the chickpea flour, scallions, and salt. Pulse to combine.
4. Shape the mixture into four patties and put them on the prepared baking sheet. Put the sheet in the preheated oven and bake for 30 minutes.
5. Remove from the oven and serve.

PER SERVING

Calories: 408, Total Fat: 18g, Total Carbohydrates: 43g, Protein: 19g, Sugar: 2g, Fiber: 12g, Sodium: 625mg

Tahini-Yogurt Roasted Brussels Sprouts

Prep time: 10 minutes | Cook time: 35 minutes | Serves: 4

1 pound (454 g) Brussels sprouts, trimmed and halved lengthwise	¼ tsp. freshly ground black pepper
	Zest and juice of 1 lemon
6 tbsp. extra-virgin olive oil, divided	¼ cup (60 ml) plain whole-milk Greek yogurt
1 tsp. salt, divided	¼ cup (60 ml) tahini
½ tsp. garlic powder	

1. Preheat the oven to 425°F (220°C). Line a baking sheet with parchment paper and set aside.
2. Put the Brussels sprouts in a large bowl. Drizzle with ½ teaspoon salt, 4 tablespoons olive oil, garlic powder, and pepper and toss well to coat.
3. Put the Brussels sprouts in a single layer on the baking sheet, reserving the bowl, and roast for 20 minutes. Take it out of the oven and give the sprouts a toss to flip. Return to the oven and continue to roast another 10 to 15 minutes until browned and crispy. Remove from the oven and put it back to the reserved bowl.
4. Whisk together the yogurt, lemon zest and juice, tahini, remaining olive oil, and remaining salt in a small bowl. Drizzle over the roasted sprouts and toss to coat. Serve.

PER SERVING

Calories: 358, Total Fat: 30g, Total Carbohydrates: 15g, Net Carbs: 9g, Protein: 7g, Fiber: 6g, Sodium: 636mg

Spiced Stuffed Peppers

Prep time: 10 minutes | Cook time: 30 minutes | Serves: 4

1 pound (454 g) ground beef	sage or 2 teaspoons dried sage
¼ cup, plus 2 tbsps. extra-virgin olive oil, divided	1 tsp. salt
	1 tsp. ground allspice
	½ tsp. freshly ground black pepper
2 large red bell peppers	
1 tbsp. freshly squeezed orange juice	½ cup chopped fresh flat-leaf Italian parsley
2 garlic cloves, minced	½ cup chopped walnuts
1 small onion, finely chopped	½ cup chopped baby arugula leaves
2 tbsps. chopped fresh	

1. Preheat the oven to 425°F (220°C).
2. In a rimmed baking sheet, drizzle 1 tablespoon olive oil and swirl to coat the bottom.
3. Cut peppers in half lengthwise, remove the stems, the seeds and membranes. Put cut-side down on the prepared baking sheet and roast 5 to 8 minutes. Remove from the oven and cool down.
4. Meanwhile, heat 1 tablespoon olive oil over medium-high heat in a large skillet. Add the beef and onions and sauté 8 to 10 minutes until the meat is browned and cooked through. Add the allspice, garlic, salt, sage, and pepper and sauté for another 2 minutes.
5. Remove from the heat and let it cool slightly. Stir in the arugula, parsley, orange juice, walnuts, and remaining olive oil and mix well.
6. Stuff the filling into each pepper half. Back to the oven and cook for 5 minutes. Serve warm.

PER SERVING

Calories: 521, Total Fat: 44g, Total Carbohydrates: 9g, Net Carbs: 6g, Protein: 25g, Fiber: 3g, Sodium: 665mg

Grilled Carrot, Zucchini and Bell Pepper

Prep time: 10 minutes | Cook time: 6 minutes | Serves: 4

4 carrots, peeled and cut in half
2 onions, quartered
1 zucchini, cut into ½-inch rounds
1 red bell pepper, seeded and cut into cubes
¼ cup olive oil
Sea salt and freshly ground pepper, to taste
Balsamic vinegar

1. Heat the grill to medium-high.
2. Brush the vegetables lightly with olive oil, and season with sea salt and freshly ground pepper.
3. Place the carrots and onions on the grill first because they take the longest. Cook the vegetables for 3–4 minutes on each side.
4. Transfer to a serving dish, and drizzle with olive oil and balsamic vinegar.

PER SERVING
Calories: 177, Fat: 13.93g, Carbohydrates: 13.12g, Protein: 2.02g, Sugar: 5.83g, Fiber: 3.6g, Sodium: 35mg

Green Beans with Potatoes and Tomato Sauce

Prep time: 15 minutes | Cook time: 56 minutes | Serves: 6

1 onion, chopped fine
2 tablespoons minced fresh oregano or 2 teaspoons dried
4 garlic cloves, minced
1½ cups water
1½ pounds (680 g) green beans, trimmed and cut into 2-inch lengths
1 pound (454 g) Yukon Gold potatoes, peeled and cut into 1-inch pieces
½ teaspoon baking soda
1 (14½-ounce / 411-g) can diced tomatoes, drained with juice reserved, chopped
1 tablespoon tomato paste
Salt and pepper, to taste
3 tablespoons chopped fresh basil
Lemon juice

1. Adjust oven rack to lower-middle position and heat oven to 275°F (135°C). Heat 3 tablespoons oil in Dutch oven over medium heat until shimmering. Add onion and cook until softened, about 5 minutes. Stir in oregano and garlic and cook until fragrant, about 30 seconds. Stir in water, green beans, potatoes, and baking soda, bring to simmer, and cook, stirring occasionally, for 10 minutes.
2. Stir in tomatoes and their juice, tomato paste, 2 teaspoons salt, and ¼ teaspoon pepper. Cover, transfer pot to oven, and cook until sauce is slightly thickened and green beans can be cut easily with side of fork, 40 to 50 minutes.
3. Stir in basil and season with salt, pepper, and lemon juice to taste. Transfer green beans to serving bowl and drizzle with remaining 2 tablespoons oil. Serve.

PER SERVING
Calories: 121, Fat: 0.89g, Carbohydrates: 27.01g, Protein: 4.19g, Sugar: 6.66g, Fiber: 6.1g, Sodium: 203mg

Sautéed Lemony Zucchini Ribbons

Prep time: 5 minutes | Cook time: 3 minutes | Serves: 4 to 6

1 small garlic clove, minced
1 teaspoon grated lemon zest plus 1 tablespoon juice
4 (6- to 8-ounce / 170- to 227-g) zucchini or yellow summer squash, trimmed
2 tablespoons plus 1 teaspoon extra-virgin olive oil
Salt and pepper, to taste
1½ tablespoons chopped fresh parsley

1. Combine garlic and lemon juice in large bowl and set aside for at least 10 minutes. Using vegetable peeler, shave off 3 ribbons from 1 side of summer squash, then turn squash 90 degrees and shave off 3 more ribbons. Continue to turn and shave ribbons until you reach seeds, discard core. Repeat with remaining squash.
2. Whisk 2 tablespoons oil, ¼ teaspoon salt, ⅛ teaspoon pepper, and lemon zest into garlic–lemon juice mixture.
3. Heat remaining 1 teaspoon oil in 12-inch nonstick skillet over medium-high heat until just smoking. Add summer squash and cook, tossing occasionally with tongs, until squash has softened and is translucent, 3 to 4 minutes. Transfer squash to bowl with dressing, add parsley, and gently toss to coat. Season with salt and pepper to taste. Serve.

PER SERVING
Calories: 57, Fat: 2.91g, Carbohydrates: 6.89g, Protein: 2.53g, Sugar: 4.69g, Fiber: 2.2g, Sodium: 17mg

Slow-Cooked Mediterranean Vegetable Stew

Prep time: 15 minutes | Cook time: 8 hours | Serves: 10

1 butternut squash, peeled, seeded, and cubed
2 cups unpeeled cubed eggplant
2 cups cubed zucchini
10 ounces (283 g) fresh okra, cut into slices
1 (8-ounce / 227-g) can tomato sauce
1 large yellow onion, chopped
1 ripe tomato, chopped
1 carrot, thinly sliced
½ cup vegetable stock
⅓ cup raisins
2 cloves garlic, minced
½ teaspoon ground cumin
½ teaspoon ground turmeric
¼ teaspoon red pepper flakes
¼ teaspoon ground cinnamon
1 teaspoon paprika

1. In the slow cooker, combine the butternut squash, eggplant, zucchini, okra, tomato sauce, onion, tomato, carrot, vegetable stock, raisins, and garlic. Sprinkle in the cumin, turmeric, red pepper flakes, cinnamon, and paprika.
2. Cover and cook on low for 8 to 10 hours, or until the vegetables are fork-tender. Serve hot.

PER SERVING
Calories: 46, Fat: 1.3g, Carbohydrates: 8.21g, Protein: 1.64g, Sugar: 2.94g, Fiber: 2.8g, Sodium: 61mg

Ratatouille and Spaghetti

Prep time: 10 minutes | Cook time: 25 minutes | Serves: 6

1 small eggplant, cut into ½-inch cubes
2 small green zucchini, diced
1 tbsp. olive oil
1 large sweet onion, chopped
3 tsp.minced garlic
1 red bell pepper, seeded and diced
2 large tomatoes, diced
6 cups multigrain spaghetti, cooked
½ tsp. freshly ground pepper
Pinch of red pepper flakes
2 tbsps. chopped fresh basil

1. Heat olive oil over medium-high heat in a large skillet.
2. Add onion and garlic and sauté about 4 minutes until tender.
3. Add zucchini, eggplant, and bell pepper. Sauté about 10 minutes until softened.
4. Add tomato, red pepper flakes and pepper.
5. Continue to cook about 7 minutes, stirring occasionally, until vegetables are tender and liquid reduces to a sauce texture.
6. Stir in basil and cooked pasta, and cook about 4 minutes until pasta is warmed through, stirring occasionally. Serve hot.

PER SERVING
Calories: 394, Fat: 4.7g, Carbohydrates: 73.9g, Protein: 14.1g, Sodium: 9mg, Fiber: 14.7g

Green Beans with Cheese and Pine Nuts

Prep time: 10 minutes | Cook time: 21 minutes | Serves: 4 to 6

1½ pounds (680 g) green beans, trimmed
¼ cup extra-virgin olive oil
¾ teaspoon sugar
Salt and pepper, to taste
2 garlic cloves, minced
1 teaspoon grated lemon zest plus 1 tablespoon
juice
1 teaspoon Dijon mustard
2 tablespoons chopped fresh basil
¼ cup shredded Pecorino Romano cheese
2 tablespoons pine nuts, toasted

1. Adjust oven rack to lowest position and heat oven to 475°F (245°C). Toss green beans with 1 tablespoon oil, sugar, ¼ teaspoon salt, and ½ teaspoon pepper. Transfer to rimmed baking sheet and spread into single layer.
2. Cover sheet tightly with aluminum foil and roast for 10 minutes. Remove foil and continue to roast until green beans are spotty brown, about 10 minutes, stirring halfway through roasting.
3. Meanwhile, combine garlic, lemon zest, and remaining 3 tablespoons oil in medium bowl and microwave until bubbling, about 1 minute. Let mixture steep for 1 minute, then whisk in lemon juice, mustard, ⅛ teaspoon salt, and ¼ teaspoon pepper until combined.
4. Transfer green beans to bowl with dressing, add basil, and toss to combine. Season with salt and pepper to taste. Transfer green beans to serving platter and sprinkle with Pecorino and pine nuts. Serve.

PER SERVING
Calories: 190, Fat: 16.15g, Carbohydrates: 9.76g, Protein: 3.94g, Sugar: 1.86g, Fiber: 3.5g, Sodium: 131mg

Harissa Roasted Eggplant with Mint

Prep time: 10 minutes | Cook time: 35 minutes | Serves: 4

2 medium eggplants, cut into ½-inch cubes
¼ cup store-bought harissa
¼ cup chopped scallions, green part only

4 tbsps. extra-virgin olive oil
1 tsp. salt
¼ tsp. freshly ground black pepper
1 cup chopped fresh mint

1. Preheat the oven to 425°F (220ºC). Line a baking sheet with parchment paper.
2. Put the eggplant, salt, olive oil, and pepper in a large bowl and toss to coat.
3. Put the eggplant on the prepared baking sheet, reserving the bowl, and roast for 15 minutes. Take the eggplant out from the oven and toss the pieces to flip. Return to the oven and roast until golden and cooked through for 15 to 20 more minutes.
4. After the eggplant is cooked, remove from the oven and put it back to the large bowl. Add the harissa, mint, and scallions and toss to combine. Serve warm or refrigerated for up to 2 days.

PER SERVING
Calories: 300, Total Fat: 28g, Total Carbohydrates: 15g, Net Carbs: 7g, Protein: 3g, Fiber: 8g, Sodium: 589mg

Pesto Cauliflower Pizza

Prep time: 10 minutes | Cook time: 35 minutes | Serves: 4

1 head cauliflower, trimmed
¼ cup (60 ml) extra-virgin olive oil
1 tsp. salt
½ tsp. freshly ground black pepper
1 tsp. garlic powder

4 tbsps. store-bought pesto
½ cup crumbled feta cheese
1 cup shredded whole-milk mozzarella or Italian cheese blend

1. Preheat the oven to 425°F (220ºC).
2. Remove the stem and bottom leaves from the cauliflower and carefully break into large florets. Thinly slice each floret to about ¼-inch thickness.
3. Line a large rimmed baking sheet with aluminum foil and drizzle with the olive oil to coat the foil.

Place the cauliflower in a single layer on the oiled sheet. Sprinkle with pepper, salt, and garlic powder.

4. Put in the oven and roast 15 to 20 minutes until softened. Remove from the oven and spread the pesto evenly over the cauliflower. Sprinkle with the shredded cheese and feta, return to the oven and roast for another 10 minutes, or until the cauliflower is soft and the cheese is melted.
5. Turn the broiler to low and broil 3 to 5 minutes until browned and bubbly on top. Take it out of the oven, cool down slightly, and cut into large squares to serve.

PER SERVING
Calories: 346, Total Fat: 30g, Total Carbohydrates: 7g, Net Carbs: 5g, Protein: 12g, Fiber: 2g, Sodium: 938mg

Vegetable Fruit Bowl with Lentil

Prep time: 20 minutes | Cook time: 40 minutes | Serves: 4-6

1 (15-ounce (425g)) can lentils, drained and rinsed
4 cups cooked brown rice
1 cup red lentils
2 cups water
Chicken Lettuce Wraps sauce
1 small jicama, peeled and cut into thin sticks,

divided
1 head radicchio, cored and torn into pieces, divided
2 scallions, sliced, divided
2 red Bartlett (or other) ripe pears, cored, quartered, and sliced, divided

1. Mix the red lentils and water in a medium bowl. Put the lid on and put it in the refrigerator overnight. When you are ready to prepare the salad, remove the lentils and drain them.
2. Put the brown rice and canned lentils in a medium bowl and mix. Add half of the chicken lettuce wrap sauce. Let the mixture sit for at least 30 minutes or overnight.
3. Divide the lentil and rice mixture into several small bowls. Put an equal amount of drained red lentils on each bowl. Sprinkle with chicory, jicama, pear, and green onion separately for garnish.
4. Finally, top with some remaining chicken lettuce roll sauce and enjoy.

PER SERVING
Calories: 989, Total Fat: 31g, Total Carbohydrates: 151g, Protein: 31g, Sugar: 16g, Fiber: 35g, Sodium: 272mg

Easy Quinoa-Broccolini Sauté

Prep time: 10 minutes | Cook time: 10 minutes | Serves: 4

1 tbsp. coconut oil
2 garlic cloves, chopped
2 leeks, white part only, sliced
½ cup vegetable broth, or water
4 cups chopped broccolini
2 cups cooked quinoa
1 tbsp. coconut aminos
1 tsp. curry powder

1. Put the coconut oil in a saucepan and melt at high temperature. Add the leeks and garlic and stir fry for about 2 minutes, until tender.
2. Pour the broccoli and vegetable soup. Cover the pot and simmer for 5 minutes.
3. Put curry powder, quinoa and coconut amino into the pot. Without covering the lid, continue to cook for 2 to 3 minutes until the quinoa is soft.
4. Serve hot or as a salad at room temperature.

PER SERVING
Calories: 273, Total Fat: 6g, Total Carbohydrates: 44g, Sugar: 5g, Protein: 11g, Fiber: 6g, Sodium: 54mg

Bulgur with Spinach and Chickpeas

Prep time: 15 minutes | Cook time: 20 minutes | Serves: 4 to 6

3 tbsps. extra-virgin olive oil, divided
1 onion, chopped fine
1½ cups (360 ml) water
½ tsp. table salt
2 tbsps. za'atar, divided
1 cup medium-grind bulgur, rinsed
1 (15-ounce, 425 g) can chickpeas, rinsed
3 garlic cloves, minced
5 ounces (5 cups, 142 g) baby spinach, chopped
1 tbsp. lemon juice, plus lemon wedges for serving

1. In Instant Pot, use highest sauté function, heat 2 tablespoons oil until shimmering. Add onion and salt and cook about 5 minutes. Stir in garlic and 1 tablespoon za'atar and cook about 30 seconds until fragrant. Stir in chickpeas, bulgur, and water.
2. Lock lid and close pressure release valve. Choose high pressure cook function and cook for 1 minute. Turn off and quick-release pressure. Carefully remove lid, letting steam escape away from you.

3. Gently fluff bulgur with fork. Lay clean dish towel over pot to replace lid, and set aside for 5 minutes. Add lemon juice, spinach, remaining za'atar, and remaining oil and gently toss to combine. Season with salt and pepper. Serve with lemon wedges.

PER SERVING
Calories: 200, Total Fat: 8g, Sat Fat: 1g, Total Carbohydrates: 28g, Protein: 6g, Sugar: 2g, Sodium: 320mg, Fiber: 6g

Vegetable Kebabs

Prep time: 15 minutes | Cook time: 10 minutes | Serves: 4

4 tbsps. olive oil
2 tbsps. balsamic vinegar
Freshly ground pepper
2 small zucchinis, cut into 16 chunks
2 small white or red onions, peeled and cut into quarters
2 red, yellow, or green bell peppers, seeded and cut into 8 slices each
8 wooden skewers,
soaked in water for 30 minutes
16 cherry tomatoes
16 medium button mushrooms
1 cup broccoli florets
1 tsp. minced garlic
½ tsp. chopped fresh thyme
½ tsp. chopped fresh oregano

1. Whisk together olive oil, garlic, thyme, vinegar, oregano, and pepper in a small bowl.
2. Pour marinade into a large resealable plastic bag, and add zucchini, tomatoes, mushrooms, onions and bell peppers.
3. Shake to coat, and put in fridge for at least 30 minutes.
4. Preheat oven to broil, and adjust an oven rack about 6 inches from broiler heat.
5. Take marinating vegetables out of fridge, and thread onto skewers, dividing evenly. On each skewer, place 2 zucchini pieces, 2 tomatoes, 2 mushrooms, 1 piece of onion and 2 pieces of bell pepper.
6. Pour remaining marinade in a small bowl to baste vegetables.
7. Place skewers on a baking sheet or oven grill rack, and broil, flipping and basting with reserved marinade for about 10 minutes, until vegetables are tender. Serve hot.

PER SERVING
Calories: 210, Fat: 8.5g, Carbohydrates: 30.9g, Protein: 8.3g, Sodium: 37mg, Fiber: 9.5g

Ginger Sweet Potatoes with Pea Hash

Prep time: 10 minutes | Cook time: 10 minutes | Serves: 4

2 tbsps. coconut oil
3 garlic cloves, minced
4 scallions, sliced
1 tsp. salt
2 tsps. minced fresh ginger
1 tsp. curry powder
½ tsp. ground turmeric
2 medium sweet potatoes, roasted in their skins, peeled, and chopped
2 cups cooked brown rice
½ cup chopped cashews
1 tbsp. coconut aminos
1 cup frozen peas
¼ cup chopped fresh cilantro

1. Melt coconut oil in a large saucepan over medium high heat. Then add onion, garlic, ginger, curry powder, salt and turmeric.
2. Stir-fry for 2 minutes, or fry until fragrant. Finally add sweet potatoes, peas, brown rice and coconut amino.
3. Stir-fry for 5 minutes. Transfer the hash to a serving plate, sprinkle with coriander and cashew nuts, and serve immediately.

PER SERVING
Calories: 511, Total Fat: 17g, Total Carbohydrates: 83g, Protein: 11g, Sugar: 4g, Fiber: 10g, Sodium: 633mg

Carrots with Orange Marmalade Glaze

Prep time: 10 minutes | Cook time: 4 hours | Serves: 8

3 pounds (1.4kg) carrots, peeled and cut into ¼-inch slices on the bias
1½ cups water, plus extra hot water as needed
1 tablespoon honey
1 teaspoon sea salt
½ cup orange marmalade
2 tablespoons unsalted butter, softened
1½ teaspoons fresh sage, minced
Black pepper (optional)

1. Combine the carrots, 1½ cups water, honey, and 1 teaspoon salt in the slow cooker. Cover and cook on low until the carrots are tender, 4 to 6 hours.
2. Drain the carrots, and then return to the slow cooker. Stir in the marmalade, butter, and sage. Season with additional salt and some pepper, if needed. Serve hot. (If needed, you may keep this dish on the warm setting for 1 to 2 hours before serving. Stir in some hot water before serving if it gets too thick.)

PER SERVING
Calories: 146, Fat: 2.36g, Carbohydrates: 31.99g, Protein: 1.81g, Sugar: 22.22g, Fiber: 5g, Sodium: 422mg

Zucchini Boats Loaded with White Bean

Prep time: 15 minutes | Cook time: 20 minutes | Serves: 4

2 tbsps. extra-virgin olive oil, plus additional for brushing
1 (15-ounce, 425 g) can white beans, drained and rinsed
4 large zucchini, halved lengthwise
½ cup chopped pitted green olives
½ tsp. salt, plus additional for seasoning
Freshly ground black pepper
Pinch ground rosemary
2 garlic cloves, minced
1 cup coarsely chopped arugula
¼ cup chopped fresh parsley
1 tbsp. apple cider vinegar

1. Preheat the oven to 375°F(190°C).
2. Use olive oil to brush a rimmed baking sheet.
3. Scoop out the seeds from the zucchini halves with a small spoon or melon baller, and discard the seeds.
4. Use olive oil to brush the scooped-out section of each zucchini boat and lightly season the inside of each boat with salt, pepper, and rosemary.
5. On the prepared baking sheet, place the zucchini, cut-side up. Place the sheet in the preheated oven and roast for 15 to 20 minutes, or until the zucchini are tender and lightly browned.
6. Use a fork to lightly mash the white beans in a medium bowl.
7. Mix in the olives, garlic, arugula, parsley, cider vinegar, the remaining ½ teaspoon of salt, and the remaining 2 tablespoons of olive oil. Season with pepper and mix well.
8. Place the bean mixture into the zucchini boats and serve.

PER SERVING
Calories: 269, Total Fat: 12g, Total Carbohydrates: 38g, Sugar: 6g, Fiber: 10g, Protein: 13g, Sodium: 873mg

Warm Zucchini Casserole

Prep time: 10 minutes | Cook time: 4½ hours | Serves: 4

1 medium red onion, sliced
1 green bell pepper, cut into thin strips
4 medium zucchini, sliced
1 (15-ounce / 425-g) can diced tomatoes, with the juice

1 teaspoon sea salt
½ teaspoon black pepper
½ teaspoon basil
1 tablespoon extra-virgin olive oil
¼ cup grated Parmesan cheese

1. Combine the onion slices, bell pepper strips, zucchini slices, and tomatoes in the slow cooker. Sprinkle with the salt, pepper, and basil.
2. Cover and cook on low for 3 hours.
3. Drizzle the olive oil over the casserole and sprinkle with the Parmesan. Cover and cook on low for 1½ hours more. Serve hot.

PER SERVING
Calories: 79, Fat: 5.46g, Carbohydrates: 5.64g, Protein: 3.06g, Sugar: 2.99g, Fiber: 2.4g, Sodium: 824mg

Vegetable Stew with Chickpea

Prep time: 15 minutes | Cook time: 35 minutes | Serves: 6 to 8

1 (15-ounce, 425 g) can chickpeas, rinsed
¼ cup extra-virgin olive oil, plus extra for drizzling
1 onion, chopped fine
2 red bell peppers, stemmed, seeded, and cut into 1-inch pieces
4 garlic cloves, minced
½ tsp. table salt
½ tsp. pepper
1½ tbsp. baharat
1 tbsp. tomato paste
4 cups (960 ml) vegetable

or chicken broth
1 (28-ounce, 794 g) can whole peeled tomatoes, drained with juice reserved, chopped
1 pound (454 g) Yukon Gold potatoes, peeled and cut into ½-inch pieces
2 zucchini, quartered lengthwise and sliced 1 inch thick
⅓ cup chopped fresh mint

1. In Instant Pot, use highest sauté function, heat oil until shimmering. Add bell pepper, salt, onion, and pepper and cook 5 to 7 minutes until vegetables are softened and lightly browned. Stir in garlic, baharat, and tomato paste and cook about 1 minute until fragrant. Add broth and tomatoes and reserved juice, scraping up any browned bits, then mix in potatoes.
2. Lock lid and close pressure release valve. Choose high pressure cook function and cook for 9 minutes. Turn off and quick-release pressure. Carefully remove lid, letting steam escape away from you.
3. Stir zucchini and chickpeas into stew and cook with highest sauté function for 10 to 15 minutes, until zucchini is tender. Turn off multicooker. Season with salt and pepper. Drizzle each portion with extra oil, sprinkle with mint and serve.

PER SERVING
Calories: 200, Total Fat: 8g, Sat Fat: 1g, Total Carbohydrates: 28g, Protein: 5g, Sugar: 7g, Sodium: 740mg, Fiber: 5g

Simple Roasted Cauliflower with Almond Sauce

Prep time: 15 minutes | Cook time: 20 minutes | Serves: 4

¼ cup extra-virgin olive oil
½ tsp. ground turmeric
1 head cauliflower, cut into florets
1 cup plain unsweetened almond yogurt
1 ½ tsps. salt, divided
1 scallion, sliced

¼ cup almond butter
½ tsp. freshly ground black pepper, divided
1 tbsp. chopped fresh parsley
1 garlic clove, minced
1 tbsp. maple syrup
1 tbsp. freshly squeezed lemon juice

1. Preheat the oven to 400°F in advance.
2. Put the cauliflower, olive oil, turmeric, 1 tsp. salt and 1/4 tsps. pepper in a large bowl and mix together.
3. Put the mixed cauliflower on the baking tray and place it in a single layer. Place in a preheated oven and bake for 20 to 30 minutes, until the cauliflower is light brown and soft.
4. Put the yogurt, almond butter, green onions, garlic, parsley, lemon juice, maple syrup, the remaining ½ teaspoon of salt and the remaining ¼ teaspoon of pepper in a blender and beat until smooth.
5. Spoon the almond paste on the roasted cauliflower. Enjoy.

PER SERVING
Calories: 277, Total Fat: 23g, Total Carbohydrates: 15g, Protein: 7g, Sugar: 6g, Fiber: 4g, Sodium: 945mg

Green Beans with Pine Nuts

Prep time: 10 minutes | Cook time: 5 minutes | Serves: 6

Juice from 1 lemon
1½ cups water
2 pounds (907 g) green beans, trimmed
1 cup chopped toasted pine nuts

1 cup Feta cheese, crumbled
6 tablespoons olive oil
½ teaspoon salt
Black pepper, to taste

1. Add water and set the rack over the water and the steamer basket on the rack. Loosely heap green beans into the steamer basket. Seal lid and cook on High Pressure for 5 minutes. Release pressure quickly. Drop green beans into a salad bowl. Top with the olive oil, Feta cheese, pepper, and pine nuts.

PER SERVING
Calories: 386, Fat: 34.57g, Carbohydrates: 15.3g, Protein: 9.47g, Sugar: 6.96g, Fiber: 5g, Sodium: 434mg

Lentil Spread with Parmesan Cheese

Prep time: 10 minutes | Cook time: 2 minutes | Serves: 6

1 pound (454 g) of lentils, cooked
1 cup sweet corn
2 tomatoes, diced
3 tablespoons tomato paste
½ teaspoon dried oregano, ground

2 tablespoons Parmesan Cheese
1 teaspoon salt
½ teaspoon red pepper flakes
3 tablespoons olive oil
1 cup water
¼ cup red wine

1. Heat oil on Sauté and add tomatoes, tomato paste, and ½ cup of water. Sprinkle with salt and oregano and stir-fry for 5 minutes. Press Cancel and add lentils, sweet corn, and wine.
2. Pour in the remaining water and seal the lid. Cook on High Pressure for 2 minutes. Do a quick release. Set aside to cool completely and refrigerate for 30 minutes. Sprinkle with Parmesan Cheese before serving.

PER SERVING
Calories: 195, Fat: 7.94g, Carbohydrates: 28.25g, Protein: 8.78g, Sugar: 3.63g, Fiber: 2.5g, Sodium: 546mg

Vegetable Mash with Parmesan

Prep time: 10 minutes | Cook time: 10 minutes | Serves: 6

3 pounds (1.4kg) Yukon Gold potatoes, chopped
1½ cups cauliflower, broken into florets
1 carrot, chopped
1 cup Parmesan Cheese,

shredded
¼ cup butter, melted
¼ cup milk
1 teaspoon salt
1 garlic clove, minced
Fresh parsley for garnish

1. Into the pot, add veggies, salt and cover with enough water. Seal the lid and cook on High Pressure for 10 minutes. Release the pressure quickly. Drain the vegetables and mash them with a potato masher.
2. Add garlic, butter and milk, and Whisk until everything is well incorporated. Serve topped with Parmesan cheese and chopped parsley.

PER SERVING
Calories: 330, Fat: 12.96g, Carbohydrates: 44.91g, Protein: 10.36g, Sugar: 3.3g, Fiber: 5.8g, Sodium: 782mg

Cranberry and Nut Stuffed Acorn Squash

Prep time: 5 minutes | Cook time: 5 hours | Serves: 4

1 acorn squash
1 tablespoon honey
1 tablespoon olive oil (not extra-virgin)
¼ cup chopped pecans

or walnuts
¼ cup chopped dried cranberries
Sea salt, to taste

1. Cut the squash in half. Remove the seeds and pulp from the middle. Cut the halves in half again so you have quarters.
2. Place the squash quarters cut-side up in the slow cooker.
3. Combine the honey, olive oil, pecans, and cranberries in a small bowl.
4. Spoon the pecan mixture into the center of each squash quarter. Season the squash with salt. Cook on low for 5 to 6 hours, or until the squash is tender. Serve hot.

PER SERVING
Calories: 145, Fat: 6.85g, Carbohydrates: 22.48g, Protein: 1.64g, Sugar: 9.37g, Fiber: 2.4g, Sodium: 585mg

Pressure-Cooked Green Minestrone

Prep time: 10 minutes | Cook time: 4 minutes | Serves: 4

2 tablespoons olive oil
1 head broccoli, cut into florets
4 celery stalks, chopped thinly
1 leek, chopped thinly
1 zucchini, chopped
1 cup green beans
2 cups vegetable broth
3 whole black peppercorns
Salt, to taste
Water to cover
2 cups chopped kale

1. Add broccoli, leek, beans, salt, peppercorns, zucchini, and celery. Mix in vegetable broth, oil, and water. Seal the lid and cook on High Pressure for 4 minutes. Release pressure naturally for 5 minutes, then release the remaining pressure quickly. Stir in kale, set on Sauté, and cook until tender.

PER SERVING
Calories: 171, Fat: 8.59g, Carbohydrates: 20.75g, Protein: 7.03g, Sugar: 3.33g, Fiber: 3.7g, Sodium: 918mg

Celery Root with Sesame Yogurt and Cilantro

Prep time: 10 minutes | Cook time: 41 minutes | Serves: 6

3 (2½-pound / 1.1-kg) celery roots, peeled, halved, and sliced ½ inch thick
3 tablespoons extra-virgin olive oil
Salt and pepper, to taste
¼ cup plain yogurt
¼ teaspoon grated lemon zest plus 1 teaspoon
juice
1 teaspoon sesame seeds, toasted
1 teaspoon coriander seeds, toasted and crushed
¼ teaspoon dried thyme
¼ cup fresh cilantro leaves

1. Adjust oven rack to lowest position and heat oven to 425°F (220°C). Toss celery root with oil, ½ teaspoon salt, and ¼ teaspoon pepper and arrange in rimmed baking sheet in single layer. Roast celery root until sides touching sheet toward back of oven are well browned, 25 to 30 minutes. Rotate sheet and continue to roast until sides touching sheet toward back of oven are well browned, 6 to 10 minutes.

2. Use metal spatula to flip each piece and continue to roast until celery root is very tender and sides touching sheet are browned, 10 to 15 minutes.

3. Transfer celery root to serving platter. Whisk yogurt, lemon zest and juice, and pinch salt together in bowl. In separate bowl, combine sesame seeds, coriander seeds, thyme, and pinch salt. Drizzle celery root with yogurt sauce and sprinkle with seed mixture and cilantro. Serve.

PER SERVING
Calories: 100, Fat: 7.74g, Carbohydrates: 6.43g, Protein: 1.81g, Sugar: 2.95g, Fiber: 3.2g, Sodium: 152mg

Italian Eggplant with Capers and Mint

Prep time: 10 minutes | Cook time: 12 minutes | Serves: 4 to 6

1½ pounds (680 g) Italian eggplant, sliced into 1-inch-thick rounds
Kosher salt and pepper, to taste
¼ cup extra-virgin olive oil
4 teaspoons red wine vinegar
1 tablespoon capers, rinsed and minced
1 garlic clove, minced
½ teaspoon grated lemon zest
½ teaspoon minced fresh oregano
3 tablespoons minced fresh mint

1. Spread eggplant on paper towel–lined baking sheet, sprinkle both sides with ½ teaspoon salt, and let sit for 30 minutes.

2. Adjust oven rack 4 inches from broiler element and heat broiler. Thoroughly pat eggplant dry with paper towels, arrange on aluminum foil–lined rimmed baking sheet in single layer, and lightly brush both sides with 1 tablespoon oil. Broil eggplant until mahogany brown and lightly charred, 6 to 8 minutes per side.

3. Whisk remaining 3 tablespoons oil, vinegar, capers, garlic, lemon zest, oregano, and ¼ teaspoon pepper together in large bowl. Add eggplant and mint and gently toss to combine. Let eggplant cool to room temperature, about 1 hour. Season with pepper to taste and serve.

PER SERVING
Calories: 57, Fat: 1.22g, Carbohydrates: 11.54g, Protein: 1.98g, Sugar: 6.41g, Fiber: 5.5g, Sodium: 55mg

Roasted Broccoli with Cashews

Prep time: 10 minutes | Cook time: 20 minutes | Serves: 4

2 tbsps. extra-virgin olive oil
6 cups broccoli florets
1 tsp. salt
½ cup toasted cashews
1 tbsp. coconut aminos

1. Preheat the oven to 375°F.
2. Put the broccoli, olive oil and salt in a large bowl, mix and stir.
3. Put the mixed broccoli on the baking tray and spread evenly into a single layer.
4. Place it in the preheated oven and bake for 15 to 20 minutes, or until the broccoli is tender.
5. Put the roasted broccoli in a large bowl, stir with coconut amino and cashews, and serve.

PER SERVING
Calories: 209, Total Fat: 15g, Total Carbohydrates: 15g, Protein: 6g, Sugar: 3g, Fiber: 4g, Sodium: 633mg

Rice and Mushroom Stuffed Bell peppers

Prep time: 10 minutes | Cook time: 17 minutes | Serves: 4

5 bell peppers, seeds and stems removed
1 onion, peeled, chopped
6 ounces (170 g) button mushrooms, chopped
4 garlic cloves, peeled, crushed
4 tablespoons olive oil
1 teaspoon salt
¼ teaspoon freshly ground black pepper
1 cup rice
½ tablespoons of paprika
2 cups vegetable stock

1. Warm 2 tablespoons of olive oil on Sauté. Add onions and garlic, and stir-fry until fragrant and translucent, for about 2 minutes. Press Cancel and set aside. In a bowl, combine rice and mushrooms with the mixture from the pot. Season with salt, pepper, and paprika, and stuff each bell pepper with this mixture.
2. Place them in the instant pot, filled side up, and pour in broth. Seal the lid and cook on High for 15 minutes. Release the pressure naturally for about 5 minutes.

PER SERVING
Calories: 404, Fat: 15.69g, Carbohydrates: 64.24g, Protein: 9.73g, Sugar: 9.82g, Fiber: 8.7g, Sodium: 883mg

Asparagus with Feta Cheese

Prep time: 5 minutes | Cook time: 1 minute | Serves: 4

1 cup water
1 pound (454 g) asparagus spears, ends trimmed
1 tablespoon olive oil
Salt and freshly ground black pepper, to taste
1 lemon, cut into wedges
1 cup Feta cheese, cubed

1. Into the pot, add water and set trivet over the water. Place steamer basket on the trivet. Place the asparagus into the steamer basket. Seal the lid and cook on High Pressure for 1 minute.
2. Release the Pressure quickly. Add olive oil in a bowl and toss in asparagus until well coated. Season with pepper and salt. Serve alongside Feta cheese and lemon wedges.

PER SERVING
Calories: 153, Fat: 11.52g, Carbohydrates: 6.46g, Protein: 7.9g, Sugar: 3.71g, Fiber: 2.6g, Sodium: 348mg

Apple Cider-Glazed Beets with Rosemary

Prep time: 10 minutes | Cook time: 8 hours | Serves: 7

2 pounds (907 g) beets, peeled and cut into wedges
2 tablespoons fresh lemon juice
2 tablespoons extra-virgin olive oil
2 tablespoons honey
1 tablespoon apple cider vinegar
¾ teaspoon sea salt
½ teaspoon black pepper
2 sprigs fresh rosemary
½ teaspoon lemon zest

1. Place the beets in the slow cooker.
2. Whisk the lemon juice, extra-virgin olive oil, honey, apple cider vinegar, salt, and pepper together in a small bowl. Pour over the beets.
3. Add the sprigs of rosemary to the slow cooker.
4. Cover and cook on low for 8 hours, or until the beets are tender.
5. Remove and discard the rosemary sprigs. Stir in the lemon zest. Serve hot.

PER SERVING
Calories: 110, Fat: 4.11g, Carbohydrates: 17.86g, Protein: 2.15g, Sugar: 13.82g, Fiber: 3.7g, Sodium: 351mg

Homemade Zucchini Noodles

Prep time: 5 minutes | Cook time: 0 minutes | Serves: 4

2 medium to large zucchini

1. Cut off and discard the ends of each zucchini and, using a spiralizer set to the smallest setting, spiralize the zucchini to create zoodles.
2. To serve, simply place a ½ cup or so of spiralized zucchini into the bottom of each bowl and spoon a hot sauce over top to "cook" the zoodles to al dente consistency. Use with any of your favorite sauces, or just toss with warmed pesto for a simple and quick meal.

PER SERVING
Calories: 48, Total Fat: 1g, Total Carbs: 7g, Net Carbs: 4g, Protein: 6g, Fiber: 3g, Sodium: 7mg

Italian-Style Vegetable Stew

Prep time: 10 minutes | Cook time: 15 minutes | Serves: 4

3 zucchinis, peeled, chopped
1 eggplant, peeled, chopped
3 red bell peppers, chopped
½ cup fresh tomato juice

2 teaspoons Italian Seasoning
½ teaspoon salt
2 tablespoons olive oil

1. Add all ingredients and give it a good stir. Pour 1 cup of water. Seal the lid and cook on High pressure for 15 minutes. Do a quick release. Set aside to cool completely. Serve as a cold salad or a side dish.

PER SERVING
Calories: 119, Fat: 7.27g, Carbohydrates: 13.18g, Protein: 2.52g, Sugar: 7.56g, Fiber: 5g, Sodium: 403mg

Broiled Eggplant with Fresh Basil

Prep time: 5 minutes | Cook time: 8 minutes | Serves: 4 to 6

1½ pounds (680 g) eggplant, sliced into ¼-inch-thick rounds
Kosher salt and pepper, to taste

3 tablespoons extra-virgin olive oil
2 tablespoons chopped fresh basil

1. Spread eggplant on paper towel–lined baking sheet, sprinkle both sides with 1½ teaspoons salt, and let sit for 30 minutes.
2. Adjust oven rack 4 inches from broiler element and heat broiler. Thoroughly pat eggplant dry with paper towels, arrange on aluminum foil–lined rimmed baking sheet in single layer, and brush both sides with oil. Broil eggplant until mahogany brown and lightly charred, about 4 minutes per side. Transfer eggplant to serving platter, season with pepper to taste, and sprinkle with basil. Serve.

PER SERVING
Calories: 134, Fat: 10.46g, Carbohydrates: 10.4g, Protein: 1.77g, Sugar: 6.01g, Fiber: 5.3g, Sodium: 4mg

Chapter 4 Fish and Seafood

Golden Salmon Cakes with Tzatziki Sauce

Prep time: 15 minutes | Cook time: 11 minutes | Serves: 2

For the Tzatziki Sauce:
½ cup plain Greek yogurt
1 teaspoon dried dill
¼ cup minced cucumber
Salt, to taste
Freshly ground black pepper, to taste
For the Salmon Cakes:
6 ounces (170 g) cooked salmon
3 tablespoons olive oil, divided

¼ cup minced celery
¼ cup minced onion
½ teaspoon dried dill
1 tablespoon fresh minced parsley
Salt, to taste
Freshly ground black pepper, to taste
1 egg, beaten
½ cup unseasoned bread crumbs

Make the Tzatziki Sauce
1. Combine the yogurt, dill, and cucumber in a small bowl. Season with salt and pepper and set aside.

Make the Salmon Cakes
1. Remove any skin from the salmon. Place the salmon in a medium bowl and break it into small flakes with a fork. Set it aside.
2. Heat 1 tablespoon of olive oil in a nonstick skillet over medium-high heat. Add the celery and onion and sauté for 5 minutes.
3. Add the celery and onion to the salmon and stir to combine. Add the dill and parsley, and season with salt and pepper.
4. Add the beaten egg and bread crumbs and stir until mixed thoroughly.
5. Wipe the skillet clean and add the remaining 2 tablespoons of oil. Heat the pan over medium-high heat.
6. Form the salmon mixture into 4 patties, and place them two at a time into the hot pan.
7. Cook for 3 minutes per side, or until they're golden brown. Carefully flip them over with a spatula and cook for another 3 minutes on the second side.
8. Repeat with the remaining salmon cakes and serve topped with the tzatziki sauce.

PER SERVING
Calories: 555, Total Fat: 41g, Total Carbohydrates: 18g, Fiber: 2g, Sugar: 4g, Protein: 31g, Sodium: 303mg

Hake Fillet in Saffron Broth

Prep time: 15 minutes | Cook time: 9 minutes | Serves: 4

2 tablespoons extra-virgin olive oil, divided, plus extra for drizzling
1 onion, chopped
4 ounces (113 g) Spanish-style chorizo sausage, sliced ¼ inch thick
4 garlic cloves, minced
1 (8-ounce / 227-g) bottle clam juice
¾ cup water
½ cup dry white wine

8 ounces (227 g) small red potatoes, unpeeled, quartered
¼ teaspoon saffron threads, crumbled
1 bay leaf
4 (4-ounce / 113-g) skinless hake fillets, 1½ inches thick
½ teaspoon table salt
¼ teaspoon pepper
2 tablespoons minced fresh parsley

1. Using highest sauté function, heat 1 tablespoon oil in Instant Pot until shimmering. Add onion and chorizo and cook until onion is softened and lightly browned, 5 to 7 minutes. Stir in garlic and cook until fragrant, about 30 seconds. Stir in clam juice, water, and wine, scraping up any browned bits. Turn off Instant Pot, then stir in potatoes, saffron, and bay leaf.
2. Fold sheet of aluminum foil into 16 by 6-inch sling. Brush hake with remaining 1 tablespoon oil and sprinkle with salt and pepper. Arrange hake skinned side down in center of sling. Using sling, lower hake into Instant Pot on top of potato mixture, allow narrow edges of sling to rest along sides of insert. Lock lid in place and close pressure release valve. Select high pressure cook function and cook for 3 minutes.
3. Turn off Instant Pot and quick-release pressure. Carefully remove lid, allowing steam to escape away from you. Using sling, transfer hake to large plate. Tent with aluminum foil and let rest while finishing potato mixture.
4. Discard bay leaf. Stir parsley into potato mixture and season with salt to taste. Serve cod with potato mixture and broth, drizzling individual portions with extra oil.

PER SERVING
Calories: 410, Total Fat: 19g, Sat Fat: 5g, Sodium: 870mg, Total Carbohydrates: 14g, Protein: 39g, Sugar: 2g, Fiber: 2g

Salmon with Broccoli Rabe and Cannellini Beans

Prep time: 10 minutes | Cook time: 11 minutes | Serves: 4

2 tablespoons extra-virgin olive oil, plus extra for drizzling
4 garlic cloves, sliced thin
½ cup chicken or vegetable broth
¼ teaspoon red pepper flakes
1 lemon, sliced ¼ inch thick, plus lemon wedges for serving

4 (6-ounce / 170-g) skinless salmon fillets, 1½ inches thick
½ teaspoon table salt
¼ teaspoon pepper
1 pound (454 g) broccoli rabe, trimmed and cut into 1-inch pieces
1 (15-ounce / 425-g) can cannellini beans, rinsed

1. Using highest sauté function, cook oil and garlic in Instant Pot until garlic is fragrant and light golden brown, about 3 minutes. Using slotted spoon, transfer garlic to paper towel–lined plate and season with salt to taste, set aside for serving. Turn off Instant Pot, then stir in broth and pepper flakes.
2. Fold sheet of aluminum foil into 16 by 6-inch sling. Arrange lemon slices widthwise in 2 rows across center of sling. Sprinkle flesh side of salmon with salt and pepper, then arrange skinned side down on top of lemon slices. Using sling, lower salmon into Instant Pot, allow narrow edges of sling to rest along sides of insert. Lock lid in place and close pressure release valve. Select high pressure cook function and cook for 3 minutes.
3. Turn off Instant Pot and quick-release pressure. Carefully remove lid, allowing steam to escape away from you. Using sling, transfer salmon to large plate. Tent with foil and let rest while preparing broccoli rabe mixture.
4. Stir broccoli rabe and beans into cooking liquid, partially cover, and cook, using highest sauté function, until broccoli rabe is tender, about 5 minutes. Season with salt and pepper to taste. Gently lift and tilt salmon fillets with spatula to remove lemon slices. Serve salmon with broccoli rabe mixture and lemon wedges, sprinkling individual portions with garlic chips and drizzling with extra oil.

PER SERVING
Calories: 510, Total Fat: 30g, Sat Fat: 6g, Total Carbohydrates: 15g, Protein: 43g, Sugar: 2g, Fiber: 6g, Sodium: 650mg

Red Snapper with Citrus Vinaigrette

Prep time: 10 minutes | Cook time: 15 minutes | Serves: 4

6 tablespoons extra-virgin olive oil
¼ cup minced fresh cilantro
2 teaspoons grated lime zest plus 2 tablespoons juice
2 teaspoons grated orange zest plus 2 tablespoons juice

1 small shallot, minced
⅛ teaspoon red pepper flakes
Salt and pepper, to taste
2 (1½- to 2-pound / 680- to 907-g) whole red snapper, scaled, gutted, fins snipped off with scissors

1. Adjust oven rack to middle position and heat oven to 500ºF (260ºC). Line rimmed baking sheet with parchment paper and grease parchment. Whisk ¼ cup oil, cilantro, lime juice, orange juice, shallot, and pepper flakes together in bowl. Season with salt and pepper to taste, set aside for serving.
2. In separate bowl, combine lime zest, orange zest, 1½ teaspoons salt, and ½ teaspoon pepper. Rinse each snapper under cold running water and pat dry with paper towels inside and out. Using sharp knife, make 3 or 4 shallow slashes, about 2 inches apart, on both sides of snapper. Open cavity of each snapper and sprinkle 1 teaspoon salt mixture on flesh. Brush 1 tablespoon oil on outside of each snapper and season with remaining salt mixture, transfer to prepared sheet and let sit for 10 minutes.
3. Roast until snapper flakes apart when gently prodded with paring knife and registers 140ºF (60ºC), 15 to 20 minutes. (To check for doneness, peek into slashed flesh or into interior through opened bottom area of each fish.)
4. Carefully transfer snapper to carving board and let rest for 5 minutes. Fillet snapper by making vertical cut just behind head from top of fish to belly. Make another cut along top of snapper from head to tail. Use spatula to lift meat from bones, starting at head end and running spatula over bones to lift out fillet. Repeat on other side of snapper. Discard head and skeleton. Whisk dressing to recombine and serve with snapper.

PER SERVING
Calories: 588, Fat: 25.65g, Carbohydrates: 2.28g, Protein: 82.35g, Sugar: 1g, Fiber: 0.4g, Sodium: 258mg

Cod with Green Salad and Dukkah

Prep time: 10 minutes | Cook time: 8 minutes | Serves: 4

¼ cup extra-virgin olive oil, divided, plus extra for drizzling
1 shallot, sliced thin
2 garlic cloves, minced
1½ pounds (680 g) small beets, scrubbed, trimmed, and cut into ½-inch wedges
½ cup chicken or vegetable broth
1 tablespoon dukkah, plus extra for sprinkling
¼ teaspoon table salt
4 (6-ounce / 170-g) skinless cod fillets, 1½ inches thick
1 tablespoon lemon juice
2 ounces (57 g) baby arugula

1. Using highest sauté function, heat 1 tablespoon oil in Instant Pot until shimmering. Add shallot and cook until softened, about 2 minutes. Stir in garlic and cook until fragrant, about 30 seconds. Stir in beets and broth. Lock lid in place and close pressure release valve. Select high pressure cook function and cook for 3 minutes. Turn off Instant Pot and quick-release pressure. Carefully remove lid, allowing steam to escape away from you.
2. Fold sheet of aluminum foil into 16 by 6-inch sling. Combine 2 tablespoons oil, dukkah, and salt in bowl, then brush cod with oil mixture. Arrange cod skinned side down in center of sling. Using sling, lower cod into Instant Pot, allow narrow edges of sling to rest along sides of insert. Lock lid in place and close pressure release valve. Select high pressure cook function and cook for 2 minutes.
3. Turn off Instant Pot and quick-release pressure. Carefully remove lid, allowing steam to escape away from you. Using sling, transfer cod to large plate. Tent with foil and let rest while finishing beet salad.
4. Combine lemon juice and remaining 1 tablespoon oil in large bowl. Using slotted spoon, transfer beets to bowl with oil mixture. Add arugula and gently toss to combine. Season with salt and pepper to taste. Serve cod with salad, sprinkling individual portions with extra dukkah and drizzling with extra oil.

PER SERVING
Calories: 340, Total Fat: 16g, Sat Fat: 2.5g, Carbohydrates: 14g, Protein: 33g, Sugar: 9g, Sodium: 460mg, Total Fiber: 4g

Sea Bass with Orange-Olive Salad

Prep time: 10 minutes | Cook time: 4 minutes | Serves: 4

2 oranges
1 red grapefruit
¼ cup pitted kalamata olives, chopped
2 tablespoons minced fresh parsley
½ teaspoon ground cumin
½ teaspoon paprika
Pinch cayenne pepper
Salt and pepper, to taste
4 (4- to 6-ounce / 113- to 170-g) skinless sea bass fillets, 1 to 1½ inches thick
2 tablespoons extra-virgin olive oil

1. Cut away peel and pith from oranges and grapefruit. Quarter oranges, then slice crosswise into ½-inch-thick pieces. Cut grapefruit into 8 wedges, then slice wedges crosswise into ½-inch-thick pieces. Combine oranges, grapefruit, olives, parsley, cumin, paprika, and cayenne in bowl. Season with salt to taste, cover, and set aside for serving.
2. Pat sea bass dry with paper towels, rub with oil, and season with salt and pepper.
3. For a charcoal grill, open bottom vent completely. Light large chimney starter filled with charcoal briquettes (6 quarts). When top coals are partially covered with ash, pour evenly over half of grill. Set cooking grate in place, cover, and open lid vent completely. Heat grill until hot, about 5 minutes.
4. For a gas grill, turn all burners to high, cover, and heat grill until hot, about 15 minutes. Leave primary burner on high and turn other burner(s) to medium-low.
5. Clean cooking grate, then repeatedly brush grate with well-oiled paper towels until grate is black and glossy, 5 to 10 times. Place sea bass on hotter part of grill and cook, uncovered, until well browned, about 10 minutes, gently flipping fillets using 2 spatulas halfway through cooking.
6. Gently move sea bass to cooler part of grill and cook, uncovered, until fish flakes apart when gently prodded with paring knife and registers 140°F (60°C), 3 to 6 minutes. Serve with salad.

PER SERVING
Calories: 270, Fat: 10.74g, Carbohydrates: 19.05g, Protein: 25.54g, Sugar: 4.57g, Fiber: 5g, Sodium: 153mg

Oven-Poached Cod Fillet

Prep time: 10 minutes | Cook time: 30 minutes | Serves: 4

4 (6-ounce / 170-g) cod filets
½ teaspoon salt
½ teaspoon freshly ground black pepper
½ cup dry white wine
½ cup seafood or

vegetable stock
2 garlic cloves, minced
1 bay leaf
1 teaspoon chopped fresh sage
4 rosemary sprigs for garnish

1. Preheat the oven to 375°F (190°C).
2. Season each filet with salt and pepper and place in a large ovenproof skillet or baking pan. Add the wine, stock, garlic, bay leaf, and sage and cover. Bake until the fish flakes easily with a fork, about 20 minutes.
3. Use a spatula to remove the filet from the skillet. Place the poaching liquid over high heat and cook, stirring frequently, until reduced by half, about 10 minutes. (Do this in a small saucepan if you used a baking pan.)
4. To serve, place a filet on each plate and drizzle with the reduced poaching liquid. Garnish each with a fresh rosemary sprig.

PER SERVING
Calories: 94, Fat: 0.97g, Carbohydrates: 2.55g, Protein: 18.14g, Sugar: 0.06g, Fiber: 1.3g, Sodium: 645mg

Sea Scallops with White Bean Purée

Prep time: 10 minutes | Cook time: 10 minutes | Serves: 2

4 tablespoons olive oil, divided
2 garlic cloves
2 teaspoons minced fresh rosemary
1 (15-ounce / 425-g) can white cannellini beans, drained and rinsed

½ cup low-sodium chicken stock
Salt, to taste
Freshly ground black pepper, to taste
6 (10 ounce / 283-g) sea scallops

1. To make the bean purée, heat 2 tablespoons of olive oil in a saucepan over medium-high heat. Add the garlic and sauté for 30 seconds, or just until it's fragrant. Don't let it burn. Add the rosemary and remove the pan from the heat.
2. Add the white beans and chicken stock to the

pan, return it to the heat, and stir. Bring the beans to a boil. Reduce the heat to low and simmer for 5 minutes.
3. Transfer the beans to a blender and purée them for 30 seconds, or until they're smooth. Taste and season with salt and pepper. Let them sit in the blender with the lid on to keep them warm while you prepare the scallops.
4. Pat the scallops dry with a paper towel and season them with salt and pepper.
5. Heat the remaining 2 tablespoons of olive oil in a large sauté pan. When the oil is shimmering, add the scallops, flat-side down.
6. Cook the scallops for 2 minutes, or until they're golden on the bottom. Flip them over and cook for another 1 to 2 minutes, or until opaque and slightly firm.
7. To serve, divide the bean purée between two plates and top with the scallops.

PER SERVING
Calories: 465, Total Fat: 29g, Total Carbohydrates: 21g, Fiber: 8g, Sugar: 1g, Protein: 30g, Sodium: 319mg

Almond-Crusted Salmon Steaks

Prep time: 10 minutes | Cook time: 8 minutes | Serves: 4

¼ cup olive oil
1 tablespoon honey
¼ cup breadcrumbs
½ cup finely chopped almonds, lightly toasted

½ teaspoon dried thyme
Sea salt and freshly ground pepper, to taste
4 salmon steaks

1. Preheat the oven to 350°F (180°C).
2. Combine the olive oil with the honey. (Soften the honey in the microwave for 15 seconds, if necessary, for easier blending.)
3. In a shallow dish, combine the breadcrumbs, almonds, thyme, sea salt, and freshly ground pepper.
4. Coat the salmon steaks with the olive oil mixture, then the almond mixture.
5. Place on a baking sheet brushed with olive oil and bake 8 to 12 minutes, or until the almonds are lightly browned and the salmon is firm.

PER SERVING
Calories: 619, Fat: 28.61g, Carbohydrates: 5.89g, Protein: 80.07g, Sugar: 4.45g, Fiber: 0.3g, Sodium: 209mg

Littleneck Clams Steamed in White Wine

Prep time: 10 minutes | Cook time: 7 minutes | Serves: 4 to 6

1½ cups dry white wine
3 shallots, minced
4 garlic cloves, minced
1 bay leaf
4 pounds (1.8 kg) littleneck clams, scrubbed

3 tablespoons extra-virgin olive oil
2 tablespoons minced fresh parsley
Lemon wedges

1. Bring wine, shallots, garlic, and bay leaf to simmer in Dutch oven over high heat and cook for 3 minutes. Add clams, cover, and cook, stirring twice, until clams open, 4 to 8 minutes. Using slotted spoon, transfer clams to serving bowl, discarding any that refuse to open.
2. Off heat, whisk oil into cooking liquid until combined. Pour sauce over clams and sprinkle with parsley. Serve with lemon wedges.

PER SERVING
Calories: 490, Fat: 14.55g, Carbohydrates: 18.79g, Protein: 66.96g, Sugar: 0.66g, Fiber: 0.3g, Sodium: 2729mg

Oven-Steamed Mussels in White Wine

Prep time: 10 minutes | Cook time: 17 minutes | Serves: 4 to 6

3 tablespoons extra-virgin olive oil
3 garlic cloves, minced
Pinch red pepper flakes
1 cup dry white wine
3 sprigs fresh thyme
2 bay leaves

4 pounds (1.8 kg) mussels, scrubbed and debearded
¼ teaspoon salt
2 tablespoons minced fresh parsley

1. Adjust oven rack to lowest position and heat oven to 500°F (260°C). Heat 1 tablespoon oil, garlic, and pepper flakes in large roasting pan over medium heat and cook, stirring constantly, until fragrant, about 30 seconds. Stir in wine, thyme sprigs, and bay leaves, bring to boil, and cook until wine is slightly reduced, about 1 minute.
2. Stir in mussels and salt. Cover pan tightly with aluminum foil and transfer to oven. Cook until most mussels have opened (a few may remain closed), 15 to 18 minutes.
3. Remove pan from oven. Discard thyme sprigs, bay leaves, and any mussels that refuse to open. Drizzle with remaining 2 tablespoons oil, sprinkle with parsley, and toss to combine. Serve.

PER SERVING
Calories: 568, Fat: 26.26g, Carbohydrates: 19.42g, Protein: 60.39g, Sugar: 0.75g, Fiber: 0.4g, Sodium: 1316mg

Squid Stew with Tomatoes and Olives

Prep time: 15 minutes | Cook time: 31 minutes | Serves: 4 to 6

¼ cup extra-virgin olive oil, plus extra for serving
2 onions, chopped fine
2 celery ribs, sliced thin
8 garlic cloves, minced
¼ teaspoon red pepper flakes
½ cup dry white wine or dry vermouth
2 pounds (907 g) small squid, bodies sliced crosswise into 1-inch-thick rings, tentacles

halved
Salt and pepper, to taste
3 (28-ounce / 794-g) cans whole peeled tomatoes, drained and chopped coarse
⅓ cup pitted brine-cured green olives, chopped coarse
1 tablespoon capers, rinsed
3 tablespoons minced fresh parsley

1. Heat oil in Dutch oven over medium-high heat until shimmering. Add onions and celery and cook until softened, about 5 minutes. Stir in garlic and pepper flakes and cook until fragrant, about 30 seconds. Stir in wine, scraping up any browned bits, and cook until nearly evaporated, about 1 minute.
2. Pat squid dry with paper towels and season with salt and pepper. Stir squid into pot. Reduce heat to medium-low, cover, and simmer gently until squid has released its liquid, about 15 minutes. Stir in tomatoes, olives, and capers, cover, and continue to cook until squid is very tender, 30 to 35 minutes.
3. Off heat, stir in parsley and season with salt and pepper to taste. Serve, drizzling individual portions with extra oil.

PER SERVING
Calories: 503, Fat: 18.52g, Carbohydrates: 45.91g, Protein: 42.66g, Sugar: 26g, Fiber: 14.3g, Sodium: 856mg

Cod Gratin with Olives and Leeks

Prep time: 10 minutes | Cook time: 20 minutes | Serves: 4

½ cup olive oil, divided
1 pound (454 g) fresh cod
1 cup black olives, pitted and chopped
4 leeks, trimmed and sliced

1 cup whole-wheat breadcrumbs
¾ cup low-salt chicken stock
Sea salt and freshly ground pepper, to taste

1. Preheat the oven to 350°F (180°C).
2. Brush 4 gratin dishes with the olive oil.
3. Place the cod on a baking dish, and bake for 5 to 7 minutes. Cool and cut into 1-inch pieces.
4. Heat the remaining olive oil in a large skillet.
5. Add the olives and leeks, and cook over medium-low heat until the leeks are tender.
6. Add the breadcrumbs and chicken stock, stirring to mix.
7. Gently fold in the pieces of cod. Divide the mixture between the 4 gratin dishes, and drizzle with olive oil.
8. Season with sea salt and freshly ground pepper. Bake for 15 minutes or until warmed through.

PER SERVING

Calories: 468, Fat: 32.44g, Carbohydrates: 23.49g, Protein: 22.12g, Sugar: 4.88g, Fiber: 3.8g, Sodium: 746mg

Dilly Baked Salmon Fillet

Prep time: 10 minutes | Cook time: 15 minutes | Serves: 4

4 (6-ounce / 170-g) salmon filets
2 tablespoons extra-virgin olive oil
½ teaspoon salt
¼ teaspoon freshly ground black pepper

Juice of large Valencia orange or tangerine
4 teaspoons orange or tangerine zest
4 tablespoons chopped fresh dill

1. Preheat the oven to 375°F (190°C). Prepare four 10-inch-long pieces of aluminum foil.
2. Rub each salmon filet on both sides with the olive oil. Season each with salt and pepper and place one in the center of each piece of foil.
3. Drizzle the orange juice over each piece of fish and top with 1 teaspoon orange zest and 1 tablespoon dill.

4. For each packet, fold the two long sides of the foil together and then fold the short ends in to make a packet. Make sure to leave about 2 inches of air space within the foil so the fish can steam. Place the packets on a baking sheet.
5. Bake for 15 minutes. Open the packets carefully (they will be very steamy), transfer the fish to 4 serving plates, and pour the sauce over the top of each.

PER SERVING

Calories: 347, Fat: 17.28g, Carbohydrates: 10.21g, Protein: 37.74g, Sugar: 5.98g, Fiber: 1.9g, Sodium: 486mg

Sicilian Tuna and Veggie Bowl

Prep time: 10 minutes | Cook time: 16 minutes | Serves: 6

1 pound (454 g) kale, chopped, center ribs removed
3 tablespoons extra-virgin olive oil
1 cup chopped onion
3 garlic cloves, minced
1 (2¼-ounce / 64-g) can sliced olives, drained
¼ cup capers
¼ teaspoon crushed red pepper
2 teaspoons coconut

sugar
2 (6-ounce / 170-g) cans tuna in olive oil, undrained
1 (15-ounce / 425-g) can cannellini beans or great northern beans, drained and rinsed
¼ teaspoon freshly ground black pepper
¼ teaspoon kosher or sea salt

1. Fill a large stockpot three-quarters full of water, and bring to a boil. Add the kale and cook for 2 minutes. (This is to make the kale less bitter.) Drain the kale in a colander and set aside.
2. Set the empty pot back on the stove over medium heat, and pour in the oil. Add the onion and cook for 4 minutes, stirring often. Add the garlic and cook for 1 minute, stirring often. Add the olives, capers, and crushed red pepper, and cook for 1 minute, stirring often. Add the partially cooked kale and sugar, stirring until the kale is completely coated with oil. Cover the pot and cook for 8 minutes.
3. Remove the kale from the heat, mix in the tuna, beans, pepper, and salt, and serve.

PER SERVING

Calories: 636g, Total Fat: 60g, Saturated Fat:8g, Total Carbs: 22g, Protein: 8g, Fiber: 8g, Sugar: 4g, Sodium: 452mg

Sea Bass with Salmoriglio Sauce

Prep time: 10 minutes | Cook time: 12 minutes | Serves: 4

For the Salmoriglio Sauce:	oil
1 small garlic clove, minced	For the Fish:
1 tablespoon lemon juice	2 (1½- to 2-pound) whole sea bass, scaled, gutted, fins snipped off with scissors
⅛ teaspoon salt	
⅛ teaspoon pepper	
1½ tablespoons minced fresh oregano	3 tablespoons extra-virgin olive oil
¼ cup extra-virgin olive	Salt and pepper, to taste

Make the Salmoriglio Sauce:
1. Whisk all ingredients together in bowl until combined, cover and set aside for serving.

Make the Fish:
1. For a charcoal grill, open bottom vent completely. Light large chimney starter filled with charcoal briquettes (6 quarts). When top coals are partially covered with ash, pour evenly over grill. Set cooking grate in place, cover, and open lid vent completely. Heat grill until hot, about 5 minutes.
2. For a gas grill, turn all burners to high, cover, and heat grill until hot, about 15 minutes. Leave all burners on high.
3. Rinse each sea bass under cold running water and pat dry with paper towels inside and out. Using sharp knife, make 3 or 4 shallow slashes, about 2 inches apart, on both sides of sea bass. Rub sea bass with oil and season generously with salt and pepper inside and outside.
4. Clean cooking grate, then repeatedly brush grate with well-oiled paper towels until black and glossy, 5 to 10 times. Place sea bass on grill and cook (covered if using gas) until skin is browned and beginning to blister on first side, 6 to 8 minutes. Using spatula, lift bottom of thick backbone edge of sea bass from cooking grate just enough to slide second spatula under fish. Remove first spatula, then use it to support raw side of sea bass as you use second spatula to flip fish over. Cook (covered if using gas) until second side is browned, beginning to blister, and sea bass registers 140°F (60°C), 6 to 8 minutes.
5. Carefully transfer sea bass to carving board and let rest for 5 minutes. Fillet sea bass by making vertical cut just behind head from top of fish to belly. Make another cut on top of sea bass from head to tail. Use spatula to lift meat from bones, starting at head end and running spatula over bones to lift out fillet. Repeat on other side of sea bass. Discard head and skeleton. Serve with sauce.

PER SERVING
Calories: 278, Fat: 25g, Carbohydrates: 1.81g, Protein: 12.13g, Sugar: 0.16g, Fiber: 0.7g, Sodium: 122mg

Fish Fillet on Lemons

Prep time: 5 minutes | Cook time: 6 minutes | Serves: 4

4 (4-ounce/ 113-g) fish fillets, such as tilapia, salmon, catfish, cod, or your favorite fish	1 tablespoon extra-virgin olive oil
Nonstick cooking spray	¼ teaspoon freshly ground black pepper
3 to 4 medium lemons	¼ teaspoon kosher or sea salt

1. Using paper towels, pat the fillets dry and let stand at room temperature for 10 minutes. Meanwhile, coat the cold cooking grate of the grill with nonstick cooking spray, and preheat the grill to 400°F (205°C), or medium-high heat. Or preheat a grill pan over medium-high heat on the stove top.
2. Cut one lemon in half and set half aside. Slice the remaining half of that lemon and the remaining lemons into ¼-inch-thick slices. (You should have about 12 to 16 lemon slices.) Into a small bowl, squeeze 1 tablespoon of juice out of the reserved lemon half.
3. Add the oil to the bowl with the lemon juice, and mix well. Brush both sides of the fish with the oil mixture, and sprinkle evenly with pepper and salt.
4. Carefully place the lemon slices on the grill (or the grill pan), arranging 3 to 4 slices together in the shape of a fish fillet, and repeat with the remaining slices. Place the fish fillets directly on top of the lemon slices, and grill with the lid closed. (If you're grilling on the stove top, cover with a large pot lid or aluminum foil.) Turn the fish halfway through the cooking time only if the fillets are more than half an inch thick. The fish is done and ready to serve when it just begins to separate into flakes (chunks) when pressed gently with a fork.

PER SERVING
Calories: 208g, Total Fat: 12g, Saturated Fat: 4g, Total Carbs: 2g, Fiber: 0g, Protein: 21g, Sugar: 1g, Sodium: 249mg

Grilled Lemony Squid

Prep time: 10 minutes | Cook time: 8 minutes | Serves: 4

5 tablespoons extra-virgin olive oil
1 tablespoon lemon juice, plus lemon wedges for serving
2 teaspoons minced fresh parsley

1 garlic clove, minced
Salt and pepper, to taste
1 pound (454 g) small squid
2 tablespoons baking soda

1. Combine 3 tablespoons oil, lemon juice, parsley, garlic, and ¼ teaspoon pepper in large bowl, set aside for serving.
2. Using kitchen shears, cut squid bodies lengthwise down one side. Open squid bodies and flatten into planks. Dissolve baking soda and 2 tablespoons salt in 3 cups cold water in large container. Submerge squid bodies and tentacles in brine, cover, and refrigerate for 15 minutes. Remove squid from brine and spread in even layer in rimmed baking sheet lined with clean kitchen towel. Place second clean kitchen towel on top of squid and press gently on towel to blot liquid. Let squid sit at room temperature, covered with towel, for 10 minutes.
3. Toss squid with remaining 2 tablespoons oil and season with pepper. Thread tentacles onto two 12-inch metal skewers.
4. For a charcoal, grill Open bottom vent completely. Light large chimney starter mounded with charcoal briquettes (7 quarts). When top coals are partially covered with ash, pour evenly over half of grill. Set cooking grate in place, cover, and open lid vent completely. Heat grill until hot, about 5 minutes.
5. For a gas grill, turn all burners to high, cover, and heat grill until hot, about 15 minutes. Leave all burners on high.
6. Clean cooking grate, then repeatedly brush grate with well-oiled paper towels until black and glossy, 5 to 10 times. Place squid bodies and tentacles on grill (directly over coals if using charcoal), draping long tentacles over skewers to prevent them from falling through grates. Cook (covered if using gas) until squid is opaque and lightly charred, about 5 minutes, flipping halfway through cooking. Transfer bodies to plate and tent loosely with aluminum foil. Continue to grill tentacles until ends are browned and crisp, about 3 minutes, transfer to plate with bodies.
7. Using tongs, remove tentacles from skewers.

Transfer bodies to cutting board and slice into ½-inch-thick strips. Add tentacles and bodies to bowl with oil mixture and toss to coat. Serve with lemon wedges.

PER SERVING
Calories: 262, Fat: 18.51g, Carbohydrates: 5.72g, Protein: 17.94g, Sugar: 1.12g, Fiber: 0.3g, Sodium: 1982mg

Panko-Crusted Fish Sticks

Prep time: 10 minutes | Cook time: 5 minutes | Serves: 4

2 large eggs, lightly beaten 1 tablespoon 2% milk
1 pound (454 g) skinned fish fillets (cod, tilapia, or other white fish) about ½ inch thick, sliced into 20 (1-inch-wide) strips
½ cup yellow cornmeal
½ cup whole-wheat

panko bread crumbs or whole-wheat bread crumbs
¼ teaspoon smoked paprika
¼ teaspoon kosher or sea salt
¼ teaspoon freshly ground black pepper
Nonstick cooking spray

1. Place a large, rimmed baking sheet in the oven. Preheat the oven to 400°F (205°C) with the pan inside.
2. In a large bowl, mix the eggs and milk. Using a fork, add the fish strips to the egg mixture and stir gently to coat.
3. Put the cornmeal, bread crumbs, smoked paprika, salt, and pepper in a quart-size zip-top plastic bag. Using a fork or tongs, transfer the fish to the bag, letting the excess egg wash drip off into the bowl before transferring. Seal the bag and shake gently to completely coat each fish stick.
4. With oven mitts, carefully remove the hot baking sheet from the oven and spray it with nonstick cooking spray. Using a fork or tongs, remove the fish sticks from the bag and arrange them on the hot baking sheet, with space between them so the hot air can circulate and crisp them up.
5. Bake for 5 to 8 minutes, until gentle pressure with a fork causes the fish to flake, and serve.

PER SERVING
Calories: 238g, Total Fat: 3g, Saturated Fat: 1g, Total Carbs: 28g, Fiber: 2g, Protein: 22g, Sugar: 1g, Sodium: 494mg

Braised Octopus in Red Wine

Prep time: 15 minutes | Cook time: 42 minutes | Serves: 4

1 (4-pound) octopus, rinsed
1 tablespoon extra-virgin olive oil
2 tablespoons tomato paste
4 garlic cloves, peeled and smashed
1 sprig fresh rosemary
2 bay leaves
Pepper, to taste
Pinch ground cinnamon
Pinch ground nutmeg
1 cup dry red wine
2 tablespoons red wine vinegar
2 tablespoons unflavored gelatin
2 teaspoons chopped fresh parsley

1. Using sharp knife, separate octopus mantle (large sac) and body (lower section with tentacles) from head (midsection containing eyes), discard head. Place octopus in large pot, cover with water by 2 inches, and bring to simmer over high heat. Reduce heat to low, cover, and simmer gently, flipping octopus occasionally, until skin between tentacle joints tears easily when pulled, 45 minutes to 1¼ hours.
2. Transfer octopus to cutting board and let cool slightly. Measure out and reserve 3 cups octopus cooking liquid, discard remaining liquid and wipe pot dry with paper towels.
3. While octopus is still warm, use paring knife to cut mantle into quarters, then trim and scrape away skin and interior fibers, transfer to bowl. Using your fingers, remove skin from body, being careful not to remove suction cups from tentacles. Cut tentacles from around core of body in three sections, discard core. Separate tentacles and cut into 2-inch lengths, transfer to bowl.
4. Heat oil in now-empty pot over medium-high heat until shimmering. Add tomato paste and cook, stirring constantly, until beginning to darken, about 1 minute. Stir in garlic, rosemary sprig, bay leaves, ½ teaspoon pepper, cinnamon, and nutmeg and cook until fragrant, about 30 seconds. Stir in reserved octopus cooking liquid, wine, vinegar, and gelatin, scraping up any browned bits. Bring to boil and cook, stirring occasionally, for 20 minutes.
5. Stir in octopus and any accumulated juices and bring to simmer. Cook, stirring occasionally, until octopus is tender and sauce has thickened slightly and coats back of spoon, 20 to 25 minutes. Off heat, discard rosemary sprig and bay leaves. Stir in parsley and season with pepper to taste. Serve.

PER SERVING
Calories: 438, Fat: 8.4g, Carbohydrates: 15.22g, Protein: 68.45g, Sugar: 2.18g, Fiber: 1.1g, Sodium: 1061mg

Pan-Roasted Halibut Steaks with Chermoula

Prep time: 15 minutes | Cook time: 11 minutes | Serves: 8

For the Chermoula:
¾ cup fresh cilantro leaves
¼ cup extra-virgin olive oil
2 tablespoons lemon juice
4 garlic cloves, minced
½ teaspoon ground cumin
½ teaspoon paprika
¼ teaspoon salt
⅛ teaspoon cayenne pepper
For the Fish:
2 (1¼-pound / 567-g) skin-on full halibut steaks, 1 to 1½ inches thick and 10 to 12 inches long, trimmed
Salt and pepper, to taste
2 tablespoons extra-virgin olive oil

Make the Chermoula
1. Process all ingredients in food processor until smooth, about 1 minute, scraping down sides of bowl as needed, set aside for serving.

Make the Fish
1. Adjust oven rack to middle position and heat oven to 325°F (163°C). Pat halibut dry with paper towels and season with salt and pepper. Heat oil in 12-inch ovensafe nonstick skillet over medium-high heat until just smoking. Place halibut in skillet and cook until well browned on first side, about 5 minutes.
2. Gently flip halibut using 2 spatulas and transfer skillet to oven. Roast until halibut flakes apart when gently prodded with paring knife and registers 140°F (60°C), 6 to 9 minutes.
3. Carefully transfer halibut to cutting board, tent loosely with aluminum foil, and let rest for 5 minutes. Remove skin from steaks and separate each quadrant of meat from bones by slipping knife or spatula between them. Serve with chermoula.

PER SERVING
Calories: 359, Fat: 29.96g, Carbohydrates: 1.15g, Protein: 20.59g, Sugar: 0.15g, Fiber: 0.2, Sodium: 188mg

Squid in Herb White Wine

Prep time: 10 minutes | Cook time: 6 minutes | Serves: 3

1 pound (454 g) fresh squid rings
1 cup dry white wine
1 cup olive oil
2 garlic cloves, crushed
1 lemon, juiced
2 cups fish stock
¼ teaspoon red pepper flakes
¼ teaspoon dried oregano
1 tablespoon fresh rosemary, chopped
1 teaspoon sea salt

1. In a bowl, mix wine, olive oil, lemon juice, garlic, flakes, oregano, rosemary, and salt. Submerge squid rings in this mixture and cover with a lid.
2. Refrigerate for 1 hour. Remove the squid from the fridge and place them in the pot along with stock and half of the marinade. Seal the lid.
3. Cook on High Pressure for 6 minutes. Release the Pressure naturally, for 10 minutes. Transfer the rings to a plate and drizzle with some marinade to serve.

PER SERVING
Calories: 814, Fat: 75.44g, Carbohydrates: 7.82g, Protein: 27.74g, Sugar: 1.47g, Fiber: 0.3g, Sodium: 1092mg

Cod Fillet with Swiss Chard

Prep time: 10 minutes | Cook time: 12 minutes | Serves: 4

1 teaspoon salt
½ teaspoon dried oregano
½ teaspoon dried thyme
½ teaspoon garlic powder
4 cod fillets
½ white onion, thinly
sliced
2 cups Swiss chard, washed, stemmed, and torn into pieces
¼ cup olive oil
1 lemon, quartered

1. Preheat the air fryer to 380ºF (193ºC).
2. In a small bowl, whisk together the salt, oregano, thyme, and garlic powder.
3. Tear off four pieces of aluminum foil, with each sheet being large enough to envelop one cod fillet and a quarter of the vegetables.
4. Place a cod fillet in the middle of each sheet of foil, then sprinkle on all sides with the spice mixture.
5. In each foil packet, place a quarter of the onion slices and ½ cup Swiss chard, then drizzle 1 tablespoon olive oil and squeeze ¼ lemon over the contents of each foil packet.
6. Fold and seal the sides of the foil packets and then place them into the air fryer basket. Steam for 12 minutes.
7. Remove from the basket, and carefully open each packet to avoid a steam burn.

PER SERVING
Calories: 252, Total Fat: 14g, Saturated Fat: 2g, Total Carbohydrates: 4g, Protein: 26g, Fiber: 1g, Sugar: 1g

Jumbo Shrimp with Fresh Parsley

Prep time: 10 minutes | Cook time: 6 minutes | Serves: 4 to 6

¼ cup salt
2 pounds (907 g) shell-on jumbo shrimp
¼ cup extra-virgin olive oil
6 garlic cloves, minced
1 teaspoon anise seeds
½ teaspoon red pepper flakes
¼ teaspoon pepper
2 tablespoons minced fresh parsley
Lemon wedges

1. Dissolve salt in 4 cups cold water in large container. Using kitchen shears or sharp paring knife, cut through shell of shrimp and devein but do not remove shell. Using paring knife, continue to cut shrimp ½ inch deep, taking care not to cut in half completely. Submerge shrimp in brine, cover, and refrigerate for 15 minutes.
2. Adjust oven rack 4 inches from broiler element and heat broiler. Combine oil, garlic, anise seeds, pepper flakes, and pepper in large bowl. Remove shrimp from brine and pat dry with paper towels. Add shrimp and parsley to oil mixture and toss well, making sure oil mixture gets into interior of shrimp. Arrange shrimp in single layer on wire rack set in rimmed baking sheet.
3. Broil shrimp until opaque and shells are beginning to brown, 2 to 4 minutes, rotating sheet halfway through broiling. Flip shrimp and continue to broil until second side is opaque and shells are beginning to brown, 2 to 4 minutes, rotating sheet halfway through broiling. Serve with lemon wedges.

PER SERVING
Calories: 327, Fat: 14.82g, Carbohydrates: 3.34g, Protein: 46.19g, Sugar: 0.65g, Fiber: 0.4g, Sodium: 734.3mg

Grouper Fillet with Tomato and Olive

Prep time: 10 minutes | Cook time: 10 minutes | Serves: 4

4 grouper fillets	olives
½ teaspoon salt	¼ cup fresh dill, roughly
3 garlic cloves, minced	chopped
1 tomato, sliced	Juice of 1 lemon
¼ cup sliced Kalamata	¼ cup olive oil

1. Preheat the air fryer to 380ºF (193ºC).
2. Season the grouper fillets on all sides with salt, then place into the air fryer basket and top with the minced garlic, tomato slices, olives, and fresh dill.
3. Drizzle the lemon juice and olive oil over the top of the grouper, then bake for 10 to 12 minutes, or until the internal temperature reaches 145ºF (63ºC),

PER SERVING

Calories: 271, Total Fat: 16g, Saturated Fat: 2g, Total Carbohydrates: 3g, Protein: 28g, Fiber: 1g, Sugar: 1g

Hake Fillet with Garlicky Potatoes

Prep time: 10 minutes | Cook time: 27 minutes | Serves: 4

1½ pounds (680 g) russet potatoes, unpeeled, sliced into ¼-inch-thick rounds	Salt and pepper, to taste 4 (4- to 6-ounce / 113- to 170-g) skinless hake fillets, 1 to 1½ inches thick
¼ cup extra-virgin olive oil	4 sprigs fresh thyme
3 garlic cloves, minced	1 lemon, sliced thin

1. Adjust oven rack to lower-middle position and heat oven to 425ºF (220ºC). Toss potatoes with 2 tablespoons oil and garlic in bowl and season with salt and pepper. Microwave, uncovered, until potatoes are just tender, 12 to 14 minutes, stirring halfway through microwaving.
2. Transfer potatoes to 13 by 9-inch baking dish and press gently into even layer. Pat hake dry with paper towels, season with salt and pepper, and arrange skinned side down on top of potatoes. Drizzle hake with remaining 2 tablespoons oil, then place thyme sprigs and lemon slices on top. Bake until hake flakes apart when gently prodded with paring knife and registers 140ºF (60ºC), 15 to 18 minutes. Slide spatula underneath potatoes and hake and carefully transfer to individual plates. Serve.

PER SERVING

Calories: 341, Fat: 14.17g, Carbohydrates: 32.73g, Protein: 21.61g, Sugar: 1.38g, Fiber: 2.5g, Sodium: 361mg

Shrimp with White Beans and Arugula

Prep time: 10 minutes | Cook time: 13 minutes | Serves: 4

1 pound (454 g) extra-large shrimp, peeled and deveined	chopped fine 2 garlic cloves, minced
Pinch coconut sugar	¼ teaspoon red pepper flakes
Salt and pepper, to taste	2 (15-ounce / 425-g) cans
5 tablespoons extra-virgin olive oil	cannellini beans, rinsed
1 red bell pepper, stemmed, seeded, and chopped fine	2 ounces (57 g) baby arugula, chopped coarse
1 small red onion,	2 tablespoons lemon juice

1. Pat shrimp dry with paper towels and season with sugar, salt, and pepper. Heat 1 tablespoon oil in 12-inch nonstick skillet over high heat until just smoking. Add shrimp to skillet in single layer and cook, without stirring, until spotty brown and edges turn pink on first side, about 1 minute.
2. Off heat, flip shrimp and let sit until opaque throughout, about 30 seconds. Transfer shrimp to bowl and cover to keep warm.
3. Heat remaining ¼ cup oil in now-empty skillet over medium heat until shimmering. Add bell pepper, onion, and ½ teaspoon salt and cook until softened, about 5 minutes. Stir in garlic and pepper flakes and cook until fragrant, about 30 seconds. Stir in beans and cook until heated through, about 5 minutes.
4. Add arugula and shrimp along with any accumulated juices and gently toss until arugula is wilted, about 1 minute. Stir in lemon juice and season with salt and pepper to taste. Serve.

PER SERVING

Calories: 300, Fat: 18.31g, Carbohydrates: 11.25g, Protein: 25.35g, Sugar: 3.71g, Fiber: 3.5g, Sodium: 726mg

Easy Tuna Steaks

Prep time: 10 minutes | Cook time: 8 minutes | Serves: 4

1 teaspoon garlic powder	oregano
½ teaspoon salt	4 tuna steaks
¼ teaspoon dried thyme	2 tablespoons olive oil
¼ teaspoon dried	1 lemon, quartered

1. Preheat the air fryer to 380°F (193°C).
2. In a small bowl, whisk together the garlic powder, salt, thyme, and oregano.
3. Coat the tuna steaks with olive oil. Season both sides of each steak with the seasoning blend. Place the steaks in a single layer in the air fryer basket.
4. Cook for 5 minutes, then flip and cook for an additional 3 to 4 minutes.

PER SERVING

Calories: 269, Total Fat: 14g, Saturated Fat: 3g, Total Carbohydrates: 1g, Protein: 33g, Fiber: 0g, Sugar: 0g

Seared Sea Scallops with Tangy Dressing

Prep time: 10 minutes | Cook time: 3 minutes | Serves: 4 to 6

1½ pounds (680 g) large sea scallops, tendons removed	2 tablespoons lime juice
	1 small shallot, minced
6 tablespoons extra-virgin olive oil	1 tablespoon minced fresh cilantro
2 tablespoons orange juice	⅛ teaspoon red pepper flakes
	Salt and pepper, to taste

1. Place scallops in rimmed baking sheet lined with clean kitchen towel. Place second clean kitchen towel on top of scallops and press gently on towel to blot liquid. Let scallops sit at room temperature, covered with towel, for 10 minutes.
2. Whisk ¼ cup oil, orange juice, lime juice, shallot, cilantro, and pepper flakes together in bowl. Season with salt to taste and set aside for serving.
3. Heat 1 tablespoon oil in 12-inch nonstick skillet over medium-high heat until just smoking. Add half of scallops to skillet in single layer and cook, without moving them, until well browned on first side, about 1½ minutes. Flip scallops and continue to cook, without moving them, until well browned on second side, about 1½

minutes. Transfer scallops to serving platter and tent loosely with aluminum foil. Repeat with remaining 1 tablespoon oil and remaining scallops. Whisk dressing to recombine and serve with scallops.

PER SERVING

Calories: 306, Fat: 21.12g, Carbohydrates: 7.88g, Protein: 20.76g, Sugar: 1.05g, Fiber: 0.3g, Sodium: 668mg

Grilled Sardines with Lemon Wedges

Prep time: 5 minutes | Cook time: 6 minutes | Serves: 4 to 6

12 (2- to 3-ounce) whole sardines, scaled, gutted, fins snipped off with scissors	2 tablespoons low fat yogurt
	½ teaspoon honey
	Lemon wedges
Pepper, to taste	

1. Rinse each sardine under cold running water and pat dry with paper towels inside and out. Open cavity of each sardine and season flesh with pepper. Combine low fat yogurt and honey, then brush mixture evenly on exterior of each fish.
2. For a charcoal grill, open bottom vent completely. Light large chimney starter filled with charcoal briquettes (6 quarts). When top coals are partially covered with ash, pour evenly over grill. Set cooking grate in place, cover, and open lid vent completely. Heat grill until hot, about 5 minutes.
3. For a gas grill, turn all burners to high, cover, and heat grill until hot, about 15 minutes. Leave all burners on high.
4. Clean cooking grate, then repeatedly brush grate with well-oiled paper towels until grate is black and glossy, 5 to 10 times. Place sardines on grill and cook (covered if using gas) until skin is browned and beginning to blister, 2 to 4 minutes. Gently flip sardines using spatula and continue to cook until second side is browned and beginning to blister, 2 to 4 minutes. Serve with lemon wedges.

PER SERVING

Calories: 405, Fat: 22.39g, Carbohydrates: 3.6g, Protein: 44.86g, Sugar: 2.48g, Fiber: 0.4g, Sodium: 886mg

Roasted Shrimp-Gnocchi Bake

Prep time: 10 minutes | Cook time: 20 minutes | Serves: 4

1 cup chopped fresh tomato
2 tablespoons extra-virgin olive oil
2 garlic cloves, minced
½ teaspoon freshly ground black pepper
¼ teaspoon crushed red pepper
1 (12-ounce / 340-g) jar roasted red peppers, drained and coarsely

chopped
1 pound (454 g) fresh raw shrimp (or frozen and thawed shrimp), shells and tails removed
1 pound (454 g) frozen gnocchi (not thawed)
½ cup cubed Feta cheese
⅓ cup fresh torn basil leaves

1. Preheat the oven to 425°F (220°C).
2. In a baking dish, mix the tomatoes, oil, garlic, black pepper, and crushed red pepper. Roast in the oven for 10 minutes.
3. Stir in the roasted peppers and shrimp. Roast for 10 more minutes, until the shrimp turn pink and white.
4. While the shrimp cooks, cook the gnocchi on the stove top according to the package directions. Drain in a colander and keep warm.
5. Remove the dish from the oven. Mix in the cooked gnocchi, Feta, and basil, and serve.

PER SERVING
Calories: 146g, Total Fat: 5g, Saturated Fat:1g, Total Carbs: 1g, Protein: 23g, Fiber: 0g, Sugar: 1g, Sodium: 669mg

Mussels Simmered with White Wine

Prep time: 10 minutes | Cook time: 5 minutes | Serves: 4

4 pounds (1.8 kg) fresh, live mussels
2 cups dry white wine
½ teaspoon sea salt
6 garlic cloves, minced
4 teaspoons diced shallot
½ cup chopped fresh

parsley, divided
4 tablespoons extra-virgin olive oil
Juice of ½ lemon
a crusty, whole-grain baguette

1. In a large colander, scrub and rinse the mussels under cold water. Discard any mussels that do not close when tapped. Use a paring knife to remove the beard from each mussel.
2. In a large stockpot over medium-high heat, bring the wine, salt, garlic, shallots, and ¼ cup of the parsley to a steady simmer.
3. Add the mussels, cover, and simmer just until all of the mussels open, 5 to 7 minutes. Do not overcook.
4. Using a slotted spoon, divide the mussels among 4 large, shallow bowls.
5. Add the olive oil and lemon juice to the pot, stir, and pour the broth over the mussels. Garnish each serving with 1 tablespoon of the remaining fresh parsley and serve with a crusty, whole-grain baguette.

PER SERVING
Calories: 545, Fat: 23.97g, Carbohydrates: 23.72g, Protein: 55.68g, Sugar: 2g, Fiber: 0.6g, Sodium: 1632mg

Beer-Battered Haddock with Crushed Potatoes

Prep time: 10 minutes | Cook time: 15 minutes | Serves: 4

8 ounces (227 g) beer
2 eggs
1 cup whole-wheat flour
½ tablespoons cayenne powder
1 tablespoon cumin powder

Salt and pepper, to taste
4 haddock fillets
Nonstick cooking spray
4 potatoes, cut into ¼- to ½-inch matchsticks
2 tablespoons olive oil

1. In a bowl, whisk beer and eggs. In another bowl, combine flour, cayenne, cumin, black pepper, and salt. Coat each fish piece in the egg mixture, then dredge in the flour mixture, coating all sides well.
2. Spray a baking dish with nonstick cooking spray. Place in the fish fillets, pour ¼ cup of water and grease with cooking spray. Place the potatoes in the pot and cover with water and place a trivet over the potatoes.
3. Lay the baking dish on top and seal the lid. Cook on High Pressure for 15 minutes. Do a quick release. Drain and crush the potatoes with olive oil and serve with the fish.

PER SERVING
Calories: 683, Fat: 14.07g, Carbohydrates: 89.67g, Protein: 48.05g, Sugar: 4.28g, Fiber: 11.9g, Sodium: 534mg

Cod Fillet on Millet

Prep time: 10 minutes | Cook time: 7 minutes | Serves: 4

1 tablespoon olive oil
1 cup millet
1 yellow bell pepper, diced
1 red bell pepper, diced
2 cups chicken broth
1 cup breadcrumbs
4 tablespoons melted almond butter
¼ cup minced fresh cilantro
1 teaspoon salt
4 cod fillets

1. Combine oil, millet, yellow and red bell peppers in the pot, and cook for 1 minute on Sauté. Mix in the chicken broth. Place a trivet atop. In a bowl, mix crumbs, butter, cilantro, lemon zest, juice, and salt.
2. Spoon the breadcrumb mixture evenly on the cod fillet. Lay the fish on the trivet. Seal the lid and cook on High for 6 minutes. Do a quick release and serve immediately.

PER SERVING
Calories: 699, Fat: 34.15g, Carbohydrates: 68.03g, Protein: 30.28g, Sugar: 3.5g, Fiber: 11.3g, Sodium: 826mg

Shrimp, Mushrooms, Basil Cheese Pasta

Prep time: 10 minutes | Cook time: 10 minutes | Serves: 6

1 pound (454 g) small shrimp, peeled and deveined
¼ cup plus 1 tablespoon olive oil, divided
¼ teaspoon garlic powder
¼ teaspoon cayenne
1 pound (454 g) whole grain pasta
5 garlic cloves, minced
8 ounces (227 g) baby bella mushrooms, sliced
½ cup Parmesan, plus more for serving (optional)
1 teaspoon salt
½ teaspoon black pepper
½ cup fresh basil

1. Preheat the air fryer to 380ºF (193ºC).
2. In a small bowl, combine the shrimp, 1 tablespoon olive oil, garlic powder, and cayenne. Toss to coat the shrimp.
3. Place the shrimp into the air fryer basket and roast for 5 minutes. Remove the shrimp and set aside.
4. Cook the pasta according to package directions. Once done cooking, reserve ½ cup pasta water,

then drain.
5. Meanwhile, in a large skillet, heat ¼ cup of olive oil over medium heat. Add the garlic and mushrooms and cook down for 5 minutes.
6. Pour the pasta, reserved pasta water, Parmesan, salt, pepper, and basil into the skillet with the vegetable-and-oil mixture, and stir to coat the pasta.
7. Toss in the shrimp and remove from heat, then let the mixture sit for 5 minutes before serving with additional Parmesan, if desired.

PER SERVING
Calories: 457, Total Fat: 15g, Saturated Fat: 3g, Total Carbohydrates: 60g, Protein: 25g, Fiber: 7g, Sugar: 1g

Pressure-Cooked Mussels

Prep time: 10 minutes | Cook time: 6 minutes | Serves: 4

1 tablespoon extra-virgin olive oil, plus extra for drizzling
1 fennel bulb, 1 tablespoon fronds minced, stalks discarded, bulb halved, cored, and sliced thin
1 leek, ends trimmed, leek halved lengthwise,
sliced 1 inch thick, and washed thoroughly
4 garlic cloves, minced
3 sprigs fresh thyme
¼ teaspoon red pepper flakes
¼ cup dry white wine
2 pounds (0.9kg) mussels, scrubbed and debearded

1. Using highest sauté function, heat oil in Instant Pot until shimmering. Add fennel and leek and cook until softened, about 5 minutes. Stir in garlic, thyme sprigs, and pepper flakes and cook until fragrant, about 30 seconds. Stir in wine, then add mussels.
2. Lock lid in place and close pressure release valve. Select high pressure cook function and set cook time for 0 minutes. Once Instant Pot has reached pressure, immediately turn off pot and quick-release pressure. Carefully remove lid, allowing steam to escape away from you.
3. Discard thyme sprigs and any mussels that have not opened. Transfer mussels to individual serving bowls, sprinkle with fennel fronds, and drizzle with extra oil. Serve.

PER SERVING
Calories: 380, Total Fat: 11g, Sat Fat: 2g, Carbohydrates: 22g, Protein: 42g, Sugar: 3g, Sodium: 794mg, Total Fiber: 2g

Sautéed Sole Fillet

Prep time: 5 minutes | Cook time: 3 minutes | Serves: 4

½ cup whole-fat flour
8 (2- to 3-ounce / 57- to 85-g) skinless sole fillets, ¼ to ½ inch thick
Salt and pepper, to taste
¼ cup extra-virgin olive oil
Lemon wedges

1. Place flour in shallow dish. Pat sole dry with paper towels and season with salt and pepper. Working with 1 fillet at a time, dredge in flour to coat, shaking off any excess.
2. Heat 2 tablespoons oil in 12-inch nonstick skillet over medium-high heat until shimmering. Place half of sole in skillet and cook until lightly browned on first side, 2 to 3 minutes. Gently flip sole using 2 spatulas and continue to cook until fish flakes apart when gently prodded with paring knife, 30 to 60 seconds.
3. Carefully transfer sole to serving platter and tent loosely with aluminum foil. Wipe skillet clean with paper towels and repeat with remaining 2 tablespoons oil and fillets. Serve with lemon wedges.

PER SERVING
Calories: 168, Fat: 3.97g, Carbohydrates: 13.12g, Protein: 19.31g, Sugar: 0.35g, Fiber: 0.6g, Sodium: 420mg

Pan-Roasted Sea Bass Fillet

Prep time: 5 minutes | Cook time: 10 minutes | Serves: 4

4 (4- to 6-ounce / 113- to 170-g) skinless sea bass fillets, 1 to 1½ inches thick
Salt and pepper, to taste
½ teaspoon coconut sugar
1 tablespoon extra-virgin olive oil
Lemon wedges

1. Adjust oven rack to middle position and heat oven to 425°F (220°C). Pat sea bass dry with paper towels, season with salt and pepper, and sprinkle sugar evenly on 1 side of each fillet.
2. Heat oil in 12-inch ovensafe skillet over medium-high heat until just smoking. Place sea bass sugared side down in skillet and press lightly to ensure even contact with skillet. Cook until browned on first side, about 2 minutes. Gently flip sea bass using 2 spatulas, transfer skillet to oven, and roast until fish flakes apart

when gently prodded with paring knife and registers 140°F (60°C), 7 to 10 minutes. Serve with lemon wedges.

PER SERVING
Calories: 160, Fat: 6g, Carbohydrates: 1.52g, Protein: 6g, Sugar: 0.62g, Fiber: 0.2g, Sodium: 88mg

Braised Halibut with Leeks and Parsley

Prep time: 10 minutes | Cook time: 33 minutes | Serves: 4

4 (4- to 6-ounce / 113- to 170-g) skinless halibut fillets, ¾ to 1 inch thick
Salt and pepper, to taste
¼ cup extra-virgin olive oil, plus extra for serving
1 pound (454 g) leeks, white and light green
parts only, halved lengthwise, sliced thin, and washed thoroughly
1 teaspoon Dijon mustard
¾ cup dry white wine
1 tablespoon minced fresh parsley
Lemon wedges

1. Pat halibut dry with paper towels and sprinkle with ½ teaspoon salt. Heat oil in 12-inch skillet over medium heat until warm, about 15 seconds. Place halibut skinned side up in skillet and cook until bottom half of halibut begins to turn opaque (halibut should not brown), about 4 minutes. Carefully transfer halibut raw side down to large plate.
2. Add leeks, mustard, and ¼ teaspoon salt to oil left in skillet and cook over medium heat, stirring frequently, until softened, 10 to 12 minutes. Stir in wine and bring to simmer. Place halibut raw side down on top of leeks. Reduce heat to medium-low, cover, and simmer gently until halibut flakes apart when gently prodded with paring knife and registers 140°F (60°C), 6 to 10 minutes. Carefully transfer halibut to serving platter, tent loosely with aluminum foil, and let rest while finishing leeks.
3. Return leeks to high heat and simmer briskly until mixture is thickened slightly, 2 to 4 minutes. Season with salt and pepper to taste. Arrange leek mixture around halibut, drizzle with extra oil, and sprinkle with parsley. Serve with lemon wedges.

PER SERVING
Calories: 955, Fat: 70.4g, Carbohydrates: 17.85g, Protein: 60.72g, Sugar: 5.23g, Fiber: 2.3, Sodium: 367mg

Crab-Meat with Asparagus and Broccoli Pilaf

Prep time: 10 minutes | Cook time: 14 minutes | Serves: 4

½ pound (227 g) asparagus, trimmed and cut into 1-inch pieces	1 small onion, chopped
½ pound (227 g) broccoli florets	1 cup rice
	⅓ cup white wine
Salt, to taste	3 cups vegetable stock
2 tablespoons olive oil	8 ounces (227 g) lump crabmeat

1. Heat oil on Sauté and cook onions for 3 minutes, until soft. Stir in rice and cook for 1 minute. Pour in the wine. Cook for 2 to 3 minutes, stirring, until the liquid has almost evaporated.
2. Add vegetable stock and salt, stir to combine. Place a trivet atop. Arrange the broccoli and asparagus on the trivet. Seal the lid and cook on High Pressure for 8 minutes. Do a quick release.
3. Remove the vegetables to a bowl. Fluff the rice with a fork and add in the crabmeat, heat for a minute. Taste and adjust the seasoning. Serve immediately topped with broccoli and asparagus.

PER SERVING
Calories: 261, Fat: 9.33g, Carbohydrates: 28.4g, Protein: 17.91g, Sugar: 5.28g, Fiber: 5.5g, Sodium: 1198mg

Oregano Shrimp Puttanesca

Prep time: 10 minutes | Cook time: 9 minutes | Serves: 4

2 tablespoons extra-virgin olive oil	1 (2¼-ounce / 64-g) can sliced black olives, drained
3 anchovy fillets, drained and chopped, or 1½ teaspoons anchovy paste	2 tablespoons capers
3 garlic cloves, minced	1 tablespoon chopped fresh oregano or 1 teaspoon dried oregano
½ teaspoon crushed red pepper	½ pound fresh raw shrimp (or frozen and thawed shrimp), shells and tails removed
1 (14½-ounce / 411-g) can low-sodium or no-salt-added diced tomatoes, undrained	

1. In a large skillet over medium heat, heat the oil. Mix in the anchovies, garlic, and crushed red pepper. Cook for 3 minutes, stirring frequently and mashing up the anchovies with a wooden spoon, until they have melted into the oil.
2. Stir in the tomatoes with their juices, olives, capers, and oregano. Turn up the heat to medium-high, and bring to a simmer.
3. When the sauce is lightly bubbling, stir in the shrimp. Reduce the heat to medium, and cook the shrimp for 6 to 8 minutes, or until they turn pink and white, stirring occasionally, and serve.

PER SERVING
Calories: 362g, Total Fat: 13g, Saturated Fat:6g, Total Carbs: 31g, Protein: 30g, Sugar: 28g, Fiber: 2g, Sodium: 786mg

Tilapia Fillet with Onion and Avocado

Prep time: 5 minutes | Cook time: 3 minutes | Serves: 4

1 tablespoon extra-virgin olive oil	fillets, more oblong than square, skin-on or skinned
1 tablespoon freshly squeezed orange juice	¼ cup chopped red onion
¼ teaspoon kosher or sea salt	1 avocado, pitted, skinned, and sliced
4 (4-ounce/ 113-g) tilapia	

1. In a 9-inch glass pie dish, use a fork to mix together the oil, orange juice, and salt. Working with one fillet at a time, place each in the pie dish and turn to coat on all sides. Arrange the fillets in a wagon-wheel formation, so that one end of each fillet is in the center of the dish and the other end is temporarily draped over the edge of the dish. Top each fillet with 1 tablespoon of onion, then fold the end of the fillet that's hanging over the edge in half over the onion. When finished, you should have 4 folded-over fillets with the fold against the outer edge of the dish and the ends all in the center.
2. Cover the dish with plastic wrap, leaving a small part open at the edge to vent the steam. Microwave on high for about 3 minutes. The fish is done when it just begins to separate into flakes (chunks) when pressed gently with a fork.
3. Top the fillets with the avocado and serve.

PER SERVING
Calories: 210g, Total Fat: 11g, Saturated Fat: 2g, Total Carbs: 5g, Fiber: 4g, Protein: 25g, Sugar: 1g, Sodium: 240mg

Steamed Oregano Salmon Fillet

Prep time: 10 minutes | Cook time: 10 minutes | Serves: 4

1 pound (454 g) fresh salmon fillets, skin on
¼ cup olive oil
½ cup freshly squeezed lemon juice
2 garlic cloves, crushed
1 tablespoon fresh oregano leaves, chopped
1 teaspoon sea salt
¼ teaspoon chili flakes
2 cups fish stock

1. In a bowl, mix oil, lemon juice, garlic, oregano leaves, salt, and flakes. Brush the fillets with the mixture and refrigerate for 30 minutes. Pour the stock in, and insert the trivet. Pat-dry the salmon and place on the steamer rack. Seal the lid, and cook on Steam for 10 minutes on High. Do a quick release and serve.

PER SERVING
Calories: 284, Fat: 18.84g, Carbohydrates: 2.86g, Protein: 25.72g, Sugar: 0.81g, Fiber: 0.3g, Sodium: 826mg

Shrimp and Veggie Pita

Prep time: 15 minutes | Cook time: 6 minutes | Serves: 4

1 pound (454 g) medium shrimp, peeled and deveined
2 tablespoons olive oil
1 teaspoon dried oregano
½ teaspoon dried thyme
½ teaspoon garlic powder
¼ teaspoon onion powder
½ teaspoon salt
¼ teaspoon black pepper
4 whole wheat pitas
4 ounces (113 g) Feta cheese, crumbled
1 cup shredded lettuce
1 tomato, diced
¼ cup black olives, sliced
1 lemon

1. Preheat the oven to 380ºF (193ºC).
2. In a medium bowl, combine the shrimp with the olive oil, oregano, thyme, garlic powder, onion powder, salt, and black pepper.
3. Pour shrimp in a single layer in the air fryer basket and cook for 6 to 8 minutes, or until cooked through.
4. Remove from the air fryer and divide into warmed pitas with Feta, lettuce, tomato, olives, and a squeeze of lemon.

PER SERVING
Calories: 395, Total Fat: 16g, Saturated Fat: 6g, Total Carbohydrates: 40g, Protein: 26g, Sugar: 3g, Fiber: 5g

Anchovy, Raisin, and Onion Stuffed Squid

Prep time: 15 minutes | Cook time: 1¼ hours | Serves: 4

2 tablespoons extra-virgin olive oil
3 onions, chopped fine
16 medium squid bodies, plus 6 ounces (170 g) tentacles, chopped
¼ cup pine nuts, toasted
1 tablespoon dried mint
Salt and pepper, to taste
½ cup plain dried bread crumbs
5 tablespoons minced fresh parsley
¼ cup golden raisins
4 anchovy fillets, rinsed and minced
1 garlic clove, minced
½ cup dry white wine
1 (15-ounce / 425-g) can tomato sauce

1. Heat 1 tablespoon oil in 12-inch nonstick skillet over medium-high heat until shimmering. Add two-thirds of onions and cook until softened, about 5 minutes. Stir in squid tentacles and cook until no longer translucent, 1 to 2 minutes. Stir in pine nuts, mint, and ¼ teaspoon pepper and cook until fragrant, about 1 minute. Transfer mixture to large bowl and stir in bread crumbs, ¼ cup parsley, raisins, and anchovies. Season with salt and pepper to taste and let cool slightly.
2. Using small soup spoon, portion 2 tablespoons filling into each squid body, pressing on filling gently to create 1-inch space at top. Thread toothpick through opening of each squid to secure closed.
3. Heat remaining 1 tablespoon oil in now-empty skillet over medium-high heat until shimmering. Add remaining onions and cook until softened, about 5 minutes. Stir in garlic, ¼ teaspoon salt, and ¼ teaspoon pepper and cook until fragrant, about 30 seconds. Stir in wine and tomato sauce and bring to simmer.
4. Nestle squid into sauce. Reduce heat to low, cover, and simmer gently until sauce has thickened slightly and squid is easily pierced with paring knife, about 1 hour, turning squid halfway through cooking. Season sauce with salt and pepper to taste. Remove toothpicks from squid and sprinkle with remaining 1 tablespoon parsley. Serve.

PER SERVING
Calories: 622, Fat: 24.25g, Carbohydrates: 47.42g, Protein: 54.65g, Sugar: 22.7g, Fiber: 6.1g, Sodium: 653mg

Dill and Garlic Stuffed Red Snapper

Prep time: 10 minutes | Cook time: 35 minutes | Serves: 4

1 teaspoon salt
½ teaspoon black pepper
½ teaspoon ground cumin
¼ teaspoon cayenne
1 (1- to 1½-pound / 454- to 680-g) whole red

snapper, cleaned and patted dry
2 tablespoons olive oil
2 garlic cloves, minced
¼ cup fresh dill
Lemon wedges, for serving

1. Preheat the air fryer to 360ºF (182ºC)
2. In a small bowl, mix together the salt, pepper, cumin, and cayenne.
3. Coat the outside of the fish with olive oil, then sprinkle the seasoning blend over the outside of the fish. Stuff the minced garlic and dill inside the cavity of the fish.
4. Place the snapper into the basket of the air fryer and roast for 20 minutes. Flip the snapper over, and roast for 15 minutes more, or until the snapper reaches an internal temperature of 145ºF (63ºC).

PER SERVING
Calories: 125, Total Fat: 2g, Saturated Fat: 0g, Total Carbohydrates: 2g, Protein: 23g, Fiber: 0g, Sugar: 0g

Provençal Hake Fillet

Prep time: 10 minutes | Cook time: 16 minutes | Serves: 4

2 tablespoons extra-virgin olive oil, plus extra for serving
1 onion, halved and sliced thin
1 fennel bulb, stalks discarded, bulb halved, cored, and sliced thin
Salt and pepper, to taste
4 garlic cloves, minced
1 teaspoon minced fresh thyme or ¼ teaspoon

dried
1 (14½-ounce / 411-g) can diced tomatoes, drained
½ cup dry white wine
4 (4- to 6-ounce / 113- to 170-g) skinless hake fillets, 1 to 1½ inches thick
2 tablespoons minced fresh parsley

1. Heat oil in 12-inch skillet over medium heat until shimmering. Add onion, fennel, and ½ teaspoon salt and cook until softened, about 5 minutes. Stir in garlic and thyme and cook until fragrant, about 30 seconds. Stir in tomatoes and wine

and bring to simmer.
2. Pat hake dry with paper towels and season with salt and pepper. Nestle hake skinned side down into skillet, spoon some sauce over top, and bring to simmer. Reduce heat to medium-low, cover, and cook until hake flakes apart when gently prodded with paring knife and registers 140ºF (60ºC), 10 to 12 minutes.
3. Carefully transfer hake to individual shallow bowls. Stir parsley into sauce and season with salt and pepper to taste. Spoon sauce over hake and drizzle with extra oil. Serve.

PER SERVING
Calories: 185, Fat: 7.67g, Carbohydrates: 10.1g, Protein: 19.79g, Sugar: 5.54g, Fiber: 4.2, Sodium: 511mg

Apple Cider-Glazed Salmon Steak

Prep time: 10 minutes | Cook time: 18 minutes | Serves: 3

1 pound (454 g) salmon steaks
1 teaspoon garlic powder
½ teaspoon rosemary powder

1 cup olive oil
½ cup apple cider vinegar
1 teaspoon salt
¼ cup lemon juice
½ teaspoon white pepper

1. In a bowl, mix garlic, rosemary, olive oil, apple cider vinegar, salt, lemon juice, and pepper. Pour the mixture into a Ziploc bag along with the salmon. Seal the bag and shake to coat well. Refrigerate for 30 minutes. Pour in 3 cups of water in the instant pot and insert the trivet. Remove the fish from the Ziploc bag and place on top.
2. Reserve the marinade. Seal lid and cook on Steam mode for 15 minutes on High Pressure. When ready, do a quick release and remove the steaks. Discard the liquid and wipe clean the pot. Grease with some of the marinade and hit Sauté. Add salmon steaks and brown on both sides for 3 to 4 minutes.

PER SERVING
Calories: 885, Fat: 82.91g, Carbohydrates: 2.83g, Protein: 31.48g, Sugar: 0.7g, Fiber: 0.3g, Sodium: 1434mg

Poached Turbot Fillet

Prep time: 10 minutes | Cook time: 40 minutes | Serves: 4

1 cup vegetable or chicken stock
½ cup dry white wine
1 yellow onion, sliced
1 lemon, sliced
4 sprigs fresh dill
½ teaspoon sea salt
4 (6-ounce / 170-g) turbot fillets

1. Combine the stock and wine in the slow cooker. Cover and heat on high for 20 to 30 minutes.
2. Add the onion, lemon, dill, salt, and turbot to the slow cooker. Cover and cook on high for about 20 minutes, until the turbot is opaque and cooked through according to taste. Serve hot.

PER SERVING
Calories: 461, Fat: 16.3g, Carbohydrates: 5.3g, Protein: 69.64g, Sugar: 1.55g, Fiber: 0.9g, Sodium: 1265mg

Salmon Steaks with Tomatoes and Olives

Prep time: 10 minutes | Cook time: 15 minutes | Serves: 4

1 tablespoon olive oil, divided
4 salmon steaks
Sea salt and freshly ground pepper, to taste
2 Roma tomatoes, chopped
¼ cup green olives, pitted
and chopped
1 clove garlic, minced
Juice of ½ lemon
1 teaspoon capers, rinsed and drained
½ teaspoon honey
½ cup dry breadcrumbs

1. Preheat the oven to 375°F (190°C).
2. Brush a baking dish with the olive oil. Place the salmon fillets in the dish. Season with sea salt and freshly ground pepper.
3. In a large bowl, combine all the remaining ingredients.
4. Top the salmon fillets with the tomato mixture, then the breadcrumbs. Drizzle with the remaining olive oil and bake for 15 minutes, or until medium rare.

PER SERVING
Calories: 577, Fat: 19.22g, Carbohydrates: 13.97g, Protein: 82.28g, Sugar: 3.35g, Fiber: 1.6g, Sodium: 354mg

Pollock and Vegetable Pitas

Prep time: 10 minutes | Cook time: 15 minutes | Serves: 4

1 pound (454 g) pollock, cut into 1-inch pieces
¼ cup olive oil
1 teaspoon salt
½ teaspoon dried oregano
½ teaspoon dried thyme
½ teaspoon garlic powder
¼ teaspoon cayenne
4 whole wheat pitas
1 cup shredded lettuce
2 Roma tomatoes, diced
Nonfat plain Greek yogurt
Lemon, quartered

1. Preheat the air fryer to 380°F (193°C).
2. In a medium bowl, combine the pollock with olive oil, salt, oregano, thyme, garlic powder, and cayenne.
3. Put the pollock into the air fryer basket and cook for 15 minutes.
4. Serve inside pitas with lettuce, tomato, and Greek yogurt with a lemon wedge on the side.

PER SERVING
Calories: 368, Total Fat: 16g, Saturated Fat: 2g, Total Carbohydrates: 38g, Protein: 21g, Sugar: 2g, Fiber: 6g

Balsamic Shrimp on Tomato and Olive

Prep time: 10 minutes | Cook time: 6 minutes | Serves: 4

½ cup olive oil
4 garlic cloves, minced
1 tablespoon balsamic vinegar
¼ teaspoon cayenne pepper
¼ teaspoon salt
1 Roma tomato, diced
¼ cup Kalamata olives
1 pound (454 g) medium shrimp, cleaned and deveined

1. Preheat the air fryer to 380°F (193°C).
2. In a small bowl, combine the olive oil, garlic, balsamic, cayenne, and salt.
3. Divide the tomatoes and olives among four small ramekins. Then divide shrimp among the ramekins, and pour a quarter of the oil mixture over the shrimp.
4. Cook for 6 to 8 minutes, or until the shrimp are cooked through.

PER SERVING
Calories: 160, Total Fat: 9g, Saturated Fat: 1g, Total Carbohydrates: 4g, Protein: 16g, Fiber: 1g, Sugar: 1g

Salmon Fillets with Dill

Prep time: 5 minutes | Cook time: 8 minutes | Serves: 4

4 salmon fillets
1 cup lemon juice
2 tablespoons almond butter, softened
2 tablespoons dill
¼ teaspoon salt
¼ teaspoon pepper, freshly ground

1. Sprinkle the fillets with salt and pepper. Insert the steamer tray and place the salmon on top. Pour in the lemon juice and 2 cups of water. Seal the lid.
2. Cook on Steam mode for 5 minutes on High. When done, release the Pressure naturally, for 10 minutes. Set aside the salmon and discard the liquid.
3. Wipe the pot clean and press Sauté. Add butter and briefly brown the fillets on both sides – for 3 to 4 minutes. Sprinkle with dill, to serve.

PER SERVING
Calories: 547, Fat: 21g, Carbohydrates: 5.48g, Protein: 80.58g, Sugar: 1.69g, Fiber: 0.5g, Sodium: 398mg

Speedy White Wine Mussels

Prep time: 5 minutes | Cook time: 1 minute | Serves: 5

1 cup white wine
½ cup water
1 teaspoon garlic powder
2 pounds (907 g)
mussels, cleaned and debearded
Juice from 1 lemon

1. In the pot, mix garlic powder, water and wine. Put the mussels into the steamer basket, rounded-side should be placed facing upwards to fit as many as possible.
2. Insert rack into the cooker and lower steamer basket onto the rack. Seal the lid and cook on Low Pressure for 1 minute. Release the pressure quickly.
3. Remove unopened mussels. Coat the mussels with the wine mixture. Serve sprinkled with lemon juice with a side of French fries or slices of toasted bread.

PER SERVING
Calories: 163, Fat: 4.09g, Carbohydrates: 8.32g, Protein: 21.96g, Sugar: 0.77g, Fiber: 0.1g, Sodium: 51mg

Slow Cooked Salmon Fillet

Prep time: 10 minutes | Cook time: 1 hour | Serves: 6

6 (6-ounce / 170-g) salmon fillets
½ cup honey
2 tablespoons lime juice
3 tablespoons
Worcestershire sauce
1 tablespoon water
2 cloves garlic, minced
1 teaspoon ground ginger
½ teaspoon black pepper

1. Place the salmon fillets in the slow cooker.
2. In medium bowl, whisk the honey, lime juice, Worcestershire sauce, water, garlic, ginger, and pepper. Pour sauce over salmon.
3. Cover and cook on high for 1 hour.

PER SERVING
Calories: 572, Fat: 14.96g, Carbohydrates: 26.06g, Protein: 79.98g, Sugar: 24.16g, Fiber: 0.2g, Sodium: 283mg

Sea Bass with Roasted Root Veggie

Prep time: 10 minutes | Cook time: 15 minutes | Serves: 15

1 carrot, diced small
1 parsnip, diced small
1 rutabaga, diced small
¼ cup olive oil
2 teaspoons salt, divided
4 sea bass fillets
½ teaspoon onion powder
2 garlic cloves, minced
1 lemon, sliced, plus additional wedges for serving

1. Preheat the air fryer to 380ºF (193ºC).
2. In a small bowl, toss the carrot, parsnip, and rutabaga with olive oil and 1 teaspoon salt.
3. Lightly season the sea bass with the remaining 1 teaspoon of salt and the onion powder, then place it into the air fryer basket in a single layer.
4. Spread the garlic over the top of each fillet, then cover with lemon slices.
5. Pour the prepared vegetables into the basket around and on top of the fish. Roast for 15 minutes.
6. Serve with additional lemon wedges if desired.

PER SERVING
Calories: 299, Total Fat: 16g, Saturated Fat: 3g, Total Carbohydrates: 13g, Protein: 25g, Fiber: 3g, Sugar: 5g

Honey-Garlic Glazed Salmon

Prep time: 5 minutes | Cook time: 10 minutes | Serves: 4

¼ cup raw honey
4 garlic cloves, minced
1 tablespoon olive oil

½ teaspoon salt
Olive oil cooking spray
4 (1½-inch-thick) salmon fillets

1. Preheat the air fryer to 380°F (193°C).
2. In a small bowl, mix together the honey, garlic, olive oil, and salt.
3. Spray the bottom of the air fryer basket with olive oil cooking spray, and place the salmon in a single layer on the bottom of the air fryer basket.
4. Brush the top of each fillet with the honey-garlic mixture, and roast for 10 to 12 minutes, or until the internal temperature reaches 145°F (63°C).

PER SERVING
Calories: 260, Total Fat: 11g, Saturated Fat: 2g, Total Carbohydrates: 18g, Protein: 23g, Fiber: 0g, Sugar: 17g

Steamed White Wine Catfish Fillets

Prep time: 10 minutes | Cook time: 8 minutes | Serves: 3

1 pound (454 g) catfish fillet
1 lemon, juiced
½ cup parsley leaves, chopped
2 garlic cloves, crushed
1 onion, finely chopped
1 tablespoon fresh dill, chopped

1 tablespoon fresh rosemary
2 cups white wine
2 tablespoons Dijon mustard
1 cup extra virgin olive oil
3 cups fish stock

1. In a bowl, mix lemon juice, parsley, garlic, onion, fresh dill, rosemary, wine, mustard, and oil. Stir well to combine. Submerge fillets in this mixture and cover with a tight lid. Refrigerate for 1 hour.
2. Insert the trivet, remove the fish from the fridge and place it on the rack. Pour in stock along with the marinade and seal the lid. Cook on Steam for 8 minutes on High. Release the pressure quickly and serve.

PER SERVING
Calories: 886, Fat: 79.07g, Carbohydrates: 14.37g, Protein: 32.93g, Sugar: 7.84g, Fiber: 2.4g, Sodium: 571mg

Salmon Fillet with Spinach

Prep time: 10 minutes | Cook time: 5 minutes | Serves: 4

1 pound (454 g) salmon filets, boneless
1 pound (454 g) fresh spinach, torn
4 tablespoons olive oil
2 garlic cloves, chopped

2 tablespoons lemon juice
1 tablespoon fresh dill, chopped
1 teaspoon sea salt
¼ teaspoon black pepper, ground

1. Place spinach in the pot, cover with water and lay the trivet on top. Rub the salmon filets with half of the olive oil, dill, salt, pepper and garlic. Lay on the trivet. Seal the lid and cook on Steam for 5 minutes on High.
2. Do a quick release. Remove salmon to a serving plate. Drain the spinach in a colander. Serve the fish on a bed of spinach. Season with salt and drizzle with lemon juice.

PER SERVING
Calories: 328, Fat: 22.34g, Carbohydrates: 6.16g, Protein: 27.04g, Sugar: 0.68g, Fiber: 2.9g, Sodium: 1163mg

Chapter 5 Beans

Green Bean and Halloumi Cheese Salad

Prep time: 15 minutes | Cook time: 6 minutes | Serves: 2

For the Dressing:
¼ cup plain kefir or buttermilk
1 tablespoon olive oil
2 teaspoons freshly squeezed lemon juice
¼ teaspoon onion powder
¼ teaspoon garlic powder
Pinch salt
Pinch freshly ground black pepper
For the Salad:
½ pound (227 g) very

fresh green beans, trimmed
2 ounces (57 g) Halloumi cheese, sliced into 2 (½-inch-thick) slices
½ cup cherry or grape tomatoes, halved
¼ cup very thinly sliced sweet onion
2 ounces (57 g) prosciutto, cooked crisp and crumbled

Make the Dressing
1. Combine the kefir or buttermilk, olive oil, lemon juice, onion powder, garlic powder, salt, and pepper in a small bowl and whisk well. Set the dressing aside.

Make the Salad
1. Fill a medium-size pot with about 1 inch of water and add the green beans. Cover and steam them for about 3 to 4 minutes, or just until beans are tender. Do not overcook. Drain beans, rinse them immediately with cold water, and set them aside to cool.
2. Heat a nonstick skillet over medium-high heat and place the slices of Halloumi in the hot pan. After about 2 minutes, check to see if the cheese is golden on the bottom. If it is, flip the slices and cook for another minute or until the second side is golden.
3. Remove cheese from the pan and cut each piece into cubes (about 1-inch square)
4. Place the green beans, halloumi, tomatoes, and sliced onion in a large bowl and toss to combine.
5. Drizzle dressing over the salad and toss well to combine. Sprinkle prosciutto over the top.

PER SERVING
Calories: 273, Total Fat: 18g, Total Carbohydrates: 16g, Protein: 15g, Fiber: 5g, Sugar: 7g, Sodium: 506mg

Black Bean and Sweet Potato Burgers

Prep time: 20 minutes | Cook time: 10 minutes | Serves: 4

1 (15-ounce / 425-g) can black beans, drained and rinsed
1 cup mashed sweet potato
½ teaspoon dried oregano
¼ teaspoon dried thyme
¼ teaspoon dried marjoram
1 garlic clove, minced
¼ teaspoon salt
¼ teaspoon black pepper

1 tablespoon lemon juice
1 cup cooked brown rice
¼ to ½ cup whole wheat bread crumbs
1 tablespoon olive oil
For Serving:
Whole wheat buns or whole wheat pitas
Plain Greek yogurt
Avocado
Lettuce
Tomato
Red onion

Preheat the air fryer to 380ºF (193ºC).
1. In a large bowl, use the back of a fork to mash the black beans until there are no large pieces left.
2. Add the mashed sweet potato, oregano, thyme, marjoram, garlic, salt, pepper, and lemon juice, and mix until well combined.
3. Stir in the cooked rice.
4. Add in ¼ cup of the whole wheat bread crumbs and stir. Check to see if the mixture is dry enough to form patties. If it seems too wet and loose, add an additional ¼ cup bread crumbs and stir.
5. Form the dough into 4 patties. Place them into the air fryer basket in a single layer, making sure that they don't touch each other.
6. Brush half of the olive oil onto the patties and bake for 5 minutes.
7. Flip the patties over, brush the other side with the remaining oil, and bake for an additional 4 to 5 minutes.
8. Serve on toasted whole wheat buns or whole wheat pitas with a spoonful of yogurt and avocado, lettuce, tomato, and red onion as desired.

PER SERVING (JUST THE PATTIES)
Calories: 263, Total Fat: 5g, Saturated Fat: 1g, Total Carbohydrates: 47g, Protein: 9g, Fiber: 8g, Sugar: 4g

Bean Balls with Marinara

Prep time: 15 minutes | Cook time: 30 minutes | Serves: 2 to 4

Bean Balls:
1 tablespoon extra-virgin olive oil
½ yellow onion, minced
1 teaspoon fennel seeds
2 teaspoons dried oregano
½ teaspoon crushed red pepper flakes
1 teaspoon garlic powder
1 (15-ounce / 425-g) can white beans (cannellini or navy), drained and rinsed
½ cup whole-grain bread crumbs
Sea salt and ground black pepper, to taste
Marinara:
1 tablespoon extra-virgin olive oil
3 garlic cloves, minced
Handful basil leaves
1 (28-ounce / 794-g) can chopped tomatoes with juice reserved
Sea salt, to taste

Make the Bean Balls
1. Preheat the oven to 350°F (180°C). Line a baking sheet with parchment paper.
2. Heat the olive oil in a nonstick skillet over medium heat until shimmering.
3. Add the onion and sauté for 5 minutes or until translucent.
4. Sprinkle with fennel seeds, oregano, red pepper flakes, and garlic powder, then cook for 1 minute or until aromatic.
5. Pour the sautéed mixture in a food processor and add the beans and bread crumbs. Sprinkle with salt and ground black pepper, then pulse to combine well and the mixture holds together.
6. Shape the mixture into balls with a 2-ounce (57-g) cookie scoop, then arrange the balls on the baking sheet.
7. Bake in the preheated oven for 30 minutes or until lightly browned. Flip the balls halfway through the cooking time.

Make the Marinara
1. While baking the bean balls, heat the olive oil in a saucepan over medium-high heat until shimmering.
2. Add the garlic and basil and sauté for 2 minutes or until fragrant.
3. Fold in the tomatoes and juice. Bring to a boil. Reduce the heat to low. Put the lid on and simmer for 15 minutes. Sprinkle with salt.
4. Transfer the bean balls on a large plate and baste with marinara before serving.

PER SERVING
Calories: 351, Fat: 16.4g, Protein: 11.5g, Total Carbohydrates: 42.9g, Fiber: 10.3g, Sodium: 377mg

Cannellini Salad with Squid and Pepperoncini

Prep time: 15 minutes | Cook time: 8 minutes | Serves: 4 to 6

1 tablespoon baking soda
Salt and pepper, to taste
1 pound (454 g) squid, bodies sliced crosswise into ½-inch-thick rings, tentacles halved
6 tablespoons extra-virgin olive oil
1 red onion, chopped fine
3 garlic cloves, minced
2 (15-ounce / 425-g) cans
cannellini beans, rinsed
⅓ cup pepperoncini, stemmed and sliced into ¼-inch-thick rings, plus 2 tablespoons brine
2 tablespoons sherry vinegar
½ cup fresh parsley leaves
3 scallions, green parts only, sliced thin

1. Dissolve baking soda and 1 tablespoon salt in 3 cups cold water in medium container. Add squid, cover, and refrigerate for 15 minutes. Dry squid thoroughly with paper towels and toss with 1 tablespoon oil.
2. Heat 1 tablespoon oil in medium saucepan over medium heat until shimmering. Add onion and ¼ teaspoon salt and cook, stirring occasionally, until softened and lightly browned, 5 to 7 minutes. Stir in garlic and cook until fragrant, about 30 seconds. Stir in beans and ¼ cup water and bring to simmer. Reduce heat to low, cover, and continue to simmer, stirring occasionally, for 2 to 3 minutes, set aside.
3. Heat 1 tablespoon oil in 12-inch nonstick skillet over high heat until just smoking. Add half of squid in single layer and cook, without moving, until well browned, about 3 minutes. Flip squid and continue to cook, without moving, until well browned on second side, about 2 minutes, transfer to bowl. Wipe skillet clean with paper towels and repeat with 1 tablespoon oil and remaining squid.
4. Whisk remaining 2 tablespoons oil, pepperoncini brine, and vinegar together in large bowl. Add beans and any remaining cooking liquid, squid, parsley, scallions, and pepperoncini and toss to combine. Season with salt and pepper to taste. Serve.

PER SERVING
Calories: 346, Fat: 22.65g, Carbohydrates: 16.51g, Protein: 20.58g, Sugar: 3.62g, Fiber: 4.2g, Sodium: 1006mg

Italian-Style Baked Beans

Prep time: 10 minutes | Cook time: 15 minutes | Serves: 6

2 teaspoons extra-virgin olive oil	¼ teaspoon ground cinnamon
½ cup minced onion	½ cup water
1 (12-ounce / 340-g) can low-sodium tomato paste	2 (15-ounce / 425-g) cans cannellini or great northern beans, undrained
¼ cup red wine vinegar	
2 tablespoons honey	

1. In a medium saucepan over medium heat, heat the oil. Add the onion and cook for 5 minutes, stirring frequently. Add the tomato paste, vinegar, honey, cinnamon, and water, and mix well. Turn the heat to low.
2. Drain and rinse one can of the beans in a colander and add to the saucepan. Pour the entire second can of beans (including the liquid) into the saucepan. Let it cook for 10 minutes, stirring occasionally, and serve.

PER SERVING
Calories: 434g, Total Fat: 2g, Saturated Fat: 1g, Total Carbs: 80g, Protein: 26g, Fiber: 24g, Sugar: 11g, Sodium: 73mg

Hot Chickpeas with Turnips

Prep time: 15 minutes | Cook time: 31 minutes | Serves: 4 to 6

2 tablespoons extra-virgin olive oil	¼ teaspoon cayenne pepper
2 onions, chopped	2 (15-ounce / 425-g) cans chickpeas
2 red bell peppers, stemmed, seeded, and chopped	12 ounces (340 g) turnips, peeled and cut into ½-inch pieces
Salt and pepper, to taste	
¼ cup tomato paste	¾ cup water, plus extra as needed
1 jalapeño chile, stemmed, seeded, and minced	¼ cup chopped fresh parsley
5 garlic cloves, minced	2 tablespoons lemon juice, plus extra for seasoning
¾ teaspoon ground cumin	

1. Heat oil in Dutch oven over medium heat until shimmering. Add onions, bell peppers, ½ teaspoon salt, and ¼ teaspoon pepper and cook until softened and lightly browned, 5 to 7 minutes. Stir in tomato paste, jalapeño, garlic, cumin, and cayenne and cook until fragrant, about 30 seconds.
2. Stir in chickpeas and their liquid, turnips, and water. Bring to simmer and cook until turnips are tender and sauce has thickened, 25 to 35 minutes.
3. Stir in parsley and lemon juice. Season with salt, pepper, and extra lemon juice to taste. Adjust consistency with extra hot water as needed. Serve.

PER SERVING
Calories: 323, Fat: 11.02g, Carbohydrates: 45.71g, Protein: 13.75g, Sugar: 11.95g, Fiber: 13.2g, Sodium: 346mg

Stewed Oregano Chickpeas with Veggies

Prep time: 10 minutes | Cook time: 51 minutes | Serves: 6

¼ cup extra-virgin olive oil	2 bay leaves
2 onions, chopped	1 pound (454 g) eggplant, cut into 1-inch pieces
1 green bell pepper, stemmed, seeded, and chopped fine	1 (28-ounce / 794-g) can whole peeled tomatoes, drained with juice reserved, chopped coarse
Salt and pepper, to taste	
3 garlic cloves, minced	
1 tablespoon minced fresh oregano or 1 teaspoon dried	2 (15-ounce / 425-g) cans chickpeas, drained with 1 cup liquid reserved

1. Adjust oven rack to lower-middle position and heat oven to 400°F (205°C). Heat oil in Dutch oven over medium heat until shimmering. Add onions, bell pepper, ½ teaspoon salt, and ¼ teaspoon pepper and cook until softened, about 5 minutes. Stir in garlic, 1 teaspoon oregano, and bay leaves and cook until fragrant, about 30 seconds.
2. Stir in eggplant, tomatoes and reserved juice, and chickpeas and reserved liquid and bring to boil. Transfer pot to oven and cook, uncovered, until eggplant is very tender, 45 to 60 minutes, stirring twice during cooking.
3. Discard bay leaves. Stir in remaining 2 teaspoons oregano and season with salt and pepper to taste. Serve.

PER SERVING
Calories: 259, Fat: 11.66g, Carbohydrates: 33.73g, Protein: 8.52g, Sugar: 11.59g, Fiber: 11.2g, Sodium: 345mg

Chickpeas with Parsley

Prep time: 10 minutes | Cook time: 18 minutes | Serves: 4 to 6

¼ cup extra-virgin olive oil	2 (15-ounce / 425-g) cans chickpeas, rinsed
4 garlic cloves, sliced thin	1 cup chicken or vegetable broth
⅛ teaspoon red pepper flakes	2 tablespoons minced fresh parsley
1 onion, chopped fine	2 teaspoons lemon juice
Salt and pepper, to taste	

1. Cook 3 tablespoons oil, garlic, and pepper flakes in 12-inch skillet over medium heat, stirring frequently, until garlic turns golden but not brown, about 3 minutes. Stir in onion and ¼ teaspoon salt and cook until softened and lightly browned, 5 to 7 minutes. Stir in chickpeas and broth and bring to simmer. Reduce heat to medium-low, cover, and cook until chickpeas are heated through and flavors meld, about 7 minutes.
2. Uncover, increase heat to high, and continue to cook until nearly all liquid has evaporated, about 3 minutes. Off heat, stir in parsley and lemon juice. Season with salt and pepper to taste and drizzle with remaining 1 tablespoon oil. Serve.

PER SERVING
Calories: 333, Fat: 17.25g, Carbohydrates: 36.8g, Protein: 10.3g, Sugar: 9.67g, Fiber: 9.1g, Sodium: 538mg

Mashed Fava Beans with Cumin and Garlic

Prep time: 10 minutes | Cook time: 8 minutes | Serves: 4 to 6

4 garlic cloves, minced	for serving
1 tablespoon extra-virgin olive oil, plus extra for serving	Salt and pepper, to taste
	1 tomato, cored and cut into ½-inch pieces
1 teaspoon ground cumin	1 small onion, chopped fine
2 (15-ounce / 425-g) cans fava beans	
3 tablespoons tahini	2 tablespoons minced fresh parsley
2 tablespoons lemon juice, plus lemon wedges	2 hard-cooked large eggs, chopped

1. Cook garlic, oil, and cumin in medium saucepan over medium heat until fragrant, about 2 minutes. Stir in beans and their liquid and tahini.

Bring to simmer and cook until liquid thickens slightly, 8 to 10 minutes.
2. Off heat, mash beans to coarse consistency using potato masher. Stir in lemon juice and 1 teaspoon pepper. Season with salt and pepper to taste. Transfer to serving dish, top with tomato, onion, parsley, and eggs, if using, and drizzle with extra oil. Serve with lemon wedges.

PER SERVING
Calories: 192, Fat: 13.03g, Carbohydrates: 14.75g, Protein: 7.66g, Sugar: 2.86g, Fiber: 4.7g, Sodium: 62mg

Turkish-Inspired Pinto Bean Salad

Prep time: 10 minutes | Cook time: 3 minutes | Serves: 4 to 6

¼ cup extra-virgin olive oil, divided	1 tablespoon ground dried Aleppo pepper, plus extra for serving
3 garlic cloves, lightly crushed and peeled	8 ounces (227 g) cherry tomatoes, halved
2 (15-ounce / 425-g) cans pinto beans, rinsed	¼ red onion, sliced thinly
2 cups plus 1 tablespoon water	½ cup fresh parsley leaves
Salt and pepper, to taste	2 hard-cooked large eggs, quartered
¼ cup tahini	
3 tablespoons lemon juice	1 tablespoon toasted sesame seeds

1. Add 1 tablespoon of the olive oil and garlic to a medium saucepan over medium heat. Cook for about 3 minutes, stirring constantly, or until the garlic turns golden but not brown.
2. Add the beans, 2 cups of the water and 1 teaspoon salt and bring to a simmer. Remove from the heat, cover and let sit for 20 minutes. Drain the beans and discard the garlic.
3. In a large bowl, whisk together the remaining 3 tablespoons of the oil, tahini, lemon juice, Aleppo, the remaining 1 tablespoon of the water and ¼ teaspoon salt. Stir in the beans, tomatoes, onion and parsley. Season with salt and pepper to taste.
4. Transfer to a serving platter and top with the eggs. Sprinkle with the sesame seeds and extra Aleppo before serving.

PER SERVING
Calories: 402, Fat: 18.9g, Total Carbohydrates: 44.4g, Protein: 16.2g, Fiber: 11.2g, Sodium: 456mg

Rich Chickpea Salad

Prep time: 10 minutes | Cook time: 3 minutes | Serves: 6

2 (15-ounce / 425-g) cans chickpeas, rinsed
¼ cup extra-virgin olive oil
2 tablespoons lemon juice
Salt and pepper, to taste

Pinch cayenne pepper
3 carrots, peeled and shredded
1 cup baby arugula, chopped coarse
½ cup pitted kalamata olives, chopped coarse

1. Microwave chickpeas in medium bowl until hot, about 2 minutes. Stir in oil, lemon juice, ¾ teaspoon salt, ½ teaspoon pepper, and cayenne and let sit for 30 minutes.
2. Add carrots, arugula, and olives and toss to combine. Season with salt and pepper to taste. Serve.

PER SERVING
Calories: 147, Fat: 4.24g, Carbohydrates: 22.48g, Protein: 6.39g, Sugar: 4.41g, Fiber: 6.7g, Sodium: 304mg

Chickpeas with Coriander and Sage

Prep time: 15 minutes | Cook time: 21 minutes | Serves: 6 to 8

1½ tablespoons table salt, for brining
1 pound (454 g) dried chickpeas, picked over and rinsed
2 tablespoons extra-virgin olive oil, plus extra for drizzling
2 onions, halved and sliced thin
¼ teaspoon table salt
1 tablespoon coriander

seeds, cracked
¼ to ½ teaspoon red pepper flakes
2½ cups chicken broth
¼ cup fresh sage leaves
2 bay leaves
1½ teaspoons grated lemon zest plus 2 teaspoons juice
2 tablespoons minced fresh parsley

1. Dissolve 1½ tablespoons salt in 2 quarts cold water in large container. Add chickpeas and soak at room temperature for at least 8 hours or up to 24 hours. Drain and rinse well.
2. Using highest sauté function, heat oil in Instant Pot until shimmering. Add onions and ¼ teaspoon salt and cook until onions are softened and well browned, 10 to 12 minutes. Stir in coriander and pepper flakes and cook

until fragrant, about 30 seconds. Stir in broth, scraping up any browned bits, then stir in chickpeas, sage, and bay leaves.
3. Lock lid in place and close pressure release valve. Select low pressure cook function and cook for 10 minutes. Turn off Instant Pot and let pressure release naturally for 15 minutes. Quick-release any remaining pressure, then carefully remove lid, allowing steam to escape away from you.
4. Discard bay leaves. Stir lemon zest and juice into chickpeas and season with salt and pepper to taste. Sprinkle with parsley. Serve, drizzling individual portions with extra oil.

PER SERVING
Calories: 190, Total Fat: 6g, Sat Fat: 0.5g, Total Carbohydrates: 40g, Protein: 11g, Sugar: 3g, Sodium: 360mg, Fiber: 1g

Garbanzo and Fava Bean Fūl

Prep time: 10 minutes | Cook time: 10 minutes | Serves: 6

1 (16-ounce / 454-g) can garbanzo beans, rinsed and drained
1 (15-ounce / 425-g) can fava beans, rinsed and drained
3 cups water

½ cup lemon juice
3 cloves garlic, peeled and minced
1 teaspoon salt
3 tablespoons extra-virgin olive oil

1. In a 3-quart pot over medium heat, cook the garbanzo beans, fava beans, and water for 10 minutes.
2. Reserving 1 cup of the liquid from the cooked beans, drain the beans and put them in a bowl.
3. Mix the reserved liquid, lemon juice, minced garlic, and salt together and add to the beans in the bowl. Using a potato masher, mash up about half the beans in the bowl.
4. After mashing half the beans, give the mixture one more stir to make sure the beans are evenly mixed.
5. Drizzle the olive oil over the top.
6. Serve warm or cold with pita bread.

PER SERVING
Calories: 199, Total Fat: 9g, Saturated Fat: 1g, Total Carbohydrates: 25g, Protein: 10g, Sugar: 4g, Fiber: 9g, Sodium: 395mg

Sicilian Cannellini Beans and Escarole

Prep time: 10 minutes | Cook time: 21 minutes | Serves: 4

1 tablespoon extra-virgin olive oil, plus extra for serving
2 onions, chopped fine
Salt and pepper, to taste
4 garlic cloves, minced
⅛ teaspoon red pepper flakes
1 (1-pound / 454-g) head

escarole, trimmed and sliced 1 inch thick
1 (15-ounce / 425-g) can cannellini beans, rinsed
1 cup chicken or vegetable broth
1 cup water
2 teaspoons lemon juice

1. Heat oil in Dutch oven over medium heat until shimmering. Add onions and ½ teaspoon salt and cook until softened and lightly browned, 5 to 7 minutes. Stir in garlic and pepper flakes and cook until fragrant, about 30 seconds.
2. Stir in escarole, beans, broth, and water and bring to simmer. Cook, stirring occasionally, until escarole is wilted, about 5 minutes. Increase heat to high and cook until liquid is nearly evaporated, 10 to 15 minutes. Stir in lemon juice and season with salt and pepper to taste. Drizzle with extra oil and serve.

PER SERVING
Calories: 157, Fat: 7.41g, Carbohydrates: 21.29g, Protein: 4.2g, Sugar: 9.58g, Fiber: 6.5g, Sodium: 716mg

White Bean Lettuce Wraps

Prep time: 10 minutes | Cook time: 9 minutes | Serves: 4

1 tablespoon extra-virgin olive oil
½ cup diced red onion
¾ cup chopped fresh tomatoes
¼ teaspoon freshly ground black pepper
1 (15-ounce / 425-g) can cannellini or great

northern beans, drained and rinsed
¼ cup finely chopped fresh curly parsley
½ cup lemony garlic hummus or ½ cup prepared hummus
8 romaine lettuce leaves

1. In a large skillet over medium heat, heat the oil. Add the onion and cook for 3 minutes, stirring occasionally. Add the tomatoes and pepper and cook for 3 more minutes, stirring occasionally. Add the beans and cook for 3 more minutes,

stirring occasionally. Remove from the heat, and mix in the parsley.
2. Spread 1 tablespoon of hummus over each lettuce leaf. Evenly spread the warm bean mixture down the center of each leaf. Fold one side of the lettuce leaf over the filling lengthwise, then fold over the other side to make a wrap and serve.

PER SERVING
Calories: 188g, Total Fat: 5g, Saturated Fat: 1g, Total Carbs: 28g, Protein: 10g, Sugar: 2g, Fiber: 9g, Sodium: 115mg, Phosphorus: 201mg, Potassium: 625mg

Bulgur with Za'Atar, Chickpeas, and Spinach

Prep time: 10 minutes | Cook time: 7 minutes | Serves: 4 to 6

3 tablespoons extra-virgin olive oil, divided
1 onion, chopped fine
½ teaspoon table salt
3 garlic cloves, minced
2 tablespoons za'atar, divided
1 cup medium-grind bulgur, rinsed

1 (15-ounce / 425-g) can chickpeas, rinsed
1½ cups water
5 ounces (142 g) baby spinach, chopped
1 tablespoon lemon juice, plus lemon wedges for serving

1. Using highest sauté function, heat 2 tablespoons oil in Instant Pot until shimmering. Add onion and salt and cook until onion is softened, about 5 minutes. Stir in garlic and 1 tablespoon za'atar and cook until fragrant, about 30 seconds. Stir in bulgur, chickpeas, and water.
2. Lock lid in place and close pressure release valve. Select high pressure cook function and cook for 1 minute. Turn off Instant Pot and quick-release pressure. Carefully remove lid, allowing steam to escape away from you.
3. Gently fluff bulgur with fork. Lay clean dish towel over pot, replace lid, and let sit for 5 minutes. Add spinach, lemon juice, remaining 1 tablespoon za'atar, and remaining 1 tablespoon oil and gently toss to combine. Season with salt and pepper to taste. Serve with lemon wedges.

PER SERVING
Calories: 200, Total Fat: 8g, Sat Fat: 1g, Total Carbohydrates: 28g, Protein: 6g, Sugar: 2g, Fiber: 6g, Sodium: 320mg

Cannellini Bean Salad

Prep time: 10 minutes | Cook time: 8 minutes | Serves: 6 to 8

¼ cup extra-virgin olive oil
3 garlic cloves, peeled and smashed
2 (15-ounce / 425-g) cans cannellini beans, rinsed
Salt and pepper, to taste
2 teaspoons sherry vinegar
1 small shallot, minced
1 red bell pepper, stemmed, seeded, and cut into ¼-inch pieces
¼ cup chopped fresh parsley
2 teaspoons chopped fresh chives

1. Cook 1 tablespoon oil and garlic in medium saucepan over medium heat, stirring often, until garlic turns golden but not brown, about 3 minutes. Add beans, 2 cups water, and 1 teaspoon salt and bring to simmer. Remove from heat, cover, and let sit for 20 minutes.
2. Meanwhile, combine vinegar and shallot in large bowl and let sit for 20 minutes. Drain beans and remove garlic. Add beans, remaining 3 tablespoons oil, bell pepper, parsley, and chives to shallot mixture and gently toss to combine. Season with salt and pepper to taste. Let sit for 20 minutes. Serve.

PER SERVING
Calories: 112, Fat: 9.52g, Carbohydrates: 6.52g, Protein: 1.55g, Sugar: 1.57g, Fiber: 2.3g, Sodium: 5mg

Lentil and Cheese Stuffed Tomatoes

Prep time: 19 minutes | Cook time: 15 minutes | Serves: 4

4 tomatoes
½ cup cooked red lentils
1 garlic clove, minced
1 tablespoon minced red onion
4 basil leaves, minced
¼ teaspoon salt
¼ teaspoon black pepper
4 ounces (113 g) Goat cheese
2 tablespoons shredded Parmesan cheese

1. Preheat the air fryer to 380ºF (193ºC).
2. Slice the top off of each tomato.
3. Using a knife and spoon, cut and scoop out half of the flesh inside of the tomato. Place it into a medium bowl.
4. To the bowl with the tomato, add the cooked lentils, garlic, onion, basil, salt, pepper, and Goat cheese. Stir until well combined.
5. Spoon the filling into the scooped-out cavity of each of the tomatoes, then top each one with ½ tablespoon of shredded Parmesan cheese.
6. Place the tomatoes in a single layer in the air fryer basket and bake for 15 minutes.

PER SERVING
Calories: 138, Total Fat: 7g, Saturated Fat: 5g, Total Carbohydrates: 11g, Protein: 9g, Fiber: 4g, Sugar: 4g

North African Veggie and Bean Stew

Prep time: 20 minutes | Cook time: 27 minutes | Serves: 6 to 8

1 tablespoon extra-virgin olive oil
1 onion, chopped fine
8 ounces (227 g) Swiss chard, stems chopped fine, leaves cut into ½-inch pieces
4 garlic cloves, minced
1 teaspoon ground cumin
½ teaspoon paprika
½ teaspoon ground coriander
¼ teaspoon ground cinnamon
2 tablespoons tomato paste
2 tablespoons all-purpose flour
7 cups vegetable broth
2 carrots, peeled and cut into ½-inch pieces
1 (15-ounce / 425-g) can chickpeas, rinsed
1 (15-ounce / 425-g) can butter beans, rinsed
½ cup small pasta, such as ditalini, tubettini, or elbow macaroni
⅓ cup minced fresh parsley
6 tablespoons harissa
Salt and pepper, to taste

1. Heat oil in Dutch oven over medium heat until shimmering. Add onion and chard stems and cook until softened, about 5 minutes. Stir in garlic, cumin, paprika, coriander, and cinnamon and cook until fragrant, about 30 seconds. Stir in tomato paste and flour and cook for 1 minute.
2. Slowly stir in broth and carrots, scraping up any browned bits and smoothing out any lumps, and bring to boil. Reduce to gentle simmer and cook for 10 minutes. Stir in chard leaves, chickpeas, beans, and pasta and simmer until vegetables and pasta are tender, 10 to 15 minutes. Stir in parsley and ¼ cup harissa. Season with salt and pepper to taste. Serve, passing remaining harissa separately.

PER SERVING
Calories: 279, Fat: 6.55g, Carbohydrates:46.96g, Protein: 11.51g, Sugar: 12.44g, Fiber: 10.9g, Sodium: 1098mg

Greek Baked Two Beans

Prep time: 15 minutes | Cook time: 30 minutes | Serves: 4

Olive oil cooking spray
1 (15-ounce / 425-g) can cannellini beans, drained and rinsed
1 (15-ounce / 425-g) can great northern beans, drained and rinsed
½ yellow onion, diced
1 (8-ounce) can tomato sauce
1½ tablespoons raw honey

¼ cup olive oil
2 garlic cloves, minced
2 tablespoons chopped fresh dill
½ teaspoon salt
½ teaspoon black pepper
1 bay leaf
1 tablespoon balsamic vinegar
2 ounces (57 g) Feta cheese, crumbled, for serving

1. Preheat the air fryer to 360°F (182°C). Lightly coat the inside of a 5-cup capacity casserole dish with olive oil cooking spray. (The shape of the casserole dish will depend upon the size of the air fryer, but it needs to be able to hold at least 5 cups.)
2. In a large bowl, combine all ingredients except the Feta cheese and stir until well combined.
3. Pour the bean mixture into the prepared casserole dish.
4. Bake in the air fryer for 30 minutes.
5. Remove from the air fryer and remove and discard the bay leaf. Sprinkle crumbled Feta over the top before serving.

PER SERVING
Calories: 397, Total Fat: 18g, Saturated Fat: 4g, Total Carbohydrates: 48g, Protein: 14g, Fiber: 16g, Sugar: 11g

Butter Beans Casserole with Parsley

Prep time: 10 minutes | Cook time: 30 minutes | Serves: 4

Olive oil cooking spray
1 (15-ounce / 425-g) can cooked butter beans, drained and rinsed
1 cup diced fresh tomatoes
½ tablespoon tomato

paste
2 garlic cloves, minced
½ yellow onion, diced
½ teaspoon salt
¼ cup olive oil
¼ cup fresh parsley, chopped

1. Preheat the air fryer to 380°F (193°C). Lightly coat the inside of a 5-cup capacity casserole dish with olive oil cooking spray. (The shape of the casserole dish will depend upon the size of the air fryer, but it needs to be able to hold at least 5 cups.)
2. In a large bowl, combine the butter beans, tomatoes, tomato paste, garlic, onion, salt, and olive oil, mixing until all ingredients are combined.
3. Pour the mixture into the prepared casserole dish and top with the chopped parsley.
4. Bake in the air fryer for 15 minutes. Stir well, then return to the air fryer and bake for 15 minutes more.

PER SERVING
Calories: 212, Total Fat: 14g, Saturated Fat: 2g, Total Carbohydrates: 17g, Protein: 5g, Fiber: 1g, Sugar: 2g

Mediterranean Green Peas with Parmesan

Prep time: 15 minutes | Cook time: 25 minutes | Serves: 8

1 cup cauliflower florets, fresh or frozen
½ white onion, roughly chopped
2 tablespoons olive oil
½ cup unsweetened almond milk
3 cups green peas, fresh or frozen
3 garlic cloves, minced

2 tablespoons fresh thyme leaves, chopped
1 teaspoon fresh rosemary leaves, chopped
½ teaspoon salt
½ teaspoon black pepper
Shredded Parmesan cheese, for garnish
Fresh parsley, for garnish

1. Preheat the air fryer to 380°F (193°C).
2. In a large bowl, combine the cauliflower florets and onion with the olive oil and toss well to coat.
3. Put the cauliflower-and-onion mixture into the air fryer basket in an even layer and bake for 15 minutes.
4. Transfer the cauliflower and onion to a food processor. Add the almond milk and pulse until smooth.
5. In a medium saucepan, combine the cauliflower puree, peas, garlic, thyme, rosemary, salt, and pepper and mix well. Cook over medium heat for an additional 10 minutes, stirring regularly.
6. Serve with a sprinkle of Parmesan cheese and chopped fresh parsley.

PER SERVING
Calories: 87, Total Fat: 4g, Saturated Fat: 1g, Total Carbohydrates: 10g, Protein: 4g, Fiber: 3g, Sugar: 4g

Herb Green Lentil Rice Balls

Prep time: 10 minutes | Cook time: 10 minutes | Serves: 6

½ cup cooked green lentils
2 garlic cloves, minced
¼ white onion, minced
¼ cup parsley leaves

5 basil leaves
1 cup cooked brown rice
1 tablespoon lemon juice
1 tablespoon olive oil
½ teaspoon salt

1. Preheat the air fryer to 380ºF (193ºC).
2. In a food processor, pulse the cooked lentils with the garlic, onion, parsley, and basil until mostly smooth. (You will want some bits of lentils in the mixture.)
3. Pour the lentil mixture into a large bowl, and stir in brown rice, lemon juice, olive oil, and salt. Stir until well combined.
4. Form the rice mixture into 1-inch balls. Place the rice balls in a single layer in the air fryer basket, making sure that they don't touch each other.
5. Fry for 6 minutes. Turn the rice balls and then fry for an additional 4 to 5 minutes, or until browned on all sides.

PER SERVING
Calories: 80, Total Fat: 3g, Saturated Fat: 0g, Total Carbohydrates: 12g, Protein: 2g, Fiber: 2g, Sugar: 1g

Roasted White Beans with Herb

Prep time: 10 minutes | Cook time: 15 minutes | Serves: 4

Olive oil cooking spray
2 (15-ounce / 425-g) cans white beans, or cannellini beans, drained and rinsed
1 red bell pepper, diced
½ red onion, diced

3 garlic cloves, minced
1 tablespoon olive oil
¼ to ½ teaspoon salt
½ teaspoon black pepper
1 rosemary sprig
1 bay leaf

1. Preheat the air fryer to 360ºF (182ºC). Lightly coat the inside of a 5-cup capacity casserole dish with olive oil cooking spray. (The shape of the casserole dish will depend upon the size of the air fryer, but it needs to be able to hold at least 5 cups.)
2. In a large bowl, combine the beans, bell pepper, onion, garlic, olive oil, salt, and pepper.
3. Pour the bean mixture into the prepared casserole dish, place the rosemary and bay leaf on top, and then place the casserole dish into the air fryer.

4. Roast for 15 minutes.
5. Remove the rosemary and bay leaves, then stir well before serving.

PER SERVING
Calories: 196, Total Fat: 5g, Saturated Fat: 0g, Total Carbohydrates: 30g, Protein: 10g, Fiber: 1g, Sugar: 2g

Ritzy Cranberry Beans

Prep time: 10 minutes | Cook time: 1¾ hours | Serves: 6 to 8

Salt and pepper, to taste
1 pound (454 g) dried cranberry beans, picked over and rinsed
3 tablespoons extra-virgin olive oil
½ fennel bulb, 2 tablespoons fronds chopped, stalks discarded, bulb cored

and chopped
1 cup plus 2 tablespoons red wine vinegar
¼ cup coconut sugar
1 teaspoon fennel seeds
6 ounces (170 g) seedless red grapes, halved
½ cup pine nuts, toasted

1. Dissolve 3 tablespoons salt in 4 quarts cold water in large container. Add beans and soak at room temperature for at least 8 hours or up to 24 hours. Drain and rinse well.
2. Bring beans, 4 quarts water, and 1 teaspoon salt to boil in Dutch oven. Reduce to simmer and cook, stirring occasionally, until beans are tender, 1 to 1½ hours. Drain beans and set aside.
3. Wipe Dutch oven clean with paper towels. Heat oil in now-empty pot over medium heat until shimmering. Add fennel, ¼ teaspoon salt, and ¼ teaspoon pepper and cook until softened, about 5 minutes. Stir in 1 cup vinegar, sugar, and fennel seeds until sugar is dissolved. Bring to simmer and cook until liquid is thickened to syrupy glaze and edges of fennel are beginning to brown, about 10 minutes.
4. Add beans to vinegar-fennel mixture and toss to coat. Transfer to large bowl and let cool to room temperature. Add grapes, pine nuts, fennel fronds, and remaining 2 tablespoons vinegar and toss to combine. Season with salt and pepper to taste and serve.

PER SERVING
Calories: 204, Fat: 14.94g, Carbohydrates: 15.98g, Protein: 2.94g, Sugar: 10.23g, Fiber: 2.9g, Sodium: 16mg

Golden Falafel

Prep time: 10 minutes | Cook time: 6 minutes | Makes 24

Salt and pepper, to taste
12 ounces (340 g) dried chickpeas, picked over and rinsed
10 scallions, chopped coarse
1 cup fresh parsley leaves
1 cup fresh cilantro leaves
6 garlic cloves, minced
½ teaspoon ground cumin
⅛ teaspoon ground cinnamon
2 cups vegetable oil

1. Dissolve 3 tablespoons salt in 4 quarts cold water in large container. Add chickpeas and soak at room temperature for at least 8 hours or up to 24 hours. Drain and rinse well.
2. Process chickpeas, scallions, parsley, cilantro, garlic, 1 teaspoon salt, 1 teaspoon pepper, cumin, and cinnamon in food processor until smooth, about 1 minute, scraping down sides of bowl as needed. Pinch off and shape chickpea mixture into 2-tablespoon-size disks, about 1½ inches wide and 1 inch thick, and place on parchment paper–lined baking sheet. (Falafel can be refrigerated for up to 2 hours.)
3. Adjust oven rack to middle position and heat oven to 200°F (93°C). Set wire rack in rimmed baking sheet. Heat oil in 12-inch skillet over medium-high heat to 375°F (190°C). Fry half of falafel until deep golden brown, 2 to 3 minutes per side. Adjust burner, if necessary, to maintain oil temperature of 375°F (190°C). Using slotted spoon, transfer falafel to prepared sheet and keep warm in oven. Return oil to 375°F (190°C) and repeat with remaining falafel. Serve.

PER SERVING
Calories: 219, Fat: 19.08g, Carbohydrates: 10.03g, Protein: 3.19g, Sugar: 1.83g, Fiber: 2.1g, Sodium: 14mg

Turkish Pinto Bean Salad with Tomatoes, Eggs, and Parsley

Prep time: 15 minutes | Cook time: 3 minutes | Serves: 4 to 6

¼ cup extra-virgin olive oil
3 garlic cloves, lightly crushed and peeled
2 (15-ounce / 425-g) cans
pinto beans, rinsed
Salt and pepper, to taste
¼ cup tahini
3 tablespoons lemon juice
1 tablespoon ground dried Aleppo pepper, plus extra for serving
8 ounces (227 g) cherry tomatoes, halved
¼ red onion, sliced thin
½ cup fresh parsley leaves
2 hard-cooked large eggs, quartered
1 tablespoon toasted sesame seeds

1. Cook 1 tablespoon oil and garlic in medium saucepan over medium heat, stirring often, until garlic turns golden but not brown, about 3 minutes. Add beans, 2 cups water, and 1 teaspoon salt and bring to simmer. Remove from heat, cover, and let sit for 20 minutes.
2. Drain beans and discard garlic. Whisk remaining 3 tablespoons oil, tahini, lemon juice, Aleppo, 1 tablespoon water, and ¼ teaspoon salt together in large bowl. Add beans, tomatoes, onion, and parsley and gently toss to combine. Season with salt and pepper to taste. Transfer to serving platter and arrange eggs on top. Sprinkle with sesame seeds and extra Aleppo and serve.

PER SERVING
Calories: 442, Fat: 26.68g, Carbohydrates: 37.68g, Protein: 16.91g, Sugar: 3.58g, Fiber: 10.7g, Sodium: 400mg

Lentils with Spinach and Toasted Garlic

Prep time: 10 minutes | Cook time: 58 minutes | Serves: 6

2 tablespoons extra-virgin olive oil
4 garlic cloves, sliced thin
Salt and pepper, to taste
1 onion, chopped fine
1 teaspoon ground coriander
1 teaspoon ground cumin
2½ cups water
1 cup green or brown lentils, picked over and rinsed
8 ounces (227 g) curly-leaf spinach, stemmed and chopped coarse
1 tablespoon red wine vinegar

1. Cook oil and garlic in large saucepan over medium-low heat, stirring often, until garlic turns crisp and golden but not brown, about 5 minutes. Using slotted spoon, transfer garlic to paper towel–lined plate and season lightly with salt, set aside.
2. Add onion and ½ teaspoon salt to oil left in saucepan and cook over medium heat until softened and lightly browned, 5 to 7 minutes. Stir in coriander and cumin and cook until fragrant, about 30 seconds.

3. Stir in water and lentils and bring to simmer. Reduce heat to low, cover, and simmer gently, stirring occasionally, until lentils are mostly tender but still intact, 45 to 55 minutes.
4. Stir in spinach, 1 handful at a time. Cook, uncovered, stirring occasionally, until spinach is wilted and lentils are completely tender, about 8 minutes. Stir in vinegar and season with salt and pepper to taste. Transfer to serving dish, sprinkle with toasted garlic, and serve.

PER SERVING
Calories: 88, Fat: 4.87g, Carbohydrates: 9.95g, Protein: 2.98g, Sugar: 3.49g, Fiber: 1.7g, Sodium: 68mg

Spicy Brown Lentil Patties

Prep time: 20 minutes | Cook time: 10 minutes | Serves: 4

1 cup cooked brown lentils	½ teaspoon onion powder
¼ cup fresh parsley leaves	½ teaspoon smoked paprika
½ cup shredded carrots	½ teaspoon dried oregano
¼ red onion, minced	¼ teaspoon salt
¼ red bell pepper, minced	¼ teaspoon black pepper
1 jalapeño, seeded and minced	½ cup whole wheat bread crumbs
2 garlic cloves, minced	For Serving:
1 egg	Whole wheat buns or whole wheat pitas
2 tablespoons lemon juice	Plain Greek yogurt
2 tablespoons olive oil, divided	Tomato
	Lettuce
	Red Onion

1. Preheat the air fryer to 380°F (193°C).
2. In a food processor, pulse the lentils and parsley mostly smooth. (You will want some bits of lentils in the mixture.)
3. Pour the lentils into a large bowl, and combine with the carrots, onion, bell pepper, jalapeño, garlic, egg, lemon juice, and 1 tablespoon olive oil.
4. Add the onion powder, paprika, oregano, salt, pepper, and bread crumbs. Stir everything together until the seasonings and bread crumbs are well distributed.
5. Form the dough into 4 patties. Place them into the air fryer basket in a single layer, making sure that they don't touch each other. Brush the remaining 1 tablespoon of olive oil over the patties.
6. Bake for 5 minutes. Flip the patties over and bake for an additional 5 minutes.
7. Serve on toasted whole wheat buns or whole wheat pitas with a spoonful of yogurt and lettuce, tomato, and red onion as desired.

PER SERVING (JUST THE PATTIES)
Calories: 206, Total Fat: 9g, Saturated Fat: 1g, Total Carbohydrates: 25g, Protein: 8g, Fiber: 6g, Sugar: 3g

Warm Spiced Cranberry Beans

Prep time: 15 minutes | Cook time: 1½ hours | Serves: 6 to 8

Salt and pepper, to taste	paste
1 pound (454 g) dried cranberry beans, picked over and rinsed	½ teaspoon ground cinnamon
¼ cup extra-virgin olive oil	½ cup dry white wine
1 onion, chopped fine	4 cups chicken or vegetable broth
2 carrots, peeled and chopped fine	2 tablespoons lemon juice, plus extra for seasoning
4 garlic cloves, sliced thin	2 tablespoons minced fresh mint
1 tablespoon tomato	

1. Dissolve 3 tablespoons salt in 4 quarts cold water in large container. Add beans and soak at room temperature for at least 8 hours or up to 24 hours. Drain and rinse well.
2. Adjust oven rack to lower-middle position and heat oven to 350°F (180°C). Heat oil in Dutch oven over medium heat until shimmering. Add onion and carrots and cook until softened, about 5 minutes. Stir in garlic, tomato paste, cinnamon, and ¼ teaspoon pepper and cook until fragrant, about 1 minute. Stir in wine, scraping up any browned bits. Stir in broth, ½ cup water, and beans and bring to boil. Cover, transfer pot to oven, and cook until beans are tender, about 1½ hours, stirring every 30 minutes.
3. Stir in lemon juice and mint. Season with salt, pepper, and extra lemon juice to taste. Adjust consistency with extra hot water as needed. Serve.

PER SERVING
Calories: 89, Fat: 3.36g, Carbohydrates: 11.55g, Protein: 4.78g, Sugar: 5.13g, Fiber: 2.8g, Sodium: 779mg

White Cannellini Bean Stew

Prep time: 10 minutes | Cook time: 30 minutes | Serves: 4 to 6

3 tablespoons extra-virgin olive oil
1 large onion, chopped
1 (15-ounce / 425-g) can diced tomatoes
2 (15-ounce / 425-g) cans white cannellini beans
1 cup carrots, chopped
4 cups vegetable broth
1 teaspoon salt
1 (1-pound / 454-g) bag baby spinach, washed

1. In a large pot over medium heat, cook the olive oil and onion for 5 minutes.
2. Add the tomatoes, beans, carrots, broth, and salt. Stir and cook for 20 minutes.
3. Add the spinach, a handful at a time, and cook for 5 minutes, until the spinach has wilted.
4. Serve warm.

PER SERVING

Calories: 356, Total Fat: 12g, Saturated Fat: 2g, Total Carbohydrates: 47g, Protein: 15g, Sugar: 10g, Fiber: 16g, Sodium: 627mg

Lush Tuscan Bean Stew

Prep time: 15 minutes | Cook time: 1½ hours | Serves: 8

Salt and pepper, to taste
1 pound (454 g) dried cannellini beans, picked over and rinsed
1 tablespoon extra-virgin olive oil, plus extra for serving
6 ounces (170 g) pancetta, cut into ¼-inch pieces
1 large onion, chopped
2 carrots, peeled and cut into ½-inch pieces
2 celery ribs, cut into ½-inch pieces
8 garlic cloves, peeled and smashed
4 cups chicken broth
3 cups water
2 bay leaves
1 pound (454 g) kale or collard greens, stemmed and chopped
1 (14½-ounce / 411-g) can diced tomatoes, drained
1 sprig fresh rosemary

1. Dissolve 3 tablespoons salt in 4 quarts cold water in large container. Add beans and soak at room temperature for at least 8 hours or up to 24 hours. Drain and rinse well.
2. Adjust oven rack to lower-middle position and heat oven to 250 degrees. Heat oil and pancetta in Dutch oven over medium heat. Cook, stirring occasionally, until pancetta is lightly browned and fat has rendered, 6 to 10 minutes. Add onion, carrots, and celery and cook, stirring occasionally, until softened and lightly browned, 10 to 16 minutes. Stir in garlic and cook until fragrant, about 1 minute. Stir in broth, water, bay leaves, and beans and bring to boil. Cover, transfer pot to oven, and cook until beans are almost tender (very center of beans will still be firm), 45 minutes to 1 hour.
3. Stir in kale and tomatoes, cover, and cook until beans and greens are fully tender, 30 to 40 minutes.
4. Remove pot from oven and submerge rosemary sprig in stew. Cover and let sit for 15 minutes. Discard bay leaves and rosemary sprig and season stew with salt and pepper to taste. If desired, use back of spoon to press some beans against side of pot to thicken stew. Serve, drizzling individual portions with extra oil.

PER SERVING

Calories: 167, Fat: 5.81g, Carbohydrates: 22.83g, Protein: 10.69g, Sugar:9.48g, Fiber: 7.4g, Sodium: 530mg

Chili Black Bean with Mangoes

Prep time: 10 minutes | Cook time: 10 minutes | Serves: 4

2 tablespoons coconut oil
1 onion, chopped
2 (15-ounce / 425-g) cans black beans, drained and rinsed
1 tablespoon chili powder
1 teaspoon sea salt
¼ teaspoon freshly ground black pepper
1 cup water
2 ripe mangoes, sliced thinly
¼ cup chopped fresh cilantro, divided
¼ cup sliced scallions, divided

1. Heat the coconut oil in a pot over high heat until melted.
2. Put the onion in the pot and sauté for 5 minutes or until translucent.
3. Add the black beans to the pot. Sprinkle with chili powder, salt, and ground black pepper. Pour in the water. Stir to mix well.
4. Bring to a boil. Reduce the heat to low, then simmering for 5 minutes or until the beans are tender.
5. Turn off the heat and mix in the mangoes, then garnish with scallions and cilantro before serving.

PER SERVING

Calories: 430, Fat: 9.1g, Total Carbohydrates: 71.9g, Protein: 20.2g, Fiber: 22.0g, Sodium: 608mg

Chapter 6 Grain and Rice

Basmati Rice with Pomegranate and Cilantro

Prep time: 15 minutes | Cook time: 34 minutes | Serves: 8 to 10

1 (2-pound / 907-g) head cauliflower, cored and cut into ¾-inch florets
¼ cup extra-virgin olive oil
Salt and pepper, to taste
½ teaspoon ground cumin
1 onion, chopped coarse
1½ cups basmati rice, rinsed
4 garlic cloves, minced
½ teaspoon ground cinnamon
½ teaspoon ground turmeric
2¼ cups water
½ cup pomegranate seeds
2 tablespoons chopped fresh cilantro
2 tablespoons chopped fresh mint

1. Adjust oven rack to lowest position and heat oven to 475ºF (245ºC). Toss cauliflower with 2 tablespoons oil, ½ teaspoon salt, ½ teaspoon pepper, and ¼ teaspoon cumin. Arrange cauliflower in single layer in rimmed baking sheet and roast until just tender, 10 to 15 minutes, set aside.
2. Heat remaining 2 tablespoons oil in large saucepan over medium heat until shimmering. Add onion and ¼ teaspoon salt and cook until softened and lightly browned, 5 to 7 minutes. Add rice, garlic, cinnamon, turmeric, and remaining ¼ teaspoon cumin and cook, stirring frequently, until grain edges begin to turn translucent, about 3 minutes.
3. Stir in water and bring to simmer. Reduce heat to low, cover, and simmer gently until rice is tender and water is absorbed, 16 to 18 minutes.
4. Off heat, lay clean dish towel underneath lid and let pilaf sit for 10 minutes. Add roasted cauliflower to pilaf and fluff gently with fork to combine. Season with salt and pepper to taste. Transfer to serving platter and sprinkle with pomegranate seeds, cilantro, and mint. Serve.

PER SERVING
Calories: 227, Fat: 16.28g, Carbohydrates: 22.53g, Protein: 7.48g, Sugar: 4.7g, Fiber: 8.3g, Sodium: 41mg

Buckwheat Groats with Root Vegetables

Prep time: 15 minutes | Cook time: 40 minutes | Serves: 6

Olive oil cooking spray
2 large potatoes, cubed
2 carrots, sliced
1 small rutabaga, cubed
2 celery stalks, chopped
½ teaspoon smoked paprika
¼ cup plus 1 tablespoon
olive oil, divided
2 rosemary sprigs
1 cup buckwheat groats
2 cups vegetable broth
2 garlic cloves, minced
½ yellow onion, chopped
1 teaspoon salt

1. Preheat the air fryer to 380ºF (193ºC). Lightly coat the inside of a 5-cup capacity casserole dish with olive oil cooking spray. (The shape of the casserole dish will depend upon the size of the air fryer, but it needs to be able to hold at least 5 cups.)
2. In a large bowl, toss the potatoes, carrots, rutabaga, and celery with the paprika and ¼ cup olive oil.
3. Pour the vegetable mixture into the prepared casserole dish and top with the rosemary sprigs. Place the casserole dish into the air fryer and bake for 15 minutes.
4. While the vegetables are cooking, rinse and drain the buckwheat groats.
5. In a medium saucepan over medium-high heat, combine the groats, vegetable broth, garlic, onion, and salt with the remaining 1 tablespoon olive oil. Bring the mixture to a boil, then reduce the heat to low, cover, and cook for 10 to 12 minutes.
6. Remove the casserole dish from the air fryer. Remove the rosemary sprigs and discard. Pour the cooked buckwheat into the dish with the vegetables and stir to combine. Cover with aluminum foil and bake for an additional 15 minutes.
7. Stir before serving.

PER SERVING
Calories: 344, Total Fat: 13g, Saturated Fat: 2g, Total Carbohydrates: 50g, Protein: 8g, Fiber: 8g, Sugar: 4g

Barley with Carrots, Snow Peas, and Sunflower Seeds

Prep time: 15 minutes | Cook time: 30 minutes | Serves: 4

½ cup plain yogurt
1½ teaspoons grated lemon zest plus 1½ tablespoons juice
1½ tablespoons minced fresh mint
Salt and pepper, to taste
1 cup pearl barley
5 carrots, peeled
3 tablespoons extra-virgin olive oil
¾ teaspoon ground coriander
8 ounces (227 g) snow peas, strings removed, halved lengthwise
⅔ cup raw sunflower seeds
½ teaspoon ground cumin
⅛ teaspoon ground cardamom

1. Whisk yogurt, ½ teaspoon lemon zest and 1½ teaspoons juice, 1½ teaspoons mint, ¼ teaspoon salt, and ⅛ teaspoon pepper together in small bowl, cover and refrigerate until ready to serve.
2. Bring 4 quarts water to boil in Dutch oven. Add barley and 1 tablespoon salt, return to boil, and cook until tender, 20 to 40 minutes. Drain barley, return to now-empty pot, and cover to keep warm.
3. Meanwhile, halve carrots crosswise, then halve or quarter lengthwise to create uniformly sized pieces. Heat 1 tablespoon oil in 12-inch skillet over medium-high heat until just smoking. Add carrots and ½ teaspoon coriander and cook, stirring occasionally, until lightly charred and just tender, 5 to 7 minutes. Add snow peas and cook, stirring occasionally, until spotty brown, 3 to 5 minutes, transfer to plate.
4. Heat 1½ teaspoons oil in now-empty skillet over medium heat until shimmering. Add sunflower seeds, cumin, cardamom, remaining ¼ teaspoon coriander, and ¼ teaspoon salt. Cook, stirring constantly, until seeds are toasted, about 2 minutes, transfer to small bowl.
5. Whisk remaining 1 teaspoon lemon zest and 1 tablespoon juice, remaining 1 tablespoon mint, and remaining 1½ tablespoons oil together in large bowl. Add barley and carrot–snow pea mixture and gently toss to combine. Season with salt and pepper to taste. Serve, topping individual portions with spiced sunflower seeds and drizzling with yogurt sauce.

PER SERVING
Calories: 480, Fat: 24.16g, Carbohydrates: 57.26g, Protein: 13.34g, Sugar: 8.38g, Fiber: 13.6g, Sodium: 76mg

Wild Mushroom Frerotte with Parmesan

Prep time: 15 minutes | Cook time: 7 minutes | Serves: 4

1½ cups whole farro
3 tablespoons extra-virgin olive oil, divided, plus extra for drizzling
12 ounces (340 g) cremini or white mushrooms, trimmed and sliced thin
½ onion, chopped fine
½ teaspoon table salt
¼ teaspoon pepper
1 garlic clove, minced
¼ ounce (7 g) dried porcini mushrooms, rinsed and chopped fine
2 teaspoons minced fresh thyme or ½ teaspoon dried
¼ cup dry white wine
2½ cups chicken or vegetable broth, plus extra as needed
2 ounces (57 g) Parmesan cheese, grated, plus extra for serving
2 teaspoons lemon juice
½ cup chopped fresh parsley

1. Pulse farro in blender until about half of grains are broken into smaller pieces, about 6 pulses.
2. Using highest sauté function, heat 2 tablespoons oil in Instant Pot until shimmering. Add cremini mushrooms, onion, salt, and pepper, partially cover, and cook until mushrooms are softened and have released their liquid, about 5 minutes. Stir in farro, garlic, porcini mushrooms, and thyme and cook until fragrant, about 1 minute. Stir in wine and cook until nearly evaporated, about 30 seconds. Stir in broth.
3. Lock lid in place and close pressure release valve. Select high pressure cook function and cook for 12 minutes. Turn off Instant Pot and quick-release pressure. Carefully remove lid, allowing steam to escape away from you.
4. If necessary adjust consistency with extra hot broth, or continue to cook Frerotte, using highest sauté function, stirring frequently, until proper consistency is achieved. (Frerotte should be slightly thickened, and spoon dragged along bottom of multicooker should leave trail that quickly fills in.) Add Parmesan and remaining 1 tablespoon oil and stir vigorously until Frerotte becomes creamy. Stir in lemon juice and season with salt and pepper to taste. Sprinkle individual portions with parsley and extra Parmesan, and drizzle with extra oil before serving.

PER SERVING
Calories: 280, Total Fat: 10g, Sat Fat: 2.5g, Total Carbohydrates: 35g, Protein: 13g, Sugar: 2g, Sodium: 630mg, Fiber: 4g

Brown Rice Pilaf

Prep time: 10 minutes | Cook time: 23 minutes | Serves: 6

2 tablespoons olive oil
1 medium onion, diced
¼ cup pine nuts
1½ cups long-grain brown rice
2 ½ cups hot chicken stock
1 cinnamon stick
¼ cup raisins
Sea salt and freshly ground pepper, to taste

1. Heat the olive oil in a large saucepan over medium heat.
2. Sauté the onions and pine nuts for 6 to 8 minutes, or until the pine nuts are golden and the onion is translucent.
3. Add the rice and sauté for 2 minutes until lightly browned. Pour the chicken stock into the pan and bring to a boil.
4. Add the cinnamon and raisins.
5. Lower the heat, cover the pan, and simmer for 15 to 20 minutes, or until the rice is tender and the liquid is absorbed.
6. Remove from the heat and fluff with a fork. Season and serve.

PER SERVING
Calories: 177, Fat: 10.03g, Carbohydrates: 17.78g, Protein: 4.81g, Sugar: 2.75g, Fiber: 1.7g, Sodium: 146mg

Wild Parmesan Mushroom Risotto

Prep time: 10 minutes | Cook time: 23 minutes | Serves: 6

2 ounces (57 g) dried porcini mushrooms
5 cups chicken stock
2 tablespoons olive oil
1 small onion, minced
2 cups brown rice
½ cup freshly grated, low-fat Parmesan cheese
Sea salt and freshly ground pepper, to taste

1. Place the mushrooms in a bowl and cover them with hot water. Set them aside for 30 minutes. Drain them, reserving the liquid, and wash them.
2. Strain the liquid through a sieve lined with cheesecloth. Add the liquid to the chicken stock.
3. Heat the chicken stock and mushroom liquid in a small saucepan. When simmering, turn heat to lowest setting.
4. Heat the olive oil in a large saucepan over medium heat. Add the onion and sauté for 3 to 5 minutes, or until tender. Stir in the rice and mushrooms and ¾ cup of the stock.
5. Continue cooking the rice, stirring almost constantly, and adding more liquid, a ladleful at a time, as soon as the rice absorbs the liquid. There should always be some liquid visible in the pan.
6. Cook, adding liquid every few minutes, until the rice is tender, with a slightly firm center, 20 to 30 minutes.
7. Remove from the heat, and stir in the Parmesan cheese, a spoonful at a time.
8. Season to taste and serve.

PER SERVING
Calories: 218, Fat: 7.62g, Carbohydrates: 30.49g, Protein: 7.85g, Sugar: 4.1g, Fiber: 2.6g, Sodium: 291mg

Basmati Rice with Currant and Almond

Prep time: 10 minutes | Cook time: 24 minutes | Serves: 4 to 6

1 tablespoon extra-virgin olive oil
1 small onion, chopped fine
Salt and pepper, to taste
1½ cups basmati rice, rinsed
2 garlic cloves, minced
½ teaspoon ground turmeric
¼ teaspoon ground cinnamon
2¼ cups water
¼ cup currants
¼ cup sliced almonds, toasted

1. Heat oil in large saucepan over medium heat until shimmering. Add onion and ¼ teaspoon salt and cook until softened, about 5 minutes. Add rice, garlic, turmeric, and cinnamon and cook, stirring frequently, until grain edges begin to turn translucent, about 3 minutes.
2. Stir in water and bring to simmer. Reduce heat to low, cover, and simmer gently until rice is tender and water is absorbed, 16 to 18 minutes.
3. Off heat, sprinkle currants over pilaf. Cover, laying clean dish towel underneath lid, and let pilaf sit for 10 minutes. Add almonds to pilaf and fluff gently with fork to combine. Season with salt and pepper to taste. Serve.

PER SERVING
Calories: 186, Fat: 12.71g, Carbohydrates: 25.86g, Protein: 6.41g, Sugar: 1.69g, Fiber: 10.3g, Sodium: 6mg

Barley Pilaf with Parsley and Chives

Prep time: 10 minutes | Cook time: 9 minutes | Serves: 4 to 6

3 tablespoons extra-virgin olive oil	fresh thyme or ½ teaspoon dried
1 small onion, chopped fine	2½ cups water
Salt and pepper, to taste	¼ cup minced fresh parsley
1½ cups pearl barley, rinsed	2 tablespoons minced fresh chives
2 garlic cloves, minced	1½ teaspoons lemon juice
1½ teaspoons minced	

1. Heat oil in large saucepan over medium heat until shimmering. Add onion and ½ teaspoon salt and cook until softened, about 5 minutes. Stir in barley, garlic, and thyme and cook, stirring frequently, until barley is lightly toasted and fragrant, about 3 minutes.
2. Stir in water and bring to simmer. Reduce heat to low, cover, and simmer until barley is tender and water is absorbed, 20 to 40 minutes.
3. Off heat, lay clean dish towel underneath lid and let pilaf sit for 10 minutes. Add parsley, chives, and lemon juice to pilaf and fluff gently with fork to combine. Season with salt and pepper to taste. Serve.

PER SERVING
Calories: 367, Fat: 11.09g, Carbohydrates: 61.3g, Protein: 7.96g, Sugar: 1.47g, Fiber: 12.4g, Sodium: 13mg

Farro with Lemony Parsley and Mint

Prep time: 10 minutes | Cook time: 18 minutes | Serves: 4 to 6

1½ cups whole farro	¼ cup chopped fresh parsley
Salt and pepper, to taste	¼ cup chopped fresh mint
3 tablespoons extra-virgin olive oil	1 tablespoon lemon juice
1 onion, chopped fine	
1 garlic clove, minced	

1. Bring 4 quarts water to boil in Dutch oven. Add farro and 1 tablespoon salt, return to boil, and cook until grains are tender with slight chew, 15 to 30 minutes. Drain farro, return to now-empty pot, and cover to keep warm.

2. Heat 2 tablespoons oil in 12-inch skillet over medium heat until shimmering. Add onion and ¼ teaspoon salt and cook until softened, about 5 minutes. Stir in garlic and cook until fragrant, about 30 seconds.
3. Add remaining 1 tablespoon oil and farro and cook, stirring frequently, until heated through, about 2 minutes. Off heat, stir in parsley, mint, and lemon juice. Season with salt and pepper to taste. Serve.

PER SERVING
Calories: 178, Fat: 13.26g, Carbohydrates: 11.99g, Protein: 3.89g, Sugar: 8.95g, Fiber: 1.2g, Sodium: 51mg

Warm Farro with Mushrooms and Shallot

Prep time: 10 minutes | Cook time: 25 minutes | Serves: 4 to 6

1½ cups whole farro	1½ teaspoons minced fresh thyme or ½ teaspoon dried
Salt and pepper, to taste	
3 tablespoons extra-virgin olive oil	3 tablespoons dry sherry
12 ounces (340 g) cremini mushrooms, trimmed and chopped coarse	3 tablespoons minced fresh parsley
	1½ teaspoons sherry vinegar, plus extra for serving
1 shallot, minced	

1. Bring 4 quarts water to boil in Dutch oven. Add farro and 1 tablespoon salt, return to boil, and cook until grains are tender with slight chew, 15 to 30 minutes. Drain farro, return to now-empty pot, and cover to keep warm.
2. Heat 2 tablespoons oil in 12-inch skillet over medium heat until shimmering. Add mushrooms, shallot, thyme, and ¼ teaspoon salt and cook, stirring occasionally, until moisture has evaporated and vegetables start to brown, 8 to 10 minutes. Stir in sherry and cook, scraping up any browned bits, until skillet is almost dry.
3. Add remaining 1 tablespoon oil and farro and cook, stirring frequently, until heated through, about 2 minutes. Off heat, stir in parsley and vinegar. Season with salt, pepper, and extra vinegar to taste and serve.

PER SERVING
Calories: 412, Fat: 14g, Carbohydrates: 72.21g, Protein: 11.29g, Sugar: 9.03g, Fiber: 10.5g, Sodium: 56mg

Herbed Barley with Nuts

Prep time: 10 minutes | Cook time: 25 minutes | Serves: 4

2 tablespoons olive oil
½ cup diced onion
½ cup diced celery
1 carrot, peeled and diced
3 cups water or chicken broth
1 cup barley

1 bay leaf
½ teaspoon thyme
½ teaspoon rosemary
¼ cup walnuts or pine nuts
Sea salt and freshly ground pepper, to taste

1. Heat the olive oil in a medium saucepan over medium-high heat. Sauté the onion, celery, and carrot over medium heat until they are tender.
2. Add the water or chicken broth, barley, and seasonings, and bring to a boil. Reduce the heat and simmer for 25 minutes, or until tender.
3. Stir in the nuts and season to taste.

PER SERVING
Calories: 290, Fat: 10.88g, Carbohydrates: 44.5g, Protein: 6.31g, Sugar: 1.71g, Fiber: 9.8g, Sodium: 23mg

Farro with Fennel and Parmesan Cheese

Prep time: 10 minutes | Cook time: 25 minutes | Serves: 4 to 6

1½ cups whole farro
Salt and pepper, to taste
3 tablespoons extra-virgin olive oil
1 onion, chopped fine
1 small fennel bulb, stalks discarded, bulb halved, cored, and chopped fine
3 garlic cloves, minced

1 teaspoon minced fresh thyme or ¼ teaspoon dried
1 ounce (28 g) Parmesan cheese, grated
¼ cup minced fresh parsley
2 teaspoons sherry vinegar

1. Bring 4 quarts water to boil in Dutch oven. Add farro and 1 tablespoon salt, return to boil, and cook until grains are tender with slight chew, 15 to 30 minutes. Drain farro, return to now-empty pot, and cover to keep warm.
2. Heat 2 tablespoons oil in 12-inch skillet over medium heat until shimmering. Add onion, fennel, and ¼ teaspoon salt and cook, stirring occasionally, until softened, 8 to 10 minutes. Add garlic and thyme and cook until fragrant, about 30 seconds.

3. Add remaining 1 tablespoon oil and farro and cook, stirring frequently, until heated through, about 2 minutes. Off heat, stir in Parmesan, parsley, and vinegar. Season with salt and pepper to taste. Serve.

PER SERVING
Calories: 227, Fat: 15.32g, Carbohydrates: 17.32g, Protein: 6.61g, Sugar: 11.15g, Fiber: 2.9g, Sodium: 207mg

Basmati Rice and Vermicelli Pasta Pilaf

Prep time: 10 minutes | Cook time: 20 minutes | Serves: 4 to 6

1½ cups basmati rice
3 tablespoons extra-virgin olive oil
2 ounces (57 g) vermicelli pasta, broken into 1-inch lengths
1 onion, chopped fine

1 garlic clove, minced
Salt and pepper, to taste
2½ cups chicken or vegetable broth
3 tablespoons minced fresh parsley

1. Place rice in medium bowl and cover with hot tap water by 2 inches, let stand for 15 minutes.
2. Using your hands, gently swish grains to release excess starch. Carefully pour off water, leaving rice in bowl. Add cold tap water to rice and pour off water. Repeat adding and pouring off cold water 4 to 5 times, until water runs almost clear. Drain rice in fine-mesh strainer.
3. Heat oil in large saucepan over medium heat until shimmering. Add pasta and cook, stirring occasionally, until browned, about 3 minutes. Add onion and garlic and cook, stirring occasionally, until onion is softened but not browned, about 4 minutes. Add rice and cook, stirring occasionally, until edges of rice begin to turn translucent, about 3 minutes. Add broth and 1¼ teaspoons salt and bring to boil. Reduce heat to low, cover, and simmer gently until rice and pasta are tender and broth is absorbed, about 10 minutes. Off heat, lay clean dish towel underneath lid and let pilaf sit for 10 minutes. Add parsley to pilaf and fluff gently with fork to combine. Season with salt and pepper to taste. Serve.

PER SERVING
Calories: 316, Fat: 19.8g, Carbohydrates: 41.39g, Protein: 7.77g, Sugar: 7.73g, Fiber: 10.8g, Sodium: 589mg

Brown Rice with Red Pepper and Onion

Prep time: 10 minutes | Cook time: 1½ hours | Serves: 4 to 6

4 teaspoons extra-virgin olive oil	brown rice, rinsed
2 onions, chopped fine	¾ cup jarred roasted red peppers, rinsed, patted dry, and chopped
Salt and pepper, to taste	
2¼ cups water	½ cup minced fresh parsley
1 cup chicken or vegetable broth	Grated Parmesan cheese
1½ cups long-grain	Lemon wedges

1. Adjust oven rack to middle position and heat oven to 375°F (190°C). Heat oil in Dutch oven over medium heat until shimmering. Add onions and 1 teaspoon salt and cook, stirring occasionally, until softened and well browned, 12 to 14 minutes.
2. Stir in water and broth and bring to boil. Stir in rice, cover, and transfer pot to oven. Bake until rice is tender and liquid is absorbed, 65 to 70 minutes.
3. Remove pot from oven. Sprinkle red peppers over rice, cover, and let sit for 5 minutes. Add parsley to rice and fluff gently with fork to combine. Season with salt and pepper to taste. Serve with grated Parmesan and lemon wedges.

PER SERVING
Calories: 369, Fat: 7.09g, Carbohydrates: 69.79g, Protein: 7.94g, Sugar: 10.65g, Fiber: 4.7g, Sodium: 266mg

Toasted Barley and Almond Pilaf

Prep time: 10 minutes | Cook time: 5 minutes | Serves: 2

1 tablespoon olive oil	barley
1 garlic clove, minced	1½ cups low-sodium chicken stock
3 scallions, minced	
2 ounces (57 g) mushrooms, sliced	½ teaspoon dried thyme
¼ cup sliced almonds	1 tablespoon fresh minced parsley
½ cup uncooked pearled	Salt, to taste

1. Heat the oil in a saucepan over medium-high heat. Add the garlic, scallions, mushrooms, and almonds, and sauté for 3 minutes.
2. Add the barley and cook, stirring, for 1 minute to toast it.

3. Add the chicken stock and thyme and bring the mixture to a boil.
4. Cover and reduce the heat to low. Simmer the barley for 30 minutes, or until the liquid is absorbed and the barley is tender.
5. Sprinkle with fresh parsley and season with salt before serving.

PER SERVING
Calories: 333, Total Fat: 14g, Total Carbohydrates: 46g, Protein: 10g, Fiber: 10g, Sugar: 2g, Sodium: 141mg

Spiced Pilaf with Sweet Potatoes

Prep time: 15 minutes | Cook time: 20 minutes | Serves: 4 to 6

2 tbsps. extra-virgin olive oil	inch thick
1 onion, chopped fine	½ preserved lemon, pulp and white pith removed, rind rinsed and minced (2 tbsp.)
½ tsp. table salt	
1½ tsps. ground turmeric	
1 tsp. ground coriander	½ cup shelled pistachios, toasted and chopped
⅛ tsp. cayenne pepper	
2 garlic cloves, minced	2 cups (480 ml) chicken broth
1½ cups long-grain white rice, rinsed	
12 ounces (340 g) sweet potato, peeled, quartered lengthwise, and sliced ½	¼ cup pomegranate seeds
	¼ cup fresh cilantro leaves

1. In Instant Pot, use highest sauté function, heat oil until shimmering. Add onion and salt and cook about 5 minutes until onion is softened. Stir in garlic, coriander, turmeric, and cayenne and cook about 30 seconds until fragrant. Stir in rice, broth, and sweet potato.
2. Lock lid and close pressure release valve. Choose high pressure cook function and cook for 4 minutes. Turn off and quick-release pressure. Carefully remove lid, letting steam escape away from you.
3. Put in preserved lemon and gently fluff rice with fork to combine. Lay clean dish towel over pot to replace lid, and set aside for 5 minutes. Season with salt and pepper. Transfer to a dish and sprinkle with cilantro, pistachios, and pomegranate seeds. Serve.

PER SERVING
Calories: 320, Total Fat: 10g, Sat Fat: 1.5g, Total Carbohydrates: 52g, Protein: 8g, Sugar: 5g, Sodium: 500mg, Fiber: 3g

Farro Risotto with Fresh Sage

Prep time: 10 minutes | Cook time: 35 minutes | Serves: 6

Olive oil cooking spray
1½ cups uncooked farro
2 ½ cups chicken broth
1 cup tomato sauce
1 yellow onion, diced
3 garlic cloves, minced
1 tablespoon fresh sage, chopped
½ teaspoon salt
2 tablespoons olive oil
1 cup Parmesan cheese, grated, divided

1. Preheat the air fryer to 380ºF (193ºC). Lightly coat the inside of a 5-cup capacity casserole dish with olive oil cooking spray. (The shape of the casserole dish will depend upon the size of the air fryer, but it needs to be able to hold at least 5 cups.)
2. In a large bowl, combine the farro, broth, tomato sauce, onion, garlic, sage, salt, olive oil, and ½ cup of the Parmesan.
3. Pour the farro mixture into the prepared casserole dish and cover with aluminum foil.
4. Bake for 20 minutes, then uncover and stir. Sprinkle the remaining ½ cup Parmesan over the top and bake for 15 minutes more.
5. Stir well before serving.

PER SERVING
Calories: 284, Total Fat: 10g, Saturated Fat: 3g, Total Carbohydrates: 40g, Protein: 12g, Fiber: 4g, Sugar: 3g

Brown Rice and Lentils

Prep time: 10 minutes | Cook time: 1 hour | Serves: 4

2 cups green or brown lentils
1 cup brown rice
5 cups water or chicken stock
½ teaspoon sea salt
½ teaspoon freshly ground pepper
½ teaspoon dried thyme
¼ cup olive oil
3 onions, peeled and sliced

1. Place the lentils and rice in a large saucepan with water or chicken stock. Bring to a boil, cover, and simmer for 20 to 25 minutes, or until almost tender.
2. Add the seasonings and cook an additional 20 to 30 minutes, or until the rice is tender and the water is absorbed.
3. In another saucepan, heat the olive oil over medium heat. Add the onions and cook very slowly, stirring frequently, until the onions become browned and caramelized, about 20 minutes.
4. To serve, ladle the lentils and rice into bowls and top with the caramelized onions.

PER SERVING
Calories: 217, Fat: 14.16g, Carbohydrates: 20.61g, Protein: 4.83g, Sugar: 0.46g, Fiber: 1.7g, Sodium: 298mg

Oregano Wheat Berries with Veggie

Prep time: 10 minutes | Cook time: 1¼ hours | Serves: 4 to 6

1½ cups wheat berries
Salt and pepper, to taste
2 tablespoons extra-virgin olive oil
3 tablespoons red wine vinegar
1 garlic clove, minced
1 tablespoon grated lemon zest
1 tablespoon minced fresh oregano or 1½ teaspoons dried
1 zucchini, cut into ½-inch pieces
1 red onion, chopped
1 red bell pepper, stemmed, seeded, and cut into ½-inch pieces

1. Bring 4 quarts water to boil in Dutch oven. Add wheat berries and 1½ teaspoons salt, return to boil, and cook until tender but still chewy, 60 to 70 minutes.
2. Meanwhile, whisk 1 tablespoon oil, vinegar, garlic, lemon zest, and oregano together in large bowl. Drain wheat berries, add to bowl with dressing, and toss gently to coat.
3. Heat 2 teaspoons oil in 12-inch nonstick skillet over medium-high heat until just smoking. Add zucchini and ¼ teaspoon salt and cook, stirring occasionally, until deep golden brown and beginning to char in spots, 6 to 8 minutes, transfer to bowl with wheat berries.
4. Return now-empty skillet to medium-high heat and add remaining 1 teaspoon oil, onion, bell pepper, and ¼ teaspoon salt. Cook, stirring occasionally, until onion is charred at edges and pepper skin is charred and blistered, 8 to 10 minutes. Add wheat berry–zucchini mixture and cook, stirring frequently, until heated through, about 2 minutes. Season with salt and pepper to taste. Serve.

PER SERVING
Calories: 243, Fat: 8.15g, Carbohydrates: 38.55g, Protein: 7.2g, Sugar: 3.29g, Fiber: 6.2g, Sodium: 8mg

Wheat Berry Salad with Orange and Veggie

Prep time: 15 minutes | Cook time: 1 hour | Serves: 4 to 6

1½ cups wheat berries
Salt and pepper, to taste
1 orange
3 tablespoons red wine vinegar
1½ tablespoons Dijon mustard
1 small shallot, minced
1 garlic clove, minced

⅛ teaspoon grated orange zest
1½ teaspoons honey
2 tablespoons extra-virgin olive oil
3 carrots, peeled and shredded
1 tablespoon minced fresh tarragon

1. Bring 4 quarts water to boil in Dutch oven. Add wheat berries and 1½ teaspoons salt, return to boil, and cook until tender but still chewy, 60 to 70 minutes. Drain wheat berries, spread in rimmed baking sheet, and let cool completely, about 15 minutes.
2. Cut away peel and pith from orange. Quarter orange, then slice crosswise into ¼-inch-thick pieces. Whisk vinegar, mustard, shallot, garlic, orange zest, honey, and ¼ teaspoon salt together in large bowl until combined. Whisking constantly, slowly drizzle in oil. Add wheat berries, carrots, tarragon, and orange pieces and gently toss to coat. Season with salt and pepper to taste. Serve.

PER SERVING
Calories: 260, Fat: 8.26g, Carbohydrates: 43.12g, Protein: 6.96g, Sugar: 7.03g, Fiber: 7.2g, Sodium: 87mg

Polenta with Parmesan Cheese

Prep time: 10 minutes | Cook time: 31 minutes | Serves: 4 to 6

7½ cups water
Salt and pepper, to taste
Pinch baking soda
1½ cups coarse-ground cornmeal
2 ounces (57 g)

Parmesan cheese, grated, plus extra for serving
2 tablespoons extra-virgin olive oil

1. Bring water to boil in large saucepan over medium-high heat. Stir in 1½ teaspoons salt and baking soda. Slowly pour cornmeal into water in steady stream while stirring back and forth with wooden spoon or rubber spatula.

Bring mixture to boil, stirring constantly, about 1 minute. Reduce heat to lowest setting and cover.
2. After 5 minutes, whisk polenta to smooth out any lumps that may have formed, about 15 seconds. (Make sure to scrape down sides and bottom of saucepan.) Cover and continue to cook, without stirring, until polenta grains are tender but slightly al dente, about 25 minutes longer. (Polenta should be loose and barely hold its shape, it will continue to thicken as it cools.)
3. Off heat, stir in Parmesan and oil and season with pepper to taste. Cover and let sit for 5 minutes. Serve, passing extra Parmesan separately.

PER SERVING
Calories: 338, Fat: 11.75g, Carbohydrates: 49.12g, Protein: 8.27g, Sugar: 0.96g, Fiber: 2.4g, Sodium: 584mg

Wheat Berry Salad with Figs and Nuts

Prep time: 10 minutes | Cook time: 1 hour | Serves: 4 to 6

1½ cups wheat berries
Salt and pepper, to taste
2 tablespoons balsamic vinegar
1 small shallot, minced
1 teaspoon Dijon mustard
1 teaspoon honey
3 tablespoons extra-virgin

olive oil
8 ounces (227 g) figs, cut into ½-inch pieces
½ cup fresh parsley leaves
¼ cup pine nuts, toasted
2 ounces (57 g) Goat cheese, crumbled

1. Bring 4 quarts water to boil in Dutch oven. Add wheat berries and 1½ teaspoons salt, return to boil, and cook until tender but still chewy, 60 to 70 minutes. Drain wheat berries, spread onto rimmed baking sheet, and let cool completely, about 15 minutes.
2. Whisk vinegar, shallot, mustard, honey, ¼ teaspoon salt, and ¼ teaspoon pepper together in large bowl. Whisking constantly, slowly drizzle in oil. Add wheat berries, figs, parsley, and pine nuts and toss gently to combine. Season with salt and pepper to taste. Transfer to serving platter and sprinkle with Goat cheese. Serve.

PER SERVING
Calories: 524, Fat: 22.72g, Carbohydrates: 74.17g, Protein: 13.73g, Sugar: 30.9g, Fiber: 11.2g, Sodium: 87mg

Rice with Oranges, Green Olives, and Almonds

Prep time: 10 minutes | Cook time: 20 minutes | Serves: 4 to 6

1½ cups basmati rice
Salt and pepper, to taste
2 oranges, plus ¼ teaspoon grated orange zest plus 1 tablespoon juice
2 tablespoons extra-virgin olive oil
2 teaspoons sherry vinegar

1 small garlic clove, minced
⅓ cup large pitted brine-cured green olives, chopped
⅓ cup slivered almonds, toasted
2 tablespoons minced fresh oregano

1. Bring 4 quarts water to boil in Dutch oven. Meanwhile, toast rice in 12-inch skillet over medium heat until faintly fragrant and some grains turn opaque, 5 to 8 minutes. Add rice and 1½ teaspoons salt to boiling water and cook, stirring occasionally, until rice is tender but not soft, about 15 minutes. Drain rice, spread onto rimmed baking sheet, and let cool completely, about 15 minutes.
2. Cut away peel and pith from oranges. Holding fruit over bowl, use paring knife to slice between membranes to release segments. Whisk oil, vinegar, garlic, orange zest and juice, 1 teaspoon salt, and ½ teaspoon pepper together in large bowl. Add rice, orange segments, olives, almonds, and oregano, gently toss to combine, and let sit for 20 minutes. Serve.

PER SERVING
Calories: 214, Fat: 16.37g, Carbohydrates: 24.91g, Protein: 6.34g, Sugar: 0.86g, Fiber: 10.7g, Sodium: 14mg

Farrotto with Parmesan Cheese

Prep time: 10 minutes | Cook time: 39 minutes | Serves: 6

1½ cups whole farro
3 cups chicken or vegetable broth
3 cups water
3 tablespoons extra-virgin olive oil
½ onion, chopped fine
1 garlic clove, minced

2 teaspoons minced fresh thyme
Salt and pepper, to taste
2 ounces (57 g) Parmesan cheese, grated
2 tablespoons minced fresh parsley
2 teaspoons lemon juice

1. Pulse farro in blender until about half of grains are broken into smaller pieces, about 6 pulses.
2. Bring broth and water to boil in medium saucepan over high heat. Reduce heat to low, cover, and keep warm.
3. Heat 2 tablespoons oil in Dutch oven over medium-low heat. Add onion and cook until softened, about 5 minutes. Stir in garlic and cook until fragrant, about 30 seconds. Add farro and cook, stirring frequently, until grains are lightly toasted, about 3 minutes.
4. Stir 5 cups warm broth mixture into farro mixture, reduce heat to low, cover, and cook until almost all liquid has been absorbed and farro is just al dente, about 25 minutes, stirring twice during cooking.
5. Add thyme, 1 teaspoon salt, and ¾ teaspoon pepper and cook, stirring constantly, until farro becomes creamy, about 5 minutes. Off heat, stir in Parmesan, parsley, lemon juice, and remaining 1 tablespoon oil. Adjust consistency with remaining warm broth mixture as needed (you may have broth left over). Season with salt and pepper to taste. Serve.

PER SERVING
Calories: 151, Fat: 11.67g, Carbohydrates: 6.32g, Protein: 5.63g, Sugar: 4.07g, Fiber: 0.3g, Sodium: 662mg

Moroccan-Style Brown Rice and Chickpea

Prep time: 15 minutes | Cook time: 45 minutes | Serves: 6

Olive oil cooking spray
1 cup long-grain brown rice
2¼ cups chicken stock
1 (15½-ounce / 439-g) can chickpeas, drained and rinsed
½ cup diced carrot
½ cup green peas
1 teaspoon ground cumin
½ teaspoon ground

turmeric
½ teaspoon ground ginger
½ teaspoon onion powder
½ teaspoon salt
¼ teaspoon ground cinnamon
¼ teaspoon garlic powder
¼ teaspoon black pepper
Fresh parsley, for garnish

1. Preheat the air fryer to 380°F (193°C). Lightly coat the inside of a 5-cup capacity casserole dish with olive oil cooking spray. (The shape of the casserole dish will depend upon the size of the air fryer, but it needs to be able to hold at least 5 cups.)

2. In the casserole dish, combine the rice, stock, chickpeas, carrot, peas, cumin, turmeric, ginger, onion powder, salt, cinnamon, garlic powder, and black pepper. Stir well to combine.
3. Cover loosely with aluminum foil.
4. Place the covered casserole dish into the air fryer and bake for 20 minutes. Remove from the air fryer and stir well.
5. Place the casserole back into the air fryer, uncovered, and bake for 25 minutes more.
6. Fluff with a spoon and sprinkle with fresh chopped parsley before serving.

PER SERVING
Calories: 204, Total Fat: 2g, Saturated Fat: 0g, Total Carbohydrates: 40g, Protein: 7g, Fiber: 5g, Sugar: 4g

Rice Salad with Asparagus and Parsley

Prep time: 10 minutes | Cook time: 30 minutes | Serves: 4 to 6

1½ cups long-grain brown rice	asparagus, trimmed and cut into 1-inch lengths
Salt and pepper, to taste	1 shallot, minced
1 teaspoon grated lemon zest plus 3 tablespoons juice	2 ounces (57 g) Goat cheese, crumbled
3½ tablespoons extra-virgin olive oil	¼ cup slivered almonds, toasted
1 pound (454 g)	¼ cup minced fresh parsley

1. Bring 4 quarts water to boil in Dutch oven. Add rice and 1½ teaspoons salt and cook, stirring occasionally, until rice is tender, 25 to 30 minutes. Drain rice, spread onto rimmed baking sheet, and drizzle with 1 tablespoon lemon juice. Let cool completely, about 15 minutes.
2. Heat 1 tablespoon oil in 12-inch skillet over high heat until just smoking. Add asparagus, ¼ teaspoon salt, and ¼ teaspoon pepper and cook, stirring occasionally, until asparagus is browned and crisp-tender, about 4 minutes, transfer to plate and let cool slightly.
3. Whisk remaining 2½ tablespoons oil, lemon zest and remaining 2 tablespoons juice, shallot, ½ teaspoon salt, and ½ teaspoon pepper together in large bowl. Add rice, asparagus, 2 tablespoons Goat cheese, 3 tablespoons almonds, and 3 tablespoons parsley. Gently toss to combine and let sit for 10 minutes. Season with salt and pepper to taste. Transfer to serving platter and sprinkle with remaining 2 tablespoons Goat

cheese, remaining 1 tablespoon almonds, and remaining 1 tablespoon parsley. Serve.

PER SERVING
Calories: 455, Fat: 19.13g, Carbohydrates: 59.84g, Protein: 12.65g, Sugar: 3.49g, Fiber: 5.3g, Sodium: 70mg

Barley Risotto with Parmesan cheese

Prep time: 10 minutes | Cook time: 1 hour | Serves: 4 to 6

4 cups chicken or vegetable broth	1½ cups pearl barley
4 cups water	1 cup dry white wine
2 tablespoons extra-virgin olive oil	1 teaspoon minced fresh thyme or ¼ teaspoon dried
1 onion, chopped fine	2 ounces (57 g) Parmesan cheese, grated
1 carrot, peeled and chopped fine	Salt and pepper, to taste

1. Bring broth and water to simmer in medium saucepan. Reduce heat to low and cover to keep warm.
2. Heat 1 tablespoon oil in Dutch oven over medium heat until shimmering. Add onion and carrot and cook until softened, 5 to 7 minutes. Add barley and cook, stirring often, until lightly toasted and aromatic, about 4 minutes.
3. Add wine and cook, stirring frequently, until fully absorbed, about 2 minutes. Stir in 3 cups warm broth and thyme, bring to simmer, and cook, stirring occasionally, until liquid is absorbed and bottom of pot is dry, 22 to 25 minutes. Stir in 2 cups warm broth, bring to simmer, and cook, stirring occasionally, until liquid is absorbed and bottom of pot is dry, 15 to 18 minutes.
4. Continue to cook risotto, stirring often and adding warm broth as needed to prevent pot bottom from becoming dry, until barley is cooked through but still somewhat firm in center, 15 to 20 minutes. Off heat, adjust consistency with remaining warm broth as needed (you may have broth left over). Stir in Parmesan and remaining 1 tablespoon oil and season with salt and pepper to taste. Serve.

PER SERVING
Calories: 434, Fat: 12.2g, Carbohydrates: 69.7g, Protein: 14.18g, Sugar: 6.87g, Fiber: 13g, Sodium: 1209mg

Farro with Asparagu, Snap Peas, and Tomato

Prep time: 10 minutes | Cook time: 18 minutes | Serves: 4 to 6

6 ounces (170 g) asparagus, trimmed and cut into 1-inch lengths
6 ounces (170 g) sugar snap peas, strings removed, cut into 1-inch lengths
Salt and pepper, to taste
1½ cups whole farro
3 tablespoons extra-virgin olive oil

2 tablespoons lemon juice
2 tablespoons minced shallot
1 teaspoon Dijon mustard
6 ounces (170 g) cherry tomatoes, halved
3 tablespoons chopped fresh dill
2 ounces (57 g) Feta cheese, crumbled

1. Bring 4 quarts water to boil in Dutch oven. Add asparagus, snap peas, and 1 tablespoon salt and cook until crisp-tender, about 3 minutes. Using slotted spoon, transfer vegetables to large plate and let cool completely, about 15 minutes.
2. Add farro to water, return to boil, and cook until grains are tender with slight chew, 15 to 30 minutes. Drain farro, spread in rimmed baking sheet, and let cool completely, about 15 minutes.
3. Whisk oil, lemon juice, shallot, mustard, ¼ teaspoon salt, and ¼ teaspoon pepper together in large bowl. Add vegetables, farro, tomatoes, dill, and ¼ cup Feta and toss gently to combine. Season with salt and pepper to taste. Transfer to serving platter and sprinkle with remaining ¼ cup Feta. Serve.

PER SERVING
Calories: 239, Fat: 17.14g, Carbohydrates: 16.02g, Protein: 8.45g, Sugar: 9.42g, Fiber: 3.9g, Sodium: 190mg

Barley Pilaf with Mushrooms

Prep time: 10 minutes | Cook time: 35 minutes | Serves: 4

Olive oil cooking spray
2 tablespoons olive oil
8 ounces (227 g) button mushrooms, diced
½ yellow onion, diced
2 garlic cloves, minced
1 cup pearl barley

2 cups vegetable broth
1 tablespoon fresh thyme, chopped
½ teaspoon salt
¼ teaspoon smoked paprika
Fresh parsley, for garnish

1. Preheat the air fryer to 380ºF (193ºC). Lightly coat the inside of a 5-cup capacity casserole dish with olive oil cooking spray. (The shape of the casserole dish will depend upon the size of the air fryer, but it needs to be able to hold at least 5 cups.)
2. In a large skillet, heat the olive oil over medium heat. Add the mushrooms and onion and cook, stirring occasionally, for 5 minutes, or until the mushrooms begin to brown.
3. Add the garlic and cook for an additional 2 minutes. Transfer the vegetables to a large bowl.
4. Add the barley, broth, thyme, salt, and paprika.
5. Pour the barley-and-vegetable mixture into the prepared casserole dish, and place the dish into the air fryer. Bake for 15 minutes.
6. Stir the barley mixture. Reduce the heat to 360ºF (182ºC), then return the barley to the air fryer and bake for 15 minutes more.
7. Remove from the air fryer and let sit for 5 minutes before fluffing with a fork and topping with fresh parsley.

PER SERVING
Calories: 263, Total Fat: 8g, Saturated Fat: 1g, Total Carbohydrates: 44g, Protein: 7g, Fiber: 9g, Sugar: 3g

Farro with English Cucumber, Yogurt, and Mint

Prep time: 10 minutes | Cook time: 15 minutes | Serves: 4 to 6

1½ cups whole farro
Salt and pepper, to taste
3 tablespoons extra-virgin olive oil
2 tablespoons lemon juice
2 tablespoons minced shallot
2 tablespoons plain Greek yogurt

1 English cucumber, halved lengthwise, seeded, and cut into ¼-inch pieces
6 ounces (170 g) cherry tomatoes, halved
1 cup baby arugula
3 tablespoons chopped fresh mint

1. Bring 4 quarts water to boil in Dutch oven. Add farro and 1 tablespoon salt, return to boil, and cook until grains are tender with slight chew, 15 to 30 minutes. Drain farro, spread in rimmed baking sheet, and let cool completely, about 15 minutes.
2. Whisk oil, lemon juice, shallot, yogurt, ¼ teaspoon salt, and ¼ teaspoon pepper together in large bowl. Add farro, cucumber, tomatoes, arugula, and mint and toss gently to combine. Season with salt and pepper to taste. Serve.

PER SERVING
Calories: 173, Fat: 13.61g, Carbohydrates: 9.58g, Protein: 4.24g, Sugar: 7.51g, Fiber: 1.4g, Sodium: 50mg

Mediterranean Lentils and Brown Rice

Prep time: 15 minutes | Cook time: 23 minutes | Serves: 4

2¼ cups low-sodium or no-salt-added vegetable broth
½ cup uncooked brown or green lentils
½ cup uncooked instant brown rice
½ cup diced carrots
½ cup diced celery
1 (2¼-ounce / 64-g) can sliced olives, drained

¼ cup diced red onion
¼ cup chopped fresh curly-leaf parsley
1½ tablespoons extra-virgin olive oil
1 tablespoon freshly squeezed lemon juice
1 garlic clove, minced
¼ teaspoon kosher or sea salt
¼ teaspoon freshly ground black pepper

1. In a medium saucepan over high heat, bring the broth and lentils to a boil, cover, and lower the heat to medium-low. Cook for 8 minutes.
2. Raise the heat to medium, and stir in the rice. Cover the pot and cook the mixture for 15 minutes, or until the liquid is absorbed. Remove the pot from the heat and let it sit, covered, for 1 minute, then stir.
3. While the lentils and rice are cooking, mix together the carrots, celery, olives, onion, and parsley in a large serving bowl.
4. In a small bowl, whisk together the oil, lemon juice, garlic, salt, and pepper. Set aside.
5. When the lentils and rice are cooked, add them to the serving bowl. Pour the dressing on top, and mix everything together. Serve warm or cold, or store in a sealed container in the refrigerator for up to 7 days.

PER SERVING
Calories: 170g, Total Fat: 6g, Saturated Fat: 1g, Total Carbs: 25g, Fiber: 3g, Protein: 5g, Sugar: 3g, Sodium: 566mg

Chapter 7 Poultry

Chicken Kebabs with Feta Tomato Salad

Prep time: 10 minutes | Cook time: 10 minutes | Serves: 4 to 6

¼ cup extra-virgin olive oil
1 teaspoon grated lemon zest plus 3 tablespoons juice
3 garlic cloves, minced
1 tablespoon minced fresh oregano
Salt and pepper, to taste
1 pound (454 g) cherry tomatoes, halved
4 ounces (113 g) Feta cheese, crumbled
¼ cup thinly sliced red onion
¼ cup plain yogurt
1½ pounds (680 g) boneless, skinless chicken breasts, trimmed and cut into 1-inch pieces

1. Whisk oil, lemon zest and juice, garlic, oregano, ½ teaspoon salt, and ½ teaspoon pepper together in medium bowl. Reserve half of oil mixture in second medium bowl. Add tomatoes, Feta, and onion to remaining oil mixture and toss to coat. Season with salt and pepper to taste and set aside for serving.
2. Whisk yogurt into reserved oil mixture. Set aside half of yogurt dressing for serving. Add chicken to remaining yogurt dressing and toss to coat. Thread chicken onto four 12-inch metal skewers.
3. For a charcoal grill, open bottom vent completely. Light large chimney starter filled with charcoal briquettes (6 quarts). When top coals are partially covered with ash, pour evenly over grill. Set cooking grate in place, cover, and open lid vent completely. Heat grill until hot, about 5 minutes.
4. For a gas grill, turn all burners to high, cover, and heat grill until hot, about 15 minutes. Leave all burners on high.
5. Place skewers on grill and cook, turning occasionally, until chicken is well browned and registers 160°F (71°C), about 10 minutes. Using tongs, slide chicken off skewers onto serving platter. Serve chicken with salad and reserved dressing.

PER SERVING
Calories: 643, Fat: 39.64g, Carbohydrates: 25.45g, Protein: 46.2g, Sugar: 5.58g, Fiber: 2.7g, Sodium: 1082mg

Peach-Glazed Chicken Drumsticks

Prep time: 10 minutes | Cook time: 20 minutes | Serves: 4

8 chicken drumsticks (2-pound / 907-g), skin removed
Nonstick cooking spray
1 (15-ounce / 425-g) can sliced peaches in 100% juice, drained
¼ cup honey
¼ cup cider vinegar
3 garlic cloves
½ teaspoon smoked paprika
¼ teaspoon kosher or sea salt
¼ teaspoon freshly ground black pepper

1. Remove the chicken from the refrigerator.
2. Set one oven rack about 4 inches below the broiler element. Preheat the oven to 500°F (260°C). Line a large, rimmed baking sheet with aluminum foil. Place a wire cooling rack on the aluminum foil, and spray the rack with nonstick cooking spray. Set aside.
3. In a blender, combine the peaches, honey, vinegar, garlic, smoked paprika, salt, and pepper. Purée the ingredients until smooth.
4. Add the purée to a medium saucepan and bring to a boil over medium-high heat. Cook for 2 minutes, stirring constantly. Divide the sauce among two small bowls. The first bowl will be brushed on the chicken, set aside the second bowl for serving at the table.
5. Brush all sides of the chicken with about half the sauce (keeping half the sauce for a second coating), and place the drumsticks on the prepared rack. Roast for 10 minutes.
6. Remove the chicken from the oven and turn to the high broiler setting. Brush the chicken with the remaining sauce from the first bowl. Return the chicken to the oven and broil for 5 minutes. Turn the chicken, broil for 3 to 5 more minutes, until the internal temperature measures 165°F (74°C) on a meat thermometer, or until the juices run clear. Serve with the reserved sauce.

PER SERVING
Calories: 1492g, Total Fat: 26g, Saturated Fat:7g, Total Carbs: 274g, Protein: 54g, Sugar: 254g, Fiber: 20g, Sodium: 487mg

Chicken, Mushrooms, and Tarragon Pasta

Prep time: 15 minutes | Cook time: 15 minutes | Serves: 2

2 tablespoons olive oil, divided
½ medium onion, minced
4 ounces (113 g) baby bella (cremini) mushrooms, sliced
2 small garlic cloves, minced
8 ounces (227 g) chicken cutlets
2 teaspoons tomato paste
2 teaspoons dried tarragon
2 cups low-sodium chicken stock
6 ounces (170 g) pappardelle pasta
¼ cup plain full-fat Greek yogurt
Salt, to taste
Freshly ground black pepper, to taste

1. Heat 1 tablespoon of the olive oil in a sauté pan over medium-high heat. Add the onion and mushrooms and sauté for 5 minutes. Add the garlic and cook for 1 minute more.
2. Move the vegetables to the edges of the pan and add the remaining 1 tablespoon of olive oil to the center of the pan. Place the cutlets in the center and let them cook for about 3 minutes, or until they lift up easily and are golden brown on the bottom.
3. Flip the chicken and cook for another 3 minutes.
4. Mix in the tomato paste and tarragon. Add the chicken stock and stir well to combine everything. Bring the stock to a boil.
5. Add the pappardelle. Break up the pasta if needed to fit into the pan. Stir the noodles so they don't stick to the bottom of the pan.
6. Cover the sauté pan and reduce the heat to medium-low. Let the chicken and noodles simmer for 15 minutes, stirring occasionally, until the pasta is cooked and the liquid is mostly absorbed. If the liquid absorbs too quickly and the pasta isn't cooked, add more water or chicken stock, about ¼ cup at a time as needed.
7. Remove the pan from the heat.
8. Stir 2 tablespoons of the hot liquid from the pan into the yogurt. Pour the tempered yogurt into the pan and stir well to mix it into the sauce. Season with salt and pepper.
9. The sauce will tighten up as it cools, so if it seems too thick, add a few tablespoons of water.

PER SERVING
Calories: 556, Total Fat: 18g, Total Carbohydrates: 56g, Protein: 42g, Fiber: 2g, Sugar: 4g, Sodium: 190mg

Chicken Breast with Tomato and Basil

Prep time: 10 minutes | Cook time: 20 minutes | Serves: 4

Nonstick cooking spray
1 pound (454 g) boneless, skinless chicken breasts
2 tablespoons extra-virgin olive oil
¼ teaspoon freshly ground black pepper
¼ teaspoon kosher or sea salt
1 large tomato, sliced thinly
1 cup shredded Mozzarella or 4 ounces fresh Mozzarella cheese, diced
1 (14½-ounce / 411-g) can low-sodium or no-salt-added crushed tomatoes
2 tablespoons fresh torn basil leaves
4 teaspoons balsamic vinegar

1. Set one oven rack about 4 inches below the broiler element. Preheat the oven to 450°F (235°C). Line a large, rimmed baking sheet with aluminum foil. Place a wire cooling rack on the aluminum foil, and spray the rack with nonstick cooking spray. Set aside.
2. Cut the chicken into 4 pieces (if they aren't already). Put the chicken breasts in a large zip-top plastic bag. With a rolling pin or meat mallet, pound the chicken so it is evenly flattened, about ¼-inch thick. Add the oil, pepper, and salt to the bag. Reseal the bag, and massage the ingredients into the chicken. Take the chicken out of the bag and place it on the prepared wire rack.
3. Cook the chicken for 15 to 18 minutes, or until the internal temperature of the chicken is 165°F (74°C) on a meat thermometer and the juices run clear. Turn the oven to the high broiler setting. Layer the tomato slices on each chicken breast, and top with the Mozzarella. Broil the chicken for another 2 to 3 minutes, or until the cheese is melted (don't let the chicken burn on the edges). Remove the chicken from the oven.
4. While the chicken is cooking, pour the crushed tomatoes into a small, microwave-safe bowl. Cover the bowl with a paper towel, and microwave for about 1 minute on high, until hot. When you're ready to serve, divide the tomatoes among four dinner plates. Place each chicken breast on top of the tomatoes. Top with the basil and a drizzle of balsamic vinegar.

PER SERVING
Calories: 258g, Total Fat: 10g, Saturated Fat: 2g, Total Carbs: 28g, Protein: 14g, Sugar: 10g, Fiber: 4g, Sodium: 573mg

Marinated Chicken Breast

Prep time: 10 minutes | Cook time: 12 minutes | Serves: 4

½ cup olive oil
2 tablespoon fresh rosemary
1 teaspoon minced garlic
Juice and zest of 1 lemon
¼ cup chopped flat-leaf
parsley
Sea salt and freshly ground pepper, to taste
4 boneless, skinless chicken breasts

1. Mix all ingredients except the chicken together in a plastic bag or bowl.
2. Place the chicken in the container and shake/stir so the marinade thoroughly coats the chicken.
3. Refrigerate up to 24 hours.
4. Heat a grill to medium heat and cook the chicken for 6 to 8 minutes a side. Turn only once during the cooking process.
5. Serve with a Greek salad and brown rice.

PER SERVING
Calories: 573, Fat: 34.26g, Carbohydrates: 1.84g, Protein: 61.49g, Sugar: 0.34g, Fiber: 0.4g, Sodium: 126mg

Chicken Breast with Lemony Chickpea Salad

Prep time: 10 minutes | Cook time: 10 minutes | Serves: 4

6 tablespoons extra-virgin olive oil
¼ cup lemon juice
1 teaspoon honey
1 teaspoon smoked paprika
½ teaspoon ground cumin
Salt and pepper, to taste
2 (15-ounce / 425-g) cans chickpeas, rinsed
½ red onion, sliced thin
¼ cup chopped fresh mint
½ cup all-purpose flour
4 (4- to 6-ounce / 113- to 170-g) boneless, skinless chicken breasts, trimmed

1. Whisk ¼ cup oil, lemon juice, honey, paprika, cumin, ½ teaspoon salt, and ½ teaspoon pepper together in large bowl until combined. Reserve 3 tablespoons dressing for serving. Add chickpeas, onion, and mint to remaining dressing and toss to combine. Season with salt and pepper to taste and set aside for serving.
2. Spread flour in shallow dish. Pound thicker ends of chicken breasts between 2 sheets of plastic wrap to uniform ½-inch thickness. Pat chicken dry with paper towels and season with salt and pepper. Working with 1 chicken breast at a time, dredge in flour to coat, shaking off any excess.
3. Heat remaining 2 tablespoons oil in 12-inch skillet over medium-high heat until just smoking. Place chicken in skillet and cook, turning as needed, until golden brown on both sides and chicken registers 160°F (71°C), about 10 minutes. Transfer chicken to serving platter, tent loosely with aluminum foil, and let rest for 5 minutes. Drizzle reserved dressing over chicken and serve with salad.

PER SERVING
Calories: 710, Fat: 30.27g, Carbohydrates: 44.08g, Protein: 64.26g, Sugar: 7.11g, Fiber: 9.1g, Sodium: 4432mg

Poached Chicken Breat with Romesco Sauce

Prep time: 10 minutes | Cook time: 12 minutes | Serves: 6

1½ pounds (680 g) boneless, skinless chicken breasts, cut into 6 pieces
1 carrot, halved
1 celery stalk, halved
½ onion, halved
2 garlic cloves, smashed
3 sprigs fresh thyme or rosemary
1 cup romesco sauce
2 tablespoons chopped fresh flat-leaf (Italian) parsley
¼ teaspoon freshly ground black pepper

1. Put the chicken in a medium saucepan. Fill with water until there's about one inch of liquid above the chicken. Add the carrot, celery, onion, garlic, and thyme. Cover and bring it to a boil. Reduce the heat to low (keeping it covered), and cook for 12 to 15 minutes, or until the internal temperature of the chicken measures 165°F (74°C) on a meat thermometer and any juices run clear.
2. Remove the chicken from the water and let sit for 5 minutes.
3. When you're ready to serve, spread ¾ cup of romesco sauce on the bottom of a serving platter. Arrange the chicken breasts on top, and drizzle with the remaining romesco sauce. Sprinkle the tops with parsley and pepper.

PER SERVING
Calories: 270g, Total Fat: 11g, Saturated Fat:3g, Total Carbs: 31g, Protein: 13g, Sugar: 8g, Fiber: 3g, Sodium: 647mg

Lebanese-Style Grilled Chicken

Prep time: 10 minutes | Cook time: 10 minutes | Serves: 4

½ cup olive oil
¼ cup apple cider vinegar
Zest and juice of 1 lemon
4 cloves garlic, minced
2 teaspoons sea salt

1 teaspoon Arabic 7 spices (baharaat)
½ teaspoon cinnamon
1 chicken, cut into 8 pieces

1. Combine all the ingredients except the chicken in a shallow dish or plastic bag.
2. Place the chicken in the bag or dish and marinate overnight, or at least for several hours.
3. Drain, reserving the marinade. Heat the grill to medium-high.
4. Cook the chicken pieces for 10 to 14 minutes, brushing them with the marinade every 5 minutes or so.
5. The chicken is done when the crust is golden brown and an instant-read thermometer reads 180 degrees in the thickest parts. Remove skin before eating.

PER SERVING
Calories: 516, Fat: 33.56g, Carbohydrates: 2.53g, Protein: 48.81g, Sugar: 0.46g, Fiber: 0.5g, Sodium: 1344mg

Chicken Breast Marsala

Prep time: 10 minutes | Cook time: 20 minutes | Serves: 4

¼ cup olive oil
4 boneless, skinless chicken breasts, pounded thin
Sea salt and freshly ground pepper, to taste
¼ cup whole-wheat flour

½ pound (227 g) mushrooms, sliced
1 cup Marsala wine
1 cup chicken broth
¼ cup flat-leaf parsley, chopped

1. Heat the olive oil in a large skillet on medium-high heat.
2. Season the chicken breasts with sea salt and freshly ground pepper, then dredge them in flour.
3. Sauté them in the olive oil until golden brown.
4. Transfer to an oven-safe plate, and keep warm in the oven on low. Sauté the mushrooms in the same pan. Add the wine and chicken broth and bring to a simmer.
5. Simmer for 10 minutes, or until the sauce is

reduced and thickened slightly. Return the chicken to the pan, and cook it in the sauce for 10 minutes. Transfer to a serving dish and sprinkle with the parsley.

PER SERVING
Calories: 649, Fat: 21.55g, Carbohydrates: 49.63g, Protein: 68.46g, Sugar: 2.21g, Fiber: 7.6g, Sodium: 354mg

Moroccan Chicken Thighs and Vegetable Tagine

Prep time: 15 minutes | Cook time: 52 minutes | Serves: 6

½ cup extra-virgin olive oil, divided
1½ pounds (680 g) boneless skinless chicken thighs, cut into 1-inch chunks
3/4 teaspoon salt, divided
½ teaspoon freshly ground black pepper
1 small red onion, chopped
1 red bell pepper, cut into 1-inch squares
2 medium tomatoes, chopped or 1½ cups

diced canned tomatoes
1 cup water
2 medium zucchinis, sliced into ¼-inch-thick half moons
1 cup pitted halved olives (Kalamata or Spanish green work nicely)
¼ cup chopped fresh cilantro or flat-leaf Italian parsley
Riced cauliflower or sautéed spinach, for serving

1. In a Dutch oven or large rimmed skillet, heat ¼ cup olive oil over medium-high heat.
2. Season the chicken with ½ teaspoon salt and pepper and sauté until just browned on all sides, 6 to 8 minutes.
3. Add the onions and peppers and sauté until wilted, another 6 to 8 minutes.
4. Add the chopped tomatoes and water, bring to a boil, and reduce the heat to low. Cover and simmer over low heat until the meat is cooked through and very tender, 30 to 45 minutes.
5. Add the remaining ¼ cup olive oil, zucchini, olives, and cilantro, stirring to combine. Continue to cook over low heat, uncovered, until the zucchini is tender, about 10 minutes.
6. Serve warm over riced cauliflower or atop a bed of sautéed spinach.

PER SERVING
Calories: 358, Total Fat: 25g, Total Carbs: 8g, Net Carbs: 5g, Protein: 25g, Fiber: 3g, Sodium: 669mg

Stuffed Chicken Breast with Caprese

Prep time: 10 minutes | Cook time: 30 minutes | Serves: 4

8 tablespoons extra-virgin olive oil, divided
2 (6-ounce / 170 g) boneless, skinless chicken breasts
4 ounces (113 g) frozen spinach, thawed and drained well
1 cup shredded fresh Mozzarella cheese
¼ cup chopped fresh basil
2 tablespoons chopped sun-dried tomatoes (preferably marinated in oil)
1 teaspoon salt, divided
1 teaspoon freshly ground black pepper, divided
½ teaspoon garlic powder
1 tablespoon balsamic vinegar

1. Preheat the oven to 375°F (190°C).
2. Drizzle 1 tablespoon olive oil in a small deep baking dish and swirl to coat the bottom.
3. Make a deep incision about 3- to 4-inches long along the length of each chicken breast to create a pocket. Using your knife or fingers, carefully increase the size of the pocket without cutting through the chicken breast. (Each breast will look like a change purse with an opening at the top.)
4. In a medium bowl, combine the spinach, Mozzarella, basil, sun-dried tomatoes, 2 tablespoons olive oil, ½ teaspoon salt, ½ teaspoon pepper, and the garlic powder and combine well with a fork.
5. Stuff half of the filling mixture into the pocket of each chicken breast, stuffing down to fully fill the pocket. Press the opening together with your fingers. You can use a couple toothpicks to pin it closed if you wish.
6. In a medium skillet, heat 2 tablespoons olive oil over medium-high heat. Carefully sear the chicken breasts until browned, 3 to 4 minutes per side, being careful to not let too much filling escape. Transfer to the prepared baking dish, incision-side up. Scrape up any filling that fell out in the skillet and add it to baking dish. Cover the pan with foil and bake until the chicken is cooked through, 30 to 40 minutes, depending on the thickness of the breasts.
7. Remove from the oven and rest, covered, for 10 minutes. Meanwhile, in a small bowl, whisk together the remaining 3 tablespoons olive oil, balsamic vinegar, ½ teaspoon salt, and ½ teaspoon pepper.
8. To serve, cut each chicken breast in half, widthwise, and serve a half chicken breast drizzled with oil and vinegar.

PER SERVING
Calories: 434, Total Fat: 35g, Total Carbs: 3g, Net Carbs: 2g, Protein: 27g, Fiber: 1g, Sodium: 742mg

Lemon-Herb Spatchcock Chicken

Prep time: 10 minutes | Cook time: 45 minutes | Serves: 6 to 8

½ cup extra-virgin olive oil, divided
1 (3- to 4-pound / 1.4- to 1.8-kg) roasting chicken
8 garlic cloves, roughly chopped
2 to 4 tablespoons
chopped fresh rosemary
2 teaspoons salt, divided
1 teaspoon freshly ground black pepper, divided
2 lemons, thinly sliced

1. Preheat the oven to 425°F (220°C).
2. Pour 2 tablespoons olive oil in the bottom of a 9-by-13-inch baking dish or rimmed baking sheet and swirl to coat the bottom.
3. To spatchcock the bird, place the whole chicken breast-side down on a large work surface. Using a very sharp knife, cut along the backbone, starting at the tail end and working your way up to the neck. Pull apart the two sides, opening up the chicken. Flip it over, breast-side up, pressing down with your hands to flatten the bird. Transfer to the prepared baking dish.
4. Loosen the skin over the breasts and thighs by cutting a small incision and sticking one or two fingers inside to pull the skin away from the meat without removing it.
5. To prepare the filling, in a small bowl, combine ¼ cup olive oil, garlic, rosemary, 1 teaspoon salt, and ½ teaspoon pepper and whisk together.
6. Rub the garlic-herb oil evenly under the skin of each breast and each thigh. Add the lemon slices evenly to the same areas.
7. Whisk together the remaining 2 tablespoons olive oil, 1 teaspoon salt, and ½ teaspoon pepper and rub over the outside of the chicken.
8. Place in the oven, uncovered, and roast for 45 minutes, or until cooked through and golden brown. Allow to rest 5 minutes before carving to serve.

PER SERVING
Calories: 435, Total Fat: 34g, Total Carbs: 2g, Net Carbs: 2g, Protein: 28g, Fiber: 0g, Sodium: 737mg

Tahini Chicken Rice Bowls with Apricots

Prep time: 15 minutes | Cook time: 15 minutes | Serves: 4

1 cup uncooked instant brown rice
¼ cup tahini or peanut butter (tahini for nut-free)
¼ cup 2% plain Greek yogurt
2 tablespoons chopped scallions, green and white parts
1 tablespoon freshly squeezed lemon juice
1 tablespoon water
1 teaspoon ground cumin

¾ teaspoon ground cinnamon
¼ teaspoon kosher or sea salt
2 cups chopped cooked chicken breast
½ cup chopped dried apricots
2 cups peeled and chopped seedless cucumber
4 teaspoons sesame seeds
Fresh mint leaves, for serving (optional)

1. Cook the brown rice according to the package instructions.
2. While the rice is cooking, in a medium bowl, mix together the tahini, yogurt, scallions, lemon juice, water, cumin, cinnamon, and salt. Transfer half the tahini mixture to another medium bowl. Mix the chicken into the first bowl.
3. When the rice is done, mix it into the second bowl of tahini (the one without the chicken).
4. To assemble, divide the chicken among four bowls. Spoon the rice mixture next to the chicken in each bowl. Next to the chicken, place the dried apricots, and in the remaining empty section, add the cucumbers. Sprinkle with sesame seeds, and top with mint, if desired, and serve.

PER SERVING
Calories: 335g, Total Fat: 11g, Saturated Fat: 2g, Total Carbs: 30g, Protein: 31g, Sugar: 12g, Fiber: 4g, Sodium: 345mg, Potassium: 672mg

Greek Chicken Souvlaki with Tzatziki

Prep time: 10 minutes | Cook time: 8 minutes | Serves: 4

½ cup extra-virgin olive oil, plus extra for serving
¼ cup dry white wine (optional, add extra lemon juice instead, if desired)
6 garlic cloves, finely minced
Zest and juice of 1 lemon
1 tablespoon dried oregano

1 teaspoon dried rosemary
½ teaspoons salt
½ teaspoon freshly ground black pepper
1 pound (454 g) boneless, skinless chicken thighs, cut into 1½-inch chunks
1 cup tzatziki, for serving

1. In a large glass bowl or resealable plastic bag, combine the olive oil, white wine (if using), garlic, lemon zest and juice, oregano, rosemary, salt, and pepper and whisk or shake to combine well. Add the chicken to the marinade and toss to coat. Cover or seal and marinate in the refrigerator for at least 1 hour, or up to 24 hours.
2. In a bowl, submerge wooden skewers in water and soak for at least 30 minutes before using.
3. To cook, heat the grill to medium-high heat. Thread the marinated chicken on the soaked skewers, reserving the marinade.
4. Grill until cooked through, flipping occasionally so that the chicken cooks evenly, 5 to 8 minutes. Remove and keep warm.
5. Bring the reserved marinade to a boil in a small saucepan. Reduce the heat to low and simmer 3 to 5 minutes.
6. Serve chicken skewers drizzled with hot marinade, adding more olive oil if desired, and tzatziki.

PER SERVING
Calories: 677, Total Fat: 61g, Total Carbs: 8g, Net Carbs: 8g, Protein: 26g, Fiber: 0g, Sodium: 640mg

Chicken Sausage and Tomato with Farro

Prep time: 10 minutes | Cook time: 45 minutes | Serves: 2

1 tablespoon olive oil
½ medium onion, diced
¼ cup julienned sun-dried tomatoes packed in olive oil and herbs
8 ounces (227 g) hot Italian chicken sausage, removed from the casing

¾ cup farro
1½ cups low-sodium chicken stock
2 cups loosely packed arugula
4 to 5 large fresh basil leaves, sliced thin
Salt, to taste

1. Heat the olive oil in a sauté pan over medium-high heat. Add the onion and sauté for 5 minutes. Add the sun-dried tomatoes and chicken sausage, stirring to break up the sausage. Cook for 7 minutes, or until the sausage is no longer pink.
2. Stir in the farro. Let it toast for 3 minutes, stirring occasionally.
3. Add the chicken stock and bring the mixture to a boil. Cover the pan and reduce the heat to medium-low. Let it simmer for 30 minutes, or until the farro is tender.
4. Stir in the arugula and let it wilt slightly. Add the basil, and season with salt.

PER SERVING
Calories: 491, Total Fat: 19g, Total Carbohydrates: 53g, Protein: 31g, Fiber: 7g, Sugar: 4g, Sodium: 765mg

Chicken Thigh with Roasted Artichokes

Prep time: 5 minutes | Cook time: 20 minutes | Serves: 4

2 large lemons
3 tablespoons extra-virgin olive oil, divided
½ teaspoon kosher or sea salt

2 large artichokes
4 (6-ounce / 170-g) bone-in, skin-on chicken thighs

1. Put a large, rimmed baking sheet in the oven. Preheat the oven to 450°F (235°C) with the pan inside. Tear off four sheets of aluminum foil about 8-by-10 inches each, set aside.
2. Using a Microplane or citrus zester, zest 1 lemon into a large bowl. Halve both lemons and squeeze all the juice into the bowl with the zest. Whisk in 2 tablespoons of oil and the salt. Set aside.
3. Rinse the artichokes with cool water, and dry with a clean towel. Using a sharp knife, cut about 1½ inches off the tip of each artichoke. Cut about ¼ inch off each stem. Halve each artichoke lengthwise so each piece has equal amounts of stem. Immediately plunge the artichoke halves into the lemon juice and oil mixture (to prevent browning) and turn to coat on all sides. Lay one artichoke half flat-side down in the center of a sheet of aluminum foil, and close up loosely to make a foil packet. Repeat the process with the remaining three artichoke halves. Set the packets aside.
4. Put the chicken in the remaining lemon juice mixture and turn to coat.
5. Using oven mitts, carefully remove the hot baking sheet from the oven and pour on the remaining tablespoon of oil, tilt the pan to coat. Carefully arrange the chicken, skin-side down, on the hot baking sheet. Place the artichoke packets, flat-side down, on the baking sheet as well. (Arrange the artichoke packets and chicken with space between them so air can circulate around them.)
6. Roast for 20 minutes, or until the internal temperature of the chicken measures 165°F (74°C) on a meat thermometer and any juices run clear. Before serving, check the artichokes for doneness by pulling on a leaf. If it comes out easily, the artichoke is ready.

PER SERVING
Calories: 832g, Total Fat: 80g, Saturated Fat: 21g, Total Carbs: 11g, Protein: 19g, Sugar: 2g, Fiber: 5g, Sodium: 544mg, Potassium: 530mg

Chapter 8 Meat

Lamb Kofte Skewers with Yogurt Sauce

Prep time: 15 minutes | Cook time: 8 minutes | Serves: 4

1 pound (454 g) ground lamb
½ cup finely chopped fresh mint, plus 2 tablespoons
¼ cup almond or coconut flour
¼ cup finely chopped red onion
¼ cup toasted pine nuts
2 teaspoons ground cumin
3/4 teaspoon salt, divided
1 teaspoon ground cinnamon
1 teaspoon ground ginger
½ teaspoon ground nutmeg
½ teaspoon freshly ground black pepper
1 cup plain low-fat Greek yogurt
2 tablespoons extra-virgin olive oil
Zest and juice of 1 lime

1. Heat the oven broiler to the low setting. You can also bake these at high heat (450ºF (235ºC)) if you happen to have a very hot broiler. Submerge four wooden skewers in water and let soak at least 10 minutes to prevent them from burning.
2. In a large bowl, combine the lamb, ½ cup mint, almond flour, red onion, pine nuts, cumin, ½ teaspoon salt, cinnamon, ginger, nutmeg, and pepper and, using your hands, incorporate all the ingredients together well.
3. Form the mixture into 12 egg-shaped patties and let sit for 10 minutes.
4. Remove the skewers from the water, thread 3 patties onto each skewer, and place on a broiling pan or wire rack on top of a baking sheet lined with aluminum foil. Broil on the top rack until golden and cooked through, 8 to 12 minutes, flipping once halfway through cooking.
5. While the meat cooks, in a small bowl, combine the yogurt, olive oil, remaining 2 tablespoons chopped mint, remaining ¼ teaspoon salt, and lime zest and juice and whisk to combine well. Keep cool until ready to use.
6. Serve the skewers with yogurt sauce.

PER SERVING
Calories: 500, Total Fat: 42g, Total Carbs: 9g, Net Carbs: 7g, Protein: 23g, Fiber: 2g, Sodium: 633mg

Moroccan Lamb and Lentil Soup

Prep time: 15 minutes | Cook time: 35 minutes | Serves: 6 to 8

1 pound (454 g) lamb shoulder chops, 1 to 1½ inches thick, trimmed and halved
1 cup French green lentils, picked over and rinsed
¾ tsp. table salt, divided
⅛ tsp. pepper
1 tbsp. extra-virgin olive oil
1 onion, chopped fine
1 tbsp. all-purpose flour
8 cups (1920 ml) chicken broth
¼ cup harissa, plus extra for serving
1 (15-ounce, 425 g) can chickpeas, rinsed
2 tomatoes, cored and cut into ¼-inch pieces
½ cup chopped fresh cilantro

1. Pat lamb dry with paper towels. Sprinkle with ¼ teaspoon salt and pepper. In Instant Pot, use highest sauté function, heat oil for 5 minutes. Put lamb in pot and cook about 4 minutes until well browned on first side, transfer to plate.
2. Add onion and remaining salt to fat left in pot and cook about 5 minutes with highest sauté function, until softened. Stir in harissa and flour and cook about 30 seconds until fragrant. Slowly whisk in broth, scraping up any browned bits and diminish any lumps. Stir in lentils, then nestle lamb into multicooker with any accumulated juices.
3. Lock lid and close pressure release valve. Choose high pressure cook function and cook for 10 minutes. Turn off and quick-release pressure. Carefully remove lid, letting steam escape away from you.
4. Transfer lamb to cutting board, cool down slightly, then shred into bite-size pieces with 2 forks, discard excess fat and bones. Stir lamb and chickpeas into soup until heated through, about 3 minutes. Season with salt and pepper. Top each portion with tomatoes and sprinkle with cilantro. Serve with extra harissa separately.

PER SERVING
Calories: 300, Total Fat: 13g, Sat Fat: 3g, Total Carbohydrates: 24g, Protein: 22g, Sodium: 940mg, Fiber: 6g, Sugar: 4g, Added Sugar: 0g

Stuffed Pork Loin with Cheesy Tomato

Prep time: 10 minutes | Cook time: 45 minutes | Serves: 6

1 to 1½ pounds (454- to 680-g) pork tenderloin
1 cup crumbled Goat cheese
4 ounces (113 g) frozen spinach, thawed and well drained
2 tablespoons chopped sun-dried tomatoes
2 tablespoons extra-virgin olive oil (or seasoned oil marinade from sun-dried tomatoes), plus ¼ cup, divided
½ teaspoon salt
½ teaspoon freshly ground black pepper
Zucchini noodles or sautéed greens, for serving

1. Preheat the oven to 350ºF (180ºC). Cut cooking twine into eight (6-inch) pieces.
2. Cut the pork tenderloin in half lengthwise, leaving about an inch border, being careful to not cut all the way through to the other side. Open the tenderloin like a book to form a large rectangle. Place it between two pieces of parchment paper or plastic wrap and pound to about ¼-inch thickness with a meat mallet, rolling pin, or the back of a heavy spoon.
3. In a small bowl, combine the Goat cheese, spinach, sun-dried tomatoes, 2 tablespoons olive oil, salt, and pepper and mix to incorporate well.
4. Spread the filling over the surface of the pork, leaving a 1-inch border from one long edge and both short edges. To roll, start from the long edge with filling and roll towards the opposite edge. Tie cooking twine around the pork to secure it closed, evenly spacing each of the eight pieces of twine along the length of the roll.
5. In a Dutch oven or large oven-safe skillet, heat ¼ cup olive oil over medium-high heat. Add the pork and brown on all sides. Remove from the heat, cover, and bake until the pork is cooked through, 45 to 75 minutes, depending on the thickness of the pork. Remove from the oven and let rest for 10 minutes at room temperature.
6. To serve, remove the twine and discard. Slice the pork into medallions and serve over zucchini noodles or sautéed greens, spooning the cooking oil and any bits of filling that fell out during cooking over top.

PER SERVING
Calories: 270, Total Fat: 21g, Total Carbs: 2g, Net Carbs: 1g, Protein: 20g, Fiber: 1g, Sodium: 323mg

Filet Mignon with Mushroom–Red Wine Sauce

Prep time: 15 minutes | Cook time: 16 minutes | Serves: 2

2 (3-ounce / 85-g) pieces filet mignon
2 tablespoons olive oil, divided
8 ounces (227 g) baby bella (cremini) mushrooms, quartered
⅓ cup large shallot, minced
2 teaspoons flour
2 teaspoons tomato paste
½ cup red wine
1 cup low-sodium chicken stock
½ teaspoon dried thyme
1 sprig fresh rosemary
1 teaspoon herbes de Provence
¼ teaspoon salt
¼ teaspoon garlic powder
¼ teaspoon onion powder
Pinch freshly ground black pepper

1. Preheat the oven to 425ºF (220ºC) and set the oven rack to the middle position.
2. Remove the filets from the refrigerator about 30 minutes before you're ready to cook them. Pat them dry with a paper towel and let them rest while you prepare the mushroom sauce.
3. In a sauté pan, heat 1 tablespoon of olive oil over medium-high heat. Add the mushrooms and shallot and sauté for 10 minutes.
4. Add the flour and tomato paste and cook for another 30 seconds. Add the wine and scrape up any browned bits from the sauté pan. Add the chicken stock, thyme, and rosemary.
5. Stir the sauce so the flour doesn't form lumps and bring it to a boil. Once the sauce thickens, reduce the heat to the lowest setting and cover the pan to keep the sauce warm.
6. In a small bowl, combine the herbes de Provence, salt, garlic powder, onion powder, and pepper.
7. Rub the beef with the remaining 1 tablespoon of olive oil and season it on both sides with the herb mixture.
8. Heat an oven-safe sauté pan over medium-high heat. Add the beef and sear for 2½ minutes on each side. Then, transfer the pan to the oven for 5 more minutes to finish cooking. Use a meat thermometer to check the internal temperature and remove it at 130°F for medium-rare.
9. Tent the meat with foil and let it rest for 5 minutes before serving topped with the mushroom sauce.

PER SERVING
Calories: 385, Total Fat: 20g, Total Carbohydrates: 15g, Protein: 25g, Fiber: 0g, Sugar: 5g, Sodium: 330mg

Turkish Lamb Stew with Pistachios

Prep time: 20 minutes | Cook time: 14 minutes | Serves: 6

1 pound (454 g) bone-in or boneless lamb leg steak, center cut
1 tablespoon extra-virgin olive oil
1 cup chopped onion
½ cup diced carrot
1 teaspoon ground cumin
½ teaspoon ground cinnamon
¼ teaspoon kosher or sea salt
4 garlic cloves, minced
2 tablespoons tomato paste

1 tablespoon chopped canned chipotle pepper in adobo sauce
2 cups water
½ cup chopped prunes
1 (15-ounce / 425-g) can chickpeas, drained and rinsed
2 tablespoons freshly squeezed lemon juice
¼ cup chopped unsalted pistachios
Cooked couscous or bulgur, for serving (optional)

1. Slice the meat into 1-inch cubes. Pat dry with a few paper towels.
2. In a large stockpot over medium-high heat, heat the oil. Add the lamb and any bone, and cook for 4 minutes, stirring only after allowing the meat to brown on one side. Using a slotted spoon, transfer the lamb from the pot to a plate. It will not yet be fully cooked. Don't clean out the stockpot.
3. Put the onion, carrot, cumin, cinnamon, and salt in the pot and cook for 6 minutes, stirring occasionally. Push the vegetables to the edge of the pot. Add the garlic and cook for 1 minute, stirring constantly. Add the tomato paste and chipotle pepper, and cook for 1 minute more, stirring constantly while blending and mashing the tomato paste into the vegetables.
4. Return the lamb to the pot along with the water and prunes. Turn up the heat to high, and bring to a boil. Reduce the heat to medium-low and cook for 5 to 7 minutes more, until the stew thickens slightly. Stir in the chickpeas and cook for 1 minute. Remove the stew from the heat, and stir in the lemon juice. Sprinkle the pistachios on top and serve over couscous, if desired.

PER SERVING
Calories: 284g, Total Fat: 9g, Saturated Fat:2g, Total Carbs: 32g, Protein: 23g, Sugar: 4g, Fiber: 5g, Sodium: 291mg

Meatballs with Almond Sauce

Prep time: 15 minutes | Cook time: 15 minutes | Serves: 4 to 6

8 ounces (227 g) ground veal or pork
8 ounces (227 g) ground beef
½ cup finely minced onion, divided
1 large egg, beaten
¼ cup almond flour
1½ teaspoons salt, divided
1 teaspoon garlic powder
½ teaspoon freshly ground black pepper

½ teaspoon ground nutmeg
2 teaspoons chopped fresh flat-leaf Italian parsley, plus ¼ cup, divided
½ cup extra-virgin olive oil, divided
¼ cup slivered almonds
1 cup dry white wine or chicken broth
¼ cup unsweetened almond butter

1. In a large bowl, combine the veal, beef, ¼ cup onion, and the egg and mix well with a fork. In a small bowl, whisk together the almond flour, 1 teaspoon salt, garlic powder, pepper, and nutmeg. Add to the meat mixture along with 2 teaspoons chopped parsley and incorporate well. Form the mixture into small meatballs, about 1 inch in diameter, and place on a plate. Let sit for 10 minutes at room temperature.
2. In a large skillet, heat ¼ cup oil over medium-high heat. Add the meatballs to the hot oil and brown on all sides, cooking in batches if necessary, 2 to 3 minutes per side. Remove from skillet and keep warm.
3. In the hot skillet, sauté the remaining ¼ cup minced onion in the remaining ¼ cup olive oil for 5 minutes. Reduce the heat to medium-low and add the slivered almonds. Sauté until the almonds are golden, another 3 to 5 minutes.
4. In a small bowl, whisk together the white wine, almond butter, and remaining ½ teaspoon salt. Add to the skillet and bring to a boil, stirring constantly. Reduce the heat to low, return the meatballs to skillet, and cover. Cook until the meatballs are cooked through, another 8 to 10 minutes.
5. Remove from the heat, stir in the remaining ¼ cup chopped parsley, and serve the meatballs warm and drizzled with almond sauce.

PER SERVING
Calories: 449, Total Fat: 42g, Total Carbs: 3g, Net Carbs: 2g, Protein: 16g, Fiber: 1g, Sodium: 696mg

Italian Sausage Orecchiette

Prep time: 10 minutes | Cook time: 20 minutes | Serves: 2

1 tablespoon olive oil
½ medium onion, diced
2 garlic cloves, minced
2 ounces (57 g) baby bella (cremini) mushrooms, sliced
4 ounces (113 g) hot or sweet Italian sausage
½ teaspoon Italian herb seasoning
1½ cups dry orecchiette pasta
2 cups low-sodium chicken stock
2 cups packed baby spinach
¼ cup cream
Salt, to taste

1. Heat the olive oil in a sauté pan over medium-high heat. Add the onion, garlic, and mushrooms and sauté for 5 minutes.
2. Remove the sausage from its casing and add it to the pan, breaking it up well. Cook for another 5 minutes, or until the sausage is no longer pink.
3. Add the Italian herb seasoning, pasta, and chicken stock. Bring the mixture to a boil.
4. Cover the pan, reduce the heat to medium-low, and let it simmer for 10 to 15 minutes, or until the pasta is cooked. Remove from the heat.
5. Add the spinach and stir it in to let it wilt.
6. Add the cream and season with salt. The sauce will tighten up as it cools. If it seems too thick, add additional chicken stock or water.

PER SERVING
Calories: 531, Total Fat: 19g, Total Carbohydrates: 69g, Protein: 23g, Fiber: 5g, Sugar: 5g, Sodium: 569mg

Pork Tenderloin with Dijon Apple Sauce

Prep time: 10 minutes | Cook time: 20 minutes | Serves: 8

1½ tablespoons extra-virgin olive oil
1 (12-ounce / 340-g) pork tenderloin
¼ teaspoon kosher salt
¼ teaspoon freshly ground black pepper
¼ cup apple jelly
¼ cup apple juice
2 to 3 tablespoons Dijon mustard
½ tablespoon cornstarch
½ tablespoon cream

1. Preheat the oven to 325°F (163°C).
2. In a large sauté pan or skillet, heat the olive oil over medium heat.
3. Add the pork to the skillet, using tongs to turn and sear the pork on all sides. Once seared, sprinkle pork with salt and pepper, and set it on a small baking sheet.
4. In the same skillet, with the juices from the pork, mix the apple jelly, juice, and mustard into the pan juices. Heat thoroughly over low heat, stirring consistently for 5 minutes. Spoon over the pork.
5. Put the pork in the oven and roast for 15 to 17 minutes, or 20 minutes per pound. Every 10 to 15 minutes, baste the pork with the apple-mustard sauce.
6. Once the pork tenderloin is done, remove it from the oven and let it rest for 15 minutes. Then, cut it into 1-inch slices.
7. In a small pot, blend the cornstarch with cream. Heat over low heat. Add the pan juices into the pot, stirring for 2 minutes, until thickened. Serve the sauce over the pork.

PER SERVING
Calories: 146, Total Fat: 7g, Saturated Fat: 2g, Total Carbohydrates: 8g, Protein: 13g, Sugar: 5g, Fiber: 0g, Sodium: 192mg

Greek-Style Pork Butt with Leeks

Prep time: 10 minutes | Cook time: 1½ hours | Serves: 4 to 6

2 pounds (907 g) boneless pork butt roast, trimmed and cut into 1-inch pieces
Salt and pepper, to taste
3 tablespoons extra-virgin olive oil
2 pounds (907 g) leeks, white and light green parts only, halved lengthwise, sliced 1
inch thick, and washed thoroughly
2 garlic cloves, minced
1 (14½-ounce / 411-g) can diced tomatoes
1 cup dry white wine
½ cup chicken broth
1 bay leaf
2 teaspoons chopped fresh oregano

1. Adjust oven rack to lower-middle position and heat oven to 325°F (163°C). Pat pork dry with paper towels and season with salt and pepper. Heat 1 tablespoon oil in Dutch oven over medium-high heat until just smoking. Brown half of pork on all sides, about 8 minutes, transfer to bowl. Repeat with 1 tablespoon oil and remaining pork, transfer to bowl.
2. Add remaining 1 tablespoon oil, leeks, ½ teaspoon salt, and ½ teaspoon pepper to fat left in pot and cook over medium heat, stirring

occasionally, until softened and lightly browned, 5 to 7 minutes. Stir in garlic and cook until fragrant, about 30 seconds. Stir in tomatoes and their juice, scraping up any browned bits, and cook until tomato liquid is nearly evaporated, 10 to 12 minutes.

3. Stir in wine, broth, bay leaf, and pork with any accumulated juices and bring to simmer. Cover, transfer pot to oven, and cook until pork is tender and falls apart when prodded with fork, 1 to 1½ hours. Discard bay leaf. Stir in oregano and season with salt and pepper to taste. Serve.

PER SERVING
Calories: 555, Fat: 20.41g, Carbohydrates: 37.96g, Protein: 55.74g, Sugar: 12.43g, Fiber: 6.6g, Sodium: 402mg

Lamb Burgers with Harissa Mayo

Prep time: 15 minutes | Cook time: 13 minutes | Serves: 2

½ small onion, minced
1 garlic clove, minced
2 teaspoons minced fresh parsley
2 teaspoons minced fresh mint
¼ teaspoon salt
Pinch freshly ground black pepper
1 teaspoon cumin
1 teaspoon smoked paprika

¼ teaspoon coriander
8 ounces (227 g) lean ground lamb
2 tablespoons olive oil low fat yogurt
½ teaspoon harissa paste, plus more or less to taste
2 hamburger buns or pitas, fresh greens, tomato slices (optional, for serving)

1. Preheat the grill to medium-high, 350°F (180°C) to 400°F (205°C) and oil the grill grate. Alternatively, you can cook these in a heavy pan (cast iron is best) on the stovetop.
2. In a large bowl, combine the onion, garlic, parsley, mint, salt, pepper, cumin, paprika, and coriander. Add the lamb and, using your hands, combine the meat with the spices so they are evenly distributed. Form meat mixture into 2 patties.
3. Grill the burgers for 4 minutes per side, or until the internal temperature registers 160°F (71°C) for medium.
4. If cooking on the stovetop, heat the pan to medium-high and oil the pan. Cook the burgers for 5 to 6 minutes per side, or until the internal temperature registers 160°F (71°C).
5. While the burgers are cooking, combine the low fat yogurt and harissa in a small bowl.
6. Serve the burgers with the harissa low fat yogurt and slices of tomato and fresh greens on a bun or pita—or skip the bun altogether.

PER SERVING
Calories: 381, Total Fat: 20g, Total Carbohydrates: 27g, Protein: 22g, Fiber: 2g, Sugar: 4g, Sodium: 653mg

Beef Pita Sandwiches with Yogurt Sauce

Prep time: 20 minutes | Cook time: 8 minutes | Serves: 2

For the Beef:
1 tablespoon olive oil
½ medium onion, minced
2 garlic cloves, minced
6 ounces (170 g) lean ground beef
1 teaspoon dried oregano
For the Yogurt Sauce:
⅓ cup plain Greek yogurt
1 ounce (28 g) crumbled Feta cheese
1 tablespoon minced fresh parsley

1 tablespoon minced scallion
1 tablespoon freshly squeezed lemon juice
Pinch salt
For the Sandwiches:
2 large Greek-style pitas
½ cup cherry tomatoes, halved
1 cup diced cucumber
Salt, to taste
Freshly ground black pepper, to taste

Make the Beef
1. Heat the olive oil in a sauté pan over medium high-heat. Add the onion, garlic, and ground beef and sauté for 7 minutes, breaking up the meat well. When the meat is no longer pink, drain off any fat and stir in the oregano. Turn off the heat.

Make the Yogurt Sauce
1. In a small bowl, combine the yogurt, Feta, parsley, scallion, lemon juice, and salt.
2. Assemble the Sandwiches
3. Warm the pitas in the microwave for 20 seconds each.
4. To serve, spread some of the yogurt sauce over each warm pita. Top with the ground beef, cherry tomatoes, and diced cucumber. Season with salt and pepper. Add additional yogurt sauce if desired.

PER SERVING
Calories: 541, Total Fat: 21g, Total Carbohydrates: 57g, Protein: 29g, Fiber: 4g, Sugar: 9g, Sodium: 694mg

Pork Chops with Bell Peppers and Onions

Prep time: 10 minutes | Cook time: 16 minutes | Serves: 4

4 (4-ounce/ 113-g) pork chops, untrimmed
1½ teaspoons salt, divided
1 teaspoon freshly ground black pepper, divided
½ cup extra-virgin olive oil, divided
1 red or orange bell pepper, thinly sliced
1 green bell pepper, thinly sliced

1 small yellow onion, thinly sliced
2 teaspoons dried Italian herbs (such as oregano, parsley, or rosemary)
2 garlic cloves, minced
1 tablespoon balsamic vinegar

1. Season the pork chops with 1 teaspoon salt and ½ teaspoon pepper.
2. In a large skillet, heat ¼ cup olive oil over medium-high heat. Fry the pork chops in the oil until browned and almost cooked through but not fully cooked, 4 to 5 minutes per side, depending on the thickness of chops. Remove from the skillet and cover to keep warm.
3. Pour the remaining ¼ cup olive oil in the skillet and sauté the sliced peppers, onions, and herbs over medium-high heat until tender, 6 to 8 minutes. Add the garlic, stirring to combine, and return the pork to skillet. Cover, reduce the heat to low, and cook for another 2 to 3 minutes, or until the pork is cooked through.
4. Turn off the heat. Using a slotted spoon, transfer the pork, peppers, and onions to a serving platter. Add the vinegar to the oil in the skillet and whisk to combine well. Drizzle the vinaigrette over the pork and serve warm.

PER SERVING
Calories: 508, Total Fat: 40g, Total Carbs: 8g, Net Carbs: 6g, Protein: 31g, Fiber: 2g, Sodium: 972mg

Moroccan Stuffed Peppers with Beef

Prep time: 15 minutes | Cook time: 20 minutes | Serves: 4

¼ cup, plus 2 tablespoons extra-virgin olive oil, divided
2 large red bell peppers
1 pound (454 g) ground beef
1 small onion, finely chopped
2 garlic cloves, minced
2 tablespoons chopped fresh sage or 2 teaspoons dried sage

1 teaspoon salt
1 teaspoon ground allspice
½ teaspoon freshly ground black pepper
½ cup chopped fresh flat-leaf Italian parsley
½ cup chopped baby arugula leaves
½ cup chopped walnuts
1 tablespoon freshly squeezed orange juice

1. Preheat the oven to 425°F (220°C).
2. Drizzle 1 tablespoon olive oil in a rimmed baking sheet and swirl to coat the bottom.
3. Remove the stems from the peppers and cut in half lengthwise, then remove the seeds and membranes. Place cut-side down on the prepared baking sheet and roast until just softened, 5 to 8 minutes. Remove from the oven and allow to cool.
4. Meanwhile, in a large skillet, heat 1 tablespoon olive oil over medium-high heat. Add the beef and onions and sauté until the meat is browned and cooked through, 8 to 10 minutes. Add the garlic, sage, salt, allspice, and pepper and sauté for 2 more minutes.
5. Remove from the heat and cool slightly. Stir in the parsley, arugula, walnuts, orange juice, and remaining ¼ cup olive oil and mix well.
6. Stuff the filling into each pepper half. Return to the oven and cook for 5 minutes. Serve warm.

PER SERVING
Calories: 521, Total Fat: 44g, Total Carbs: 9g, Net Carbs: 6g, Protein: 25g, Fiber: 3g, Sodium: 665mg

Beef Short Ribs with Red Wine

Prep time: 10 minutes | Cook time: 1¾ hours | Serves: 4

1½ pounds (680 g) boneless beef short ribs (if using bone-in, use 3½ pounds)
1 teaspoon salt
½ teaspoon freshly ground black pepper
½ teaspoon garlic powder

¼ cup extra-virgin olive oil
1 cup dry red wine (such as cabernet sauvignon or merlot)
2 to 3 cups beef broth, divided
4 sprigs rosemary

1. Preheat the oven to 350°F (180°C).
2. Season the short ribs with salt, pepper, and garlic powder. Let sit for 10 minutes.
3. In a Dutch oven or oven-safe deep skillet, heat the olive oil over medium-high heat.
4. When the oil is very hot, add the short ribs and brown until dark in color, 2 to 3 minutes per side. Remove the meat from the oil and keep warm.
5. Add the red wine and 2 cups beef broth to the Dutch oven, whisk together, and bring to a boil. Reduce the heat to low and simmer until the liquid is reduced to about 2 cups, about 10 minutes.
6. Return the short ribs to the liquid, which should come about halfway up the meat, adding up to 1 cup of remaining broth if needed. Cover and braise until the meat is very tender, about 1½ to 2 hours.
7. Remove from the oven and let sit, covered, for 10 minutes before serving. Serve warm, drizzled with cooking liquid.

PER SERVING
Calories: 792, Total Fat: 76g, Total Carbs: 2g, Net Carbs: 2g, Protein: 25g, Fiber: 0g, Sodium: 783mg

Moroccan Cheesy Meatballs

Prep time: 10 minutes | Cook time: 16 minutes | Serves: 4

¼ cup finely chopped onion
¼ cup raisins, coarsely chopped
1 teaspoon ground cumin
½ teaspoon ground cinnamon
¼ teaspoon smoked paprika
1 large egg
1 pound (454 g) ground beef (93% lean) or ground

lamb
⅓ cup panko bread crumbs
1 teaspoon extra-virgin olive oil
1 (28-ounce / 794-g) can low-sodium or no-salt-added crushed tomatoes
Chopped fresh mint, Feta cheese, and/or fresh orange or lemon wedges, for serving (optional)

1. In a large bowl, combine the onion, raisins, cumin, cinnamon, smoked paprika, and egg. Add the ground beef and bread crumbs and mix gently with your hands. Divide the mixture into 20 even portions, then wet your hands and roll each portion into a ball. Wash your hands.
2. In a large skillet over medium-high heat, heat the oil. Add the meatballs and cook for 8 minutes, rolling around every minute or so with tongs or a fork to brown them on most sides. (They won't be cooked through.) Transfer the meatballs to a paper towel–lined plate. Drain the fat out of the pan, and carefully wipe out the hot pan with a paper towel.
3. Return the meatballs to the pan, and pour the tomatoes over the meatballs. Cover and cook on medium-high heat until the sauce begins to bubble. Lower the heat to medium, cover partially, and cook for 7 to 8 more minutes, until the meatballs are cooked through. Garnish with fresh mint, Feta cheese, and/or a squeeze of citrus, if desired, and serve.

PER SERVING
Calories: 284g, Total Fat: 17g, Saturated Fat: 6g, Total Carbs: 10g, Protein: 26g, Sugar: 6g, Fiber: 5g, Sodium: 113mg, Potassium: 753mg

Honey Garlicky Pork Chops

Prep time: 10 minutes | Cook time: 16 minutes | Serves: 4

4 pork chops, boneless or bone-in
¼ teaspoon salt
⅛ teaspoon freshly ground black pepper
3 tablespoons extra-virgin olive oil

5 tablespoons low-sodium chicken broth, divided
6 garlic cloves, minced
¼ cup honey
2 tablespoons apple cider vinegar

1. Season the pork chops with salt and pepper and set aside.
2. In a large sauté pan or skillet, heat the oil over medium-high heat. Add the pork chops and sear for 5 minutes on each side, or until golden brown.
3. Once the searing is complete, move the pork to a dish and reduce the skillet heat from medium-high to medium. Add 3 tablespoons of chicken broth to the pan, this will loosen the bits and flavors from the bottom of the skillet.
4. Once the broth has evaporated, add the garlic to the skillet and cook for 15 to 20 seconds, until fragrant. Add the honey, vinegar, and the remaining 2 tablespoons of broth. Bring the heat back up to medium-high and continue to cook for 3 to 4 minutes.
5. Stir periodically, the sauce is ready once it's thickened slightly. Add the pork chops back into the pan, cover them with the sauce, and cook for 2 minutes. Serve.

PER SERVING
Calories: 302, Total Fat: 16g, Saturated Fat: 4g, Total Carbohydrates: 19g, Protein: 22g, Sugar: 17g, Fiber: <1g, Sodium: 753mg

Flank Steak Slices with Pistou

Prep time: 10 minutes | Cook time: 12 minutes | Serves: 4

1 pound (454 g) flank steak
8 tablespoons extra-virgin olive oil, divided
1 teaspoon salt, divided
1 teaspoon freshly ground black pepper, divided
½ cup chopped fresh flat-leaf Italian parsley

¼ cup chopped fresh mint leaves
2 garlic cloves, roughly chopped
Zest and juice of 1 orange or 2 clementines
1 teaspoon red pepper flakes (optional)
1 tablespoon red wine vinegar

1. Heat the grill to medium-high heat or, if using an oven, preheat to 400°F (205°C).
2. Rub the steak with 2 tablespoons olive oil and sprinkle with ½ teaspoon salt and ½ teaspoon pepper. Let sit at room temperature while you make the pistou.
3. In a food processor, combine the parsley, mint, garlic, orange zest and juice, remaining ½ teaspoon salt, red pepper flakes (if using), and remaining ½ teaspoon pepper. Pulse until finely chopped. With the processor running, stream in the red wine vinegar and remaining 6 tablespoons olive oil until well combined. This pistou will be more oil-based than traditional basil pesto.
4. Cook the steak on the grill, 6 to 8 minutes per side. Remove from the grill and allow to rest for 10 minutes on a cutting board. If cooking in the oven, heat a large oven-safe skillet (cast iron works great) over high heat. Add the steak and sear, 1 to 2 minutes per side, until browned. Transfer the skillet to the oven and cook 10 to 12 minutes, or until the steak reaches your desired temperature.
5. To serve, slice the steak and drizzle with the pistou.

PER SERVING
Calories: 441, Total Fat: 36g, Total Carbs: 3g, Net Carbs: 3g, Protein: 25g, Fiber: 0g, Sodium: 897mg

Chapter 9 Pasta and Couscous

Farfalle with Zucchini, Tomatoes, and Basil

Prep time: **10 minutes** | Cook time: **20 minutes** | Serves: **6**

2 pounds (907 g) zucchini and/or summer squash, halved lengthwise and sliced ½ inch thick
Kosher salt and pepper, to taste
5 tablespoons extra-virgin olive oil
3 garlic cloves, minced
½ teaspoon red pepper flakes
1 pound (454 g) farfalle
12 ounces (340 g) grape tomatoes, halved
½ cup chopped fresh basil
¼ cup pine nuts, toasted
2 tablespoons balsamic vinegar
Grated Parmesan cheese

1. Toss squash with 1 tablespoon salt and let drain in colander for 30 minutes. Pat squash dry with paper towels and carefully wipe away any residual salt.
2. Heat 1 tablespoon oil in 12-inch nonstick skillet over high heat until just smoking. Add half of squash and cook, stirring occasionally, until golden brown and slightly charred, 5 to 7 minutes, reducing heat if skillet begins to scorch, transfer to large plate. Repeat with 1 tablespoon oil and remaining squash, transfer to plate.
3. Heat 1 tablespoon oil in now-empty skillet over medium heat until shimmering. Add garlic and pepper flakes and cook until fragrant, about 30 seconds. Stir in squash and cook until heated through, about 30 seconds.
4. Meanwhile, bring 4 quarts water to boil in large pot. Add pasta and 1 tablespoon salt and cook, stirring often, until al dente. Reserve ½ cup cooking water, then drain pasta and return it to pot. Add squash mixture, tomatoes, basil, pine nuts, vinegar, and remaining 2 tablespoons oil and toss to combine. Season with salt and pepper to taste and adjust consistency with reserved cooking water as needed. Serve with Parmesan.

PER SERVING
Calories: 291, Fat: 18.23g, Carbohydrates: 28.85g, Protein: 7.57g, Sugar: 14.83g, Fiber: 3.7g, Sodium: 183mg

Spaghetti with Mussels and White Wine

Prep time: **10 minutes** | Cook time: **25 minutes** | Serves: **6**

1 pound (454 g) mussels, scrubbed and debearded
½ cup dry white wine
1 tablespoon extra-virgin olive oil
2 garlic cloves, minced
½ teaspoon red pepper flakes
1 teaspoon grated lemon zest plus 2 tablespoons juice
1 pound (454 g) spaghetti or linguine
Salt and pepper, to taste
2 tablespoons minced fresh parsley

1. Bring mussels and wine to boil in 12-inch straight-sided sauté pan, cover, and cook, shaking pan occasionally, until mussels open, about 5 minutes. As mussels open, remove them with slotted spoon and transfer to bowl. Discard any mussels that refuse to open. (If desired, remove mussels from shells.) Drain steaming liquid through fine-mesh strainer lined with coffee filter into bowl, avoiding any gritty sediment that has settled on bottom of pan. Wipe skillet clean with paper towels.
2. Cook oil, garlic, and pepper flakes in now-empty pan over medium heat, stirring frequently, until garlic turns golden but not brown, about 3 minutes. Stir in reserved mussel steaming liquid and lemon zest and juice, bring to simmer, and cook until flavors meld, about 4 minutes. Stir in mussels, cover, and cook until heated through, about 2 minutes.
3. Meanwhile, bring 4 quarts water to boil in large pot. Add pasta and 1 tablespoon salt and cook, stirring often, until al dente. Reserve ½ cup cooking water, then drain pasta and return it to pot. Add sauce and parsley and toss to combine. Season with salt and pepper to taste and adjust consistency with reserved cooking water as needed. Serve.

PER SERVING
Calories: 184, Fat: 4.39g, Carbohydrates: 24.14g, Protein: 13.34g, Sugar: 1.05g, Fiber: 3.6g, Sodium: 221mg

Spaghetti al Limone with Parmesan

Prep time: 10 minutes | Cook time: 15 minutes | Serves: 6

½ cup extra-virgin olive oil
2 teaspoons grated lemon zest plus ⅓ cup lemon juice
1 small garlic clove, minced to paste

Salt and pepper, to taste
2 ounces (57 g) Parmesan cheese, grated
1 pound (454 g) spaghetti
6 tablespoons shredded fresh basil

1. Whisk oil, lemon zest and juice, garlic, ½ teaspoon salt, and ¼ teaspoon pepper together in small bowl, then stir in Parmesan until thick and creamy.
2. Meanwhile, bring 4 quarts water to boil in large pot. Add pasta and 1 tablespoon salt and cook, stirring often, until al dente. Reserve ½ cup cooking water, then drain pasta and return it to pot. Add oil mixture and basil and toss to combine. Season with salt and pepper to taste and adjust consistency with reserved cooking water as needed. Serve.

PER SERVING
Calories: 298, Fat: 21.11g, Carbohydrates: 22.96g, Protein: 6.93g, Sugar: 1.03g, Fiber: 3.6g, Sodium: 174mg

Whole-Wheat Couscous with Apricots

Prep time: 10 minutes | Cook time: 10 minutes | Serves: 4

2 tablespoons olive oil
1 small onion, diced
1 cup whole-wheat couscous
2 cups water or broth
½ cup dried apricots,

soaked in water overnight
½ cup slivered almonds or pistachios
½ teaspoon dried mint
½ teaspoon dried thyme

1. Heat the olive oil in a large skillet over medium-high heat. Add the onion and cook until translucent and soft.
2. Stir in the couscous and cook for 2 to 3 minutes.
3. Add the water or broth, cover, and cook for 8 to 10 minutes until the water is mostly absorbed.
4. Remove from the heat and let stand for a few minutes.

5. Fluff with a fork and fold in the apricots, nuts, mint, and thyme.

PER SERVING
Calories: 295, Fat: 14.59g, Carbohydrates: 37.7g, Protein: 7.84g, Sugar: 10.73g, Fiber: 6.3g, Sodium: 6mg

Orzo with Shrimp and Feta Cheese

Prep time: 15 minutes | Cook time: 13 minutes | Serves: 4 to 6

1 pound (454 g) large shrimp, peeled and deveined
1 tablespoon grated lemon zest plus 1 tablespoon juice
¼ teaspoon table salt
¼ teaspoon pepper
2 tablespoons extra-virgin olive oil, plus extra for serving
1 onion, chopped fine

2 garlic cloves, minced
2 cups orzo
2 cups chicken broth, plus extra as needed
1¼ cups water
½ cup pitted kalamata olives, chopped coarse
1 ounce (28 g) Feta cheese, crumbled, plus extra for serving
1 tablespoon chopped fresh dill

1. Toss shrimp with lemon zest, salt, and pepper in bowl, refrigerate until ready to use.
2. Using highest sauté function, heat oil in Instant Pot until shimmering. Add onion and cook until softened, about 5 minutes. Stir in garlic and cook until fragrant, about 30 seconds. Add orzo and cook, stirring frequently, until orzo is coated with oil and lightly browned, about 5 minutes. Stir in broth and water, scraping up any browned bits.
3. Lock lid in place and close pressure release valve. Select high pressure cook function and cook for 2 minutes. Turn off Instant Pot and quick-release pressure. Carefully remove lid, allowing steam to escape away from you.
4. Stir shrimp, olives, and Feta into orzo. Cover and let sit until shrimp are opaque throughout, 5 to 7 minutes. Adjust consistency with extra hot broth as needed. Stir in dill and lemon juice, and season with salt and pepper to taste. Sprinkle individual portions with extra Feta and drizzle with extra oil before serving.

PER SERVING
Calories: 320, Total Fat: 8g, Sat Fat: 2g, Total Carbohydrates: 46g, Protein: 18g, Fiber: 2g, Sodium: 670mg, Sugar: 4g

Warm Couscous

Prep time: 5 minutes | Cook time: 10 minutes | Serves: 6

2 tablespoons extra-virgin olive oil
2 cups couscous
1 cup water
1 cup chicken or vegetable broth
Salt and pepper, to taste

1. Heat oil in medium saucepan over medium-high heat until shimmering. Add couscous and cook, stirring frequently, until grains are just beginning to brown, 3 to 5 minutes. Stir in water, broth, and 1 teaspoon salt. Cover, remove saucepan from heat, and let sit until couscous is tender, about 7 minutes. Gently fluff couscous with fork and season with pepper to taste. Serve.

PER SERVING
Calories: 102, Fat: 4.68g, Carbohydrates: 12.58g, Protein: 2.29g, Sugar: 0.23g, Fiber: 0.8g, Sodium: 158mg

Linguine with Artichokes and Peas

Prep time: 10 minutes | Cook time: 5 minutes | Serves: 4 to 6

1 pound (454 g) linguine
5 cups water, plus extra as needed
1 tablespoon extra-virgin olive oil
1 teaspoon table salt
1 cup jarred whole baby artichokes packed in water, quartered
1 cup frozen peas, thawed
4 ounces (113 g) finely grated Pecorino Romano, plus extra for serving
½ teaspoon pepper
2 teaspoons grated lemon zest
2 tablespoons chopped fresh tarragon

1. Loosely wrap half of pasta in dish towel, then press bundle against corner of counter to break noodles into 6-inch lengths, repeat with remaining pasta.
2. Add pasta, water, oil, and salt to Instant Pot, making sure pasta is completely submerged. Lock lid in place and close pressure release valve. Select high pressure cook function and cook for 4 minutes. Turn off Instant Pot and quick-release pressure. Carefully remove lid, allowing steam to escape away from you.
3. Stir artichokes and peas into pasta, cover, and let sit until heated through, about 3 minutes.

Gently stir in Pecorino and pepper until cheese is melted and fully combined, 1 to 2 minutes. Adjust consistency with extra hot water as needed. Stir in lemon zest and tarragon, and season with salt and pepper to taste. Serve, passing extra Pecorino separately.

PER SERVING
Calories: 390, Total Fat: 8g, Sat Fat: 3.5g, Total Carbohydrates: 59g, Protein: 17g, Sodium: 680mg, Fiber: 4g, Sugar: 3g

Penne with Tomato Sauce and Parmesan

Prep time: 10 minutes | Cook time: 50 minutes | Serves: 6

1 shallot, sliced thin
¼ cup extra-virgin olive oil
2 pounds (907 g) cherry tomatoes, halved
3 large garlic cloves, sliced thin
1 tablespoon balsamic vinegar
1½ teaspoons coconut sugar, or to taste
Salt and pepper
¼ teaspoon red pepper flakes
1 pound (454 g) penne
¼ cup coarsely chopped fresh basil
Grated Parmesan cheese

1. Adjust oven rack to middle position and heat oven to 350°F (180°C). Toss shallot with 1 teaspoon oil in bowl. In separate bowl, gently toss tomatoes with remaining oil, garlic, vinegar, sugar, ½ teaspoon salt, ¼ teaspoon pepper, and pepper flakes. Spread tomato mixture in even layer in rimmed baking sheet, scatter shallot over tomatoes, and roast until edges of shallot begin to brown and tomato skins are slightly shriveled, 35 to 40 minutes. (Do not stir tomatoes during roasting.) Let cool for 5 to 10 minutes.
2. Meanwhile, bring 4 quarts water to boil in large pot. Add pasta and 1 tablespoon salt and cook, stirring often, until al dente. Reserve ½ cup cooking water, then drain pasta and return it to pot. Using rubber spatula, scrape tomato mixture onto pasta. Add basil and toss to combine. Season with salt and pepper to taste and adjust consistency with reserved cooking water as needed. Serve with Parmesan.

PER SERVING
Calories: 214, Fat: 9.98g, Carbohydrates: 29.48g, Protein: 3.7g, Sugar: 5.31g, Fiber: 5.7g, Sodium: 15mg

Warm Pearl Couscous

Prep time: 5 minutes | Cook time: 17 minutes | Serves: 6

2 cups pearl couscous	2½ cups water
1 tablespoon extra-virgin olive oil	½ teaspoon salt

1. Heat couscous and oil in medium saucepan over medium heat, stirring frequently, until about half of grains are golden brown, about 5 minutes. Stir in water and salt, increase heat to high, and bring to boil. Reduce heat to medium-low, cover, and simmer, stirring occasionally, until water is absorbed and couscous is tender, 9 to 12 minutes. Off heat, let couscous sit, covered, for 3 minutes. Serve.

PER SERVING
Calories: 79, Fat: 2.33g, Carbohydrates: 12.15g, Protein: 1.98g, Sugar: 0.05g, Fiber: 0.7g, Sodium: 198mg

Asparagus and Grape Tomato Pasta

Prep time: 10 minutes | Cook time: 25 minutes | Serves: 6

8 ounces uncooked small pasta, like orecchiette (little ears) or farfalle (bow ties)	¼ teaspoon freshly ground black pepper
	¼ teaspoon kosher or sea salt
1½ pounds (680 g) fresh asparagus, ends trimmed and stalks chopped into 1-inch pieces	2 cups fresh Mozzarella, drained and cut into bite-size pieces
1½ cups grape tomatoes, halved	⅓ cup torn fresh basil leaves
2 tablespoons extra-virgin olive oil	2 tablespoons balsamic vinegar

1. Preheat the oven to 400ºF (205ºC).
2. In a large stockpot, cook the pasta according to the package directions. Drain, reserving about ¼ cup of the pasta water.
3. While the pasta is cooking, in a large bowl, toss the asparagus, tomatoes, oil, pepper, and salt together. Spread the mixture onto a large, rimmed baking sheet and bake for 15 minutes, stirring twice as it cooks.
4. Remove the vegetables from the oven, and add the cooked pasta to the baking sheet. Mix with a few tablespoons of pasta water to help the sauce become smoother and the saucy vegetables stick to the pasta.
5. Gently mix in the Mozzarella and basil. Drizzle with the balsamic vinegar. Serve from the baking sheet or pour the pasta into a large bowl.
6. If you want to make this dish ahead of time or to serve it cold, follow the recipe up to step 4, then refrigerate the pasta and vegetables. When you are ready to serve, follow step 5 either with the cold pasta or with warm pasta that's been gently reheated in a pot on the stove.

PER SERVING
Calories: 147g, Total Fat: 3g, Saturated Fat:1g, Total Carbs: 17g, Protein: 16g, Sugar: 4g, Fiber: 5g, Sodium: 420mg

Dinner Meaty Baked Penne

Prep time: 5 minutes | Cook time: 50 minutes | Serves: 8

1 pound (454 g) penne pasta	sauce
	1 (1-pound / 454-g) bag baby spinach, washed
1 pound (454 g) ground beef	3 cups shredded Mozzarella cheese, divided
¼ teaspoon salt	
1 (25-ounce) jar marinara	

1. Bring a large pot of salted water to a boil, add the penne, and cook for 7 minutes. Reserve 2 cups of the pasta water and drain the pasta.
2. Preheat the oven to 350ºF (180ºC).
3. In a large saucepan over medium heat, cook the ground beef and salt. Brown the ground beef for about 5 minutes.
4. Stir in marinara sauce, and 2 cups of pasta water. Let simmer for 5 minutes.
5. Add a handful of spinach at a time into the sauce, and cook for another 3 minutes.
6. To assemble, in a 9-by-13-inch baking dish, add the pasta and pour the pasta sauce over it. Stir in 1½ cups of the Mozzarella cheese. Cover the dish with foil and bake for 20 minutes.
7. After 20 minutes, remove the foil, top with the rest of the Mozzarella, and bake for another 10 minutes. Serve warm.

PER SERVING
Calories: 497, Total Fat: 18g, Saturated Fat: 8g, Total Carbohydrates: 54g, Protein: 31g, Sugar: 7g, Fiber: 5g, Sodium: 838mg

Bow Ties with Zucchini

Prep time: 10 minutes | Cook time: 32 minutes | Serves: 4

3 tablespoons extra-virgin olive oil
2 garlic cloves, minced
3 large or 4 medium zucchini, diced
½ teaspoon freshly ground black pepper
¼ teaspoon kosher or sea salt
½ cup 2% milk

¼ teaspoon ground nutmeg
8 ounces (227 g) uncooked farfalle (bow ties) or other small pasta shape
½ cup grated Parmesan or Romano cheese
1 tablespoon freshly squeezed lemon juice

1. In a large skillet over medium heat, heat the oil. Add the garlic and cook for 1 minute, stirring frequently. Add the zucchini, pepper, and salt. Stir well, cover, and cook for 15 minutes, stirring once or twice.
2. In a small, microwave-safe bowl, warm the milk in the microwave on high for 30 seconds. Stir the milk and nutmeg into the skillet and cook uncovered for another 5 minutes, stirring occasionally.
3. While the zucchini is cooking, in a large stockpot, cook the pasta according to the package directions.
4. Drain the pasta in a colander, saving about 2 tablespoons of pasta water. Add the pasta and pasta water to the skillet. Mix everything together and remove from the heat. Stir in the cheese and lemon juice and serve.

PER SERVING
Calories: 190g, Total Fat: 10g, Saturated Fat: 3g, Total Carbs: 20g, Protein: 7g, Sugar: 2g, Fiber: 3g, Sodium: 475mg

American Baked Ziti

Prep time: 15 minutes | Cook time: 43 minutes | Serves: 8

For the Marinara Sauce:
2 tablespoons olive oil
¼ medium onion, diced
3 cloves garlic, chopped
1 (28-ounce / 794-g) can whole, peeled tomatoes, roughly chopped
Sprig of fresh thyme
½ bunch fresh basil
Sea salt and freshly

ground pepper, to taste

For the Ziti:
1 pound (454 g) whole-wheat ziti
3½ cups marinara sauce
1 cup low-fat cottage cheese
1 cup grated, low-fat Mozzarella cheese, divided

fat Parmesan cheese, ¾ cup freshly grated, low- divided

Make the Marinara Sauce
1. Heat the olive oil in a medium saucepan over medium-high heat.
2. Sauté the onion and garlic, stirring until lightly browned, about 3 minutes.
3. Add the tomatoes and the herb sprigs, and bring to a boil. Lower the heat and simmer, covered, for 10 minutes. Remove and discard the herb sprigs.
4. Stir in sea salt and season with freshly ground pepper to taste.

Make the Ziti
1. Preheat the oven to 375°F (190°C).
2. Prepare the pasta according to package directions. Drain pasta. Combine the pasta in a bowl with 2 cups marinara sauce, the cottage cheese, and half the Mozzarella and Parmesan cheeses.
3. Spread the mixture in a baking dish, and top with the remaining marinara sauce and cheese.
4. Bake for 30 to 40 minutes, or until bubbly and golden brown.

PER SERVING
Calories: 410, Fat: 14.37g, Carbohydrates: 56.54g, Protein: 17.84g, Sugar: 10.07g, Fiber: 11.6g, Sodium: 540mg

Moroccan-Style Couscous with Peas

Prep time: 15 minutes | Cook time: 14 minutes | Serves: 6

¼ cup extra-virgin olive oil, plus extra for serving
1½ cups couscous
2 carrots, peeled and chopped fine
1 onion, chopped fine
Salt and pepper
3 garlic cloves, minced
1 teaspoon ground coriander
1 teaspoon ground ginger

¼ teaspoon ground anise seed
1¾ cups chicken or vegetable broth
1 (15-ounce / 425-g) can chickpeas, rinsed
1½ cups frozen peas
½ cup chopped fresh parsley, cilantro, and/or mint
Lemon wedges

1. Heat 2 tablespoons oil in 12-inch skillet over medium-high heat until shimmering. Add couscous and cook, stirring frequently, until grains are just beginning to brown, 3 to 5 minutes. Transfer to bowl and wipe skillet clean

with paper towels.

2. Heat remaining 2 tablespoons oil in now-empty skillet over medium heat until shimmering. Add carrots, onion, and 1 teaspoon salt and cook until softened and lightly browned, 5 to 7 minutes. Stir in garlic, coriander, ginger, and anise and cook until fragrant, about 30 seconds. Stir in broth and chickpeas and bring to simmer.

3. Stir in peas and couscous. Cover, remove skillet from heat, and let sit until couscous is tender, about 7 minutes. Add parsley to couscous and gently fluff with fork to combine. Season with salt and pepper to taste and drizzle with extra oil. Serve with lemon wedges.

PER SERVING
Calories: 232, Fat: 10.66g, Carbohydrates: 28.8g, Protein: 6.82g, Sugar: 5.6g, Fiber: 5.7g, Sodium: 378mg

Penne with Cherry Tomato and Arugula

Prep time: 15 minutes | Cook time: 50 minutes | Serves: 6

1 shallot, sliced thin	sugar, or to taste
¼ cup extra-virgin olive oil	Salt and pepper, to taste
2 pounds (907 g) cherry tomatoes, halved	¼ teaspoon red pepper flakes
3 large garlic cloves, sliced thin	1 pound (454 g) penne
1 tablespoon sherry or red wine vinegar	4 ounces (113 g) baby arugula
1½ teaspoons coconut	4 ounces (113 g) Goat cheese, crumbled

1. Adjust oven rack to middle position and heat oven to 350°F (180°C). Toss shallot with 1 teaspoon oil in bowl. In separate bowl, gently toss tomatoes with remaining oil, garlic, vinegar, sugar, ½ teaspoon salt, ¼ teaspoon pepper, and pepper flakes. Spread tomato mixture in even layer in rimmed baking sheet, scatter shallot over tomatoes, and roast until edges of shallot begin to brown and tomato skins are slightly shriveled, 35 to 40 minutes. (Do not stir tomatoes during roasting.) Let cool for 5 to 10 minutes.

2. Meanwhile, bring 4 quarts water to boil in large pot. Add pasta and 1 tablespoon salt and cook, stirring often, until al dente. Reserve ½ cup cooking water, then drain pasta and return it to pot. Add arugula to pasta and toss until wilted. Using rubber spatula, scrape tomato mixture

onto pasta and toss to combine. Season with salt and pepper to taste and adjust consistency with reserved cooking water as needed. Serve, passing Goat cheese separately.

PER SERVING
Calories: 300, Fat: 16.73g, Carbohydrates: 29.92g, Protein: 9.79g, Sugar: 5.64g, Fiber: 6g, Sodium: 94mg

Whole-Wheat Fusilli with Chickpea Sauce

Prep time: 15 minutes | Cook time: 15 minutes | Serves: 4

¼ cup extra-virgin olive oil	pasta
½ large shallot, chopped	¼ teaspoon salt
5 garlic cloves, thinly sliced	⅛ teaspoon freshly ground black pepper
1 (15-ounce / 425-g) can chickpeas, drained and rinsed, reserving ½ cup canning liquid	¼ cup shaved fresh Parmesan cheese
	¼ cup chopped fresh basil
Pinch red pepper flakes	2 teaspoons dried parsley
1 cup whole-grain fusilli	1 teaspoon dried oregano
	Red pepper flakes

1. In a medium pan, heat the oil over medium heat, and sauté the shallot and garlic for 3 to 5 minutes, until the garlic is golden. Add ¾ of the chickpeas plus 2 tablespoons of liquid from the can, and bring to a simmer.

2. Remove from the heat, transfer into a standard blender, and blend until smooth. At this point, add the remaining chickpeas. Add more reserved chickpea liquid if it becomes thick.

3. Bring a large pot of salted water to a boil and cook pasta until al dente, about 8 minutes. Reserve ½ cup of the pasta water, drain the pasta, and return it to the pot.

4. Add the chickpea sauce to the hot pasta and add up to ¼ cup of the pasta water. You may need to add more pasta water to reach your desired consistency.

5. Place the pasta pot over medium heat and mix occasionally until the sauce thickens. Season with salt and pepper.

6. Serve, garnished with Parmesan, basil, parsley, oregano, and red pepper flakes.

PER SERVING (1 cup pasta)
Calories: 310, Total Fat: 17g, Saturated Fat: 3g, Total Carbohydrates: 33g, Protein: 10g, Sugar: 1g, Fiber: 7g, Sodium: 243mg

Couscous with Lamb, Chickpeas, and Almond

Prep time: 20 minutes | Cook time: 24 minutes | Serves: 6

3 tablespoons extra-virgin olive oil, plus extra for serving
1½ cups couscous
1 pound (454 g) lamb shoulder chops (blade or round bone), 1 to 1½ inches thick, trimmed and halved
Salt and pepper, to taste
1 onion, chopped fine
10 (2-inch) strips orange zest
1 teaspoon grated fresh ginger
1 teaspoon ground coriander
¼ teaspoon ground cinnamon
⅛ teaspoon cayenne pepper
½ cup dry white wine
2½ cups chicken broth
1 (15-ounce / 425-g) can chickpeas, rinsed
½ cup raisins
½ cup sliced almonds, toasted
⅓ cup minced fresh parsley

1. Adjust oven rack to lower-middle position and heat oven to 325°F (163°C). Heat 2 tablespoons oil in Dutch oven over medium-high heat until shimmering. Add couscous and cook, stirring frequently, until grains are just beginning to brown, 3 to 5 minutes. Transfer to bowl and wipe pot clean with paper towels.
2. Pat lamb dry with paper towels and season with salt and pepper. Heat remaining 1 tablespoon oil in now-empty pot over medium-high heat until just smoking. Brown lamb, about 4 minutes per side, transfer to plate.
3. Add onion to fat left in pot and cook over medium heat until softened, about 5 minutes. Stir in orange zest, ginger, coriander, cinnamon, cayenne, and ⅛ teaspoon pepper and cook until fragrant, about 30 seconds. Stir in wine, scraping up any browned bits. Stir in broth and chickpeas and bring to boil.
4. Nestle lamb into pot along with any accumulated juices. Cover, place pot in oven, and cook until fork slips easily in and out of lamb, about 1 hour.
5. Transfer lamb to cutting board, let cool slightly, then shred into bite-size pieces using 2 forks, discarding excess fat and bones. Strain cooking liquid through fine mesh strainer set over bowl. Return solids and 1½ cups cooking liquid to now-empty pot and bring to simmer over medium heat, discard remaining liquid.
6. Stir in couscous and raisins. Cover, remove pot from heat, and let sit until couscous is tender, about 7 minutes. Add shredded lamb, almonds, and parsley to couscous and gently fluff with fork to combine. Season with salt and pepper to taste and drizzle with extra oil. Serve.

PER SERVING
Calories: 302, Fat: 12.73g, Carbohydrates: 26.62g, Protein: 21.54g, Sugar: 5.27g, Fiber: 5.1g, Sodium: 547mg

Orecchiette with Italian Sausage and Broccoli

Prep time: 10 minutes | Cook time: 13 minutes | Serves: 4 to 6

2 tablespoons extra-virgin olive oil, divided
1 pound (454 g) broccoli rabe, trimmed and cut into 1½-inch pieces
¼ teaspoon table salt
8 ounces (227 g) hot or sweet Italian sausage, casings removed
6 garlic cloves, minced
¼ teaspoon red pepper flakes
¼ cup dry white wine
4½ cups chicken broth
1 pound (454 g) orecchiette
2 ounces (57 g) Parmesan cheese, grated, plus extra for serving

1. Using highest sauté function, heat 1 tablespoon oil in Instant Pot until shimmering. Add broccoli rabe and salt, partially cover, and cook, stirring occasionally, until broccoli rabe is softened, 3 to 5 minutes. Using slotted spoon, transfer broccoli rabe to bowl, set aside.
2. Add sausage and remaining 1 tablespoon oil to now-empty pot. Using highest sauté function, cook sausage, breaking up meat with wooden spoon, until lightly browned, about 5 minutes. Stir in garlic and pepper flakes and cook until fragrant, about 30 seconds. Stir in wine, scraping up any browned bits, then stir in broth and pasta.
3. Lock lid in place and close pressure release valve. Select high pressure cook function and cook for 4 minutes. Turn off Instant Pot and quick-release pressure. Carefully remove lid, allowing steam to escape away from you.
4. Stir broccoli rabe and any accumulated juices and Parmesan into pasta. Season with salt and pepper to taste. Serve, passing extra Parmesan separately.

PER SERVING
Calories: 440, Total Fat: 13g, Sat Fat: 3.5g, Total Carbohydrates: 59g, Protein: 22g, Fiber: 1g, Sugar: 2g, Sodium: 930mg

Rigatoni with Thyme Beef Ragu

Prep time: 15 minutes | Cook time: 2½ hours | Serves: 6

1½ pounds (680 g) bone-in English-style short ribs, trimmed
Salt and pepper, to taste
1 tablespoon extra-virgin olive oil
1 onion, chopped fine
3 garlic cloves, minced
1 teaspoon minced fresh thyme or ¼ teaspoon dried
½ teaspoon ground cinnamon
Pinch ground cloves
½ cup dry red wine
1 (28-ounce / 794-g) can whole peeled tomatoes, drained with juice reserved, chopped fine
1 pound (454 g) rigatoni
2 tablespoons minced fresh parsley
Grated Parmesan cheese

1. Pat ribs dry with paper towels and season with salt and pepper. Heat oil in 12-inch skillet over medium-high heat until just smoking. Brown ribs on all sides, 8 to 10 minutes, transfer to plate.
2. Pour off all but 1 teaspoon fat from skillet, add onion, and cook over medium heat until softened, about 5 minutes. Stir in garlic, thyme, cinnamon, and cloves and cook until fragrant, about 30 seconds. Stir in wine, scraping up any browned bits, and simmer until nearly evaporated, about 2 minutes.
3. Stir in tomatoes and reserved juice. Nestle ribs into sauce along with any accumulated juices and bring to simmer. Reduce heat to low, cover, and simmer gently, turning ribs occasionally, until meat is very tender and falling off bones, about 2 hours.
4. Transfer ribs to cutting board, let cool slightly, then shred meat into bite-size pieces using 2 forks, discard excess fat and bones. Using wide, shallow spoon, skim excess fat from surface of sauce. Stir shredded meat and any accumulated juices into sauce and bring to simmer over medium heat. Season with salt and pepper to taste.
5. Meanwhile, bring 4 quarts water to boil in large pot. Add pasta and 1 tablespoon salt and cook, stirring often, until al dente. Reserve ½ cup cooking water, then drain pasta and return it to pot. Add sauce and parsley and toss to combine. Season with salt and pepper to taste and adjust consistency with reserved cooking water as needed. Serve with Parmesan.

PER SERVING
Calories: 323, Fat: 15.84g, Carbohydrates: 16.87g, Protein: 29.46g, Sugar: 8.3g, Fiber: 4.4g, Sodium: 512mg

Rigatoni with Pancetta and Veggie

Prep time: 15 minutes | Cook time: 22 minutes | Serves: 4 to 6

2 ounces (56 g) pancetta, chopped fine
1 onion, chopped fine
¼ teaspoon table salt
3 garlic cloves, minced
2 anchovy fillets, rinsed, patted dry, and minced
2 teaspoons fennel seeds, lightly cracked
¼ teaspoon red pepper flakes
1 (28-ounce / 794-g) can diced tomatoes
2 cups chicken broth
1½ cups water
1 pound (454 g) rigatoni
¼ cup grated Pecorino Romano cheese, plus extra for serving
2 tablespoons minced fresh parsley

1. Using highest sauté function, cook pancetta in Instant Pot, stirring often, until browned and fat is well rendered, 6 to 10 minutes. Using slotted spoon, transfer pancetta to paper towel–lined plate, set aside for serving.
2. Add onion and salt to fat left in pot and cook, using highest sauté function, until onion is softened, about 5 minutes. Stir in garlic, anchovies, fennel seeds, and pepper flakes and cook until fragrant, about 1 minute. Stir in tomatoes and their juice, broth, and water, scraping up any browned bits, then stir in pasta.
3. Lock lid in place and close pressure release valve. Select high pressure cook function and cook for 5 minutes. Turn off Instant Pot and quick-release pressure. Carefully remove lid, allowing steam to escape away from you.
4. Stir in Pecorino and season with salt and pepper to taste. Transfer to serving dish and let sit until sauce thickens slightly, about 5 minutes. Sprinkle with parsley and reserved pancetta. Serve, passing extra Pecorino separately.

PER SERVING
Calories: 400, Total Fat: 8g, Sat Fat: 2.5g, Total Carbohydrates: 64g, Protein: 17g, Fiber: 6g, Sugar: 6g, Sodium: 922mg

Chapter 10 Soup

Spicy Lamb and Lentil Soup

Prep time: 10 minutes | Cook time: 25 minutes | Serves: 6 to 8

1 pound (454 g) lamb shoulder chops, 1 to 1½ inches thick, trimmed and halved
Salt and pepper
1 tbsp. extra-virgin olive oil
1 onion, chopped fine
1 (15-ounce, 425 g) can chickpeas, rinsed
4 plum tomatoes, cored and cut into ¾-inch pieces
1 tsp. grated fresh ginger
1 tsp. ground cumin
Pinch saffron threads, crumbled
1 tbsp. all-purpose flour
10 cups (2400 ml) chicken broth
½ tsp. paprika
¼ tsp. ground cinnamon
¼ tsp. cayenne pepper
¾ cup green or brown lentils, picked over and rinsed
⅓ cup minced fresh cilantro
¼ cup (60 ml) harissa, plus extra for serving

1. Put oven rack to lower-middle position and heat oven to 325 degrees. Pat lamb dry and season with salt and pepper. Heat oil over medium-high heat until just smoking. Brown lamb, 4 minutes per side, transfer to plate. Pour off all but leave 2 tablespoons fat in pot.
2. Add onion to fat left in pot and cook about 5 minutes over medium heat until softened. Stir in ginger, paprika, cumin, cayenne, pepper, cinnamon, and saffron and cook about 30 seconds until fragrant. Stir in flour and cook for 1 minute. Slowly stir in broth, scraping up any browned bits and smoothing out any lumps, and boil.
3. Put lamb into pot, bring to simmer, and cook for 10 minutes. Add lentils and chickpeas, cover, and place pot in oven. Cook 50 minutes to 1 hour until fork slips easily in and out of lamb and lentils are tender.
4. Transfer lamb to cutting board, cool down slightly, then shred into bite-size pieces, discarding excess fat and bones. Stir shredded lamb into soup and heat about 2 minutes. Stir in cilantro, tomatoes, and harissa and season with salt and pepper. Serve.

PER SERVING
Calories: 281, Fat: 9.81g, Carbohydrates: 30.54g, Protein: 19.7g, Sodium: 276mg, Fiber: 3.5g

Spanish Meatball Soup with Saffron

Prep time: 10 minutes | Cook time: 50 minutes | Serves: 6 to 8

MEATBALLS:
2 slices hearty white sandwich bread, torn into quarters
⅓ cup (80 ml) whole milk
2 tbsps. extra-virgin olive oil
½ tsp. salt
½ tsp. pepper
8 ounces (227 g) ground pork
1 ounce (28 g) Manchego cheese, grated (½ cup)
3 tbsps. minced fresh parsley
1 shallot, minced
8 ounces (227 g) 80 percent lean ground beef
SOUP:
1 tbsp. extra-virgin olive oil
1 onion, chopped fine
1 recipe Picada
2 tbsps. minced fresh parsley
1 tsp. paprika
¼ tsp. saffron threads, crumbled
⅛ tsp. red pepper flakes
1 red bell pepper, stemmed, seeded, and cut into ¾-inch pieces
2 garlic cloves, minced
1 cup (240 ml) dry white wine
8 cups (1920 ml) chicken broth
Salt and pepper

1. Using fork, mash bread and milk together into paste in a large bowl. Stir in ground pork, oil, parsley, Manchego, shallot, salt, and pepper until combined. Knead ground beef with your hands until combined. Pinch off and roll 2-teaspoon-size pieces of mixture into balls and arrange in rimmed baking sheet. Cover with plastic wrap and refrigerate at least 30 minutes until firm.
2. Heat oil over medium-high heat until shimmering. Add onion and bell pepper and cook 8 to 10 minutes until softened and lightly browned. Stir in saffron, garlic, paprika, and pepper flakes and cook about 30 seconds until fragrant. Add wine, scraping up any browned bits, and cook about 1 minute until almost completely evaporated.
3. Stir in broth and simmer. Gently add meatballs and simmer 10 to 12 minutes until cooked through. Off heat, stir in parsley and picada, season with salt and pepper. Serve.

PER SERVING
Calories: 787, Fat: 42g, Carbohydrates: 14.83g, Protein: 82.67g, Sodium: 282mg, Fiber: 1.8g

Farro White Bean Soup

Prep time: 10 minutes | Cook time: 2 hours | Serves: 8

2 tablespoons olive oil
1 medium onion, diced
1 celery stalk, diced
2 garlic cloves, minced
8 cups chicken broth or water
1 cup white beans, soaked overnight, rinsed, and drained

1 (14-ounce / 397-g) can diced tomatoes, with juice
1 cup farro
½ teaspoon thyme
½ teaspoon freshly ground pepper
2 bay leaves
Sea salt and freshly ground pepper, to taste

1. Heat the olive oil in a large stockpot on medium-high heat. Sauté the onion, celery, and garlic cloves just until tender.
2. Add the broth or water, beans, tomatoes, farro, and seasonings, and bring to a simmer.
3. Cover and cook for 2 hours, or until the beans and farro are tender. Season with sea salt and freshly ground pepper to taste.

PER SERVING
Calories: 163, Fat: 5.26g, Carbohydrates: 21.5g, Protein: 9.05g, Sugar: 5.04g, Fiber: 5.3g, Sodium: 952mg

Hazelnut and Leek Soup

Prep time: 10 minutes | Cook time: 15 minutes | Serves: 4

4 ounces (113 g) hazelnuts
4 tablespoons olive oil
4 leeks, white parts only, sliced
½ onion, diced

4 cups chicken stock, divided
¼ cup cream
2 tablespoons chopped chives

1. Preheat the oven to 350°F (180°C).
2. Spread the hazelnuts on a baking sheet and toast for 5 minutes.
3. Cool nuts in the refrigerator and process 3 ounces of the nuts in a food processor until fine. Reserve the remaining nuts for a garnish.
4. Heat the olive oil in a medium saucepan.
5. Add the leeks and onion, and sauté over low heat until tender.
6. Add ½ cup chicken stock, then puree the mixture in a blender until smooth. Return the chicken stock mixture to the saucepan. Add the remaining chicken stock and simmer for 10

minutes. Stir in the heavy cream until combined.
7. Pour into bowls and garnish with the unprocessed hazelnuts and chives.

PER SERVING
Calories: 473, Fat: 36.79g, Carbohydrates: 27.7g, Protein: 12.23g, Sugar: 9.65g, Fiber: 4.6g, Sodium: 368mg

Roasted Eggplant and Tomato Soup

Prep time: 10 minutes | Cook time: 50 minutes | Serves: 8

3 large eggplants, sliced lengthwise
Pinch sea salt
2 tablespoons olive oil
1 medium red onion, chopped
2 tablespoons garlic, minced
1 teaspoon dried thyme

Sea salt and freshly ground pepper, to taste
2 large ripe tomatoes, halved
5 cups chicken broth
¼ cup low-fat cream
Small bunch fresh mint, chopped

1. Preheat oven to 400°F (205°C).
2. Salt both sides of the sliced eggplant, and let sit for 20 minutes to draw out the bitter juices. Rinse the eggplant and pat dry with a paper towel.
3. Place the eggplants on a sheet pan, and put them in the oven.
4. Roast for 45 minutes. Remove from oven and allow to cool. When cool, remove all of the insides, discarding the skins.
5. Heat the olive oil in a large skillet over medium heat.
6. Add the onions and garlic, and cook for 5 minutes until soft and translucent.
7. Add the thyme and season with sea salt and freshly ground pepper.
8. Put the eggplant, tomatoes, and onion in a food processor, and process until smooth.
9. Put the chicken broth in a pot, and bring to a boil. Reduce heat to a simmer, and add the eggplant mixture.
10. Stir until well combined, and fold in the cream. Season to taste.
11. Serve the soup garnished with the fresh mint.

PER SERVING
Calories: 123, Fat: 5.33g, Carbohydrates: 17.32g, Protein: 4.27g, Sugar: 10.12g, Fiber: 7.1g, Sodium: 870mg

Curried Lentil Soup with Spinach

Prep time: 5 minutes | Cook time: 15 minutes | Serves: 6

1 teaspoon olive oil	powder
1 cup onion, chopped	6 cups water
1½ cups lentils	12 ounces (340 g)
1 tablespoon curry	spinach

1. Heat the olive oil and sauté the onion. Add the lentils and curry powder and stir.
2. Add the water and cook until lentils are tender, about 15 to 20 minutes. Add the spinach and stir until wilted.
3. Serve with toasted whole-wheat bread and a green salad.

PER SERVING
Calories: 51, Fat: 1.24g, Carbohydrates: 8.7g, Protein: 3.71g, Sugar: 1.08g, Fiber: 2.4g, Sodium: 53mg

French Chicken Soup

Prep time: 15 minutes | Cook time: 35 minutes | Serves: 6 to 8

2 fennel bulbs, 2 tbsps. fronds minced, stalks discarded, bulbs halved, cored, and cut into ½-inch pieces	2 anchovy fillets, minced
	1 (14.5-ounce, 411 g) can diced tomatoes, drained
	2 carrots, peeled, halved lengthwise, and sliced ½ inch thick
1 tbsp. extra-virgin olive oil	2 (12-ounce, 340 g) bone-in split chicken breasts, trimmed
4 garlic cloves, minced	
1 onion, chopped	
1¾ tsp. table salt	4 (5- to 7-ounce, 142g to 198 g) bone-in chicken thighs, trimmed
2 tbsps. tomato paste	
7 cups water, divided	
1 tbsp. minced fresh thyme or 1 teaspoon dried	½ cup pitted brine-cured green olives, chopped
	1 tsp. grated orange zest

1. In Instant Pot, use highest sauté function, heat oil until shimmering. Add fennel pieces, onion, and salt and cook about 5 minutes until softened. Stir in tomato paste, thyme, garlic, and anchovies and cook about 30 seconds until fragrant. Stir in 5 cups water, scraping up any browned bits, then add tomatoes and carrots. Nestle chicken breasts and thighs in pot.
2. Close the lid and close pressure release valve. Select high pressure cook function and cook for 20 minutes. Turn off and quick-release pressure.

Carefully remove lid, letting steam escape away from you.

3. Transfer chicken to cutting board, cool down slightly, then shred into bite-size pieces with 2 forks, discard skin and bones.
4. Skim excess fat from surface of soup with a wide, shallow spoon. Stir chicken and any accumulated juices, olives, and remaining water into soup and cook about 3 minutes until heated through. Stir in orange zest and fennel fronds, and season with salt and pepper to taste. Serve.

PER SERVING
Calories: 170, Total Fat: 5g, Total Carbohydrates: 11g, Protein: 19g, Sat Fat: 1g, Sodium: 870mg, Fiber: 3g, Sugar: 5g

Cinnamon Tomato Soup

Prep time: 15 minutes | Cook time: 15 minutes | Serves: 6

2 tablespoons olive oil	1 cinnamon stick
1 large onion, coarsely chopped	1 teaspoon honey
	Sea salt and freshly
8 large tomatoes, seeded and coarsely chopped	ground pepper, to taste
	Juice of 1 lemon
1 teaspoon paprika	1 small bunch flat-leaf
1 teaspoon fresh ginger, finely chopped	parsley, chopped
	2 tablespoons chopped
1 teaspoon ground cumin	cilantro
2 cups chicken broth	

1. Heat a large Dutch oven over medium-high heat.
2. Add the olive oil and onion, and cook until soft and translucent. Add the tomatoes and the seasonings and stir.
3. Pour in the chicken broth, and add the cinnamon stick and honey.
4. Simmer for 15 minutes, and puree the soup in a food processor or blender (remove the cinnamon stick for this step and return it when done).
5. Pour back into the pot, and season with sea salt and freshly ground pepper to taste.
6. Stir in the lemon juice and serve garnished with the cilantro and parsley.

PER SERVING
Calories: 112, Fat: 5.43g, Carbohydrates: 15.37g, Protein: 3.44g, Sugar: 9.11g, Fiber: 4.2g, Sodium: 311mg

Spinach Leaves and Brown Rice Soup

Prep time: 10 minutes | Cook time: 53 minutes | Serves: 6

1 tablespoon olive oil
1 large onion, chopped
2 cloves garlic, minced
3 pounds (1.4kg) spinach leaves, stems removed and leaves chopped

8 cups chicken broth
½ cup long-grain brown rice
Sea salt and freshly ground pepper, to taste

1. Heat the olive oil in a large Dutch oven over medium heat, and add the onion and garlic.
2. Cook until the onions are soft and translucent, about 5 minutes. Add the spinach and stir.
3. Cover the pot and cook the spinach until wilted, about 3 more minutes.
4. Using a slotted spoon, remove the spinach and onions from the pot, leaving the liquid.
5. Put the spinach mixture in a food processor or blender, and process until smooth, then return to the pot.
6. Add the chicken broth and bring to a boil.
7. Add the rice, reduce heat, and simmer until rice is cooked, about 45 minutes.
8. Season to taste.
9. Serve hot.

PER SERVING
Calories: 161, Fat: 4.32g, Carbohydrates: 24.51g, Protein: 10.21g, Sugar: 3.58g, Fiber: 6.1g, Sodium: 1413mg

Feta Roasted Red Pepper Soup

Prep time: 10 minutes | Cook time: minutes | Serves: 6

10 red peppers, peeled, roasted, seeded, and chopped
2 red chili peppers, peeled, roasted, and seeded
2 tablespoons olive oil
1 medium red onion, chopped
4 garlic cloves, minced

2 teaspoons finely chopped fresh oregano
6 cups chicken broth
Sea salt and freshly ground pepper, to taste
¼ cup cream
Juice of 1 lemon
6 tablespoons crumbled Greek Feta

1. Put all of the roasted peppers in a food processor and process until smooth.
2. Heat the olive oil in a large Dutch oven on medium-high heat and add the onion and garlic. Cook until soft and translucent, about 5 minutes.
3. Add the pepper mixture and oregano, followed by the broth.
4. Bring to a boil on high heat and season with sea salt and freshly ground pepper to taste.
5. Reduce heat to low and simmer for 15 minutes. Stir in the cream and lemon juice.
6. Pour into bowls, top with the crumbled Feta, and serve immediately.

PER SERVING
Calories: 258, Fat: 17.94g, Carbohydrates: 15.76g, Protein: 10.81g, Sugar: 10.6g, Fiber: 2.3g, Sodium: 1678mg

Farro, Pancetta, and Leek Soup

Prep time: 10 minutes | Cook time: 16 minutes | Serves: 6 to 8

1 cup whole farro
1 tablespoon extra-virgin olive oil, plus extra for drizzling
3 ounces (85 g) pancetta, chopped fine
1 pound (454 g) leeks, ends trimmed, chopped, and washed thoroughly

2 carrots, peeled and chopped
1 celery rib, chopped
6 cups chicken broth, plus extra as needed
½ cup minced fresh parsley
Grated Parmesan cheese

1. Pulse farro in blender until about half of grains are broken into smaller pieces, about 6 pulses, set aside.
2. Using highest sauté function, heat oil in Instant Pot until shimmering. Add pancetta and cook until lightly browned, 3 to 5 minutes. Stir in leeks, carrots, and celery and cook until softened, about 5 minutes. Stir in broth, scraping up any browned bits, then stir in farro.
3. Lock lid in place and close pressure release valve. Select high pressure cook function and cook for 8 minutes. Turn off Instant Pot and quick-release pressure. Carefully remove lid, allowing steam to escape away from you.
4. Adjust consistency with extra hot broth as needed. Stir in parsley and season with salt and pepper to taste. Drizzle individual portions with extra oil and top with Parmesan before serving.

PER SERVING
Calories: 180, Fat: 6.2g, Total Carbohydrates: 24.8g, Protein: 22.1g, Fiber: 1.2g, Sodium: 850mg

White Bean, Kale, and Tomato Soup

Prep time: 10 minutes | Cook time: 26 minutes | Serves: 4

2 tablespoons olive oil
1 small onion, chopped
2 cloves garlic, minced
1 bunch kale, torn into bite-sized pieces
6 cups chicken or vegetable broth
2 pints cherry tomatoes, halved
2 cans white beans of your choice, drained and rinsed
Sea salt and freshly ground pepper, to taste
Freshly grated, low-fat Parmesan cheese

1. Heat the olive oil in a large soup pot or Dutch oven over medium heat. Add the onions and cook for 5 minutes, or until soft and translucent. Add the garlic and cook for 1 more minute.
2. Add the kale and stir until well coated with the olive oil. Add the broth and bring to boil on high heat.
3. Reduce heat to low, and simmer for 15 minutes, until kale is softened. Add the tomatoes and beans, and simmer for 5 more minutes. Season with sea salt and freshly ground pepper to taste.
4. To serve, ladle into bowls, and sprinkle with freshly grated, low-fat Parmesan cheese.

PER SERVING
Calories: 263, Fat: 8.95g, Carbohydrates: 34.89g, Protein: 13.01g, Sugar: 4.73g, Fiber: 9g, Sodium: 1645mg

Shrimp and Leek Soup

Prep time: 10 minutes | Cook time: 38 minutes | Serves: 6

2 tablespoons olive oil
3 stalks celery, chopped
1 leek, both whites and light green parts, sliced
1 medium fennel bulb, chopped
1 clove garlic, minced
Sea salt and freshly ground pepper, to taste
1 tablespoon fennel seeds
4 cups vegetable or chicken broth
1 pound (454 g) medium shrimp, peeled and deveined
2 tablespoons light cream
Juice of 1 lemon

1. Heat the oil in a large Dutch oven over medium heat.
2. Add the celery, leek, and fennel, and cook for about 15 minutes, until vegetables are browned and very soft.

3. Add the garlic and season with sea salt and freshly ground pepper to taste. Add the fennel seed and stir.
4. Add the broth and bring to a boil, then reduce to a simmer and cook about 20 more minutes.
5. Add the shrimp to the soup and cook until just pink, about 3 minutes. Add the cream and lemon juice, and serve immediately.

PER SERVING
Calories: 142, Fat: 6.88g, Carbohydrates: 8.29g, Protein: 12.45g, Sugar: 3.29g, Fiber: 2.2g, Sodium: 1042mg

Chicken Wing Broth

Prep time: 15 minutes | Cook time: 1.5 hours | Serves: 3 quarts

3 pounds (1.4 kg) chicken wings
1 tbsp. vegetable oil
1 onion, chopped
12 cups (2880 ml) water, divided
½ tsp. table salt
3 bay leaves
3 garlic cloves, lightly crushed and peeled

1. Pat chicken wings dry with paper towels. In Instant Pot, use highest sauté function, heat oil for 5 minutes. Brown half of chicken wings for about 10 minutes, transfer to bowl. Repeat with remaining chicken wings.
2. Add onion to fat left in pot and cook 8 to 10 minutes until softened and well browned. Stir in garlic and cook about 30 seconds until fragrant. Add 1 cup water, scraping up any browned bits. Stir in remaining 11 cups water, bay leaves, salt, and chicken and any accumulated juices.
3. Lock lid and close pressure release valve. Choose high pressure cook function and cook for 1 hour. Turn off and let pressure release naturally for 15 minutes. Quick-release any remaining pressure and carefully remove lid, letting steam escape away from you.
4. Strain broth through colander into large container, pressing on solids to extract as much liquid as possible, throw away solids. Skim excess fat from surface of broth with a wide, shallow spoon. (Broth can be refrigerated for up to 4 days or frozen for 2 months.)

PER SERVING
Calories: 20, Total Fat: 0g, Sat Fat: 0g, Total Carbohydrates: 0g, Protein: 4g, Fiber: 0g, Sugar: 0g Sodium: 95mg

Turkish Green Lentil Soup

Prep time: 10 minutes | Cook time: 1 hour | Serves: 6

2 tablespoons olive oil
1 small onion, diced
2 tablespoons flour
4 cups water or chicken stock
1½ cups green lentils

1 carrot, peeled and diced
½ teaspoon dried thyme
1 teaspoon sea salt
½ teaspoon freshly ground pepper

1. Heat the olive oil in a large stockpot on medium-high heat. Sauté the onions just until tender and translucent.
2. Whisk in the flour, stirring for 30 seconds until thickened into a paste.
3. Slowly, whisk in the water or chicken stock ¼ cup at a time, and bring to a boil, stirring frequently.
4. Add the lentils, carrot, and seasonings. Cover and simmer for 1 hour, or until lentils are tender.

PER SERVING
Calories: 78, Fat: 4.66g, Carbohydrates: 8.11g, Protein: 2.2g, Sugar: 0.77g, Fiber: 0.8g, Sodium: 395mg

Creamy Cauliflower Gazpacho

Prep time: 15 minutes | Cook time: 25 minutes | Serves: 4 to 6

1 small head cauliflower, stalk removed and broken into florets (about 3 cups)
2 garlic cloves, finely minced
1 cup raw almonds
½ tsp. salt
½ cup (120 ml) extra-

virgin olive oil, plus 1 tbsp., divided
1 small white onion, minced
2 cups (480 ml) chicken or vegetable stock
1 tbsp. red wine vinegar
¼ tsp. freshly ground black pepper

1. Boil water in a small pot. Add the almonds to the water and boil for 1 minute, being careful to not boil longer or the almonds will become soggy. Drain in a colander and rinse under cold water. Pat dry and, squeeze the meat of each almond out of its skin. Discard the skins.
2. In a food processor, blend together the almonds and salt. With the processor running, drizzle in ½ cup extra-virgin olive oil, and scrape down the sides. Set the almond paste aside.
3. In a large stockpot, heat the remaining olive oil over medium-high heat. Add the onion and sauté 3 to 4 minutes until golden. Add the cauliflower florets and sauté for another 3 to 4 minutes. Add the garlic and sauté for 1 minute more.
4. Put in 2 cups stock and bring to a boil. Cover, reduce the heat to medium-low, and simmer the vegetables for 8 to 10 minutes until tender. Remove from the heat and cool down slightly.
5. Put in vinegar and pepper. Use an immersion blender to blend smoothly. With the blender running, add the almond paste and blend until smooth.
6. Serve warm, or chill in refrigerator at least 4 to 6 hours to serve a cold gazpacho.

PER SERVING
Calories: 505, Total Fat: 45g, Total Carbohydrates: 15g, Protein: 10g, Net Carbs: 10g, Fiber: 5g, Sodium: 484mg

Traditional Zuppa di Fagioli

Prep time: 10 minutes | Cook time: 2 hours | Serves: 8

2 tablespoons olive oil
3 carrots, peeled and diced
1 onion, chopped
2 cloves garlic, chopped
8 cups water or chicken broth
2 cups dried beans, soaked overnight, rinsed,

and drained
1 teaspoon fresh thyme
1 bay leaf
Sea salt and freshly ground pepper, to taste
8 slices whole-wheat bread
Freshly grated, low-fat Parmesan cheese

1. Heat the olive oil in a large stockpot on medium heat.
2. Add the carrots and onion, and sauté until the onions are translucent. Add the garlic and sauté 1 minute more.
3. Add the water or chicken broth, the beans, and the seasonings, and cover.
4. Bring to a boil on high heat, then reduce heat and simmer for 2 hours, or until the beans are tender.
5. Season to taste, and top with a slice of toasted whole-wheat bread and grated Parmesan cheese.

PER SERVING
Calories: 144, Fat: 5.5g, Carbohydrates: 18.61g, Protein: 5.78g, Sugar: 2.89g, Fiber: 3.5g, Sodium: 185mg

Tomato and Red Pepper Hummus Soup

Prep time: 5 minutes | Cook time: 0 minutes | Serves: 2

1 (14½-ounce / 411-g) can crushed tomatoes with basil	Salt, to taste
1 cup roasted red pepper hummus	¼ cup fresh basil leaves, thinly sliced (optional, for garnish)
2 cups low-sodium chicken stock	Garlic croutons (optional, for garnish)

1. Combine the canned tomatoes, hummus, and chicken stock in a blender and blend until smooth. Pour the mixture into a saucepan and bring it to a boil.
2. Season with salt and fresh basil if desired. Serve with garlic croutons as a garnish, if desired.

PER SERVING
Calories: 148, Fat: 6.2g, Total Carbohydrates: 18.8g, Protein: 5.1g, Fiber: 4.2g, Sodium: 680mg

Beans and Kale Fagioli

Prep time: 15 minutes | Cook time: 46 minutes | Serves: 2

1 tablespoon olive oil	stemmed and chopped
2 medium carrots, diced	1 (15-ounce / 425-g) can red kidney beans, drained and rinsed
2 medium celery stalks, diced	1 (15-ounce / 425-g) can cannellini beans, drained and rinsed
½ medium onion, diced	
1 large garlic clove, minced	½ cup fresh basil, chopped
3 tablespoons tomato paste	Salt, to taste
4 cups low-sodium vegetable broth	Freshly ground black pepper, to taste
1 cup packed kale,	

1. Heat the olive oil in a stockpot over medium-high heat. Add the carrots, celery, onion, and garlic and sauté for 10 minutes, or until the vegetables start to turn golden.
2. Stir in the tomato paste and cook for about 30 seconds.
3. Add the vegetable broth and bring the soup to a boil. Cover, and reduce the heat to low. Cook the soup for 45 minutes, or until the carrots are tender.
4. Using an immersion blender, purée the soup so that it's partly smooth, but with some chunks of vegetables. If you don't have an immersion blender, scoop out about ⅓ of the soup and blend it in a blender, then add it back to the pot.
5. Add the kale, beans, and basil. Season with salt and pepper.

PER SERVING
Calories: 215, Fat: 4.2g, Total Carbohydrates: 35.8g, Protein: 11.1g, Fiber: 11.2g, Sodium: 486mg

Greek Gigante Bean Soup

Prep time: 8 hours | Cook time: 30 minutes | Serves: 6 to 8

1½ tbsp. table salt, for brining	1 onion, chopped
1 pound (2½ cups, 454 g) dried gigante beans, picked over and rinsed	4 garlic cloves, minced
	4 cups (960 ml) vegetable or chicken broth
2 tbsps. extra-virgin olive oil, plus extra for drizzling	4 cups (960 ml) water
	½ cup pitted kalamata olives, chopped
5 celery ribs, cut into ½-inch pieces, plus ½ cup leaves, minced	2 bay leaves
	2 tbsps. minced fresh marjoram
½ tsp. table salt	Lemon wedges

1. Add 1½ tablespoons salt in 2 quarts cold water in large container. Put beans in and soak at room temperature for at least 8 hours or up to 24 hours. Drain and rinse well.
2. In Instant Pot, use highest sauté function, heat oil until shimmering. Add onion, celery pieces, and ½ teaspoon salt and cook about 5 minutes until vegetables are softened. Stir in garlic and cook about 30 seconds until fragrant. Stir in broth, beans, water, and bay leaves.
3. Lock lid and close pressure release valve. Choose high pressure cook function and cook for 6 minutes. Turn off and let pressure release naturally for 15 minutes. Quick-release any remaining pressure and carefully remove lid, letting steam escape away from you.
4. Combine olives, celery leaves, and marjoram in bowl. Throw away bay leaves. Season soup with salt and pepper. Top each portion with celery-olive mixture. Drizzle with extra oil and serve with lemon wedges.

PER SERVING
Calories: 250, Total Fat: 4.5g, Total Carbohydrates: 40g, Protein: 13g, Sat Fat: 0.5g, Sodium: 660mg, Fiber: 11g, Sugar: 6g, Added Sugar: 0g

Spicy Fava Bean Soup

Prep time: 10 minutes | Cook time: 2 hours | Serves: 4 to 6

1 onion, chopped
Salt and pepper
5 garlic cloves, minced
3 tbsps. extra-virgin olive oil, plus extra for serving
6 cups (1440 ml) chicken or vegetable broth, plus extra as needed
2 cups (480 ml) water
¼ cup (60 ml) lemon juice (2 lemons)
2 tsps. paprika, plus extra for serving
2 tsps. cumin, plus extra for serving
1 pound (3 cups, 454 g) dried split fava beans, picked over and rinsed

1. Heat oil over medium heat until shimmering. Add onion, salt, and pepper and cook 5 to 7 minutes until softened and lightly browned. Add garlic, paprika, and cumin and cook about 30 seconds until fragrant.
2. Stir in broth, beans and water and bring to boil. Cover, reduce heat to low, and simmer gently for 1½ to 2 hours, stirring occasionally, until beans are soft and broken down.
3. Off heat, whisk soup for about 30 seconds until broken down to coarse puree. Add lemon juice and season with salt and pepper. Serve, drizzling with extra oil and sprinkling with extra cumin and paprika.

PER SERVING
Calories: 192, Fat: 9.77g, Carbohydrates: 22.19g, Protein: 9.87g, Sodium: 267mg, Fiber: 7.7g

Whole Farro and Leek Soup

Prep time: 15 minutes | Cook time: 30 minutes | Serves: 6 to 8

1 cup whole farro
1 tbsp. extra-virgin olive oil, plus extra for drizzling
3 ounces (85 g) pancetta, chopped fine
1 pound (454 g) leeks, ends trimmed, chopped, and washed thoroughly
1 celery rib, chopped
2 carrots, peeled and chopped
½ cup minced fresh parsley
8 cups (1920 ml) chicken broth, plus extra as needed
Grated Parmesan cheese

1. Pulse farro in blender for about 6 pulses until about half of grains are broken into smaller pieces, set aside.
2. In Instant Pot, use highest sauté function, heat oil until shimmering. Add pancetta and cook 3 to 5 minutes until lightly browned. Stir in carrots, leeks, and celery and cook about 5 minutes until softened. Add broth, scraping up any browned bits, then stir in farro.
3. Lock lid and close pressure release valve. Choose high pressure cook function and cook for 8 minutes. Turn off and quick-release pressure. Carefully remove lid, letting steam escape away from you.
4. Adjust consistency with extra hot broth if you like. Stir in parsley and season with salt and pepper. Drizzle each portion with extra oil and top with Parmesan. Serve.

PER SERVING
Calories: 169, Fat: 6.22g, Carbohydrates: 21g, Protein: 12.35g, Fiber: 4g, Sodium: 831mg

Ultimate Tuscan Bean Soup with Kale

Prep time: 20minutes | Cook time: 25minutes | Serves: 4

2 tbsps. extra-virgin olive oil
1 (15-ounce, 425g) can no-salt-added or low-sodium cannellini beans, drained and rinsed
1 onion, diced
1 carrot, diced
1 celery stalk, diced
4 cups no-salt-added vegetable stock
1 tsp. kosher salt
1 tbsp. fresh thyme, chopped
1 tbsp. fresh sage, chopped
1 tbsp. fresh oregano, chopped
¼ tsp. freshly ground black pepper
1 bunch kale, stemmed and chopped
¼ cup grated Parmesan cheese (optional)

1. Heat the olive oil in a large pot over medium-high heat. Add the onion, carrot, celery, and salt and sauté until translucent and slightly golden, for 5 to 6 minutes.
2. Add the vegetable stock, beans, thyme, sage, oregano, and black pepper and bring to a boil. Turn down the heat to low, and simmer for 10 minutes. Stir in the kale and let it wilt, about 5 minutes.
3. Sprinkle 1 tablespoon Parmesan cheese over each bowl before serving, if desired.

PER SERVING
Calories: 235, Total fat: 8g, Saturated fat: 1g, Total Carbohydrates: 35g, Protein: 9g, Fiber: 7g, Sugar: 6g, Sodium: 540mg

Beans and Zucchini Soup

Prep time: 10 minutes | Cook time: 20 minutes | Serves: 5

1 tablespoon olive oil
1 onion, chopped
2 cloves garlic, minced
5 cups vegetable broth
1 cup dried chickpeas
½ cup dried pinto beans, soaked overnight
½ cup dried navy beans, soaked overnight
3 carrots, chopped
1 large celery stalk, chopped
1 teaspoon dried thyme
16 ounces (454 g) zucchini noodles
Salt and black pepper, to taste

1. Warm oil on Sauté. Stir in garlic and onion and cook for 5 minutes until golden brown. Mix in pepper, broth, carrots, salt, celery, beans, and thyme.
2. Seal the lid and cook for 15 minutes on High Pressure. Release the pressure naturally for 10 minutes.
3. Mix zucchini noodles into the soup and stir until wilted. Taste and adjust the seasoning.

PER SERVING
Calories: 371, Fat: 6.17g, Carbohydrates: 62.19g, Protein: 20.18g, Sugar: 10.22g, Fiber: 13.7g, Sodium: 985mg

Avocado and Tomato Gazpacho

Prep time: 15 minutes | Cook time: 0 minutes | Serves: 4

2 cups chopped tomatoes
2 large ripe avocados, halved and pitted
1 large cucumber, peeled and seeded
1 medium bell pepper (red, orange or yellow), chopped
1 cup plain whole-milk Greek yogurt
¼ cup extra-virgin olive oil
¼ cup chopped fresh cilantro
¼ cup chopped scallions, green part only
2 tablespoons red wine vinegar
Juice of 2 limes or 1 lemon
½ to 1 teaspoon salt
¼ teaspoon freshly ground black pepper

1. In a blender or in a large bowl, if using an immersion blender, combine the tomatoes, avocados, cucumber, bell pepper, yogurt, olive oil, cilantro, scallions, vinegar, and lime juice. Blend until smooth. If using a stand blender, you may need to blend in two or three batches.

2. Season with salt and pepper and blend to combine the flavors.
3. Chill in the refrigerator for 1 to 2 hours before serving. Serve cold.

PER SERVING
Calories: 392, Fat: 32.2g, Total Carbohydrates: 20.4g, Protein: 6.1g, Fiber: 9.2g, Sodium: 335mg

Lentil and Chorizo Sausage Soup

Prep time: 15 minutes | Cook time: 18 minutes | Serves: 6 to 8

1 tablespoon extra-virgin olive oil, plus extra for drizzling
8 ounces (227 g) Spanish-style chorizo sausage, quartered lengthwise and sliced thin
4 garlic cloves, minced
1½ teaspoons smoked paprika
5 cups water
1 pound (454 g) French green lentils, picked over and rinsed
4 cups chicken broth
1 tablespoon sherry vinegar, plus extra for seasoning
2 bay leaves
½ teaspoon table salt
1 large onion, peeled
2 carrots, peeled and halved crosswise
½ cup slivered almonds, toasted
½ cup minced fresh parsley

1. Using highest sauté function, heat oil in Instant Pot until shimmering. Add chorizo and cook until lightly browned, 3 to 5 minutes. Stir in garlic and paprika and cook until fragrant, about 30 seconds. Stir in water, scraping up any browned bits, then stir in lentils, broth, vinegar, bay leaves, and salt. Nestle onion and carrots into pot.
2. Lock lid in place and close pressure release valve. Select high pressure cook function and cook for 14 minutes. Turn off Instant Pot and quick-release pressure. Carefully remove lid, allowing steam to escape away from you.
3. Discard bay leaves. Using slotted spoon, transfer onion and carrots to food processor and process until smooth, about 1 minute, scraping down sides of bowl as needed. Stir vegetable mixture into lentils and season with salt, pepper, and extra vinegar to taste. Drizzle individual portions with extra oil, and sprinkle with almonds and parsley before serving.

PER SERVING
Calories: 360, Fat: 16.2g, Total Carbohydrates: 29.8g, Protein: 21.1g, Fiber: 7.2g, Sodium: 841mg

Red Lentil and Carrot Soup

Prep time: 10 minutes | Cook time: 20 minutes | Serves: 6 to 8

1 cup red lentils, picked over and rinsed	olive oil
½ cup long grain or basmati rice, rinsed	1 large onion, finely chopped
10 cups water	2 cups carrots, finely diced
1 teaspoon salt	1 teaspoon turmeric
3 tablespoons extra-virgin	1 lemon, cut into wedges

1. In a large pot over medium heat, heat the lentils, rice, water, and salt. Bring to a simmer for 40 minutes, stirring occasionally.
2. In a small skillet over medium-low heat, cook the olive oil and onions for 5 minutes until the onions are golden brown.
3. Add the cooked onions, carrots, and turmeric to the soup and cook for 15 minutes, stirring occasionally.
4. Serve the soup with a big squeeze of lemon over the top and a lemon wedge on the side.

PER SERVING
Calories: 230, Fat: 7.2g, Total Carbohydrates: 36.8g, Protein: 9.1g, Fiber: 9.2g, Sodium: 706mg

Chorizo Sausage and Tomato Soup

Prep time: 10 minutes | Cook time: 13 minutes | Serves: 6

1 tablespoon olive oil	1 tablespoon red wine vinegar
2 shallots, chopped	3 chorizo sausage, chopped
3 cloves garlic, minced	½ teaspoon ground black pepper
1 teaspoon salt	½ cup thinly chopped fresh basil
4 cups beef broth	
28 ounces (794 g) fire-roasted diced tomatoes	
½ cup fresh ripe tomatoes	

1. Warn oil on Sauté and cook chorizo until crispy. Remove to a to a plate lined with paper towel.
2. Add in garlic and onion and cook for 5 minutes until soft. Season with salt. Stir in red wine vinegar, broth, diced tomatoes, sun-dried tomatoes, and black pepper into the cooker.
3. Seal the lid and cook on High Pressure for 8 minutes. Release the ´pressure quickly. Pour the soup into a blender and process until smooth.

Divide into bowls, top with chorizo and decorate with basil.

PER SERVING
Calories: 104, Fat: 6.68g, Carbohydrates: 6.51g, Protein: 5.5g, Sugar: 0.8g, Fiber: 1.6g, Sodium: 1160mg

Pasta e Fagioli with Tomato and Fennel

Prep time: 10 minutes | Cook time: 35 minutes | Serves: 8 to 10

1 tbsp. extra-virgin olive oil, plus extra for serving	1 Parmesan cheese rind, plus grated Parmesan for serving
3 ounces (85 g) pancetta, chopped fine	2 (15-ounce, 425 g) cans cannellini beans, rinsed
1 onion, chopped fine	1 cup orzo
1 fennel bulb, stalks discarded, bulb halved, cored, and chopped fine	¼ cup minced fresh parsley
1 celery rib, minced	3½ cups (840 ml) chicken broth
4 garlic cloves, minced	2½ (600 ml) cups water
3 anchovy fillets, rinsed and minced	Salt and pepper
1 tbsp. minced fresh oregano or 1 teaspoon dried	2 tsps. grated orange zest
1 (28-ounce, 800 g) can diced tomatoes	½ tsp. fennel seeds
	¼ tsp. red pepper flakes

1. Heat oil over medium-high heat until shimmering. Add pancetta and cook 3 to 5 minutes., stirring occasionally until beginning to brown. Combine onion, fennel, and celery and cook 5 to 7 minutes until vegetables are softened. Stir in garlic, orange zest, anchovies, fennel seeds, oregano, and pepper flakes and cook about 1 minute until fragrant.
2. Stir in tomatoes and their juice, scraping up any browned bits. Add Parmesan rind and beans, simmer and cook about 10 minutes until flavors meld.
3. Stir in water, broth, and 1 teaspoon salt. Increase heat to high and boil. Stir in pasta and cook about 10 minutes until al dente. Off heat, discard Parmesan rind. Stir in parsley and season with salt and pepper. Serve, drizzling with extra oil and sprinkling with grated Parmesan.

PER SERVING
Calories: 115, Fat: 3.66g, Carbohydrates: 16.33g, Protein: 6.6g, Sodium: 283mg, Fiber: 4.9g

Fennel and Cod Chowder with Mushrooms

Prep time: 20 minutes | Cook time: 35 minutes | Serves: 4

1 cup (240 ml) extra-virgin olive oil, divided
1 small head cauliflower, core removed and broken into florets
1 small white onion, thinly sliced
1 fennel bulb, white part only, trimmed and thinly sliced
½ cup (120 ml) dry white wine (optional)
2 garlic cloves, minced
1 tsp. salt
¼ tsp. freshly ground

black pepper
4 cups Fish Stock
1 pound (454 g) thick cod fillet, cut into ¾-inch cubes
4 ounces (113 g) shiitake mushrooms, stems trimmed and thinly sliced (⅛-inch slices)
¼ cup chopped Italian parsley, for garnish (optional)
¼ cup (60 ml) plain whole-milk Greek yogurt, for garnish (optional)

1. In large stockpot, heat ¼ cup olive oil over medium-high heat. Add the onion, cauliflower florets, and fennel and sauté for 10 to 12 minutes. Add the salt, white wine, garlic, and pepper and sauté for another 1 to 2 minutes.
2. Add 4 cups fish stock and bring to a boil. Cover, lower the heat to medium-low, and simmer until vegetables are very tender, another 8 to 10 minutes. Remove from the heat and allow to cool slightly.
3. Using an immersion blender, purée the vegetable mixture, slowly streaming in ½ cup olive oil, until very smooth and silky.
4. Turn the heat back to medium-high and bring the soup to a low simmer. Add the cod pieces and cook, covered, about 5 minutes. Remove from the heat and keep covered.
5. In a medium skillet, heat the remaining olive oil over medium-high heat. When very hot, add the mushrooms and fry until crispy. Remove with a slotted spoon and transfer to a plate. Toss the mushrooms with a sprinkle of salt.
6. Serve the chowder hot, topped with fried mushrooms and drizzled with 1 tablespoon reserved frying oil. Garnish with chopped fresh parsley and Greek yogurt.

PER SERVING
Calories: 658, Total Fat: 54g, Total Carbohydrates: 15g, Protein: 28g, Net Carbs: 10g, Fiber: 5g, Sodium: 832mg

Almond and Cauliflower Gazpacho

Prep time: 10 minutes | Cook time: 16 minutes | Serves: 4 to 6

1 cup raw almonds
½ teaspoon salt
½ cup extra-virgin olive oil, plus 1 tablespoon, divided
1 small white onion, minced
1 small head cauliflower, stalk removed and broken into florets (about

3 cups)
2 garlic cloves, finely minced
2 cups chicken or vegetable stock or broth, plus more if needed
1 tablespoon red wine vinegar
¼ teaspoon freshly ground black pepper

1. Bring a small pot of water to a boil. Add the almonds to the water and boil for 1 minute, being careful to not boil longer or the almonds will become soggy. Drain in a colander and run under cold water. Pat dry and, using your fingers, squeeze the meat of each almond out of its skin. Discard the skins.
2. In a food processor or blender, blend together the almonds and salt. With the processor running, drizzle in ½ cup extra-virgin olive oil, scraping down the sides as needed. Set the almond paste aside.
3. In a large stockpot, heat the remaining 1 tablespoon olive oil over medium-high heat. Add the onion and sauté until golden, 3 to 4 minutes. Add the cauliflower florets and sauté for another 3 to 4 minutes. Add the garlic and sauté for 1 minute more.
4. Add 2 cups stock and bring to a boil. Cover, reduce the heat to medium-low, and simmer the vegetables until tender, 8 to 10 minutes. Remove from the heat and allow to cool slightly.
5. Add the vinegar and pepper. Using an immersion blender, blend until smooth. Alternatively, you can blend in a stand blender, but you may need to divide the mixture into two or three batches. With the blender running, add the almond paste and blend until smooth, adding extra stock if the soup is too thick.
6. Serve warm, or chill in refrigerator at least 4 to 6 hours to serve a cold gazpacho.

PER SERVING
Calories: 505, Fat: 45.2g, Total Carbohydrates: 10.4g, Protein: 10.1g, Fiber: 5.2g, Sodium: 484mg

Homemade Chicken Chili with Beans

Prep time: 15 minutes | Cook time: 4 hours | Serves: 6

4 boneless skinless chicken breasts, cut into 1-inch pieces

2 tbsps. extra-virgin olive oil

2 onions, chopped

4 garlic cloves, minced

2 celery stalks, chopped

2 tsps. ground cumin

1 tsp. dried oregano

1 bay leaf

1 (28-ounce, 794 g) can chopped tomatoes

2 ½ cups (600 ml) chicken broth, plus additional as needed

2 (15-ounce, 425 g) cans white beans, drained and rinsed

¼ cup chopped fresh parsley, divided

1 tsp. salt

1 tsp. chipotle powder

½ tsp. freshly ground black pepper

1. Combine the onions, olive oil, celery, garlic, cumin, chipotle powder, salt, pepper, oregano, chicken, chicken broth, tomatoes, bay leaf, and white beans in the slow cooker. Set to high and cook for 4 hours.
2. If the mixture gets too thick, add some water or a little more chicken broth.
3. Garnish each serving with parsley. Serve alone or over brown rice or quinoa.

PER SERVING

Calories: 423, Total Fat: 13g, Total Carbohydrates: 41g, Protein: 42g, Sugar: 6g, Fiber: 10g, Sodium: 857mg

Healthy Sweet Potato Lentil Soup

Prep time: 15 minutes | Cook time: 30minutes | Serves: 6

1 tbsp. extra-virgin olive oil

1 onion, diced

1 carrot, diced

1 celery stalk, diced

1 sweet potato, unpeeled and diced

1 cup green or brown lentils

1 dried bay leaf

4 cups no-salt-added vegetable stock

1 tsp. ground turmeric

1 tsp. ground cumin

1 tsp. kosher salt

¼ tsp. freshly ground black pepper

1. Heat the olive oil in a large stockpot over medium-high heat. Add the onion, carrot, celery, and sweet potato and sauté 5 to 6 minutes. Add the lentils, bay leaf, turmeric, cumin, salt,

and black pepper and cook for 30 seconds to 1 minute more.

2. Add the stock, bring to a boil, then lower the heat to low, and simmer, covered for 20 to 30 minutes, or until the lentils and sweet potato are tender. If you find the soup becoming thick and stew-like, feel free to add additional stock or water as it cooks.

PER SERVING

Calories: 145, Total fat: 3g, Saturated fat: 0g, Total Carbohydrates: 25g, Protein: 7g, Sodium: 350mg, Potassium: 455mg, Fiber: 7g, Sugar: 6g, Magnesium: 35mg, Calcium: 30mg

Paella Soup

Prep time: 15 minutes | Cook time: 24 minutes | Serves: 6

1 cup frozen green peas

2 tablespoons extra-virgin olive oil

1 cup chopped onion

1½ cups coarsely chopped red bell pepper

1½ cups coarsely chopped green bell pepper

2 garlic cloves, chopped

1 teaspoon ground turmeric

1 teaspoon dried thyme

2 teaspoons smoked

paprika

2½ cups uncooked instant brown rice

2 cups low-sodium or no-salt-added chicken broth

2½ cups water

1 (28-ounce / 794-g) can low-sodium or no-salt-added crushed tomatoes

1 pound (454 g) fresh raw medium shrimp (or frozen raw shrimp completely thawed), shells and tails removed

1. Put the frozen peas on the counter to partially thaw as the soup is being prepared.
2. In a large stockpot over medium-high heat, heat the oil. Add the onion, red and green bell peppers, and garlic. Cook for 8 minutes, stirring occasionally. Add the turmeric, thyme, and smoked paprika, and cook for 2 minutes more, stirring often. Stir in the rice, broth, and water. Bring to a boil over high heat. Cover, reduce the heat to medium-low, and cook for 10 minutes.
3. Stir the peas, tomatoes, and shrimp into the soup. Cook for 4 to 6 minutes, until the shrimp is cooked, turning from gray to pink and white. The soup will be very thick, almost like stew, when ready to serve.

PER SERVING

Calories: 275, Fat: 5.2g, Total Carbohydrates: 41.8g, Protein: 18.1g, Fiber: 6.2g, Sodium: 644mg

Slow-Cooker Mixed Vegetable Broth

Prep time: 10 minutes | Cook time: 6 hours | Serves: 6-7

1 fennel bulb, halved
1 onion, halved
2 carrots, cut into 2-inch pieces
1 garlic head, halved widthwise
2 leeks, halved
lengthwise
3 fresh parsley sprigs
1 fresh rosemary sprig
1 tbsp. apple cider vinegar
6 cups water

1. Add the leeks, fennel, onion, carrots, garlic, parsley, rosemary, cider vinegar, and water to the slow cooker, mix well. Cook on high for 6 hours.
2. Set a fine-mesh strainer, strain the broth and discard the solids.
3. Keep the broth in airtight containers, and store in the refrigerator or freezer.

PER SERVING
Calories: 36, Total Fat: 0g, Total Carbohydrates: 5g, Protein: 1g, Sugar: 1g, Fiber: 1g, Sodium: 21mg

Silky Tomato Soup with Tofu

Prep time: 20minutes | Cook time: 15minutes | Serves: 4

1 tbsp. extra-virgin olive oil
8 ounces(227g) silken tofu, drained
2 pounds(907g) tomatoes, chopped
1 cup cherry tomatoes, quartered
1 onion, diced
2 garlic cloves, sliced
1 tbsp. no-salt-added tomato paste
½ cup no-salt-added vegetable stock
¾ cup fresh basil, chopped and divided
1 tsp. kosher salt
¼ tsp. freshly ground black pepper

1. Heat the olive oil in a large saucepan over medium-high heat. Add the onion and sauté until slightly golden, about 5 to 6 minutes.
2. Add the garlic and sauté for 30 seconds. Then add the tomato paste and sauté for 30 seconds.
3. Add the tomatoes and cook down a bit, for 5 to 10 minutes. Add the stock, ½ cup of the basil, the salt, and black pepper.
4. Carefully transfer the mixture, in batches, to a high-powered blender or Vitamix. Add the tofu, and purée. Return the soup to the saucepan and

simmer for 10 minutes.
5. Divide the cherry tomatoes among 4 bowls. Ladle the soup into the bowls. Garnish with the remaining ¼ cup basil.

PER SERVING
Calories: 130, Total fat: 6g, Saturated fat: 1g, Total Carbohydrates: 17g, Protein: 6g, Fiber: 4g, Sugar: 10g, Sodium: 325mg

Sicilian Chickpea Soup with Escarole

Prep time: 10 minutes | Cook time: 1.5 hours | Serves: 6 to 8

1 head escarole (1 pound), trimmed and cut into 1-inch pieces
1 large tomato, cored and chopped
2 tsps. minced fresh oregano or ½ teaspoon dried
¼ tsp. red pepper flakes
Salt and pepper
2 fennel bulbs, stalks discarded, bulbs halved, cored, and chopped fine
1 small onion, chopped
5 garlic cloves, minced
5 cups (1200 ml) chicken or vegetable broth
1 Parmesan cheese rind, plus grated Parmesan for serving
2 bay leaves
1 (3-inch) strip orange zest
1 pound (2¾ cups, 454 g) dried chickpeas, picked over and rinsed
2 tbsps. extra-virgin olive oil, plus extra for serving

1. Put 3 tablespoons salt in 4 quarts cold water in a large container. Add chickpeas and soak for at least 8 hours or up to 24 hours. Drain and rinse well.
2. Heat oil in over medium heat until shimmering. Add onion, fennel, and 1 teaspoon salt and cook 7 to 10 minutes until vegetables are softened. Stir in oregano, garlic, and pepper flakes and cook about 30 seconds until fragrant.
3. Stir in 7 cups water, broth, Parmesan rind, soaked chickpeas, bay leaves, and orange zest and boil. Reduce heat to simmer and cook 1¼ to 1¾ hours until chickpeas are tender.
4. Add escarole and tomato and cook 5 to 10 minutes until escarole is wilted. Off heat, discard bay leaves and Parmesan rind. Season with salt and pepper. Serve, drizzling with extra oil and sprinkling with grated Parmesan.

PER SERVING
Calories: 354, Fat: 10.39g, Carbohydrates: 52.17g, Protein: 16.66g, Sodium: 283mg, Fiber: 12.8g

Lemony Avocado Gazpacho

Prep time: 15 minutes | Cook time: 0 | Serves: 4

2 cups chopped tomatoes
2 large ripe avocados, halved and pitted
1 large cucumber, peeled and seeded
1 medium bell pepper, chopped
2 tbsps. red wine vinegar
Juice of 2 limes or 1 lemon
1 cup (240 ml) plain

whole-milk Greek yogurt
¼ cup (60 ml) extra-virgin olive oil
¼ cup chopped fresh cilantro
¼ cup chopped scallions, green part only
½ to 1 tsp. salt
¼ tsp. freshly ground black pepper

1. In a blender, combine the tomatoes, cucumber, avocados, yogurt, bell pepper, olive oil, cilantro, vinegar, scallions, and lime juice. Blend until smooth.
2. Season with salt and pepper and blend to mix the flavors.
3. Chill in the refrigerator for 1 to 2 hours before serving.

PER SERVING

Calories: 392, Total Fat: 32g, Total Carbohydrates: 20g, Protein: 6g, Net Carbs: 11g, Fiber: 9g, Sodium: 335mg

Lemony Coconut Fish Stew

Prep time: 15 minutes | Cook time: 10 minutes | Serves: 4

1 ½ pounds (680 g) firm white fish fillet, cut into 1-inch cubes
2 tbsps. coconut oil
1 white onion, sliced thin
2 zucchini, sliced thin
2 garlic cloves, sliced thin
1 (4-inch) piece lemongrass (white part only), bruised with the

back of a knife
1 (13.5-ounce, 383 g) can coconut milk
½ cup slivered scallions
¼ cup chopped cilantro
3 tbsps. freshly squeezed lemon juice
1 tsp. salt
¼ tsp. freshly ground white pepper

1. Melt the coconut oil in a large pot over medium heat.
2. Add the garlic, onion, and zucchini. Sauté for 5 minutes.
3. Add the lemongrass, fish, salt, coconut milk, and white pepper to the pot. Add enough water if the liquid doesn't cover the fish. Bring to a boil,

then lower the heat to simmer, and cook for 5 minutes.
4. Garnish the soup with the cilantro, scallions, and lemon juice.

PER SERVING

Calories: 608, Total Fat: 43g, Total Carbohydrates: 13g, Protein: 46g, Sugar: 7g, Fiber: 4g, Sodium: 725mg

Mediterranean Fish Stew

Prep time: 15 minutes | Cook time: 20 minutes | Serves: 4 to 6

1½ pounds (680 g) skinless swordfish steak, cut into 1-inch pieces
2 tbsps. extra-virgin olive oil
2 onions, chopped fine
1 tsp. table salt
½ tsp. pepper
1 tsp. minced fresh thyme or ¼ teaspoon dried
Pinch red pepper flakes
4 garlic cloves, minced, divided
1 (28-ounce, 794 g)

can whole peeled tomatoes, drained with juice reserved, chopped coarse
1 (8-ounce, 227 g) bottle clam juice
¼ cup (60 ml) dry white wine
¼ cup golden raisins
2 tbsps. capers, rinsed
¼ cup pine nuts, toasted
¼ cup minced fresh mint
1 tsp. grated orange zest

1. In Instant Pot, use highest sauté function, heat oil until shimmering. Add onions, salt, and pepper and cook about 5 minutes until onions are softened. Stir in pepper flakes, thyme, and 3/4 garlic and cook about 30 seconds until fragrant. Stir in tomatoes and reserved juice, wine, clam juice, raisins, and capers. Nestle swordfish into pot and spoon cooking liquid over top.
2. Lock lid and close pressure release valve. Choose high pressure cook function and cook for 1 minute. Turn off and quick-release pressure. Carefully remove lid, letting steam escape away from you.
3. Combine pine nuts, orange zest, mint, and remaining garlic in bowl. Season stew with salt and pepper. Sprinkle each portion with pine nut mixture and serve.

PER SERVING

Calories: 320, Total Fat: 16g, Sat Fat: 3g, Total Carbohydrates: 16g, Protein: 25g, Sodium: 920mg, Fiber: 3g, Sugar: 10g, Added Sugar: 0g

Classic Picada

¼ cup slivered almonds
2 tbsps. extra-virgin olive oil
⅛ tsp. salt

2 slices hearty white sandwich bread, torn into quarters
Pinch pepper

1. Put oven rack to middle position and heat oven to 375 degrees. Pulse almonds in food processor to fine crumbs, about 20 pulses.
2. Add oil, salt, bread and pepper and pulse bread to coarse crumbs, about 10 pulses.
3. Spread mixture evenly on rimmed baking sheet and bake about 10 minutes, stirring often, until golden brown. Set aside to cool down.

PER SERVING
Calories: 460, Fat: 30.65g, Carbohydrates: 36.24g, Protein: 11.12g, Sodium: 293mg, Fiber: 6.4g

Moroccan Lamb Chops and Lentil Soup

1 pound (454 g) lamb shoulder chops (blade or round bone), 1 to 1½ inches thick, trimmed and halved
¾ teaspoon table salt, divided
⅛ teaspoon pepper
1 tablespoon extra-virgin olive oil
1 onion, chopped fine
¼ cup harissa, plus extra for serving

1 tablespoon all-purpose flour
8 cups chicken broth
1 cup French green lentils, picked over and rinsed
1 (15-ounce / 425-g) can chickpeas, rinsed
2 tomatoes, cored and cut into ¼-inch pieces
½ cup chopped fresh cilantro

1. Pat lamb dry with paper towels and sprinkle with ¼ teaspoon salt and pepper. Using highest sauté function, heat oil in Instant Pot for 5 minutes (or until just smoking). Place lamb in pot and cook until well browned on first side, about 4 minutes, transfer to plate.
2. Add onion and remaining ½ teaspoon salt to fat left in pot and cook, using highest sauté function, until softened, about 5 minutes. Stir in harissa and flour and cook until fragrant, about 30 seconds. Slowly whisk in broth, scraping up

any browned bits and smoothing out any lumps. Stir in lentils, then nestle lamb into multicooker and add any accumulated juices.
3. Lock lid in place and close pressure release valve. Select high pressure cook function and cook for 10 minutes. Turn off Instant Pot and quick-release pressure. Carefully remove lid, allowing steam to escape away from you.
4. Transfer lamb to cutting board, let cool slightly, then shred into bite-size pieces using 2 forks, discard excess fat and bones. Stir lamb and chickpeas into soup and let sit until heated through, about 3 minutes. Season with salt and pepper to taste. Top individual portions with tomatoes and sprinkle with cilantro. Serve, passing extra harissa separately.

PER SERVING
Calories: 300, Fat: 13.2g, Total Carbohydrates: 23.8g, Protein: 22.1g, Fiber: 6.2g, Sodium: 940mg

Classic Avgolemono

8 cups (1920 ml)chicken broth
½ cup long-grain white rice
1½ tsp. salt
2 large eggs plus 2 large yolks, room temperature
12 (4-inch) strips lemon zest plus ¼ cup juice (2

lemons)
4 green cardamom pods, crushed, or 2 whole cloves
1 bay leaf
1 scallion, sliced thin, or 3 tbsps. chopped fresh mint

1. Boil broth in a saucepan over high heat. Stir in bay leaf, lemon zest, rice, cardamom pods, and salt. Reduce to simmer and cook 16 to 20 minutes until rice is tender and broth is aromatic.
2. Whisk whole eggs, egg yolks, and lemon juice together in a bowl until combined. Discard cardamom, bay leaf, and zest strips. Reduce heat to low. Stir constantly, slowly ladle about 2 cups hot broth into egg mixture and mix. Pour egg mixture back into saucepan and cook about 5 minutes, stirring constantly, until soup is slightly thickened (do not simmer or boil). Sprinkle with scallion and serve immediately.

PER SERVING
Calories: 100, Fat: 2.1g, Carbohydrates: 16.76g, Protein: 4.32g, Sodium: 299mg, Fiber: 1.6g

Vegetable Gazpacho Soup

Prep time: 10 minutes | Cook time: 0 minutes | Serves: 6 to 8

½ cup of water
2 slices of white bread, crust removed
2 pounds (907 g) ripe tomatoes
1 Persian cucumber, peeled and chopped
1 clove garlic, finely chopped
⅓ cup extra-virgin olive oil, plus more for garnish
2 tablespoons red wine vinegar
1 teaspoon salt
½ teaspoon freshly ground black pepper

1. Soak the bread in the water for 5 minutes, discard water when done.
2. Blend the bread, tomatoes, cucumber, garlic, olive oil, vinegar, salt, and black pepper in a food processor or blender until completely smooth.
3. Pour the soup into a glass container and store in the fridge until completely chilled.
4. When you are ready to serve, pour the soup into a bowl and top with a drizzle of olive oil.

PER SERVING
Calories: 163, Fat: 13.2g, Total Carbohydrates: 12.4g, Protein: 2.1g, Fiber: 2.2g, Sodium: 442mg

Feta Potato and Leek Gazpacho

Prep time: 10 minutes | Cook time: 15 minutes | Serves: 4

3 large leeks
3 tablespoons almond butter
1 onion, thinly chopped
1 pound (454 g) potatoes, chopped
5 cups vegetable stock
2 teaspoons lemon juice
¼ teaspoon nutmeg
¼ teaspoon ground coriander
1 bay leaf
5 ounces (142 g) Feta, crumbled
Salt and white pepper, to taste
Freshly snipped chives, to garnish

1. Remove most of the green parts of the leeks. Slice the white parts very finely. Melt butter on Sauté, and stir-fry leeks and onion for 5 minutes without browning. Add potatoes, stock, juice, nutmeg, coriander and bay leaf. Season to taste with salt and pepper, and seal the lid.
2. Press Manual/Pressure Cook and set the timer to 10 minutes. Cook on High Pressure. Do a quick release and discard the bay leaf. Process the soup in a food processor until smooth. Season to taste, add Feta. Serve the soup sprinkled with freshly snipped chives.

PER SERVING
Calories: 343, Fat: 16.65g, Carbohydrates: 41.56g, Protein: 9.2g, Sugar: 11.67g, Fiber: 4.7g, Sodium: 1596mg

Provençal Hake Soup

Prep time: 10 minutes | Cook time: 50 minutes | Serves: 6 to 8

1 tbsp. extra-virgin olive oil, plus extra for serving
6 ounces (170 g) pancetta, chopped fine
1 fennel bulb, 2 tablespoons fronds minced, stalks discarded, bulb halved, cored, and cut into ½-inch pieces
4 garlic cloves, minced
1 tsp. paprika
⅛ tsp. red pepper flakes
2 (8-ounce, 227 g) bottles clam juice
2 bay leaves
Pinch saffron threads, crumbled
1 cup (240 ml) dry white wine or dry vermouth
4 cups (960 ml) water
2 tbsps. minced fresh parsley
1 tbsp. grated orange zest
2 pounds (907 g) skinless hake fillets, 1 to 1½ inches thick, sliced crosswise into 6 equal pieces
1 onion, chopped
2 celery ribs, halved lengthwise and cut into ½-inch pieces
Salt and pepper

1. Heat oil over medium heat until shimmering. Add pancetta and cook 3 to 5 minutes, stirring occasionally until beginning to brown. Stir in onion, fennel pieces, celery, and salt and cook 12 to 14 minutes until vegetables are softened and lightly browned. Stir in pepper flakes, garlic, paprika and saffron and cook about 30 seconds until fragrant.
2. Add wine, scraping up any browned bits. Stir in clam juice, water, and bay leaves. Bring to simmer and cook 15 to 20 minutes until flavors meld.
3. Off heat, discard bay leaves. Put hake into cooking liquid, cover, and let sit 8 to 10 minutes until fish flakes apart when gently prodded with paring knife and registers 140 degrees. Gently put in parsley, orange zest and fennel fronds, break fish into large pieces. Season with salt and pepper. Serve, drizzling with extra oil.

PER SERVING
Calories: 431, Fat: 20.33g, Carbohydrates: 23.9g, Protein: 37.42g, Sodium: 280mg, Fiber: 2.6g

White Bean and Carrot Soup

Prep time: 10 minutes | Cook time: 20 minutes | Serves: 6

3 tablespoons extra-virgin olive oil
1 large onion, finely chopped
3 large garlic cloves, minced
2 cups carrots, diced
2 cups celery, diced

2 (15-ounce / 425-g) cans white beans, rinsed and drained
8 cups vegetable broth
1 teaspoon salt
½ teaspoon freshly ground black pepper

1. In a large pot over medium heat, cook the olive oil, onion, and garlic for 2 to 3 minutes.
2. Add the carrots and celery, and cook for another 3 to 5 minutes, stirring occasionally.
3. Add the beans, broth, salt, and pepper. Stir and let simmer for 15 to 17 minutes, stirring occasionally. Serve warm.

PER SERVING
Calories: 244, Fat: 7.2g, Total Carbohydrates: 36.4g, Protein: 9.1g, Fiber: 10.2g, Sodium: 503mg

Spanish Turkey Meatball Soup

Prep time: 15 minutes | Cook time: 35 minutes | Serves: 6 to 8

8 ounces (227 g) kale, stemmed and chopped
1 pound (454 g) ground turkey
1 slice hearty white sandwich bread, torn into quarters
¼ cup (60 ml) whole milk
1 ounce (28 g) Manchego cheese, grated (½ cup), plus extra for serving
5 tbsp. minced fresh parsley, divided

½ tsp. table salt
4 garlic cloves, minced
1 tbsp. extra-virgin olive oil
1 onion, chopped
1 red bell pepper, stemmed, seeded, and cut into ¾-inch pieces
2 tsps. smoked paprika
½ cup (120 ml) dry white wine
8 cups (1920 ml) chicken broth

1. Mash bread and milk together into paste with a fork in large bowl. Stir in 3 tablespoons parsley, Manchego, and salt until combined. Add turkey and knead mixture with your hands until well mixed. Roll 2-teaspoon-size pieces of pinched off mixture into balls and place on large plate (you should have about 35 meatballs), set aside.
2. In Instant Pot, use highest sauté function, heat oil until shimmering. Add onion and bell pepper and cook 5 to 7 minutes until softened

and lightly browned. Stir in garlic and paprika and cook about 30 seconds until fragrant. Stir in wine, scraping up any browned bits, and cook about 5 minutes until almost completely evaporated. Stir in kale and broth, then gently submerge meatballs.

3. Lock lid and close pressure release valve. Cook with high pressure cook function for 3 minutes. Turn off and quick-release pressure. Carefully remove lid, letting steam escape away from you.
4. Stir in remaining parsley and season with salt and pepper. Serve with extra Manchego separately.

PER SERVING
Calories: 170, Total Carbohydrates: 9g, Total Fat: 4.5g, Sat Fat: 2.5g, Protein: 21g, Fiber: 2g, Sugar: 4g, Sodium: 750mg

Parmesan Mushroom-Barley Soup

Prep time: 10 minutes | Cook time: minutes | Serves: 6

2 tablespoons extra-virgin olive oil
1 cup chopped onion
1 cup chopped carrots
5½ cups chopped mushrooms
6 cups low-sodium or no-salt-added vegetable broth
1 cup uncooked pearled

barley
¼ cup red wine
2 tablespoons tomato paste
4 sprigs fresh thyme or ½ teaspoon dried thyme
1 dried bay leaf
6 tablespoons grated Parmesan cheese

1. In a large stockpot over medium heat, heat the oil. Add the onion and carrots and cook for 5 minutes, stirring frequently. Turn up the heat to medium-high and add the mushrooms. Cook for 3 minutes, stirring frequently.
2. Add the broth, barley, wine, tomato paste, thyme, and bay leaf. Stir, cover the pot, and bring the soup to a boil. Once it's boiling, stir a few times, reduce the heat to medium-low, cover, and cook for another 12 to 15 minutes, until the barley is cooked through.
3. Remove the bay leaf and serve in soup bowls with 1 tablespoon of cheese sprinkled on top of each.

PER SERVING
Calories: 195, Fat: 4.2g, Total Carbohydrates: 33.8g, Protein: 7.1g, Fiber: 6.2g, Sodium: 173mg

Authentic Red Gazpacho

Prep time: 15 minutes | Cook time: 0 |
Serves: 4

⅓ cup extra-virgin olive oil	chunks
2 pounds(907g) tomatoes, cut into chunks	1 garlic clove, smashed
	2 tsps. sherry vinegar
1 bell pepper, cut into chunks	½ tsp. kosher salt
	¼ tsp. freshly ground black pepper
1 cucumber, cut into chunks	¼ cup fresh chives, chopped, for garnish
1 small red onion, cut into	Lemon juice (optional)

1. In a high-speed blender or Vitamix, add the tomatoes, bell pepper, cucumber, onion, garlic, vinegar, salt, and black pepper. Blend until smooth.
2. With the motor running, add the olive oil and purée until smooth. Add more vinegar or a spritz of lemon juice if needed.
3. Garnish with the chives.

PER SERVING
Calories: 240, Total fat: 19g, Saturated fat: 3g, Total Carbohydrates: 18g, Protein: 4g, Fiber: 5g, Sugar: 11g, Sodium: 155mg

Rib Stew with Eggplant and Potatoes

Prep time: 15 minutes | Cook time: 50 minutes | Serves: 6 to 8

2 pounds (907 g) boneless short ribs, trimmed and cut into 1-inch pieces	1 tsp. ground cardamom
	¾ tsp. ground cinnamon
	4 cups (960 ml) chicken broth
1½ tsp. table salt, divided	1 cup (240 ml) water
2 tbsps. extra-virgin olive oil	1 pound (454 g) eggplant, cut into 1-inch pieces
1 onion, chopped fine	1 pound (454 g) Yukon Gold potatoes, unpeeled, cut into 1-inch pieces
3 tbsps. tomato paste	
¼ cup all-purpose flour	
3 garlic cloves, minced	½ cup chopped fresh mint or parsley
1 tbsp. ground cumin	
1 tsp. ground turmeric	

1. Pat beef dry with paper towels. Sprinkle with 1 teaspoon salt. In Instant Pot, use highest sauté function, heat oil for 5 minutes. Brown half of beef on all sides for 7 to 9 minutes and transfer it to bowl. Set aside remaining uncooked beef.

2. Add onion to fat left in pot and cook with highest sauté function for about 5 minutes, until softened. Stir in tomato paste, garlic, flour, cumin, cardamom, turmeric, cinnamon, and remaining salt. Cook about 1 minute until fragrant. Slowly add broth and water, scraping up any browned bits. Stir in eggplant and potatoes. Nestle remaining uncooked beef into pot along with browned beef with any accumulated juices.

3. Lock lid and close pressure release valve. Choose high pressure cook function and cook for 30 minutes. Turn off and quick-release pressure. Carefully remove lid, letting steam escape away from you.

4. 4 Skim excess fat from surface of stew with a wide, shallow spoon. Stir in mint and season with salt and pepper. Serve.

PER SERVING
Calories: 330, Total Carbohydrates: 22g, Protein: 26g, Total Fat: 15g, Sat Fat: 5g, Sodium: 790mg, Fiber: 4g, Sugar: 4g

Turkish Herb Leek and Potato Soup

Prep time: 10 minutes | Cook time: 18 minutes | Serves: 5

2 tablespoons almond butter	½ cup sour cream
	2 tablespoons rosemary
3 leeks, white part only, chopped	2 bay leaves
	Salt and ground black pepper to taste
2 cloves garlic, minced	
4 cups vegetable broth	2 tablespoons fresh chives, to garnish
3 potatoes, peeled and cubed	

1. Melt butter on Sauté mode. Stir in garlic and leeks and cook for 3 to 4 minutes, until soft. Stir in bay leaves, potatoes, and broth. Seal the lid and cook on High Pressure for 15 minutes. Release pressure quickly. Remove the bay leaves and cobs and discard.

2. Transfer soup to immersion blender and puree soup to obtain a smooth consistency. Season with salt and pepper. Top with diced chives and sour cream.

PER SERVING
Calories: 289, Fat: 7.49g, Carbohydrates: 51.33g, Protein: 6.33g, Sugar: 5.5g, Fiber: 6.2g, Sodium: 832mg

Fall Spanish Soup

Prep time: 10 minutes | Cook time: 30 minutes | Serves: 4

3 sweet potatoes, chopped	pumpkin
1 teaspoon sea salt	1 large onion, chopped
2 fennel bulb, chopped	1 tablespoon olive oil
16 ounces (454 g) pureed	4 cups water
	1 tablespoon sour cream

1. Heat the oil on Sauté, and add onion and fennel bulb. Cook for 3 to 5 minutes, until tender and translucent. Add the remaining ingredients and seal the lid. Cook on High pressure for 25 minutes. Do a quick release, transfer the soup to a blender and blend for 20 seconds until creamy. Top with sour cream and serve.

PER SERVING

Calories: 126, Fat: 4.21g, Carbohydrates: 21.94g, Protein: 3.76g, Sugar: 9.32g, Fiber: 6.2g, Sodium: 654mg

Spicy and Creamy Carrot Soup

Prep time: 15 minutes | Cook time: 35 minutes | Serves: 6 to 8

2 tbsps. extra-virgin olive oil	2 pounds (907 g) carrots, peeled and cut into 2-inch pieces
2 onions, chopped	½ tsp. baking soda
1 tsp. table salt	2 tbsps. pomegranate molasses
1 tbsp. grated fresh ginger	½ cup (120 ml) plain Greek yogurt
1 tbsp. ground coriander	½ cup hazelnuts, toasted, skinned, and chopped
1 tbsp. ground fennel	½ cup chopped fresh cilantro or mint
1 tsp. ground cinnamon	
4 cups (960 ml) vegetable or chicken broth	
2 cups (480 ml) water	

1. In Instant Pot, use highest sauté function, heat oil until shimmering. Add onions and salt and cook about 5 minutes until onions are softened. Stir in ginger, fennel, coriander, and cinnamon and cook about 30 seconds until fragrant. Add broth, carrots, water, and baking soda.
2. Lock lid and close pressure release valve. Choose high pressure cook function and cook for 3 minutes. Turn off and quick-release pressure. Carefully remove lid, letting steam escape away from you.
3. Working in batches, process soup in blender for

1 to 2 minutes until smooth. Put processed soup back to Instant Pot and simmer with highest sauté function. Season with salt and pepper. Drizzle each portion with pomegranate molasses and top with hazelnuts, yogurt and cilantro. Serve.

PER SERVING

Calories: 190, Total Fat: 11g, Sat Fat: 2.5g, Total Carbohydrates: 20g, Protein: 4g, Sodium: 820mg, Fiber: 5g, Sugar: 10g

Creamy Roasted Eggplant Soup

Prep time: 15 minutes | Cook time: 40minutes | Serves: 6

Olive oil cooking spray	4 rosemary sprigs
2 tbsps. extra-virgin olive oil	1 to 2 cups no-salt-added vegetable stock
2 pounds (907g, 1 to 2 medium to large) eggplant, halved lengthwise	1 tsp. pure maple syrup
	1 tsp. ground cumin
	1 tsp. ground coriander
2 beefsteak tomatoes, halved	1 tsp. kosher salt
	¼ tsp. freshly ground black pepper
2 onions, halved	Lemon juice (optional)
4 garlic cloves, smashed	

1. Preheat the oven to 400°F(204°C). Line two baking sheets with parchment paper or foil. Lightly spray with olive oil cooking spray. Spread the eggplant, tomatoes, onions, and garlic on the prepared baking sheets, cut-side down. Nestle the rosemary sprigs among the vegetables. Drizzle with the olive oil and roast for 40 minutes, checking halfway through and removing the garlic before it gets brown.
2. When cool enough to touch, remove the eggplant flesh and tomato flesh from the skin and add to a high-powered blender(food processor, or Vitamix). Add the rosemary leaves, onions, garlic, 1 cup of the vegetable stock, maple syrup, cumin, coriander, salt, and black pepper. Purée until smooth. The soup should be thick and creamy. If the soup is too thick, add another cup of stock slowly, until your desired consistency is reached.
3. Spritz with lemon juice, if desired.

PER SERVING

Calories: 185, Total fat: 8g, Saturated fat: 1g, Total Carbohydrates: 29g, Protein: 4g, Sodium: 400mg, Fiber: 9g, Sugar: 17g

Italian-Style Broccoli and Potato Soup

1 pound (454 g) broccoli, cut into florets
2 potatoes, peeled, chopped
4 cups vegetable broth
½ teaspoon dried rosemary
½ teaspoon salt
½ cup sour cream

1. Place broccoli and potatoes in the pot. Pour the broth and seal the lid. Cook on Soup/Broth for 20 minutes on High. Do a quick release and remove to a blender. Pulse to combine. Stir in sour cream and add salt.

PER SERVING
Calories: 218, Fat: 3.78g, Carbohydrates: 40.53g, Protein: 8.33g, Sugar: 3.93g, Fiber: 7.1g, Sodium: 1303mg

Spicy Chicken and Lentil Soup

1½ pounds (680 g) bone-in split chicken breasts, trimmed
Salt and pepper
1 tbsp. extra-virgin olive oil
1 onion, chopped fine
¼ tsp. ground cinnamon
¼ tsp. cayenne pepper
Pinch saffron threads, crumbled
1 tsp. grated fresh ginger
1 tsp. ground cumin
½ tsp. paprika
1 tbsp. all-purpose flour
10 cups (2400 ml) chicken broth
¾ cup green or brown lentils, picked over and rinsed
⅓ cup minced fresh cilantro
¼ cup (60 ml) harissa, plus extra for serving
1 (15-ounce, 425 g) can chickpeas, rinsed
4 plum tomatoes, cored and cut into ¾-inch pieces

1. Pat chicken dry and season with salt and pepper. Heat oil over medium-high heat until just smoking. Brown chicken for 3 minutes per side, transfer to plate.
2. Add onion to fat left in pot and cook about 5 minutes over medium heat until softened. Stir in ginger, cinnamon, cumin, paprika, pepper, cayenne, and saffron and cook about 30 seconds until fragrant. Stir in flour and cook for 1 minute. Slowly stir in broth, scraping up any browned bits and smoothing out any lumps, and boil.
3. Add lentils and chickpeas, then put chicken into pot and simmer. Cover, reduce heat to low, and simmer 15 to 20 minutes until chicken registers 160 degrees.
4. Transfer chicken to cutting board, cool down slightly, then shred into bite-size pieces, discarding skin and bones. Meanwhile, continue to simmer lentils for for 25 to 30 minutes, covered.
5. Add shredded chicken and cook about 2 minutes until heated through. Stir in cilantro, tomatoes, and harissa and season with salt and pepper. Serve.

PER SERVING
Calories: 236, Fat: 5g, Carbohydrates: 29.2g, Protein: 20.34g, Sodium: 266mg, Fiber: 3g

Greek Chicken Soup with Artichokes

4 cups (960 ml) Chicken Stock
2 cups Riced Cauliflower, divided
2 large egg yolks
¼ cup freshly squeezed lemon juice (about 2 lemons)
¾ cup (180 ml) extra-
virgin olive oil, divided
8 ounces (227 g) cooked chicken, coarsely chopped
1 (13.75-ounce, 390 g) can artichoke hearts, drained and quartered
¼ cup chopped fresh dill

1. Bring the stock to a low boil in a large saucepan. Lower the heat and simmer, covered.
2. Transfer 1 cup of the hot stock to a blender. Add ½ cup raw riced cauliflower, the egg yolks, and lemon juice and purée. While the processor is running, stream in ½ cup olive oil and blend until smooth.
3. Whisking constantly, pour the purée into the simmering stock until well blended together and smooth. Add the chicken and artichokes and simmer 8 to 10 minutes until thickened slightly. Stir in the dill and remaining riced cauliflower. Serve warm, drizzled with the remaining olive oil.

PER SERVING
Calories: 566, Total Fat: 46g, Total Carbohydrates: 14g, Protein: 24g, Net Carbs: 7g, Fiber: 7g, Sodium: 754mg

Paprika Asparagus Soup

Prep time: 10 minutes | Cook time: 22 minutes | Serves: 4

2 pounds (907 g) fresh asparagus, trimmed, 1-inch thick	2 tablespoons almond butter
2 onions, peeled and finely chopped	1 tablespoon olive oil
1 cup cream	½ teaspoon salt
4 cups vegetable broth	½ teaspoon dried oregano
	½ teaspoon paprika

1. Warm butter and oil on Sauté. Stir-fry the onions for 2 minutes, until translucent. Add asparagus, oregano, salt, and paprika. Stir well and cook until asparagus soften, for a few minutes. Pour in the broth. Seal the lid and cook on Soup/Broth for 20 minutes on High. Do a quick release and whisk in the cream. Serve chilled or warm.

PER SERVING
Calories: 309, Fat: 21.17g, Carbohydrates: 26.75g, Protein: 8.05g, Sugar: 16.81g, Fiber: 6.4g, Sodium: 1318mg

Healthy Garlicky Roasted Vegetable Soup

Prep time: 30 minutes | Cook time: 40 minutes | Serves: 6-8

½ cup extra-virgin olive oil	squash
4 carrots, halved lengthwise	4 garlic cloves
½ head cauliflower, broken into florets	3 shallots, halved lengthwise
3 Roma tomatoes, quartered	1 tsp. salt
2 cups cubed butternut	¼ tsp. freshly ground black pepper
	4 to 6 cups water or vegetable broth

1. Preheat the oven to 400°F(205°C).
2. Add the carrots, cauliflower, tomatoes, butternut squash, garlic, and shallots into a large bowl, combine them together. Add the olive oil, salt, and pepper and toss the vegetables to coat.
3. Place the vegetables in a single layer on a rimmed baking sheet. Put the sheet in the preheated oven, and roast the vegetables until they start to brown, about 25 minutes.
4. After roasting, transfer the roasted vegetables to a large Dutch oven, coved with enough water and bring to a boil over high heat. Lower the heat to a simmer and cook the soup for 10 minutes.
5. In a blender, pour the soup, working in batches if necessary, and purée until smooth.

PER SERVING
Calories: 197, Total Fat: 17g, Total Carbohydrates: 13g, Protein: 2g, Sugar: 5g, Fiber: 3g, Sodium: 426mg

Spanish Chorizo and Lentil Soup

Prep time: 15 minutes | Cook time: 30 minutes | Serves: 6 to 8

8 ounces (227 g) Spanish-style chorizo sausage, quartered lengthwise and sliced thin	g) French green lentils, picked over and rinsed
1 large onion, peeled	4 cups (960 ml) chicken broth
1 tbsp. extra-virgin olive oil, plus extra for drizzling	1 tbsp. sherry vinegar, plus extra for seasoning
2 carrots, peeled and halved crosswise	2 bay leaves
4 garlic cloves, minced	1 tsp. table salt
1½ tsp. smoked paprika	½ cup slivered almonds, toasted
5 cups (1200 ml) water	½ cup minced fresh parsley
1 pound (2¼ cups, 454	

1. In Instant Pot, use highest sauté function, heat oil until shimmering. Add chorizo and cook 3 to 5 minutes until lightly browned. Stir in garlic and paprika and cook about 30 seconds until fragrant. Add water, scraping up any browned bits, then stir in lentils, bay leaves, vinegar, broth, and salt. Nestle carrots and onion into pot.
2. Lock lid and close pressure release valve. Choose high pressure cook function and cook for 14 minutes. Turn off and quick-release pressure. Carefully remove lid, letting steam escape away from you.
3. Throw away bay leaves. Transfer onion and carrots to food processor with a slotted spoon and process about 1 minute until smooth, scraping down sides of bowl if you like. Stir vegetable mixture into lentils and season with pepper, salt, and extra vinegar. Drizzle each portion with extra oil, sprinkle with almonds and parsley and serve.

PER SERVING
Calories: 360, Total Fat: 16g, Sat Fat: 4.5g, Total Carbohydrates: 30g, Protein: 21g, Fiber: 7g, Sugar: 5g, Sodium: 950mg

Red Lentil Soup with Turmeric

Prep time: 15 minutes | Cook time: 30minutes | Serves: 6

1 tbsp. extra-virgin olive oil
1 onion, diced
1 carrot, diced
1 celery stalk, diced
3 garlic cloves, minced
4 cups no-salt-added vegetable stock
1 tsp. ground cumin
1 tsp. ground coriander

1 tsp. ground turmeric
1 tsp. kosher salt
¼ tsp. freshly ground black pepper
1 tbsp. no-salt-added tomato paste
2 cups water
1 cup red lentils
3 tbsps lemon juice
¼ cup fresh parsley, chopped

1. Heat the olive oil in a large stock pot over medium-high heat. Add the cumin, coriander, turmeric, salt, and black pepper and cook and stir for 30 seconds. Add the tomato paste then cook and stir for 30 seconds to 1 minute. Add the onion, carrot, and celery and sauté 5 to 6 minutes. Add the garlic and sauté 30 seconds.
2. Add the vegetable stock, water, and lentils and bring to a boil. Turn down the heat to low, and simmer, covering partially, until the lentils are tender, about 20 minutes.
3. Mix in the lemon juice and parsley.

PER SERVING
Calories: 170, Total fat: 3g, Saturated fat: 0g, Total Carbohydrates: 27g, Protein: 9g, Sodium: 340mg, Fiber: 6g, Sugar: 5g

Spiced Chicken Soup with Chickpeas and Squash

Prep time: 15 minutes | Cook time: 35 minutes | Serves: 6 to 8

1½ pounds butternut squash, peeled, seeded, and cut into 1½-inch pieces (4 cups)
2 tbsps. extra-virgin olive oil
7 cups water, divided
1¾ tsp. table salt
2 tbsps. tomato paste
4 garlic cloves, minced
1 tbsp. ground coriander
1½ tsp. ground cumin
1 tsp. ground cardamom

½ tsp. ground allspice
¼ tsp. cayenne pepper
2 (12-ounce, 340 g) bone-in split chicken breasts, trimmed
4 (5- to 7-ounce, 142g to 198 g) bone-in chicken thighs, trimmed
1 onion, chopped
1 (15-ounce, 425 g) can chickpeas, rinsed
½ cup chopped fresh cilantro

1. In Instant Pot, use highest sauté function, heat oil until shimmering. Add onion and salt and cook about 5 minutes until softened. Stir in tomato paste, coriander, garlic, cumin, allspice, cardamom, and cayenne and cook about 30 seconds until fragrant. Stir in 5 cups water, scraping up any browned bits. Nestle chicken breasts and thighs in pot, then place squash evenly around chicken.
2. Lock lid and close pressure release valve. Choose high pressure cook function and cook for 20 minutes. Turn off and quick-release pressure. Carefully remove lid, letting steam escape away from you.
3. Transfer chicken to cutting board, cool down slightly, then shred into bite-size pieces with 2 forks, discard skin and bones.
4. Skim excess fat from surface of soup with a wide, shallow spoon, then break squash into bite-size pieces. Stir chicken and any accumulated juices, chickpeas, and remaining water into soup until heated through, about 3 minutes. Stir in cilantro and season with salt and pepper. Serve.

PER SERVING
Calories: 190, Total Carbohydrates: 16g, Total Fat: 7g, Sat Fat: 1g, Protein: 20g, Fiber: 4g, Sugar: 3g, Sodium: 700mg

Black Bean Stew with Mango and Onion

Prep time: 10 minutes | Cook time: 10 minutes | Serves: 4

2 tbsps. coconut oil
2 (15-ounce, 425 g) cans black beans, drained and rinsed
1 onion, chopped
2 ripe mangoes, sliced thin
¼ cup chopped fresh cilantro, divided

¼ cup sliced scallions, divided
1 tbsp. chili powder
1 tsp. salt
¼ tsp. freshly ground black pepper
1 cup water

1. Add the coconut oil into a large pot, melt over high heat.
2. Place the onion into the pot and sauté for 5 minutes.
3. Stir in the black beans, chili powder, salt, pepper, and water. Bring to a boil. Lower the heat to simmer and cook for 5 minutes.
4. Take the pot off the heat, stir in the mangoes just before serving. Garnish each serving with the cilantro and scallions.

PER SERVING
Calories: 431, Total Fat: 9g, Total Carbohydrates: 72g, Protein: 20g, Sugar: 17g, Fiber: 22g, Sodium: 609mg

Shrimp Soup with Leeks and Wine

Prep time: 10 minutes | Cook time: 40 minutes | Serves: 6 to 8

2 tbsps. extra-virgin olive oil, plus extra for serving
12 ounces (340 g) large shrimp (26 to 30 per pound), peeled and deveined, shells reserved
12 ounces (340 g) large sea scallops, tendons removed
12 ounces (340 g) squid, bodies sliced crosswise into ½-inch-thick rings, tentacles halved
1 cup (240 ml) dry white wine or dry vermouth
4 cups (960 ml) water
1½ pounds (680 g) leeks, white and light green parts only, halved lengthwise, sliced thin, and washed

thoroughly
4 ounces (113 g) pancetta, chopped fine
1 tsp. grated fresh ginger
1 tsp. ground coriander
½ tsp. ground turmeric
⅛ tsp. red pepper flakes
3 tbsps. tomato paste
2 garlic cloves, minced
Salt and pepper
2 (8-ounce, 227g) bottles clam juice
⅓ cup minced fresh parsley

1. Heat oil over medium heat until shimmering. Add shrimp shells and cook 2 to 4 minutes, stirring frequently, until beginning to turn spotty brown and pot starts to brown. Add wine and simmer for 2 minutes, stirring occasionally. Stir in water and simmer, cook for 4 minutes. Strain mixture through fine-mesh strainer into bowl, pressing to extract as much liquid as possible.
2. Heat oil in pot over medium heat until shimmering. Add leeks and pancetta and cook about 8 minutes until leeks are softened and lightly browned. Stir in salt, tomato paste, garlic, turmeric, ginger, coriander, and pepper flakes and cook about 1 minute until fragrant. Stir in wine mixture and clam juice, scraping up any browned bits. Simmer and cook 15 to 20 minutes until flavors meld.
3. Add sea scallops, and cook for 2 minutes. Stir in shrimp and cook about 2 minutes until just opaque throughout. Off heat, stir in squid, cover, and let sit 1 to 2 minutes until just opaque and tender. Stir in parsley and season with salt and pepper. Serve, drizzling with extra oil.

PER SERVING
Calories: 305, Fat: 7.72g, Carbohydrates: 28.37g, Protein: 30.85g, Sodium: 291mg, Fiber: 2.5g

Chapter 11 Salads

Superfood Spinach Quinoa Salad with Pomegranate Citrus Dressing

Prep time: 15 minutes | Cook time: 15 minutes | Serves: 6

1 cup extra-virgin olive oil
3 cups baby spinach
1½ cups water
1 cup quinoa
¼ tsp. kosher salt
½ cup pomegranate juice
½ cup freshly squeezed orange juice
1 small shallot, minced
1 tsp. pure maple syrup
1 tsp. za'atar
½ tsp. ground sumac
½ tsp. kosher salt
¼ tsp. freshly ground black pepper
½ cup fresh parsley, coarsely chopped
½ cup fresh mint, coarsely chopped
Approximately ¾ cup pomegranate seeds, or 2 pomegranates
¼ cup pistachios, shelled and toasted
¼ cup crumbled blue cheese

TO MAKE THE QUINOA
1. Bring the water, quinoa, and salt to a boil in a small saucepan. Reduce the heat and cover, simmer for 10 to 12 minutes. Fluff with a fork.

TO MAKE THE DRESSING:
1. Whisk together the olive oil, pomegranate juice, orange juice, shallot, maple syrup, za'atar, sumac, salt, and black pepper in a medium bowl.
2. In a separate large bowl, add about ½ cup of dressing.
3. Store the remaining dressing in a glass jar or airtight container and refrigerate. The dressing can be kept up to 2 weeks. Let the chilled dressing reach room temperature before using.

TO MAKE THE SALAD:
1. Combine the spinach, parsley, and mint in the bowl with the dressing and toss gently together.
2. Add the quinoa and toss gently, then add the pomegranate seeds.
3. If using whole pomegranates: Cut the pomegranates in half. Fill a large bowl with water and hold the pomegranate half, cut side-down. Using a wooden spoon, hit the back of the pomegranate so the seeds fall into the water.
4. Immerse the pomegranate in the water and gently pull out any remaining seeds. Repeat with the remaining pomegranate. Skim the white pith off the top of the water. Drain the seeds and add them to the greens.
5. Add the pistachios and cheese and toss gently.

PER SERVING
Calories: 300, Total fat: 19g, Saturated fat: 4g, Total Carbohydrates: 28g, Protein: 8g, Sodium: 225mg, Fiber: 5g, Sugar: 8g

Best Roasted Beet, Avocado, and Watercress Salad

Prep time: 15 minutes | Cook time: 60 minutes | Serves: 4

1 tbsp. extra-virgin olive oil
1 bunch (about 1½ pounds, 680g) golden and red beets
1 bunch (about 4 ounces, 113g) watercress
1 avocado, peeled, pitted, and diced
¼ cup crumbled feta cheese
1 tbsp. white wine vinegar
½ tsp. kosher salt
¼ tsp. freshly ground black pepper
¼ cup walnuts, toasted
1 tbsp. fresh chives, chopped

1. Preheat the oven to 425°F(218°C). Wash and trim the beets (cut an inch above the beet root, leaving the long tail if desired), then wrap each beet individually in foil.
2. Place the beets on a baking sheet and roast until fully cooked, 45 to 60 minutes depending on the size of each beet. Start checking at 45 minutes, if easily pierced with a fork, the beets are cooked.
3. Remove the beets from the oven and allow them to cool. Under cold running water, slough off the skin. Cut the beets into bite-size cubes or wedges.
4. In a large bowl, whisk together the olive oil, vinegar, salt, and black pepper. Add the watercress and beets and toss well. Add the avocado, feta, walnuts, and chives and mix gently.

PER SERVING
Calories: 235, Total fat: 16g, Saturated fat: 3g, Total Carbohydrates: 21g, Protein: 6g, Sodium: 365mg, Fiber: 8g, Sugar: 12g

Italian Celery and Orange Salad

Prep time: 10 minutes | Cook time: 0 minutes | Serves: 6

3 celery stalks, including leaves, sliced diagonally into ½-inch slices
2 large oranges, peeled and sliced into rounds
½ cup green olives (or any variety)
¼ cup sliced red onion
1 tablespoon extra-virgin

olive oil
1 tablespoon olive brine
1 tablespoon freshly squeezed lemon or orange juice
¼ teaspoon kosher or sea salt
¼ teaspoon freshly ground black pepper

1. Place the celery, oranges, olives, and onion on a large serving platter or in a shallow, wide bowl.
2. In a small bowl, whisk together the oil, olive brine, and lemon juice. Pour over the salad, sprinkle with salt and pepper, and serve.

PER SERVING
Calories: 21, Fat: 1.2g, Total Carbohydrates: 1.8g, Protein: 1.1g, Fiber: 0.8g, Sodium: 138mg

Cantaloupe Caprese Salad

Prep time: 10 minutes | Cook time: 0 minutes | Serves: 6

1 cantaloupe, quartered and seeded
½ small seedless watermelon
1 cup grape tomatoes
2 cups fresh Mozzarella balls
⅓ cup fresh basil or mint leaves, torn into small

pieces
2 tablespoons extra-virgin olive oil
1 tablespoon balsamic vinegar
¼ teaspoon freshly ground black pepper
¼ teaspoon kosher or sea salt

1. Using a melon baller or a metal, teaspoon-size measuring spoon, scoop balls out of the cantaloupe. You should get about 2½ to 3 cups from one cantaloupe. (If you prefer, cut the melon into bite-size pieces instead of making balls.) Put them in a large colander over a large serving bowl.
2. Using the same method, ball or cut the watermelon into bite-size pieces, you should get about 2 cups. Put the watermelon balls in the colander with the cantaloupe.
3. Let the fruit drain for 10 minutes. Pour the juice from the bowl into a container to refrigerate and save for drinking or adding to smoothies. Wipe the bowl dry, and put in the cut fruit.

4. Add the tomatoes, Mozzarella, basil, oil, vinegar, pepper, and salt to the fruit mixture. Gently mix until everything is incorporated and serve.

PER SERVING
Calories: 58, Fat: 2.2g, Total Carbohydrates: 8.8g, Protein: 1.1g, Fiber: 0.8g, Sodium: 156mg

Barley Salad with Lemon-Tahini Sauce

Prep time: 15 minutes | Cook time: 45 minutes | Serves: 4 to 6

1½ cups pearl barley
5 tbsps. extra-virgin olive oil, divided
1½ tsps. table salt, for cooking barley
¼ cup (60 ml) tahini
1 tsp. grated lemon zest plus ¼ cup (60 ml) juice (2 lemons)
1 tbsp. sumac, divided
1 garlic clove, minced
4 scallions, sliced thin

¾ tsp. table salt
1 English cucumber, cut into ½-inch pieces
1 red bell pepper, stemmed, seeded, and chopped
1 carrot, peeled and shredded
2 tbsps. finely chopped jarred hot cherry peppers
¼ cup coarsely chopped fresh mint

1. Mix 6 cups water, 1 tablespoon oil, barley, and 1½ teaspoons salt in Instant Pot. Lock lid and close pressure release valve. Choose high pressure cook function and cook for 8 minutes. Turn off and let pressure release naturally for 15 minutes. Quick-release any remaining pressure, then carefully remove lid, letting steam escape away from you. Drain barley, spread onto rimmed baking sheet, and let cool for about 15 minutes.
2. Meanwhile, whisk remaining ¼ cup oil, 1 teaspoon sumac, 2 tablespoons water, tahini, lemon zest and juice, garlic, and ¾ teaspoon salt in large bowl until well mixed, set aside for 15 minutes.
3. Measure out and reserve ½ cup dressing for serving. Add barley, carrot, scallions, cucumber, bell pepper, and cherry peppers to bowl with dressing and gently toss. Season with salt and pepper. Transfer salad to a dish and sprinkle with mint and remaining sumac. Serve with reserved dressing separately.

PER SERVING
Calories: 370, Total Fat: 18g, Sat Fat: 2.5g, Total Carbohydrates: 47g, Protein: 8g, Sodium: 510mg, Fiber: 10g, Sugar: 3g

Moroccan Tomato and Pepper Salad

Prep time: 10 minutes | Cook time: 10 minutes | Serves: 6

2 large green bell peppers	1 small bunch flat-leaf parsley, chopped
1 hot red chili Fresno or jalapeño pepper	4 tablespoons olive oil
4 large tomatoes, peeled, seeded, and diced	1 teaspoon ground cumin
	Juice of 1 lemon
1 large cucumber, peeled and diced	Sea salt and freshly ground pepper, to taste

1. Preheat broiler on high. Broil all of the peppers and chilies until the skin blackens and blisters.
2. Place the peppers and chilies in a paper bag. Seal and set aside to cool. Combine the rest of the ingredients in a medium bowl and mix well.
3. Take peppers and chilies out from the bag and remove the skins. Seed and chop the peppers and add them to the salad.
4. Season with sea salt and freshly ground pepper.
5. Toss to combine and let sit for 15 to 20 minutes before serving.

PER SERVING
Calories: 124, Fat: 9.57g, Carbohydrates: 9.46g, Protein: 2.22g, Sugar: 5.3g, Fiber: 2.6g, Sodium: 15mg

Tuna and Stuffed Green Olive Salad

Prep time: 10 minutes | Cook time: 8 minutes | Serves: 4

1½ pounds (680 g) potatoes, quartered	½ cup pimento stuffed green olives
2 eggs	½ cup chopped roasted red peppers
3 tablespoons melted butter	2 tablespoons chopped fresh parsley
Salt and pepper, to taste	
6 pickles, chopped	10 ounces (283 g) canned tuna, drained
2 tablespoons red wine vinegar	

1. Pour 2 cups of water into the pot and add potatoes. Place a trivet over the potatoes. Lay the eggs on the trivet. Seal the lid and cook for 8 minutes on High Pressure. Do a quick release.
2. Drain and remove potatoes to a bowl. Transfer

the eggs in filled with an ice water bowl. Drizzle melted butter over the potatoes and season with salt and pepper. Peel and chop the chilled eggs.
3. Add pickles, eggs, peppers, tuna, vinegar to the potatoes and mix to coat. Serve topped with olives.

PER SERVING
Calories: 385, Fat: 16.76g, Carbohydrates: 37.8g, Protein: 23.22g, Sugar: 4.59g, Fiber: 6.7g, Sodium: 2069mg

Panzanella Salad

Prep time: 10 minutes | Cook time: 11 minutes | Serves: 2

Cooking spray	4 very thin slices of sweet onion, cut crosswise into thin rings
1 ear corn on the cob, peeled and shucked	
4 slices stale French baguette	½ cup fresh whole basil leaves
½ pint cherry or grape tomatoes, halved	2 ounces (57 g) mini Mozzarella balls (ciliegine), halved or quartered
1 medium sweet pepper, seeded and cut into 1-inch pieces	
	¼ cup honey balsamic dressing
1 medium avocado, pitted and cut into cubes	

1. Heat the grill to medium-high heat (about 350°F (180°C)) and lightly spray the cooking grates with cooking spray.
2. Grill the corn for 10 minutes, or until it is lightly charred all around.
3. Grill the bread for 30 to 45 seconds on each side, or until it has grill marks.
4. Let the corn sit until it's cool enough to handle. Cut the kernels off the cob and place them in a large bowl.
5. Cut the bread into chunks and add it to the bowl.
6. Add the tomatoes, sweet pepper, avocado, onion, basil, Mozzarella, and dressing to the bowl, and toss lightly to combine. Let the salad sit for about 15 minutes in the refrigerator, so the bread can soften and the flavors can blend.
7. This is best served shortly after it's prepared.

PER SERVING
Calories: 525, Fat: 26.2g, Total Carbohydrates: 60.8g, Protein: 16.1g, Fiber: 10.2g, Sodium: 524mg

Tabouli Salad

Prep time: 10 minutes | Cook time: 0 minutes | Serves: 8 to 10

1 cup bulgur wheat, grind
4 cups Italian parsley, finely chopped
2 cups ripe tomato, finely diced
1 cup green onion, finely chopped
½ cup lemon juice
½ cup extra-virgin olive oil
1½ teaspoons salt
1 teaspoon dried mint

1. Before you chop the vegetables, put the bulgur in a small bowl. Rinse with water, drain, and let stand in the bowl while you prepare the other ingredients.
2. Put the parsley, tomatoes, green onion, and bulgur into a large bowl.
3. In a small bowl, whisk together the lemon juice, olive oil, salt, and mint.
4. Pour the dressing over the tomato, onion, and bulgur mixture, tossing everything together. Add additional salt to taste. Serve immediately or store in the fridge for up to 2 days.

PER SERVING
Calories: 207, Fat: 14.2g, Total Carbohydrates: 19.8g, Protein: 4.1g, Fiber: 5.2g, Sodium: 462mg

Flank Steak and Baby Spinach Salad

Prep time: 10 minutes | Cook time: 10 minutes | Serves: 4

1 pound (454 g) flank steak
1 teaspoon extra-virgin olive oil
1 tablespoon garlic powder
½ teaspoon salt
½ teaspoon freshly ground black pepper
4 cups baby spinach
leaves
10 cherry tomatoes, halved
10 cremini or white mushrooms, sliced
1 small red onion, thinly sliced
½ red bell pepper, thinly sliced

1. Preheat the broiler. Line a baking sheet with aluminum foil.
2. Rub the top of the flank steak with the olive oil, garlic powder, salt, and pepper and let sit for 10 minutes before placing under the broiler. Broil for 5 minutes on each side for medium rare. Allow the meat to rest on a cutting board for 10 minutes.
3. Meanwhile, in a large bowl, combine the spinach, tomatoes, mushrooms, onion, and bell pepper and toss well.
4. To serve, divide the salad among 4 dinner plates. Slice the steak on the diagonal and place 4 to 5 slices on top of each salad. Serve with your favorite vinaigrette.

PER SERVING
Calories: 206, Fat: 7.21g, Carbohydrates: 8.46g, Protein: 26.92g, Sugar: 3.05g, Fiber: 2.5g, Sodium: 380mg

Crab Cake Lettuce Wraps

Prep time: 25 minutes, plus 15 minutes to marinate | Cook time: 25 minutes | Serves: 4

1 pound jumbo lump crab
1 large egg
6 tablespoons Roasted Garlic Aioli or avocado oil mayonnaise, divided
2 tablespoons Dijon mustard
½ cup almond flour
¼ cup minced red onion
2 teaspoons smoked paprika
1 teaspoon celery salt
1 teaspoon garlic powder
1 teaspoon dried dill (optional)
½ teaspoon freshly ground black pepper
¼ cup extra-virgin olive oil
4 large Bibb lettuce leaves, thick spine removed

1. Put the crabmeat in a large bowl and break apart the meat with a fork.
2. In a small bowl, whisk together the egg, Dijon mustard and 2 tablespoons aioli. Add to the crabmeat and blend with a fork. Put in the almond flour, paprika, red onion, celery salt, dill, garlic powder, and pepper and combine well. Set aside at room temperature for 10 to 15 minutes.
3. Shape into 8 small cakes, about 2 inches in diameter.
4. In large skillet, heat the olive oil over medium-high heat. Fry the cakes for 2 to 3 minutes per side. Cover the skillet, reduce the heat to low, and cook for another 6 to 8 minutes. Remove from the skillet.
5. Wrap 2 small crab cakes in each lettuce leaf and top with 1 tablespoon aioli. Serve.

PER SERVING
Calories: 344, Total Fat: 24g, Total Carbohydrates: 8g, Net Carbs: 6g, Protein: 24g, Fiber: 2g, Sodium: 615mg

Citrus Fennel and Pecan Salad

Prep time: 10 minutes | Cook time: 0 minutes | Serves: 2

For the Dressing:
2 tablespoons fresh orange juice
3 tablespoons olive oil
1 tablespoon blood orange vinegar, other orange vinegar, or cider vinegar
1 tablespoon honey
Salt, to taste
Freshly ground black pepper, to taste

For the Salad:
2 cups packed baby kale
1 medium navel or blood orange, segmented
½ small fennel bulb, stems and leaves removed, sliced into matchsticks
3 tablespoons toasted pecans, chopped
2 ounces (57 g) Goat cheese, crumbled

Make the Dressing
1. Combine the orange juice, olive oil, vinegar, and honey in a small bowl and whisk to combine. Season with salt and pepper. Set the dressing aside.

Make the Salad
1. Divide the baby kale, orange segments, fennel, pecans, and Goat cheese evenly between two plates.
2. Drizzle half of the dressing over each salad.

PER SERVING
Calories: 502, Fat: 39.2g, Total Carbohydrates: 30.8g, Protein: 13.1g, Fiber: 6.2g, Sodium: 158mg

Light Nutty Apple Salad

Prep time: 15 minutes | Cook time: 0 minutes | Serves: 4

6 firm apples, such as Gala or Golden Delicious, peeled, cored, and sliced
1 tablespoon freshly squeezed lemon juice
2 kiwis, peeled and diced
½ cup sliced strawberries
½ cup packaged shredded coleslaw mix, without dressing
½ cup walnut halves

¼ cup slivered almonds
¼ cup balsamic vinegar
¼ cup extra-virgin olive oil
2 tablespoons sesame seeds, plus more for garnish (optional)
¼ teaspoon salt
¼ teaspoon freshly ground black pepper

1. In a medium bowl, toss the apple slices with the lemon juice to prevent browning. Add the kiwis, strawberries, coleslaw mix, walnuts, and almonds and toss well to mix.
2. In a small bowl, whisk together the balsamic vinegar, olive oil, and sesame seeds and season with salt and pepper.
3. Pour the dressing over the salad and toss to coat.
4. To serve, spoon into small bowls and top with additional sesame seeds if desired.

PER SERVING
Calories: 338, Fat: 15.54g, Carbohydrates: 51.75g, Protein: 4.25g, Sugar: 38.3g, Fiber: 9.4g, Sodium: 275mg

Wilted Mixed Greens with Bacon and Eggs

Prep time: 20 minutes | Cook time: 25 minutes | Serves: 4

8 bacon strips
¼ tsp. ground chipotle pepper
1 tsp. packed honey
1 small red onion, halved and thinly sliced
1 tsp. coconut sugar
2 tbsps. champagne vinegar

½ tsp. pepper
4 large eggs
¼ tsp. coconut salt
8 cups spring mix salad greens (about 5 oz., 142 g)
½ cup crumbled feta cheese

1. Preheat oven to 350°F(180°C). On one half of a foil-lined 15x10x1-in. pan, add the bacon. Combine the chipotle pepper and honey, sprinkle this mixture evenly over bacon. Bake for 10 minutes, until bacon begins to shrink.
2. Move bacon to other half of pan with tongs. Add onion to bacon drippings, stirring to coat. Place it back to oven, bake for 15 minutes, until bacon is crisp. Use paper towel to drain, reserving 2 Tbsp. drippings.
3. 3. Add the sugar, vinegar, pepper and reserved bacon drippings into a small bowl, whisk them together. Coarsely chop bacon.
4. 4. Spray a large nonstick skillet with cooking spray and place over medium-high heat. Break eggs, one at a time, into skillet. Reduce heat to low, cook the eggs until desired doneness, turning after whites are set if desired. Sprinkle with salt.
5. With dressing to toss greens, divide among four dishes. Place the bacon, onion, cheese and eggs on the top. Serve immediately.

PER SERVING
Calories: 279, Fat: 20g, Carbohydrates: 10g, Protein: 17g, Sugar: 3g, Fiber: 3g, Sodium: 510mg

Riviera Balsamic Tuna Salad

Prep time: 15 minutes | Cook time: 0 minutes | Serves: 4

¼ cup olive oil	1 (6-ounce / 170-g) can
¼ cup balsamic vinegar	solid white albacore tuna,
½ teaspoon minced garlic	drained
¼ teaspoon dried oregano	1 cup canned garbanzo beans, rinsed and
Sea salt and freshly ground pepper, to taste	drained
2 tablespoons capers, drained	¼ cup low-salt olives, pitted and quartered
4 to 6 cups baby greens	2 Roma tomatoes, chopped

1. To make the vinaigrette, whisk together the olive oil, balsamic vinegar, garlic, oregano, sea salt, and pepper until emulsified.
2. Stir in the capers. Refrigerate for up to 6 hours before serving.
3. Place the baby greens in a salad bowl or on individual plates, and top with the tuna, beans, olives, and tomatoes.
4. Drizzle the vinaigrette over all, and serve immediately.

PER SERVING
Calories: 380, Fat: 19.99g, Carbohydrates: 30.13g, Protein: 21.2g, Sugar: 9.64g, Fiber: 10.4g, Sodium: 773mg

Lemony Turmeric Chicken Salad

Prep time: 15 minutes | Cook time: 20 minutes | Serves: 4

4 boneless skinless chicken breasts	oil
6 cups chopped romaine lettuce	1 tbsp. chopped fresh cilantro
1 garlic clove, minced	½ cup (120 ml) plain unsweetened almond yogurt
1 tsp. salt	
¼ tsp. ground turmeric	1 tbsp. freshly squeezed lemon juice
¼ tsp. freshly ground black pepper	1 tsp. lemon zest
1 tbsp. extra-virgin olive	½ cup chopped almonds

1. Put the chicken breast in a shallow baking dish.
2. Whisk together the olive oil, garlic, cilantro, turmeric, salt, and pepper in a small bowl. Rub the mixture all over the chicken. Cover the chicken and marinate, refrigerated for at least 30 minutes.
3. Preheat the oven to 375°F (190ºC). When the oven is hot, put the baking dish in the preheated oven and bake for 20 minutes. Remove from the oven and set aside.
4. Whisk together the lemon juice, yogurt, and lemon zest in a large bowl. Add the almonds and romaine lettuce and toss to coat them with the dressing.
5. Transfer the salad to a serving platter. Cut the chicken breast into strips and arrange them over lettuce.

PER SERVING
Calories: 418, Total Fat: 21g, Total Carbohydrates: 10g, Protein: 46g, Sugar: 3g, Fiber: 4g, Sodium: 759mg

Roasted Asparagus Salad with Quinoa

Prep time: 10 minutes | Cook time: 15 minutes | Serves: 4

1 bunch asparagus, trimmed	vinegar
2 cups cooked quinoa, cold or at room temperature	¼ cup chopped fresh mint
	¼ red onion, finely chopped
3 tbsps extra-virgin olive oil, divided	Freshly ground black pepper
1 tbsp. flaxseed	1 tsp. salt, plus additional
1 tbsp. apple cider	for seasoning

1. Preheat the oven to 400°F in advance.
2. Put the asparagus, 1 tablespoon of olive oil and 1 teaspoon of salt in a large bowl, mix and stir.
3. Wrap the asparagus in aluminum foil, and then place the wrapped asparagus on the baking tray. Put the slices in the oven and bake for 10 to 15 minutes.
4. While roasting the asparagus, in a large bowl, mix and stir the quinoa, onion, vinegar, mint, flaxseed, and the remaining 2 tablespoons of olive oil. Take out the roasted asparagus and let it stand at room temperature.
5. When the asparagus is not so hot, cut it into pieces. Add to the mixed quinoa, sprinkle with salt and pepper to taste, and enjoy.

PER SERVING
Calories: 228, Total Fat: 13g, Total Carbohydrates: 24g, Protein: 6g, Sugar: 2g, Fiber: 5g, Sodium: 592mg

Kale and Cherry Tomato Salad

Prep time: 5 minutes | Cook time: 10 minutes | Serves: 4

2 heads kale
1 tablespoon olive oil
2 cloves garlic, minced
1 cup cherry tomatoes, sliced
Sea salt and freshly ground pepper, to taste
Juice of 1 lemon

1. Rinse and dry kale.
2. Tear the kale into bite-sized pieces.
3. Heat 1 tablespoon of the olive oil in a large skillet, and add the garlic. Cook for 1 minute and then add the kale.
4. Cook just until wilted, then add the tomatoes.
5. Cook until tomatoes are softened, then remove from heat.
6. Place tomatoes and kale in a bowl, and season with sea salt and freshly ground pepper.
7. Drizzle with remaining olive oil and lemon juice, serve, and enjoy.

PER SERVING
Calories: 47, Fat: 3.58g, Carbohydrates: 3.94g, Protein: 0.88g, Sugar: 1.48g, Fiber: 1g, Sodium: 5mg

Tasty Wild Rice Salad with Chickpeas and Pickled Radish

Prep time: 20 minutes | Cook time: 45 minutes | Serves: 4 (main) or 6 (side)

FOR THE RICE
1 cup water
4 ounces (113g) (⅔ cup) wild rice
¼ tsp. kosher salt
FOR THE PICKLED RADISH
1 bunch radishes (6 to 8 small), sliced thin
½ cup white wine vinegar
½ tsp. kosher salt
FOR THE DRESSING
2 tbsps. extra-virgin olive oil
2 tbsps. white wine vinegar
½ tsp. pure maple syrup
½ tsp. kosher salt
¼ tsp. freshly ground black pepper
FOR THE SALAD
1 (15-ounce, 425g) can no-salt-added or low-sodium chickpeas, rinsed and drained
1 bulb fennel, diced
¼ cup walnuts, chopped and toasted
¼ cup crumbled feta cheese
¼ cup currants
2 tbsps. fresh dill, chopped

TO MAKE THE RICE
1. Bring the water, rice, and salt to a boil in a medium saucepan. Cover, reduce the heat, and simmer for 45 minutes.

TO MAKE THE PICKLED RADISH
1. In a medium bowl, combine the radishes, vinegar, and salt. Let sit for 15 to 30 minutes.

TO MAKE THE DRESSING
1. In a large bowl, whisk together the olive oil, vinegar, maple syrup, salt, and black pepper.

TO MAKE THE SALAD
1. While still warm, add the rice to the bowl with the dressing and mix well.
2. Add the chickpeas, fennel, walnuts, feta, currants, and dill. Mix well.
3. Garnish with the pickled radishes before serving.

PER SERVING
Calories: 310, Total fat: 16g, Saturated fat: 3g, Total Carbohydrates: 36g, Protein: 10g, Sodium: 400mg, Fiber: 7g, Sugar: 11g

Simple Mediterranean Chopped Salad

Prep time: 15 minutes | Cook time: 10 minutes | Serves: 4

2 cups packed spinach
3 large tomatoes, diced
1 tbsp. sumac
1 bunch radishes, sliced thin
1 English cucumber, peeled and diced
¼ cup extra-virgin olive oil
2 scallions, sliced
2 garlic cloves, minced
1 tbsp. chopped fresh mint
1 tbsp. chopped fresh parsley
1 cup unsweetened plain almond yogurt
1 tbsp. apple cider vinegar
3 tbsps freshly squeezed lemon juice
¼ tsp. freshly ground black pepper
1 tsp. salt

1. Put spinach, tomatoes, radishes, apple cider vinegar, green onions, garlic, cucumber, mint, yogurt, olive oil, parsley, lemon juice, salt, pepper, and sumac in a large bowl and stir to combine.
2. It is recommended to pair with cooked chicken or fish, if necessary.
3. Mediterranean tip: If following the Mediterranean Action Plan, sprinkle 3 ounces of goat cheese on top.

PER SERVING
Calories: 194, Total Fat: 14g, Total Carbohydrates: 15g, Protein: 4g, Sugar: 7g, Fiber: 5g, Sodium: 661mg

Fruited Chicken Breast Salad

Prep time: 10 minutes | Cook time: 0 minutes | Serves: 2

2 cups chopped cooked chicken breast	2 tablespoons honey Dijon mustard
2 Granny Smith apples, peeled, cored, and diced	1 tablespoon olive oil low fat yogurt
½ cup dried cranberries	½ teaspoon salt
¼ cup diced red onion	¼ teaspoon freshly ground black pepper
¼ cup diced celery	

1. In a medium bowl, combine the chicken, apples, cranberries, onion, and celery and mix well.
2. In a small bowl, combine the mustard, low fat yogurt, salt, and pepper and whisk together until well blended.
3. Stir the dressing into the chicken mixture until thoroughly combined.

PER SERVING
Calories: 401, Fat: 5.76g, Carbohydrates: 39.53g, Protein: 45.01g, Sugar: 22.51g, Fiber: 5.4g, Sodium: 855mg

Vegetable Salad with Sardine Filets

Prep time: 10 minutes | Cook time: 0 minutes | Serves: 6

½ cup olive oil	1 pound (454 g) arugula, trimmed and chopped
Juice of 1 medium lemon	1 small red onion, thinly sliced
1 teaspoon Dijon mustard	
Sea salt and freshly ground pepper, to taste	1 small bunch flat-leaf parsley, chopped
4 medium tomatoes, diced	4 whole sardine filets packed in olive oil, drained and chopped
1 large cucumber, peeled and diced	

1. For the dressing, whisk together the olive oil, lemon juice, and mustard, and season with sea salt and pepper. Set aside.
2. In a large bowl, combine all the vegetables with the parsley, and toss. Add the sardine filets on top of the salad.
3. Drizzle the dressing over the salad just before serving.

PER SERVING
Calories: 227, Fat: 19.8g, Carbohydrates: 9.53g, Protein: 5.44g, Sugar: 5.14g, Fiber: 3.2g, Sodium: 66mg

Mixed-Beans Salad

Prep time: 10 minutes | Cook time: 10 minutes | Serves: 4

½ cup white beans, cooked	1 red bell pepper, diced
½ cup black-eyed peas, cooked	1 small bunch flat-leaf parsley, chopped
½ cup fava beans, cooked	2 tablespoons olive oil
	1 teaspoon ground cumin
½ cup lima beans, cooked	Juice of 1 lemon
	Sea salt and freshly ground pepper, to taste

1. You can cook the beans a day or two in advance to speed up the preparation of this dish.
2. Combine all ingredients in a large bowl and mix well. Season to taste.
3. Allow to sit for 30 minutes, so the flavors can come together before serving.

PER SERVING
Calories: 224, Fat: 7.7g, Carbohydrates: 30.49g, Protein: 7.7g, Sugar: 3.31g, Fiber: 8.8g, Sodium: 20mg

Yellow Pepper and Tomato Salad

Prep time: 5 minutes | Cook time: 10 minutes | Serves: 6

3 large yellow peppers	4 large tomatoes, seeded and diced
¼ cup olive oil	
1 small bunch fresh basil leaves	Sea salt and freshly ground pepper, to taste
2 cloves garlic, minced	

1. Preheat broiler to high heat and broil the peppers until blackened on all sides.
2. Remove from heat and place in a paper bag. Seal and allow peppers to cool.
3. Once cooled, peel the skins off the peppers, then seed and chop them.
4. Add half of the peppers to a food processor along with the olive oil, basil, and garlic, and pulse several times to make the dressing.
5. Combine the rest of the peppers with the tomatoes and toss with the dressing.
6. Season the salad with sea salt and freshly ground pepper. Allow salad to come to room temperature before serving.

PER SERVING
Calories: 129, Fat: 9.46g, Carbohydrates: 11.24g, Protein: 2.11g, Sugar: 3.2g, Fiber: 2.4g, Sodium: 8mg

Peach and Tomato Salad

Prep time: 5 minutes | Cook time: 0 minutes | Serves: 2

2 ripe peaches, pitted and sliced into wedges
2 ripe tomatoes, cut into wedges
½ red onion, thinly sliced

Sea salt and freshly ground pepper, to taste
3 tablespoons olive oil
1 tablespoon lemon juice

1. Toss the peaches, tomatoes, and red onion in a large bowl. Season to taste.
2. Add the olive oil and lemon juice, and gently toss. Serve at room temperature.

PER SERVING
Calories: 249, Fat: 20.75g, Carbohydrates: 16.99g, Protein: 1.81g, Sugar: 13.7g, Fiber: 3g, Sodium: 2mg

Tuna Niçoise Salad

Prep time: 15 minutes | Cook time: 20 minutes | Serves: 4

2 (5-ounce, 142g) cans no-salt-added tuna packed in olive oil, drained
1 pound (454g) small red or fingerling potatoes, halved
1 pound (454g) green beans or haricots verts, trimmed

1 head romaine lettuce, chopped or torn into bite-size pieces
½ pint cherry tomatoes, halved
8 radishes, sliced thin
½ cup olives, pitted (any kind you like)
8 anchovies (optional)

1. Fill a large pot fitted with a steamer basket with 2 to 3 inches of water. Put the potatoes in the steamer basket and lay the green beans on top of the potatoes. Bring the water to a boil over high heat, lower the heat to low and simmer, cover, and cook for 7 minutes, or until the green beans are tender but crisp. Remove the green beans and continue to steam the potatoes for an additional 10 minutes.
2. Place the romaine lettuce on a serving platter. Group the potatoes, green beans, tomatoes, radishes, olives, and tuna in different areas of the platter. If using the anchovies, place them around the platter.

PER SERVING
Calories: 315, Total fat: 9g, Saturated fat: 1g, Total Carbohydrates: 33g, Protein: 28g, Sodium: 420mg, Fiber: 9g, Sugar: 8g

Balsamic Asparagus Salad

Prep time: 5 minutes | Cook time: 0 minutes | Serves: 4

1 pound (454 g) asparagus
Sea salt and freshly ground pepper, to taste

4 tablespoons olive oil
1 tablespoon balsamic vinegar
1 tablespoon lemon zest

1. Either roast the asparagus or, with a vegetable peeler, shave it into thin strips.
2. Season to taste.
3. Toss with the olive oil and vinegar, garnish with a sprinkle of lemon zest, and serve.

PER SERVING
Calories: 148, Fat: 13.66g, Carbohydrates: 5.71g, Protein: 2.59g, Sugar: 2.83g, Fiber: 2.5g, Sodium: 4mg

Nutty Rib-Eye Steak Salad

Prep time: 15 minutes | Cook time: 35 minutes | Serves: 4

1 pound (454 g) rib-eye steak, boneless
4 ounces (113 g) fresh arugula
1 large tomato, chopped
¼ cup fresh Goat's cheese
4 almonds

4 walnuts
4 hazelnuts
3 tablespoons olive oil
2 cups beef broth
2 tablespoons red wine vinegar
1 tablespoon Italian Seasoning mix

1. Whisk together vinegar, Italian mix, and olive oil. Brush each steak with this mixture and place in your instant pot. Pour in the broth and seal the lid.
2. Cook on Meat/Stew for 25 minutes on High Pressure. Release the Pressure naturally, for about 10 minutes, and remove the steaks along with the broth.
3. Grease the inner pot with oil and hit Sauté. Brown the steaks on both sides for 5 to 6 minutes. Remove from the pot and cool for 5 minutes before slicing.
4. In a bowl, mix arugula, tomato, cheese, almonds, walnuts, and hazelnuts. Top with steaks and drizzle with red wine mixture.

PER SERVING
Calories: 493, Fat: 41.34g, Carbohydrates: 5.36g, Protein: 26.14g, Sugar: 2.36g, Fiber: 1.9g, Sodium: 715mg

Apple and Baby Spinach Salad

Prep time: 5 minutes | Cook time: 0 minutes | Serves: 4

8 cups baby spinach
1 medium Granny Smith apple, diced
1 medium red apple, diced
½ cup toasted walnuts
2 ounces (57 g) low-fat,

sharp white Cheddar cheese, cubed
3 tablespoons olive oil
1 tablespoon red wine vinegar or apple cider vinegar

1. Toss the spinach, apples, walnuts, and cubed cheese together. Lightly drizzle olive oil and vinegar over top and serve.

PER SERVING
Calories: 275, Fat: 21.83g, Carbohydrates: 15.71g, Protein: 6.95g, Sugar: 9.28g, Fiber: 4.3g, Sodium: 140mg

Shredded Vegetable Slaw with Cheese and Honey

Prep time: 20 minutes | Cook time: 1 minute | Serves: 4-6

½ cup extra-virgin olive oil
2 large broccoli stems, peeled and shredded
2 carrots, peeled and shredded
½ celery root bulb, peeled and shredded
1 large beet, peeled and shredded
2 zucchinis, shredded
1 small red onion, sliced

thin
¼ cup chopped fresh Italian parsley
3 ounces (85 g) feta cheese, crumbled
½ cup apple cider vinegar
1 tbsp. raw honey or maple syrup
1 tsp. Dijon mustard
1 tsp. salt
¼ tsp. freshly ground black pepper

1. Add the olive oil, cider vinegar, honey, Dijon mustard, salt, and pepper into a large bowl, whisk them together.
2. Mix in the broccoli, carrots, celery root, beets, zucchini, onion, and Italian parsley. Toss the dressing and make it to coat the vegetables.
3. On a serving bowl, place the slaw and garnish with the feta cheese. Serve immediately.

PER SERVING
Calories: 388, Total Fat: 30g, Total Carbohydrates: 26g, Protein: 8g, Sugar: 12g, Fiber: 6g, Sodium: 981mg

Balsamic Baby Spinach Salad

Prep time: 10 minutes | Cook time: 0 minutes | Serves: 4

1 large ripe tomato
1 medium red onion
½ teaspoon fresh lemon zest
3 tablespoons balsamic vinegar

¼ cup extra-virgin olive oil
½ teaspoon salt
1 pound (454 g) baby spinach, washed, stems removed

1. Dice the tomato into ¼-inch pieces and slice the onion into long slivers.
2. In a small bowl, whisk together the lemon zest, balsamic vinegar, olive oil, and salt.
3. Put the spinach, tomatoes, and onions in a large bowl. Pour the dressing over the salad and lightly toss to coat.

PER SERVING
Calories: 172, Fat: 14.2g, Total Carbohydrates: 9.8g, Protein: 4.1g, Fiber: 4.2g, Sodium: 389mg

Traditional Greek Salad with Feta

Prep time: 10 minutes | Cook time: 0 | Serves: 4

2 large English cucumbers
4 Roma tomatoes, quartered
1 green bell pepper, cut into 1- to 1½-inch chunks
¼ small red onion, thinly sliced
4 ounces (113 g) pitted Kalamata olives
4 ounces (113 g)

crumbled traditional feta cheese
¼ cup (60 ml) extra-virgin olive oil
2 tbsps. fresh lemon juice
1 tbsp. red wine vinegar
1 tbsp. chopped fresh oregano
¼ tsp. freshly ground black pepper

1. Cut the cucumbers in half lengthwise and then into ½-inch-thick half-moons. Put in a large bowl.
2. Add the quartered tomatoes, red onion, bell pepper, and olives.
3. In a small bowl, whisk together the olive oil, oregano, vinegar, lemon juice, and pepper. Drizzle over the vegetables and toss to coat.
4. Divide between salad plates and top with feta.

PER SERVING
Calories: 278, Total Fat: 22g, Total Carbohydrates: 12g, Protein: 8g, Net Carbs: 8g, Fiber: 4g, Sodium: 572mg

Spring Creamy Egg Salad

Prep time: 10 minutes | Cook time: 5 minutes | Serves: 6

2 cups water
Cooking spray
6 eggs
¼ cup crème frâiche
2 large spring onions,
minced
1 tablespoon dill, minced
2 teaspoons mustard
Salt and black pepper, to taste

1. Grease a cake pan with cooking spray. Carefully crack the eggs into the pan. To the inner pot, add water. Set pan on the trivet.
2. Seal the lid and cook for 5 minutes on High Pressure. Do a quick release. Loosen the eggs on the edges with a knife. Transfer to a cutting board and chop into smaller sizes.
3. Transfer the chopped eggs to a bowl. Add in onion, mustard, salt, dill, crème frâiche, and black pepper.

PER SERVING
Calories: 145, Fat: 10.18g, Carbohydrates: 3.56g, Protein: 9.46g, Sugar: 2.01g, Fiber: 0.5g, Sodium: 127mg

Fennel, Tomato, and Spinach Salad

Prep time: 10 minutes | Cook time: 5 minutes | Serves: 4

4 tablespoons chicken broth
4 cups baby spinach leaves
10 cherry tomatoes, halved
Sea salt and freshly ground pepper, to taste
1 fennel bulb, sliced
¼ cup olive oil
Juice of 2 lemons

1. In a large sauté pan, heat the chicken broth over medium heat. Add the spinach and tomatoes and cook until spinach is wilted. Season with sea salt and freshly ground pepper to taste.
2. Remove from heat and toss fennel slices in with the spinach and tomatoes. Let the fennel warm in the pan, then transfer to a large bowl.
3. Drizzle with the olive oil and lemon juice, and serve immediately.

PER SERVING
Calories: 160, Fat: 13.93g, Carbohydrates: 9.1g, Protein: 2.2g, Sugar: 4.22g, Fiber: 3.2g, Sodium: 115mg

Feta Watermelon Salad

Prep time: 5 minutes | Cook time: 0 minutes | Serves: 2

3 cups packed arugula
2½ cups watermelon, cut into bite-size cubes
2 ounces (57 g) Feta
cheese, crumbled
2 tablespoons balsamic glaze

1. Divide the arugula between two plates.
2. Divide the watermelon cubes between the beds of arugula.
3. Sprinkle 1 ounce of the Feta over each salad.
4. Drizzle about 1 tablespoon of the glaze (or more if desired) over each salad.

PER SERVING
Calories: 159, Fat: 7.2g, Total Carbohydrates: 20.8g, Protein: 6.1g, Fiber: 1.2g, Sodium: 327mg

Healthy French Lentil Salad

Prep time: 20 minutes | Cook time: 25 minutes | Serves: 4

2 tbsps. extra-virgin olive oil
2 tbsps. red wine vinegar
½ tsp. ground cumin
½ tsp. kosher salt
¼ tsp. freshly ground black pepper
2 celery stalks, diced
small
1 bell pepper, diced small
½ red onion, diced small
¼ cup fresh parsley, chopped
¼ cup fresh mint, chopped

TO MAKE THE LENTILS
1. Put the lentils, garlic, and bay leaf in a large saucepan. Cover with water by about 3 inches and bring to a boil. Reduce the heat, cover, and simmer until tender, 20 to 30 minutes.
2. Drain the lentils to remove any remaining water after cooking. Remove the garlic and bay leaf.
TO MAKE THE SALAD
1. In a large bowl, whisk together the olive oil, vinegar, cumin, salt, and black pepper. Add the celery, bell pepper, onion, parsley, and mint and toss to combine.
2. Add the lentils and mix well.

PER SERVING
Calories: 200, Total fat: 8g, Saturated fat: 1g, Total Carbohydrates: 26g, Protein: 10g, Sodium: 165mg, Fiber: 10g, Sugar: 5g

Avocado and Mango Salad with Fresh Veggies

Prep time: 15 minutes | Cook time: 1 minute | Serves: 4

2 ripe mangos, cut into
1 large ripe avocado
½-inch cubes
2 romaine lettuce hearts,
chopped

1 cucumber, peeled and
cut into ¼-inch cubes
2 scallions, sliced thin
1 cup Creamy Coconut-
Herb Dressing

1. Add the romaine lettuce, cucumber, mangos, scallions, and avocado into a large serving bowl, combine them together.
2. Over the fruit and vegetables, pour in the Creamy Coconut-Herb Dressing. Toss to combine and serve.

PER SERVING

Calories: 253, Total Fat: 13g, Total Carbohydrates: 37g, Sugar: 21g, Fiber: 10g, Protein: 4g, Sodium: 363mg

Greek Vegetable Salad

Prep time: 10 minutes | Cook time: 0 minutes | Serves: 4 to 6

1 head iceberg lettuce
2 cups cherry tomatoes
1 large cucumber
1 medium onion
½ cup extra-virgin olive
oil
¼ cup lemon juice

¼ teaspoon salt
1 clove garlic, minced
1 cup Kalamata olives,
pitted
1 (6-ounce / 170-g)
package Feta cheese,
crumbled

1. Cut the lettuce into 1-inch pieces and put them in a large salad bowl.
2. Cut the tomatoes in half and add them to the salad bowl.
3. Slice the cucumber into bite-size pieces and add them to the salad bowl.
4. Thinly slice the onion and add it to the salad bowl.
5. In another small bowl, whisk together the olive oil, lemon juice, salt, and garlic. Pour the dressing over the salad and gently toss to evenly coat.
6. Top the salad with the Kalamata olives and Feta cheese and serve.

PER SERVING

Calories: 539, Fat: 50.2g, Total Carbohydrates: 17.8g, Protein: 9.1g, Fiber: 4.2g, Sodium: 785mg

Cheese and Arugula Salad

Prep time: 10 minutes | Cook time: 0 | Serves: 4

1 tbsp. red wine vinegar
½ tsp. salt
4 tbsps. extra-virgin olive
oil
Zest and juice of 2
clementines or 1 orange
¼ tsp. freshly ground
black pepper

8 cups baby arugula
1 cup crumbled goat
cheese
½ cup pomegranate
seeds
1 cup coarsely chopped
walnuts

1. Whisk together the olive oil, vinegar, zest and juice, salt and pepper in a small bowl and set aside.
2. In a large bowl, mix the arugula, goat cheese, walnuts, and pomegranate seeds. Drizzle with the dressing and toss to coat.

PER SERVING

Calories: 444, Total Fat: 40g, Total Carbohydrates: 11g, Net Carbs: 8g, Protein: 10g, Fiber: 3g, Sodium: 412mg

Pistachio-Parmesan Kale and Arugula Salad

Prep time: 10 minutes | Cook time: minutes | Serves: 6

6 cups raw kale,
center ribs removed
and discarded, leaves
coarsely chopped
¼ cup extra-virgin olive
oil
2 tablespoons freshly
squeezed lemon juice

½ teaspoon smoked
paprika
2 cups arugula
⅓ cup unsalted shelled
pistachios
6 tablespoons grated
Parmesan or Pecorino
Romano cheese

1. In a large salad bowl, combine the kale, oil, lemon juice, and smoked paprika. With your hands, gently massage the leaves for about 15 seconds or so, until all are thoroughly coated. Let the kale sit for 10 minutes.
2. When you're ready to serve, gently mix in the arugula and pistachios. Divide the salad among six serving bowls, sprinkle 1 tablespoon of grated cheese over each, and serve.

PER SERVING

Calories: 105, Fat: 9.2g, Total Carbohydrates: 3.8g, Protein: 4.1g, Fiber: 2.2g, Sodium: 176mg

Carrot Salad with Tahini-Lime Dressing

Prep time: 10 minutes | Cook time: 5 minutes | Serves: 6

4 cups grated or shredded carrots
⅓ cup shelled pistachios, roughly chopped
½ cup fresh cilantro leaves, finely chopped
3 scallions, sliced
4 Medjool dates, pitted and chopped
¼ tsp. red pepper flakes
½ cup Tahini-Lime Dressing

1. Mix together the cilantro, carrots, scallions, dates, pistachios, and red pepper flakes in a large bowl.
2. Pour the dressing over the salad and toss to coat. Serve immediately.

PER SERVING
Calories: 101, Total Fat: 2g, Saturated Fat: 0g, Carbohydrates: 22g, Protein: 2g, Fiber: 4g

Beet and Apple Salad with Celery and Spinach

Prep time: 15 minutes | Cook time: 1 minute | Serves: 4

2 green apples, cored and quartered
2 small beets, peeled and quartered
4 cups spinach
2 celery stalks, sliced thin
½ cup shredded carrots
½ red onion, sliced thin
1 tbsp. apple cider
vinegar
3 tbsps. extra-virgin olive oil
1 tbsp. raw honey or maple syrup
Salt
Freshly ground black pepper
¼ cup pumpkin seeds

1. Slice the apples and the beets with a mandoline or the slicing disk of a food processor.
2. On a large platter, put the spinach then arrange the apples and beets over the spinach. Place the celery, carrots, and red onion on top.
3. Add the cider vinegar, olive oil, and honey into a small bowl, whisk them together. Season with salt and pepper.
4. Drizzle the salad with the dressing and garnish with the pumpkin seeds. Serve.

PER SERVING
Calories: 239, Total Fat: 15g, Total Carbohydrates: 27g, Protein: 4g, Sugar: 18g, Fiber: 5g, Sodium: 121mg

Fig, Prosciutto and Arugula Salad

Prep time: 10 minutes | Cook time: 1 minute | Serves: 2

3 cups arugula
4 fresh, ripe figs (or 4 to 6 dried figs), stemmed and sliced
2 tablespoons olive oil
3 very thin slices prosciutto, trimmed of any fat and sliced lengthwise
into 1-inch strips
¼ cup pecan halves, lightly toasted
2 tablespoons crumbled blue cheese
1 to 2 tablespoons balsamic glaze

1. In a large bowl, toss the arugula and figs with the olive oil.
2. Place the prosciutto on a microwave-safe plate and heat it on high in the microwave for 60 seconds, or until it just starts to crisp.
3. Add the crisped prosciutto, pecans, and blue cheese to the bowl. Toss the salad lightly.
4. Drizzle with the balsamic glaze.

PER SERVING
Calories: 519, Fat: 38.2g, Total Carbohydrates: 29.8g, Protein: 20.1g, Fiber: 6.2g, Sodium: 482mg

Easy Crab Salad with Endive

Prep time: 10 minutes | Cook time: 10 minutes | Serves: 4

1 pound (454g) lump crabmeat
⅔ cup plain Greek yogurt
3 tbsps mayonnaise
3 tbsps fresh chives, chopped, plus additional for garnish
3 tbsps fresh parsley, chopped, plus additional for garnish
3 tbsps fresh basil, chopped, plus additional for garnish
Zest of 1 lemon
Juice of 1 lemon
½ tsp. kosher salt
¼ tsp. freshly ground black pepper
4 endives, ends cut off and leaves separated

1. Combine the crab, yogurt, mayonnaise, chives, parsley, basil, lemon zest, lemon juice, salt, and black pepper in a medium bowl, and mix until well combined.
2. Place the endive leaves on 4 salad plates. Divide the crab mixture evenly on top of the endive. Garnish with additional herbs if desired.

PER SERVING
Calories: 200, Total fat: 9g, Saturated fat: 2g, Total Carbohydrates: 44g, Protein: 25g, Sodium: 570mg, Fiber: 2g, Sugar: 2g

Lemony Kale Salad

Prep time: 10 minutes | Cook time: 10 minutes | Serves: 4

2 heads kale
Sea salt and freshly ground pepper
Juice of 1 lemon
1+ tbsp. olive oil
2 cloves garlic, minced
1 cup cherry tomatoes, sliced

1. Wash and dry kale.
2. Tear the kale into small pieces.
3. Heat olive oil in a large skillet, and add the garlic. Cook for 1 minute and then add the kale.
4. Add the tomatoes after kale wilted.
5. Cook until tomatoes are softened, then remove from heat.
6. Put tomatoes and kale together in a bowl, and season with sea salt and freshly ground pepper.
7. Drizzle with remaining olive oil and lemon juice, serve.

PER SERVING
Calories: 59, Fat: 3.83g, Carbohydrates: 5.95g, Protein: 2g, Sodium: 16mg, Fiber: 1.9 g

Chopped Salad With Tuna

Prep time: 15 minutes | Cook time: 1 minute | Serves: 4

2 tbsps. extra-virgin olive oil
2 (6-ounce, 170g) cans no-salt-added tuna packed in water, drained
12 olives, pitted and chopped
6 cups baby spinach
2 tbsps. lemon juice
2 tsps. Dijon mustard
½ tsp. kosher salt
¼ tsp. freshly ground black pepper
½ cup celery, diced
½ cup red onion, diced
½ cup red bell pepper, diced
½ cup fresh parsley, chopped

1. In a medium bowl, whisk together the olive oil, lemon juice, mustard, salt, and black pepper. Add in the olives, celery, onion, bell pepper, and parsley and mix well. Add the tuna and gently incorporate.
2. Divide the spinach evenly among 4 plates or bowls. Spoon the tuna salad evenly on top of the spinach.

PER SERVING
Calories: 220, Total fat: 11g, Saturated fat: 1g, Total Carbohydrates: 7g, Protein: 25g, Sodium: 396mg, Fiber: 2g, Sugar: 2g

Kale Salad with Anchovies

Prep time: 15 minutes, plus 30 minutes to rest | Cook time: 0 | Serves: 4

¼ cup (60 ml) extra-virgin olive oil
8 anchovy fillets, roughly chopped
1 large bunch lacinato or dinosaur kale
¼ cup toasted pine nuts
1 cup shaved or coarsely shredded fresh Parmesan cheese
2 to 3 tbsps. fresh lemon juice (from 1 large lemon)
2 tsps. red pepper flakes (optional)

1. Remove the rough center stems from the kale leaves and roughly tear each leaf into about 4x1-inch strips. Put the torn kale in a large bowl and add the pine nuts and cheese.
2. Whisk together the olive oil, lemon juice, anchovies, and red pepper flakes in a small bowl. Drizzle over the salad and toss to coat. Set aside at room temperature 30 minutes before serving.

PER SERVING
Calories: 337, Total Fat: 25g, Total Carbohydrates: 12g, Net Carbs: 10g, Protein: 16g, Fiber: 2g, Sodium: 603mg

Palm Lettuce Salad with Caesar Dressing

Prep time: 15 minutes | Cook time: 0 | Serves: 4

1 (14-ounce, 397 g) can hearts of palm, drained and sliced
½ cup sunflower seeds
2 romaine lettuce hearts, chopped
1 recipe Almost Caesar Dressing
Salt
Freshly ground black pepper

1. Add the hearts of palm, sunflower seeds and lettuce into a large bowl, combine them together.
2. Pour in the enough dressing to lightly coat the lettuce leaves. Reserve any remaining dressing for another use.
3. Use pepper and salt to season the salad, and serve immediately.

PER SERVING
Calories: 431, Total Fat: 42g, Total Carbohydrates: 14g, Protein: 6g, Sugar: 3g, Fiber: 5g, Sodium: 803mg

Pepper and Tomato Salad

Prep time: 10 minutes | Cook time: 10 minutes | Serves: 6

2 cloves garlic, minced
4 large tomatoes, seeded and diced
3 large yellow peppers
1/4 cup (60 ml) olive oil

1 small bunch fresh basil leaves
Sea salt and freshly ground pepper

1. Preheat broiler to high heat and broil the peppers until blackened.
2. Remove from heat and place peppers in a paper bag. Seal and cool down peppers.
3. Peel the skins off the peppers, then seed and chop them.
4. Add half of the peppers to a food processor with olive oil, basil, and garlic, and pulse several times to make the dressing.
5. Mix the rest of the peppers with the tomatoes and toss with the dressing.
6. Season the salad with sea salt and freshly ground pepper. Serve with room temperature.

PER SERVING
Calories: 113, Fat: 9.31g, Carbohydrates: 7.43g, Protein: 1.62g, Sodium: 8mg, Fiber: 1.9g

Quick White Bean Salad with Bell Peppers

Prep time: 15 minutes | Cook time: 0 | Serves: 4

2 tbsps. extra-virgin olive oil
3 cups cooked cannellini beans, or 2 (15-ounce, 425g) cans no-salt-added or low-sodium cannellini beans, drained and rinsed
2 tbsps. white wine vinegar

½ shallot, minced
½ tsp. kosher salt
¼ tsp. freshly ground black pepper
2 celery stalks, diced
½ red bell pepper, diced
¼ cup fresh parsley, chopped
¼ cup fresh mint, chopped

1. In a large bowl, whisk together the olive oil, vinegar, shallot, salt, and black pepper.
2. Add the beans, celery, red bell pepper, parsley, and mint, mix well.

PER SERVING
Calories: 300, Total fat: 8g, Saturated fat: 1g, Total Carbohydrates: 46g, Protein: 15g, Sodium: 175mg, Fiber: 11g, Sugar: 3g

Zucchini and Cherry Tomato Salad

Prep time: 10 minutes | Cook time: 5 minutes | Serves: 2

1 medium zucchini, shredded or sliced paper thin
6 cherry tomatoes, halved
3–4 basil leaves, thinly sliced

2 tbsps. freshly grated, low-fat Parmesan cheese
3 tbsps. olive oil
Juice of 1 lemon
Sea salt and freshly ground pepper

1. Place the zucchini slices on 2 plates in even layers. Top with the tomatoes.
2. Drizzle with lemon juice and olive oil. Season to taste.
3. Top with the basil and sprinkle with cheese. Serve.

PER SERVING
Calories: 211, Fat: 21.47g, Carbohydrates: 4.63g, Protein: 1.82g, Sodium: 80mg, Fiber: 1g

White Bean, Tuna and Arugula Salad

Prep time: 15 minutes | Cook time: 0 | Serves: 4

¼ cup extra-virgin olive oil
1 (15-ounce, 425 g) can white beans, drained and rinsed
2 (5-ounce, 142 g) cans flaked white tuna, drained
½ pint cherry tomatoes, halved lengthwise
4 cups arugula
½ cup pitted Kalamata

olives
½ red onion, finely chopped
2 tbsps. freshly squeezed lemon juice
Salt
Freshly ground black pepper
2 ounces (57 g) crumbled sheep's milk or goat's milk feta cheese

1. Add the olive oil, white beans, tuna, tomatoes, arugula, olives, onion and lemon juice to a large bowl, mix them together, then use pepper and salt to season.
2. Place feta cheese on the top of this salad, and serve.

PER SERVING
Calories: 373, Total Fat: 19g, Total Carbohydrates: 28g, Sugar: 3g, Fiber: 7g, Protein: 29g, Sodium: 388mg

Tomato and Peach Salad

Prep time: 10 minutes | Cook time: 5 minutes | Serves: 2

2 ripe peaches, pitted and sliced into wedges
2 ripe tomatoes, cut into wedges
3 tbsps. olive oil

1 tbsp. lemon juice
1/2 red onion, thinly sliced
Sea salt and freshly ground pepper

1. Toss the peaches, red onion and tomatoes in a large bowl. Season to taste.
2. Put in the olive oil and lemon juice, and gently toss. Serve.

PER SERVING
Calories: 275, Fat: 20.95g, Carbohydrates: 22.93g, Protein: 2.9g, Sodium: 8mg, Fiber: 4.5g

Roasted Cauliflower with Pomegranate and Pine Nuts

Prep time: 20 minutes | Cook time: 20 minutes | Serves: 4

2 tbsps. extra-virgin olive oil, plus more for drizzling (optional)
1 head cauliflower, trimmed and cut into 1-inch florets
5 ounces (142g) arugula
1 tsp. ground cumin

½ tsp. kosher salt
¼ tsp. freshly ground black pepper
⅓ cup pomegranate seeds
¼ cup pine nuts, toasted

1. Preheat the oven to 425°F(218°C). Line a baking sheet with parchment paper or foil.
2. In a large bowl, combine the cauliflower, olive oil, cumin, salt, and black pepper. Spread in a single layer on the prepared baking sheet and roast for 20 minutes, tossing halfway through.
3. Divide the arugula among 4 plates. Top with the cauliflower, pomegranate seeds, and pine nuts.
4. Serve with Lemon Vinaigrette dressing or a simple drizzle of olive oil.

PER SERVING
Calories: 190, Total fat: 14g, Saturated fat: 2g, Total Carbohydrates: 16g, Protein: 6g, Sodium: 210mg, Fiber: 6g, Sugar: 7g

Rice Cauliflower Tabbouleh Salad

Prep time: 15 minutes | Cook time: 0 | Serves: 4

¼ cup extra-virgin olive oil
1 pound (454g) riced cauliflower
1 English cucumber, diced
12 cherry tomatoes, halved
1 cup fresh parsley, chopped
¼ cup lemon juice
Zest of 1 lemon

¾ tsp. kosher salt
½ tsp. ground turmeric
¼ tsp. ground coriander
¼ tsp. ground cumin
¼ tsp. black pepper
⅛ tsp. ground cinnamon
½ cup fresh mint, chopped

1. In a large bowl, whisk together the olive oil, lemon juice, lemon zest, salt, turmeric, coriander, cumin, black pepper, and cinnamon.
2. Add the riced cauliflower to the bowl and mix well. Add in the cucumber, tomatoes, parsley, and mint and gently mix together.

PER SERVING
Calories: 180, Total fat: 15g, Saturated fat: 2g, Total Carbohydrates: 12g, Protein: 4g, Sodium: 260mg, Fiber: 5g, Sugar: 5g

Dilled Tuna and Avocado Sandwich

Prep time: 10 minutes | Cook time: 0 | Serves: 4

2 (4-ounce, 113 g) cans tuna, packed in olive oil
2 tbsps. Roasted Garlic Aioli, or avocado oil mayonnaise
4 Versatile Sandwich Rounds

fresh lemon juice and zest
1 ripe avocado, peeled, pitted, and mashed
1 tbsp. chopped fresh capers (optional)
1 tsp. chopped fresh dill

1. Make sandwich rounds and cut each round in half and set aside.
2. In a medium bowl, put in the tuna and the oil from cans. Add the aioli, capers, avocado, and dill and blend well with a fork.
3. Toast sandwich rounds and fill each with 1/4 tuna salad, about ⅓ cup.

PER SERVING
Calories: 436, Total Fat: 36g, Total Carbohydrates: 5g, Net Carbs: 2g, Protein: 23g, Fiber: 3g, Sodium: 790mg

Orange-Tarragon Chicken Salad Cup

Prep time: 15 minutes | Cook time: 0 | Serves: 4

2 small ripe avocados, peeled and thinly sliced
Zest of 1 clementine, or ½ small orange
½ cup (120 ml) plain whole-milk Greek yogurt
2 tbsps. Dijon mustard
2 tbsps. extra-virgin olive oil
2 tbsps. chopped fresh tarragon

½ tsp. salt
¼ tsp. freshly ground black pepper
2 cups cooked shredded chicken
½ cup slivered almonds
4 to 8 large Bibb lettuce leaves, tough stem removed

1. In a medium bowl, combine the yogurt, olive oil, mustard, orange zest, tarragon, salt, and pepper and whisk until creamy.
2. Add the shredded chicken and almonds and stir to coat.
3. Place about ½ cup chicken salad mixture in the center of lettuce leaf and top with sliced avocados.

PER SERVING
Calories: 440, Total Fat: 32g, Total Carbohydrates: 12g, Protein: 26g, Net Carbs: 4g, Fiber: 8g, Sodium: 445mg

Honey Mustard Brussels Sprout Slaw with Apple

Prep time: 15 minutes | Cook time: 1 minute | Serves: 4

1 pound (454 g) Brussels sprouts, stem ends removed and sliced thin
1 apple, cored and sliced thin
½ red onion, sliced thin
1 tsp. Dijon mustard
1 tsp. salt

1 cup plain coconut milk yogurt
2 tsps. apple cider vinegar
1 tbsp. raw honey or maple syrup
½ cup chopped toasted hazelnuts
½ cup pomegranate seeds

1. Add the Brussels sprouts, apple, and onion into a medium bowl, combine them together.
2. Add the Dijon mustard, salt, yogurt, cider vinegar, and honey to a small bowl, whisk them until well combined.
3. Combine the dressing to the Brussels sprouts, toss them until evenly coated.
4. Garnished with the hazelnuts and pomegranate seeds and serve.

PER SERVING
Calories: 189, Total Fat: 8g, Total Carbohydrates: 29g, Protein: 6g, Sugar: 13g, Fiber: 9g, Sodium: 678mg

Chapter 12 Breads, Flatbreads, Pizzas, and More

Homemade Pita Bread

Prep time: 0 minutes | Cook time: 13 minutes | Makes 8 (8-inch) pitas

3⅔ cups bread flour
2½ teaspoons instant or rapid-rise yeast
2 teaspoons salt
1⅓ cups water, room temperature
¼ cup extra-virgin olive oil
2½ teaspoons coconut sugar

1. Whisk flour, yeast, and salt together in bowl of stand mixer. Whisk water, oil, and sugar together in 4-cup liquid measuring cup until sugar has dissolved.
2. Using dough hook on low speed, slowly add water mixture to flour mixture and mix until cohesive dough starts to form and no dry flour remains, about 2 minutes, scraping down sides of bowl as needed. Increase speed to medium-low and knead until dough is smooth and elastic and clears sides of bowl, about 8 minutes.
3. Transfer dough to lightly floured counter and knead by hand to form smooth, round ball, about 30 seconds. Place dough seam side down in lightly greased large bowl or container, cover tightly with plastic wrap, and let rise until doubled in size, 1 to 1½ hours.
4. Press down on dough to deflate. Transfer dough to lightly floured counter and divide into quarters, then cut each quarter into halves (about 4 ounces each), cover loosely with greased plastic.
5. Working with 1 piece of dough at a time (keep remaining pieces covered), form into rough ball by stretching dough around your thumbs and pinching edges together so that top is smooth.
6. Generously coat 1 dough ball with flour and place on well-floured counter. Press and roll into 8-inch round of even thickness and cover loosely with greased plastic. (If dough resists stretching, let it relax for 10 to 20 minutes before trying to stretch it again.) Repeat with remaining balls. Let dough rounds rest for 20 minutes.
7. One hour before baking, adjust oven rack to lower-middle position, place baking stone on rack, and heat oven to 500°F (260°C). Gently transfer 2 dough rounds to well-floured pizza peel. Slide rounds onto stone and bake until single air pocket is just beginning to form, about

1 minute.
8. Working quickly, flip pitas using metal spatula and continue to bake until light golden brown, 1 to 2 minutes. Transfer pitas to plate and cover with dish towel. Repeat with remaining dough rounds in 3 batches, allowing oven to reheat for 5 minutes after each batch. Let pitas cool for 10 minutes before serving.

PER SERVING (1 pita)
Calories: 252, Fat: 7.62g, Carbohydrates: 38.43g, Protein: 6.6g, Sugar: 0.96g, Fiber: 1.4g, Sodium: 639mg

Mushroom-Olives Pizza with Arugula

Prep time: 10 minutes | Cook time: 15 minutes | Serves: 4

1 pizza crust
½ cup tomato paste
¼ cup water
1 teaspoon coconut sugar
1 teaspoon dried oregano
4 ounces (113 g) button mushrooms, chopped
½ cup grated gouda cheese
2 tablespoons extra virgin olive oil
12 olives
1 cup arugula for serving

1. Grease the bottom of a baking dish with one tablespoon of olive oil. Line some parchment paper. Flour the working surface and roll out the pizza dough to the approximate size of your instant pot. Gently fit the dough in the previously prepared baking dish.
2. In a bowl, combine tomato paste, water, sugar, and dry oregano. Spread the mixture over dough, make a layer with button mushrooms and grated gouda.
3. Add a trivet inside the pot and pour in 1 cup of water. Seal the lid, and cook for 15 minutes on High Pressure. Do a quick release. Remove the pizza from your pot using a parchment paper. Sprinkle with the remaining olive oil and top with olives and arugula. Cut and serve.

PER SERVING
Calories: 738, Fat: 28.76g, Carbohydrates: 73.98g, Protein: 28.6g, Sugar: 14.33g, Fiber: 9g, Sodium: 1275mg

Baked Za'atar Pizza

Prep time: 5 minutes | Cook time: 10 minutes | Serves: 4 to 6

1 sheet puff pastry	oil
¼ cup extra-virgin olive	⅓ cup za'atar seasoning

1. Preheat the oven to 350°F (180°C).
2. Put the puff pastry on a parchment-lined baking sheet. Cut the pastry into desired slices.
3. Brush the pastry with olive oil. Sprinkle with the za'atar.
4. Put the pastry in the oven and bake for 10 to 12 minutes or until edges are lightly browned and puffed up. Serve warm or at room temperature.

PER SERVING
Calories: 374, Fat: 30.1g, Total Carbohydrates: 19.9g, Protein: 3.2g, Fiber: 1.1g, Sodium: 166mg

Veggie and Double Cheese Pizza

Prep time: 15 minutes | Cook time: 15 minutes | Serves: 4

1 pound (454 g) refrigerated fresh pizza dough	ground black pepper
Nonstick cooking spray	1 tablespoon water
2 tablespoons extra-virgin olive oil, divided	1 tablespoon freshly squeezed lemon juice
½ cup thinly sliced onion	All-purpose flour, for dusting
2 garlic cloves, minced	½ cup crumbled Goat cheese
3 cups baby spinach	
3 cups arugula	¼ cup shredded Parmesan cheese
¼ teaspoon freshly	

1. Preheat the oven to 500°F (260°C). Take the pizza dough out of the refrigerator. Coat a large, rimmed baking sheet with nonstick cooking spray.
2. In a large skillet over medium heat, heat 1 tablespoon of oil. Add the onion and cook for 4 minutes, stirring often. Add the garlic and cook for 1 minute, stirring often. Add the spinach, arugula, pepper, and water. Cook for about 2 minutes, stirring often, especially at the beginning, until all the greens are coated with oil and they start to cook down (they will shrink considerably). Remove the pan from the heat and mix in the lemon juice.
3. On a lightly floured surface, form the pizza dough into a 12-inch circle or a 10-by-12-inch rectangle, using a rolling pin or by stretching with your hands. Place the dough on the prepared baking sheet. Brush the dough with the remaining tablespoon of oil. Spread the cooked greens on top of the dough to within ½ inch of the edge. Crumble the Goat cheese on top, then sprinkle with the Parmesan cheese.
4. Bake for 10 to 12 minutes, or until the crust starts to brown around the edges. Remove from the oven, and slide the pizza onto a wooden cutting board. Cut into eight pieces with a pizza cutter or a sharp knife and serve.

PER SERVING
Calories: 521, Fat: 31.1g, Total Carbohydrates: 37.9g, Protein: 23.2g, Fiber: 4.1g, Sodium: 896mg

Whole Wheat Banana and Walnut Bread

Prep time: 15 minutes | Cook time: 20 minutes | Serves: 6

Olive oil cooking spray	2 tablespoons raw honey
2 ripe medium bananas	1 cup whole wheat flour
1 large egg	¼ teaspoon salt
¼ cup nonfat plain Greek yogurt	¼ teaspoon baking soda
¼ cup olive oil	½ teaspoon ground cinnamon
½ teaspoon vanilla extract	¼ cup chopped walnuts

1. Preheat the air fryer to 360°F (182°C). Lightly coat the inside of a 8-by-4-inch loaf pan with olive oil cooking spray. (Or use two 5 ½-by-3-inch loaf pans.)
2. In a large bowl, mash the bananas with a fork. Add the egg, yogurt, olive oil, vanilla, and honey. Mix until well combined and mostly smooth.
3. Sift the whole wheat flour, salt, baking soda, and cinnamon into the wet mixture, then stir until just combined. Do not overmix.
4. Gently fold in the walnuts.
5. Pour into the prepared loaf pan and spread to distribute evenly.
6. Place the loaf pan in the air fryer basket and bake for 20 to 23 minutes, or until golden brown on top and a toothpick inserted into the center comes out clean.

PER SERVING
Calories: 255, Fat: 13.8g, Total Carbohydrates: 30.2g, Protein: 5.9g, Fiber: 4.3g, Sodium: 31mg

Pesto and Roasted Red Pepper Pizza

Prep time: 10 minutes | Cook time: 22 minutes | Serves: 5 to 6

1½ cups warm water
1 teaspoon active dry yeast
¼ cup extra-virgin olive oil
1 tablespoon coconut sugar
½ teaspoon kosher salt

4 cups all-purpose flour
10 ounces (283 g) fresh Mozzarella, shredded
¼ cup pesto
⅓ cup chopped roasted red peppers
¼ cup crumbled Feta

1. In a small bowl, microwave the water for about 15 seconds, just until it's warm. Sprinkle the yeast into the warm water and let it stand for 10 minutes, until the top layer is foamy.
2. In a large bowl, whisk together the oil, sugar, and salt. Stir this into the yeast mix, then pour it back into the large bowl and add the flour.
3. Gently combine the flour mixture with a whisk or wooden spoon. Mix in the bowl until almost all the flour is incorporated and a ball of dough is formed. Cover the bowl with a heavy kitchen towel and let stand for 1 hour at room temperature.
4. Once the hour has passed, preheat the oven to 400°F (205°C) and put a baking sheet upside-down in the oven.
5. Next, flour an area of the kitchen counter well and cut the pizza dough in half, reserving half for another pizza. Gently roll out half of the dough into a circle about 1 inch thick. The second half of the pizza dough will last for about 6 months in the freezer or 2 to 3 days in the refrigerator.
6. Reduce the heat to 375°F (190°C) and remove the baking sheet from the oven. Place it upside-down on a heatproof surface. Place the pizza dough on the back of the hot baking sheet and put it in the oven for 5 to 7 minutes.
7. Remove the pizza from the oven and add Mozzarella cheese first. Put it back into the oven and cook for 7 to 10 minutes. This will help dry out the wet, fresh Mozzarella.
8. After 7 to 10 minutes, remove the pizza and add the pesto followed by the peppers and put it back into the oven for an additional 10 minutes.
9. Remove the pizza and let it rest for 5 minutes, while it's cooling, add the crumbled Feta.

PER SERVING
Calories: 705, Fat: 32.3g, Total Carbohydrates: 78.4g, Protein: 23.1g, Fiber: 3.2g, Sodium: 776mg

Za'atar Bread Slices

Prep time: 10 minutes | Cook time: 20 minutes | Makes 1 flatbread

3½ cups bread flour
2½ teaspoons instant or rapid-rise yeast
2½ teaspoons coconut sugar
1⅓ cups ice water

½ cup plus 2 tablespoons extra-virgin olive oil
2 teaspoons salt
⅓ cup za'atar
Coarse sea salt, to taste

1. Pulse flour, yeast, and sugar in food processor until combined, about 5 pulses. With processor running, slowly add ice water and process until dough is just combined and no dry flour remains, about 10 seconds. Let dough rest for 10 minutes.
2. Add 2 tablespoons oil and salt to dough and process until dough forms satiny, sticky ball that clears sides of bowl, 30 to 60 seconds. Transfer dough to lightly floured counter and knead by hand to form smooth, round ball, about 30 seconds. Place dough seam side down in lightly greased large bowl or container, cover tightly with plastic wrap, and refrigerate for at least 24 hours or up to 3 days.
3. Remove dough from refrigerator and let sit at room temperature for 1 hour. Coat rimmed baking sheet with 2 tablespoons oil. Gently press down on dough to deflate any large gas pockets. Transfer dough to prepared sheet and, using your fingertips, press out to uniform thickness, taking care not to tear dough. (Dough may not fit snugly into corners.) Cover loosely with greased plastic and let dough rest for 1 hour.
4. Adjust oven rack to lower-middle position and heat oven to 375°F (190°C). Using your fingertips, gently press dough into corners of sheet and dimple entire surface.
5. Combine remaining 6 tablespoons oil and za'atar in bowl. Using back of spoon, spread oil mixture in even layer on entire surface of dough to edge.
6. Bake until bottom crust is evenly browned and edges are crisp, 20 to 25 minutes, rotating sheet halfway through baking. Let bread cool in sheet for 10 minutes, then transfer to cutting board with spatula. Sprinkle with sea salt, slice, and serve warm.

PER SERVING(1 flatbread)
Calories: 2740, Fat: 116.09g, Carbohydrates: 357.6g, Protein: 61.03g, Sugar: 7.89g, Fiber: 12.5g, Sodium: 7440mg

Caprese Tomato Breakfast Pizza

Prep time: 10 minutes | Cook time: 6 minutes | Serves: 2

1 whole wheat pita	¼ cup diced tomato
2 teaspoons olive oil	¼ cup Mozzarella pearls
¼ garlic clove, minced	6 fresh basil leaves
1 large egg	½ teaspoon balsamic
⅛ teaspoon salt	vinegar

1. Preheat the air fryer to 380°F (193°C).
2. Brush the top of the pita with olive oil, then spread the minced garlic over the pita.
3. Crack the egg into a small bowl or ramekin and season it with salt.
4. Place the pita into the air fryer basket, and gently pour the egg onto the top of the pita. Top with the tomato, Mozzarella pearls, and basil.
5. Bake for 6 minutes.
6. Remove the pita pizza from the air fryer and drizzle balsamic vinegar over the top.
7. Allow to cool for 5 minutes before cutting into pieces for serving.

PER SERVING
Calories: 209, Fat: 11.2g, Total Carbohydrates: 19.1g, Protein: 10.3g, Fiber: 2.9g, Sodium: 104mg

Herb Focaccia Bread

Prep time: 10 minutes | Cook time: 18 minutes | Serves: 10

1 tablespoon dried rosemary or 3 tablespoons minced fresh rosemary	oil
	1 teaspoon coconut sugar
	1 cup warm water
1 tablespoon dried thyme or 3 tablespoons minced fresh thyme leaves	1 (¼-ounce / 7-g) packet active dry yeast
½ cup extra-virgin olive	2½ cups flour, divided
	1 teaspoon salt

1. In a small bowl, combine the rosemary and thyme with the olive oil.
2. In a large bowl, whisk together the sugar, water, and yeast. Let stand for 5 minutes.
3. Add 1 cup of flour, half of the olive oil mixture, and the salt to the mixture in the large bowl. Stir to combine.
4. Add the remaining 1½ cups flour to the large bowl. Using your hands, combine dough until it starts to pull away from the sides of the bowl.

5. Put the dough on a floured board or countertop and knead 10 to 12 times. Place the dough in a well-oiled bowl and cover with plastic wrap. Put it in a warm, dry space for 1 hour.
6. Oil a 9-by-13-inch baking pan. Turn the dough onto the baking pan, and using your hands gently push the dough out to fit the pan.
7. Using your fingers, make dimples into the dough. Evenly pour the remaining half of the olive oil mixture over the dough. Let the dough rise for another 30 minutes.
8. Preheat the oven to 450°F (235°C). Place the dough into the oven and let cook for 18 to 20 minutes, until you see it turn a golden brown.

PER SERVING
Calories: 199, Fat: 11.2g, Total Carbohydrates: 22.8g, Protein: 2.9g, Fiber: 1.2g, Sodium: 232mg

Tuna and Rosemary Cheese Pizza

Prep time: 10 minutes | Cook time: 15 minutes | Serves: 4

1 cup canned tuna, oil-free	paste
	½ teaspoon dried rosemary
½ cup Mozzarella cheese, shredded	14 ounces (397 g) pizza crust
¼ cup Goat's cheese	
3 tablespoons olive oil	1 cup olives, optional
1 tablespoon tomato	

1. Grease the bottom of a baking dish with one tablespoon of olive oil. Line some parchment paper. Flour the working surface and roll out the pizza dough to the approximate size of your instant pot. Gently fit the dough in the previously prepared baking dish.
2. In a bowl, combine olive oil, tomato paste and rosemary. Whisk together and spread the mixture over the crust.
3. Sprinkle with Goat cheese, Mozzarella, and tuna. Place a trivet inside the pot and pour in 1 cup of water.
4. Seal the lid, and cook for 15 minutes on High Pressure. Do a quick release. Remove the pizza from the pot. Cut and serve.

PER SERVING
Calories: 512, Fat: 31.74g, Carbohydrates: 31.73g, Protein: 26.14g, Sugar: 4.73g, Fiber: 3.7g, Sodium: 1107mg

Flat Beef Pies

Prep time: 5 minutes | Cook time: 12 minutes | Serves: 4

½ pound (227 g) ground beef
1 small onion, finely chopped
1 medium tomato, finely diced and strained
½ teaspoon salt
½ teaspoon freshly ground black pepper
2 sheets puff pastry

1. Preheat the oven to 400ºF (205ºC).
2. In a medium bowl, combine the beef, onion, tomato, salt, and pepper. Set aside.
3. Line 2 baking sheets with parchment paper. Cut the puff pastry dough into 4-inch squares and lay them flat on the baking sheets.
4. Scoop about 2 tablespoons of beef mixture onto each piece of dough. Spread the meat on the dough, leaving a ½-inch edge on each side.
5. Put the meat pies in the oven and bake for 12 to 15 minutes until edges are golden brown.

PER SERVING
Calories: 577, Fat: 38.2g, Total Carbohydrates: 41.1g, Protein: 17.8g, Fiber: 2.3g, Sodium: 541mg

Turkish Lahmacun

Prep time: 15 minutes | Cook time: 48 minutes | Makes 4 (9-inch) flatbreads

For the Dough:
1¾ cups bread flour
1 teaspoon coconut sugar
¾ teaspoon instant or rapid-rise yeast
¾ cup ice water
2 tablespoons extra-virgin olive oil
1 teaspoon salt
For the Topping:
3 tablespoons Turkish hot pepper paste
1 tablespoon tomato paste
1 garlic clove, minced
¾ teaspoon smoked hot paprika
¾ teaspoon ground allspice
½ teaspoon salt
1 cup coarsely chopped red bell pepper
⅔ cup coarsely chopped onion
4 ounces (113 g) ground lamb
¼ cup chopped fresh parsley

Make the Dough
1. Pulse flour, sugar, and yeast in food processor until combined, about 5 pulses. With processor running, slowly add ice water and process until dough is just combined and no dry flour remains, about 10 seconds. Let dough rest for 10 minutes.
2. Add oil and salt to dough and process until dough forms satiny, sticky ball that clears sides of bowl, 30 to 60 seconds. Transfer dough to lightly floured counter and knead by hand to form smooth, round ball, about 30 seconds. Place dough seam side down in lightly greased large bowl or container, cover tightly with plastic wrap, and refrigerate for at least 24 hours or up to 3 days.
3. Press down on dough to deflate. Transfer dough to lightly floured counter, divide into quarters, and cover loosely with greased plastic. Working with 1 piece of dough at a time (keep remaining pieces covered), form into rough ball by stretching dough around your thumbs and pinching edges together so that top is smooth. Space balls 3 inches apart, cover loosely with greased plastic, and let rest for 1 hour.

Make the Topping
1. Process pepper paste, tomato paste, garlic, paprika, allspice, and salt in clean, dry workbowl until well combined, about 20 seconds, scraping down sides of bowl as needed. Add bell pepper and onion and pulse until finely ground, about 10 pulses. Add lamb and parsley and pulse until well combined, about 8 pulses.
2. Adjust oven racks to upper-middle and lower-middle positions and heat oven to 350ºF (180ºC). Grease 2 rimmed baking sheets. Generously coat 1 dough ball with flour and place on well-floured counter. Press and roll into 9-inch round. Arrange round on prepared sheet, with edges fitted snugly into 1 corner of sheet, and reshape as needed. (If dough resists stretching, let it relax for 10 to 20 minutes before trying to stretch it again.) Repeat with remaining dough balls, arranging 2 rounds on each sheet in opposite corners.
3. Using back of spoon, spread one-quarter of topping in thin layer on surface of each dough round, leaving ¼-inch border around edge.
4. Bake until edges of flatbreads are set but still pale, 10 to 12 minutes, switching and rotating sheets halfway through baking. Remove flatbreads from oven and heat broiler.
5. Return 1 sheet to upper rack and broil until edges of flatbreads are crisp and spotty brown and filling is set, 2 to 4 minutes. Transfer flatbreads to wire rack with spatula and let cool for 5 minutes before serving. Repeat broiling with remaining flatbreads.

PER SERVING (1 flatbread)
Calories: 373, Fat: 11.53g, Carbohydrates: 53g, Protein: 14.84g, Sugar: 4.9g, Fiber: 3.2g, Sodium: 933mg

Rosemary Focaccia Bread

Make the Sponge:
½ cup all-purpose flour
⅓ cup water, room temperature
¼ teaspoon instant or rapid-rise yeast

Make the Dough:
2½ cups all-purpose flour
1¼ cups water, room temperature
1 teaspoon instant or rapid-rise yeast
Kosher salt, to taste
¼ cup extra-virgin olive oil
2 tablespoons chopped fresh rosemary

Make the Sponge
1. Stir all ingredients together in large bowl with wooden spoon until well combined. Cover tightly with plastic wrap and let sit at room temperature until sponge has risen and begins to collapse, about 6 hours (sponge can sit at room temperature for up to 24 hours).

Make the Dough
1. Stir flour, water, and yeast into sponge with wooden spoon until well combined. Cover bowl tightly with plastic and let dough rest for 15 minutes.
2. Stir 2 teaspoons salt into dough with wooden spoon until thoroughly incorporated, about 1 minute. Cover bowl tightly with plastic and let dough rest for 30 minutes.
3. Using greased bowl scraper (or rubber spatula), fold dough over itself by gently lifting and folding edge of dough toward middle. Turn bowl 45 degrees and fold dough again, repeat turning bowl and folding dough 6 more times (total of 8 folds). Cover tightly with plastic and let rise for 30 minutes. Repeat folding and rising. Fold dough again, then cover bowl tightly with plastic and let dough rise until nearly doubled in size, 30 minutes to 1 hour.
4. One hour before baking, adjust oven rack to upper-middle position, place baking stone on rack, and heat oven to 500°F (260°C). Coat two 9-inch round cake pans with 2 tablespoons oil each. Sprinkle each pan with ½ teaspoon salt. Transfer dough to lightly floured counter and dust top with flour. Divide dough in half and cover loosely with greased plastic. Working with 1 piece of dough at a time (keep remaining piece covered), shape into 5-inch round by gently tucking under edges.
5. Place dough rounds seam side up in prepared pans, coat bottoms and sides with oil, then flip rounds over. Cover loosely with greased plastic and let dough rest for 5 minutes.
6. Using your fingertips, gently press each dough round into corners of pan, taking care not to tear dough. (If dough resists stretching, let it relax for 5 to 10 minutes before trying to stretch it again.) Using fork, poke surface of dough 25 to 30 times, popping any large bubbles. Sprinkle 1 tablespoon rosemary evenly over top of each loaf, cover loosely with greased plastic, and let dough rest until slightly bubbly, about 10 minutes.
7. Place pans on baking stone and reduce oven temperature to 450°F (235°C). Bake until tops are golden brown, 25 to 30 minutes, rotating pans halfway through baking. Let loaves cool in pans for 5 minutes. Remove loaves from pans and transfer to wire rack. Brush tops with any oil remaining in pans and let cool for 30 minutes. Serve warm or at room temperature.

PER SERVING(1 loaf)
Calories: 930, Fat: 28.97g, Carbohydrates: 144.2g, Protein: 20.32g, Sugar: 0.57g, Fiber: 5.5g, Sodium: 1284mg

Caramelized Onion Flatbread Squares with Arugula

4 tablespoons extra-virgin olive oil, divided
2 large onions, sliced into ¼-inch-thick slices
1 teaspoon salt, divided
1 sheet puff pastry
1 (5-ounce / 142-g) package Goat cheese
8 ounces (227 g) arugula
½ teaspoon freshly ground black pepper

1. Preheat the oven to 400°F (205°C).
2. In a large skillet over medium heat, cook 3 tablespoons olive oil, the onions, and ½ teaspoon of salt, stirring, for 10 to 12 minutes, until the onions are translucent and golden brown.
3. To assemble, line a baking sheet with parchment paper. Lay the puff pastry flat on the parchment paper. Prick the middle of the puff pastry all over with a fork, leaving a ½-inch border.
4. Evenly distribute the onions on the pastry, leaving the border.
5. Crumble the Goat cheese over the onions. Put the pastry in the oven to bake for 10 to 12 minutes, or until you see the border become golden brown.

6. Remove the pastry from the oven, set aside. In a medium bowl, add the arugula, remaining 1 tablespoon of olive oil, remaining ½ teaspoon of salt, and ½ teaspoon black pepper, toss to evenly dress the arugula.
7. Cut the pastry into even squares. Top the pastry with dressed arugula and serve.

PER SERVING
Calories: 501, Fat: 40.1g, Total Carbohydrates: 29.3g, Protein: 12.1g, Fiber: 4.4g, Sodium: 541mg

French Pissaladière

Prep time: 20 minutes | Cook time: 46 minutes | Makes 2 (14 by 8-inch) tarts

For the Dough:
3 cups bread flour
2 teaspoons coconut sugar
½ teaspoon instant or rapid-rise yeast
1⅓ cups ice water
1 tablespoon extra-virgin olive oil
1½ teaspoons salt
For the Toppings:
¼ cup extra-virgin olive oil
2 pounds (907 g) onions, halved and sliced ¼ inch thick
1 teaspoon coconut sugar
½ teaspoon salt
1 tablespoon water
½ cup pitted niçoise olives, chopped coarse
8 anchovy fillets, rinsed, patted dry, and chopped coarse, plus 12 fillets for garnish (optional)
2 teaspoons minced fresh thyme
1 teaspoon fennel seeds
½ teaspoon pepper
2 tablespoons minced fresh parsley

Make the Dough
1. Pulse flour, sugar, and yeast in food processor until combined, about 5 pulses. With processor running, slowly add ice water and process until dough is just combined and no dry flour remains, about 10 seconds. Let dough rest for 10 minutes.
2. Add oil and salt to dough and process until dough forms satiny, sticky ball that clears sides of bowl, 30 to 60 seconds. Transfer dough to lightly floured counter and knead by hand to form smooth, round ball, about 30 seconds. Place dough seam side down in lightly greased large bowl or container, cover tightly with plastic wrap, and refrigerate for at least 24 hours or up to 3 days.
Make the Toppings
1. Heat 2 tablespoons oil in 12-inch nonstick skillet over medium heat until shimmering. Stir in onions, sugar, and salt. Cover and cook, stirring occasionally, until onions are softened and have released their juice, about 10 minutes. Remove lid and continue to cook, stirring often, until onions are golden brown, 10 to 15 minutes. Transfer onions to bowl, stir in water, and let cool completely before using.
2. One hour before baking, adjust oven rack 4 inches from broiler element, set baking stone on rack, and heat oven to 500°F (260°C). Press down on dough to deflate. Transfer dough to clean counter, divide in half, and cover loosely with greased plastic. Pat 1 piece of dough (keep remaining piece covered) into 4-inch round. Working around circumference of dough, fold edges toward center until ball forms.
3. Flip ball seam side down and, using your cupped hands, drag in small circles on counter until dough feels taut and round and all seams are secured on underside. (If dough sticks to your hands, lightly dust top of dough with flour.) Repeat with remaining piece of dough. Space dough balls 3 inches apart, cover loosely with greased plastic, and let rest for 1 hour.
4. Heat broiler for 10 minutes. Meanwhile, generously coat 1 dough ball with flour and place on well-floured counter. Press and roll into 14 by 8-inch oval. Transfer oval to well-floured pizza peel and reshape as needed. (If dough resists stretching, let it relax for 10 to 20 minutes before trying to stretch it again.) Using fork, poke entire surface of oval 10 to 15 times.
5. Brush dough oval with 1 tablespoon oil, then sprinkle evenly with ¼ cup olives, half of chopped anchovies, 1 teaspoon thyme, ½ teaspoon fennel seeds, and ¼ teaspoon pepper, leaving ½-inch border around edge. Arrange half of onions on top, followed by 6 whole anchovies, if using.
6. Slide flatbread carefully onto baking stone and return oven to 500°F (260°C). Bake until bottom crust is evenly browned and edges are crisp, 13 to 15 minutes, rotating flatbread halfway through baking. Transfer flatbread to wire rack and let cool for 5 minutes. Sprinkle with 1 tablespoon parsley, slice, and serve. Heat broiler for 10 minutes. Repeat with remaining dough, oil, and toppings, returning oven to 500°F (260°C) when flatbread is placed on stone.

PER SERVING (1 tart)
Calories: 683, Fat: 41.23g, Carbohydrates: 68.37g, Protein: 14.08g, Sugar: 30.05g, Fiber: 7.5g, Sodium: 3504mg

Thin-Crust Cheese Pizza

Prep time: 15 minutes | Cook time: 16 minutes | Makes 2 (13-inch) pizzas

Make the Dough:
3 cups bread flour
2 teaspoons coconut sugar
½ teaspoon instant or rapid-rise yeast
1⅓ cups ice water
1 tablespoon extra-virgin olive oil
1½ teaspoons salt
Make the Sauce and Toppings:
1 (28-ounce / 794-g) can whole peeled tomatoes, drained with juice reserved

1 tablespoon extra-virgin olive oil
2 garlic cloves, minced
1 teaspoon red wine vinegar
1 teaspoon dried oregano
½ teaspoon salt
¼ teaspoon pepper
1 ounce (28 g) Parmesan cheese, grated fine
8 ounces (227 g) whole-milk Mozzarella cheese, shredded

Make the Dough

1. Pulse flour, sugar, and yeast in food processor until combined, about 5 pulses. With processor running, slowly add ice water and process until dough is just combined and no dry flour remains, about 10 seconds. Let dough rest for 10 minutes.
2. Add oil and salt to dough and process until dough forms satiny, sticky ball that clears sides of bowl, 30 to 60 seconds. Transfer dough to lightly oiled counter and knead by hand to form smooth, round ball, about 30 seconds. Place dough seam side down in lightly greased large bowl or container, cover tightly with plastic wrap, and refrigerate for at least 24 hours or up to 3 days.

Make the Sauce and Toppings

1. Process tomatoes, oil, garlic, vinegar, oregano, salt, and pepper in clean, dry workbowl until smooth, about 30 seconds. Transfer mixture to 2-cup liquid measuring cup and add reserved tomato juice until sauce measures 2 cups. Reserve 1 cup sauce, set aside remaining sauce for another use.
2. One hour before baking, adjust oven rack 4 inches from broiler element, set baking stone on rack, and heat oven to 500°F (260°C). Press down on dough to deflate. Transfer dough to clean counter, divide in half, and cover loosely with greased plastic. Pat 1 piece of dough (keep remaining piece covered) into 4-inch round. Working around circumference of dough, fold edges toward center until ball forms.
3. Flip ball seam side down and, using your cupped hands, drag in small circles on counter until dough feels taut and round and all seams are secured on underside. (If dough sticks to your hands, lightly dust top of dough with flour.) Repeat with remaining piece of dough. Space dough balls 3 inches apart, cover loosely with greased plastic, and let rest for 1 hour.
4. Heat broiler for 10 minutes. Meanwhile, coat 1 dough ball generously with flour and place on well-floured counter. Using your fingertips, gently flatten into 8-inch round, leaving 1 inch of outer edge slightly thicker than center. Using your hands, gently stretch dough into 12-inch round, working along edge and giving disk quarter turns.
5. Transfer dough to well-floured pizza peel and stretch into 13-inch round. Using back of spoon or ladle, spread ½ cup tomato sauce in even layer on surface of dough, leaving ¼-inch border around edge. Sprinkle ¼ cup Parmesan evenly over sauce, followed by 1 cup Mozzarella.
6. Slide pizza carefully onto baking stone and return oven to 500°F (260°C). Bake until crust is well browned and cheese is bubbly and partially browned, 8 to 10 minutes, rotating pizza halfway through baking. Transfer pizza to wire rack and let cool for 5 minutes before slicing and serving. Heat broiler for 10 minutes. Repeat with remaining dough, sauce, and toppings, returning oven to 500°F (260°C) when pizza is placed on stone.

PER SERVING(1 pizza)
Calories: 747, Fat: 45.66g, Carbohydrates: 49.66g, Protein: 37.85g, Sugar: 17.67g, Fiber: 9.9g, Sodium: 4081mg

Moroccan Chicken B'stilla

Prep time: 15 minutes | Cook time: 1¼ hours | Serves: 10 to 12

½ cup extra-virgin olive oil
1 onion, chopped fine
¾ teaspoon salt
1 tablespoon grated fresh ginger
½ teaspoon pepper
½ teaspoon ground turmeric
½ teaspoon paprika
1½ cups water
2 pounds (907 g) boneless, skinless chicken thighs, trimmed
6 large eggs
½ cup minced fresh cilantro
1 pound (454 g) (14 by 9-inch) phyllo, thawed
1½ cups slivered almonds, toasted and chopped
¼ cup coconut sugar
1 tablespoon ground cinnamon

1. Heat 1 tablespoon oil in 12-inch nonstick skillet over medium heat until shimmering. Add onion and salt and cook until softened, about 5 minutes. Stir in ginger, pepper, turmeric, and paprika and cook until fragrant, about 30 seconds. Add water and chicken and bring to simmer. Reduce heat to low, cover, and cook until chicken registers 170°F (79°C), 15 to 20 minutes. Transfer chicken to cutting board, let cool slightly, then shred into bite-size pieces using 2 forks, transfer to large bowl.
2. Whisk eggs together in small bowl. Bring cooking liquid to boil over high heat and cook until reduced to about 1 cup, about 10 minutes. Reduce heat to low. Whisking constantly, slowly pour eggs into broth and cook until mixture resembles loose scrambled eggs, 6 to 8 minutes, transfer to bowl with chicken. Stir in cilantro until combined. Wipe skillet clean with paper towels and let cool completely.
3. Adjust oven rack to middle position and heat oven to 375°F (190°C). Brush 1 phyllo sheet with oil and arrange in bottom of cooled skillet with short side against side of pan. Some phyllo will overhang edge of skillet, leave in place. Turn skillet 30 degrees. Brush second phyllo sheet with oil and arrange in skillet, leaving any overhanging phyllo in place. Repeat turning and layering with 10 more phyllo sheets in pinwheel pattern, brushing each with oil, to cover entire circumference of skillet (you should have total of 12 layers of phyllo).
4. Combine almonds, 3 tablespoons sugar, and 2 teaspoons cinnamon and sprinkle over phyllo in skillet. Lay 2 phyllo sheets evenly across top of almond mixture and brush top with oil. Rotate skillet 90 degrees and lay 2 more phyllo sheets evenly across top, do not brush with oil. Spoon chicken mixture into skillet and spread into even layer.
5. Stack 5 phyllo sheets on counter and brush top with oil. Fold phyllo in half crosswise and brush top with oil. Lay phyllo stack on center of chicken mixture.
6. Fold overhanging phyllo over filling and phyllo stack, pleating phyllo every 2 to 3 inches, and press to seal. Brush top with oil and bake until phyllo is crisp and golden, 35 to 40 minutes.
7. Combine remaining 1 tablespoon sugar and remaining 1 teaspoon cinnamon in small bowl. Let B'stilla cool in skillet for 15 minutes. Using rubber spatula, carefully slide B'stilla out onto cutting board. Dust top with cinnamon sugar, slice, and serve.

PER SERVING
Calories: 399 Fat: 20.13g, Carbohydrates: 30.4g, Protein: 23.11g, Sugar: 4.42g, Fiber: 1.7g, Sodium: 489mg

Goat Cheese, Fennel, and Olive Hand Pies

Make the Filling:
1 tablespoon extra-virgin olive oil
1 large fennel bulb, stalks discarded, bulb halved, cored, and sliced thin
3 garlic cloves, minced
½ cup dry white wine
6 ounces (170 g) Goat cheese, crumbled
¼ cup pitted kalamata olives, chopped fine
2 tablespoons chopped fresh oregano
2 teaspoons grated lemon zest plus 1 tablespoon juice
Salt and pepper, to taste
Make the Pies:
10 (14 by 9-inch) phyllo sheets, thawed
¼ cup extra-virgin olive oil

Make the Filling
1. Heat oil in 12-inch skillet over medium heat until shimmering. Add fennel and cook until softened and lightly browned, 8 to 10 minutes. Stir in garlic and cook until fragrant, about 30 seconds. Stir in wine, cover, and cook for 5 minutes. Uncover and continue to cook until liquid has evaporated and fennel is very tender, 3 to 5 minutes.
2. Transfer fennel mixture to medium bowl and let cool to room temperature, about 15 minutes. Gently stir in Goat cheese, olives, oregano, and lemon zest and juice until combined. Season with salt and pepper to taste.

Make the Pies
1. Adjust oven rack to lower-middle position and heat oven to 375ºF (190ºC). Place 1 phyllo sheet on counter with long side parallel to counter edge, brush lightly with oil, then top with second phyllo sheet. Cut phyllo vertically into three 9 by 4⅔-inch strips. Place generous 1 tablespoon filling on bottom left-hand corner of each strip. Fold up phyllo to form right-angle triangle, gently pressing on filling as needed to create even layer. Continue folding up and over, as if folding a flag, to end of strip. Brush triangle with oil and place seam side down in parchment paper–lined rimmed baking sheet. Repeat with remaining phyllo sheets and filling to make 15 triangles.
2. Bake triangles until golden brown, 10 to 15 minutes, rotating sheet halfway through baking. Let triangles cool on sheet for 5 minutes. Serve.

PER SERVING(1 triangle)
Calories: 133 Fat: 8.35g, Carbohydrates: 9.29g, Protein: 5.53g, Sugar: 1.17g, Fiber: 1.2g, Sodium: 235mg

Chapter 13 Snacks

Apple Chips with Maple Chocolate Tahini

Prep time: 10 minutes | Cook time: 0 minutes | Serves: 2

2 tablespoons tahini
1 tablespoon honey
1 tablespoon unsweetened cocoa powder

1 to 2 tablespoons warm water (or more if needed)
2 medium apples
1 tablespoon roasted, salted sunflower seeds

1. In a small bowl, mix together the tahini, honey, and cocoa powder. Add warm water, a little at a time, until thin enough to drizzle. Do not microwave it to thin it, it won't work.
2. Slice the apples crosswise into round slices, and then cut each piece in half to make a chip.
3. Lay the apple chips out on a plate and drizzle them with the chocolate tahini sauce.
4. Sprinkle sunflower seeds over the apple chips.

PER SERVING
Calories: 261, Total Fat: 11g, Total Carbohydrates: 43g, Protein: 5g, Fiber: 8g, Sugar: 29g, Sodium: 21mg

Mediterranean White Bean Harissa Dip

Prep time: 5 minutes | Cook time: 1 hour | Makes 1½ cups

1 whole head of garlic
½ cup olive oil, divided
1 (15-ounce / 425-g) can cannellini beans, drained

and rinsed
1 teaspoon salt
1 teaspoon harissa paste (or more to taste)

1. Preheat the oven to 350ºF (180ºC).
2. Cut about ½ inch off the top of a whole head of garlic and lightly wrap it in foil. Drizzle 1 to 2 teaspoons of olive oil over the top of the cut side. Place it in an oven-safe dish and roast it in the oven for about 1 hour or until the cloves are soft and tender.
3. Remove the garlic from the oven and let it cool. The garlic can be roasted up to 2 days ahead of time.
4. Remove the garlic cloves from their skin and place them in the bowl of a food processor along with the beans, salt, and harissa. Purée, drizzling in as much olive oil as needed until the beans are smooth. If the dip seems too stiff, add additional olive oil to loosen the dip.
5. Taste the dip and add additional salt, harissa, or oil as needed.
6. Store in the refrigerator for up to a week.
7. Portion out ¼ cup of dip and serve with a mixture of raw vegetables and mini pita breads.

PER SERVING (¼ cup)
Calories: 209, Total Fat: 17g, Total Carbohydrates: 12g, Protein: 4g, Fiber: 3g, Sugar: 0g, Sodium: 389mg

Strawberry Caprese Skewers with Balsamic Glaze

Prep time: 5 minutes | Cook time: 10 minutes | Serves: 2

½ cup balsamic vinegar
16 whole, hulled strawberries
12 small basil leaves or 6

large leaves, halved
12 pieces of small Mozzarella balls (ciliegine)

1. To make the balsamic glaze, pour the balsamic vinegar into a small saucepan and bring it to a boil. Reduce the heat to medium-low and simmer for 10 minutes, or until it's reduced by half and is thick enough to coat the back of a spoon.
2. On each of 4 wooden skewers, place a strawberry, a folded basil leaf, and a Mozzarella ball, repeating twice and adding a strawberry on the end. (Each skewer should have 4 strawberries, 3 basil leaves, and 3 Mozzarella balls.)
3. Drizzle 1 to 2 teaspoons of balsamic glaze over the skewers.

PER SERVING
Calories: 206, Total Fat: 10g, Total Carbohydrates: 17g, Protein: 10g, Fiber: 1g, Sugar: 14g, Sodium: 282mg

Light Pesto Cucumber Boats

Prep time: 10 minutes | Cook time: 0 minutes | Serves: 4 to 6

3 medium cucumbers
¼ teaspoon salt
1 packed cup fresh basil leaves
1 garlic clove, minced
¼ cup walnut pieces

¼ cup grated Parmesan cheese
¼ cup extra-virgin olive oil
½ teaspoon paprika

1. Cut each cucumber in half lengthwise and again in half crosswise to make 4 stocky pieces. Use a spoon to remove the seeds and hollow out a shallow trough in each piece. Lightly salt each piece and set aside on a platter.
2. In a blender or food processor, combine the basil, garlic, walnuts, Parmesan cheese, and olive oil and blend until smooth.
3. Use a spoon to spread pesto into each cucumber "boat" and sprinkle each with paprika. Serve.

PER SERVING
Calories: 198, Fat: 18.78g, Carbohydrates: 5.22g, Protein: 3.52g, Sugar: 2.25g, Fiber: 1.5g, Sodium: 262mg

Grape Leaves Stuffed Dolmades

Prep time: 15 minutes | Cook time: 35 minutes | Makes 20

1 tablespoon olive oil
3 shallots, chopped
2 cloves garlic, minced
¾ cup short-grain rice
¼ cup gold raisins
¼ cup pine nuts, toasted
Juice of 1 lemon
Sea salt and freshly ground pepper, to taste

⅔ cup water
4 green onions, chopped
1 small bunch mint leaves, finely chopped
1 small bunch flat-leaf parsley, chopped
20 preserved grape leaves

1. Heat the olive oil in large skillet over medium heat. Add the shallots and garlic, and sauté for 5 minutes.
2. Add the rice, golden raisins, pine nuts, and lemon juice. Season with sea salt and freshly ground pepper.
3. Add ⅔ cup water, bring to a boil, and cover. Reduce heat and simmer for 20 minutes.
4. Turn off heat and allow rice to cool.
5. Add the green onions and herbs to the rice filling and mix well.
6. Rinse the grape leaves in water and stuff each leaf with about 1 tablespoon of the filling.
7. Roll tightly and place each in a steamer, seam side down. Steam for about 10 minutes, until leaves are tender.
8. Serve warm.

PER SERVING(1 dolmade)
Calories: 56, Fat: 1.99g, Carbohydrates: 8.73g, Protein: 1.16g, Sugar: 1.59g, Fiber: 0.8g, Sodium: 5mg

Mascarpone Pecans Stuffed Dates

Prep time: 5 minutes | Cook time: 5 minutes | Serves: 12 to 15

1 cup pecans, shells removed
1 (8-ounce) container

Mascarpone cheese
20 medjool dates

1. Preheat the oven to 350°F (180°C). Put the pecans on a baking sheet and bake for 5 to 6 minutes, until lightly toasted and aromatic. Take the pecans out of the oven and let cool for 5 minutes.
2. Once cooled, put the pecans in a food processor fitted with a chopping blade and chop until they resemble the texture of bulgur wheat or coarse sugar.
3. Reserve ¼ cup of ground pecans in a small bowl. Pour the remaining chopped pecans into a larger bowl and add the Mascarpone cheese.
4. Using a spatula, mix the cheese with the pecans until evenly combined.
5. Spoon the cheese mixture into a piping bag.
6. Using a knife, cut one side of the date lengthwise, from the stem to the bottom. Gently open and remove the pit.
7. Using the piping bag, squeeze a generous amount of the cheese mixture into the date where the pit used to be. Close up the date and repeat with the remaining dates.
8. Dip any exposed cheese from the stuffed dates into the reserved chopped pecans to cover it up.
9. Set the dates on a serving plate, serve immediately or chill in the fridge until you are ready to serve.

PER SERVING
Calories: 253, Total Fat: 15g, Saturated Fat: 4g, Total Carbohydrates: 31g, Protein: 2g, Sugar: 27g, Fiber: 4g, Sodium: 7mg

Balsamic Artichoke Antipasto

Prep time: 5 minutes | Cook time: 0 minutes | Serves: 4

1 (12-ounce / 340-g) jar roasted red peppers, drained, stemmed, and seeded
8 artichoke hearts, either frozen (thawed), or jarred (drained)
1 (16-ounce / 454-g) can garbanzo beans, drained
1 cup whole Kalamata olives, drained
¼ cup balsamic vinegar
½ teaspoon salt

1. Cut the peppers into ½-inch slices and put them into a large bowl.
2. Cut the artichoke hearts into quarters, and add them to the bowl.
3. Add the garbanzo beans, olives, balsamic vinegar, and salt.
4. Toss all the ingredients together. Serve chilled.

PER SERVING
Calories: 281, Total Fat: 15g, Saturated Fat: 2g, Total Carbohydrates: 30g, Protein: 7g, Sugar: 3g, Fiber: 10g, Sodium: 615mg

Oven-Roasted Fresh Balsamic Beets

Prep time: 10 minutes | Cook time: 35 minutes | Serves: 8 to 10

10 medium fresh beets
4 tablespoons extra-virgin olive oil, divided
1 teaspoon salt
3 teaspoons fresh thyme
leaves, stems removed
⅓ cup balsamic vinegar
½ teaspoon freshly ground black pepper

1. Preheat the oven to 400°F (205°C).
2. Cut off the stems and roots of the beets. Wash the beets thoroughly and dry them with a paper towel.
3. Peel the beets using a vegetable peeler. Cut the beets into ½-inch pieces and put them into a large bowl.
4. Add 2 tablespoons of olive oil, the salt, and thyme to the bowl. Toss together and pour out onto a baking sheet. Spread the beets so that they are evenly distributed.
5. Bake for 35 to 40 minutes, turning once or twice with a spatula, until the beets are tender.
6. When the beets are done cooking, set them aside and let cool for 10 minutes.
7. In a small bowl, whisk together the remaining olive oil, vinegar, and black pepper.
8. Transfer the beets into a serving bowl, spoon the vinegar mixture over the beets, and serve.

PER SERVING
Calories: 111, Total Fat: 7g, Saturated Fat: 1g, Total Carbohydrates: 11g, Protein: 2g, Sugar: 7g, Fiber: 3g, Sodium: 374mg

Arabic Mixed-Spiced Roasted Chickpeas

Prep time: 15 minutes | Cook time: 25 minutes | Serves: 2

For the Seasoning Mix:
¾ teaspoon cumin
½ teaspoon coriander
½ teaspoon salt
¼ teaspoon freshly ground black pepper
¼ teaspoon paprika
¼ teaspoon cardamom
¼ teaspoon cinnamon
¼ teaspoon allspice
For the Chickpeas:
1 (15-ounce / 425-g) can chickpeas, drained and rinsed
1 tablespoon olive oil
¼ teaspoon salt

Make the Seasoning Mix
1. In a small bowl, combine the cumin, coriander, salt, freshly ground black pepper, paprika, cardamom, cinnamon, and allspice. Stir well to combine

Make the Chickpeas
1. Preheat the oven to 400°F (205°C) and set the rack to the middle position. Line a baking sheet with parchment paper.
2. Pat the rinsed chickpeas with paper towels or roll them in a clean kitchen towel to dry off any water.
3. Place the chickpeas in a bowl and season them with the olive oil and salt.
4. Add the chickpeas to the lined baking sheet (reserve the bowl) and roast them for about 25 to 35 minutes, turning them over once or twice while cooking. Most should be light brown. Taste one or two to make sure they are slightly crisp.
5. Place the roasted chickpeas back into the bowl and sprinkle them with the seasoning mix. Toss lightly to combine. Taste, and add additional salt if needed. Serve warm.

PER SERVING
Calories: 268, Total Fat: 11g, Total Carbohydrates: 35g, Protein: 11g, Fiber: 10g, Sugar: 6g, Sodium: 301mg

Citrus-Thyme Chickpeas

Prep time: 5 minutes | Cook time: 23 minutes | Serves: 4

1 (15-ounce / 425-g) can chickpeas, drained and rinsed
2 teaspoons extra-virgin olive oil
¼ teaspoon dried thyme

or ½ teaspoon chopped fresh thyme leaves
⅛ teaspoon kosher or sea salt
½ teaspoon zest of ½ orange

1. Preheat the oven to 450°F (235°C).
2. Spread the chickpeas on a clean kitchen towel, and rub gently until dry.
3. Spread the chickpeas on a large, rimmed baking sheet. Drizzle with the oil, and sprinkle with the thyme and salt. Using a Microplane or citrus zester, zest about half of the orange over the chickpeas. Mix well using your hands.
4. Bake for 10 minutes, then open the oven door and, using an oven mitt, give the baking sheet a quick shake. (Do not remove the sheet from the oven.) Bake for 10 minutes more. Taste the chickpeas (carefully!). If they are golden but you think they could be a bit crunchier, bake for 3 minutes more before serving.

PER SERVING
Calories: 97g, Total Fat: 3g, Saturated Fat: 1g, Total Carbs: 14g, Protein: 5g, Fiber: 4g, Sugar: 3g, Sodium: 232mg, Phosphorus: 51mg, Potassium: 72mg

Feta Zucchini Roulades

Prep time: 10 minutes | Cook time: 10 minutes | Serves: 6

½ cup Feta
1 garlic clove, minced
2 tablespoons fresh basil, minced
1 tablespoon capers, minced

⅛ teaspoon salt
⅛ teaspoon red pepper flakes
1 tablespoon lemon juice
2 medium zucchini
12 toothpicks

1. Preheat the air fryer to 360°F (182°C). (If using a grill attachment, make sure it is inside the air fryer during preheating.)
2. In a small bowl, combine the Feta, garlic, basil, capers, salt, red pepper flakes, and lemon juice.
3. Slice the zucchini into ⅛-inch strips lengthwise. (Each zucchini should yield around 6 strips.)
4. Spread 1 tablespoon of the cheese filling onto each slice of zucchini, then roll it up and secure

it with a toothpick through the middle.
5. Place the zucchini roulades into the air fryer basket in a single layer, making sure that they don't touch each other.
6. Bake or grill in the air fryer for 10 minutes.
7. Remove the zucchini roulades from the air fryer and gently remove the toothpicks before serving.

PER SERVING
Calories: 46, Total Fat: 3g, Saturated Fat: 1g, Total Carbohydrates: 3g, Protein: 3g, Fiber: 1g, Sugar: 2g

Ultimate Mediterranean Spicy Roasted Potatoes

Prep time: 10 minutes | Cook time: 25 minutes | Serves: 5

1½ pounds (680 g) red potatoes or gold potatoes
3 tablespoons garlic, minced
1½ teaspoons salt
¼ cup extra-virgin olive oil
½ cup fresh cilantro,

chopped
½ teaspoon freshly ground black pepper
¼ teaspoon cayenne pepper
3 tablespoons lemon juice

1. Preheat the oven to 450°F (235°C).
2. Scrub the potatoes and pat dry.
3. Cut the potatoes into ½-inch pieces and put them into a bowl.
4. Add the garlic, salt, and olive oil and toss everything together to evenly coat.
5. Pour the potato mixture onto a baking sheet, spread the potatoes out evenly, and put them into the oven, roasting for 25 minutes. Halfway through roasting, turn the potatoes with a spatula, continue roasting for the remainder of time until the potato edges start to brown.
6. Remove the potatoes from the oven and let them cool on the baking sheet for 5 minutes.
7. Using a spatula, remove the potatoes from the pan and put them into a bowl.
8. Add the cilantro, black pepper, cayenne, and lemon juice to the potatoes and toss until well mixed.
9. Serve warm.

PER SERVING
Calories: 203, Total Fat: 11g, Saturated Fat: 2g, Total Carbohydrates: 24g, Protein: 3g, Sugar: 3g, Fiber: 3g, Sodium: 728mg

Hummus Dip

Prep time: 10 minutes | Cook time: 0 minutes | Serves: 6 to 8

3 cups cooked chickpeas, slightly warmed	Sea salt and freshly ground pepper, to taste
¼ cup olive oil	½ cup pine nuts, toasted (optional)
Juice of 2 lemons	¼ cup flat-leaf parsley, chopped
2 to 3 cloves garlic	
¾ cup tahini	

1. Add the chickpeas, olive oil, lemon juice, and garlic to a food processor, and puree until smooth.
2. Add the tahini and continue to blend until creamy. If too thick, a bit of water can be used to thin it out. Season with sea salt and freshly ground pepper to taste.
3. Add the pine nuts if desired, and garnish with chopped parsley. Serve with fresh veggies or whole-wheat pita wedges.

PER SERVING
Calories: 475, Fat: 35.02g, Carbohydrates: 32.15g, Protein: 14.14g, Sugar: 4.92g, Fiber: 9.7g, Sodium: 42mg

Crispy Seedy Crackers

Prep time: 10 minutes | Cook time: 10 minutes | Makes 24 crackers

1 cup almond flour	¼ teaspoon salt
1 tablespoon sesame seeds	Freshly ground black pepper, to taste
1 tablespoon flaxseed	1 large egg, at room temperature
1 tablespoon chia seeds	
¼ teaspoon baking soda	

1. Preheat the oven to 350°F (180°C).
2. In a large bowl, combine the almond flour, sesame seeds, flaxseed, chia seeds, baking soda, salt, and pepper and stir well.
3. In a small bowl, whisk the egg until well beaten. Add to the dry ingredients and stir well to combine and form the dough into a ball.
4. Place one layer of parchment paper on your counter-top and place the dough on top. Cover with a second layer of parchment and, using a rolling pin, roll the dough to ⅛-inch thickness, aiming for a rectangular shape.
5. Cut the dough into 1- to 2-inch crackers and bake on parchment until crispy and slightly golden, 10 to 15 minutes, depending on thickness. Alternatively, you can bake the large rolled dough prior to cutting and break into free-form crackers once baked and crispy.
6. Store in an airtight container in the fridge for up to 1 week.

PER SERVING (6 crackers)
Calories: 119, Total Fat: 9g, Total Carbs: 4g, Net Carbs: 1g, Protein: 5g, Fiber: 3g, Sodium: 242mg

Manchego Cheese Crackers

Prep time: 5 minutes | Cook time: 12 minutes | Makes 40 crackers

4 tablespoons butter, at room temperature	1 teaspoon salt, divided
1 cup finely shredded Manchego cheese	¼ teaspoon freshly ground black pepper
1 cup almond flour	1 large egg

1. Using an electric mixer, cream together the butter and shredded cheese until well combined and smooth.
2. In a small bowl, combine the almond flour with ½ teaspoon salt and pepper. Slowly add the almond flour mixture to the cheese, mixing constantly until the dough just comes together to form a ball.
3. Transfer to a piece of parchment or plastic wrap and roll into a cylinder log about 1½ inches thick. Wrap tightly and refrigerate for at least 1 hour.
4. Preheat the oven to 350°F (180°C). Line two baking sheets with parchment paper or silicone baking mats.
5. To make the egg wash, in a small bowl, whisk together the egg and remaining ½ teaspoon salt.
6. Slice the refrigerated dough into small rounds, about ¼ inch thick, and place on the lined baking sheets.
7. Brush the tops of the crackers with egg wash and bake until the crackers are golden and crispy, 12 to 15 minutes. Remove from the oven and allow to cool on a wire rack.
8. Serve warm or, once fully cooled, store in an airtight container in the refrigerator for up to 1 week.

PER SERVING (10 crackers)
Calories: 243, Total Fat: 23g, Total Carbs: 2g, Net Carbs: 1g, Protein: 8g, Fiber: 1g, Sodium: 792mg

Labneh and Veggie Parfaits

Prep time: 10 minutes | Cook time: 0 minutes | Serves: 2

For the Labneh:
8 ounces (227 g) plain Greek yogurt
pinch salt
1 teaspoon za'atar seasoning
1 teaspoon freshly squeezed lemon juice

Pinch lemon zest
For the Parfaits:
½ cup peeled, chopped cucumber
½ cup grated carrots
½ cup cherry tomatoes, halved

Make the Labneh
1. Line a strainer with cheesecloth and place it over a bowl.
2. Stir together the Greek yogurt and salt and place in the cheesecloth. Wrap it up and let it sit for 24 hours in the refrigerator.
3. When ready, unwrap the labneh and place it into a clean bowl. Stir in the za'atar, lemon juice, and lemon zest.

Make the Parfaits
1. Divide the cucumber between two clear glasses.
2. Top each portion of cucumber with about 3 tablespoons of labneh.
3. Divide the carrots between the glasses.
4. Top with another 3 tablespoons of the labneh.
5. Top parfaits with the cherry tomatoes.

PER SERVING
Calories: 143, Total Fat: 7g, Total Carbohydrates: 16g, Protein: 5g, Fiber: 2g, Sugar: 13g, Sodium: 187mg

Lebanese-Style Sesame-Thyme Mano'ushe

Prep time: 5 minutes | Cook time: 10 minutes | Serves: 6

Nonstick cooking spray
1 (16-ounce / 454-g) bag whole-wheat pizza dough or 3 (6-inch) whole-wheat pita breads
3 tablespoons dried thyme

3 tablespoons sesame seeds
3 tablespoons extra-virgin olive oil
¼ teaspoon kosher or sea salt

1. Preheat the oven to 450°F (235°C). Spray a large, rimmed baking sheet with nonstick cooking spray.
2. Divide the dough into three equal balls. On a floured surface, roll each dough ball with a rolling pin into a 6-inch circle. Place all three dough circles (or pita breads) on the baking sheet.
3. In a small bowl, whisk together the thyme, sesame seeds, oil, and salt. With a pastry brush or spoon, brush the oil onto the three dough circles (or pita breads) until it's all used up.
4. Bake the dough circles for 10 minutes, or until the edges just start to brown and crisp and the oil is cooked into the dough. If using pita rounds, bake them for only 5 minutes. Remove the flatbreads from the oven, cut each circle in half, and serve.

PER SERVING
Calories: 66g, Total Fat: 6g, Saturated Fat:1g, Total Carbs: 3g, Protein: 2g, Fiber: 1g, Sugar: 0g, Sodium: 180mg

Honey Fig-Pecan Energy Bites

Prep time: 10 minutes | Cook time: 0 minutes | Serves: 6

¾ cup diced dried figs
½ cup chopped pecans
¼ cup rolled oats (old-fashioned or quick oats)
2 tablespoons ground

flaxseed or wheat germ (flaxseed for gluten-free)
2 tablespoons powdered or regular peanut butter
2 tablespoons honey

1. In a medium bowl, mix together the figs, pecans, oats, flaxseed, and peanut butter. Drizzle with the honey, and mix everything together. A wooden spoon works well to press the figs and nuts into the honey and powdery ingredients. (If you're using regular peanut butter instead of powdered, the dough will be stickier to handle, so freeze the dough for 5 minutes before making the bites.)
2. Divide the dough evenly into four sections in the bowl. Dampen your hands with water—but don't get them too wet or the dough will stick to them. Using your hands, roll three bites out of each of the four sections of dough, making 12 total energy bites.
3. Enjoy immediately or chill in the freezer for 5 minutes to firm up the bites before serving. The bites can be stored in a sealed container in the refrigerator for up to 1 week.

PER SERVING
Calories: 158g, Total Fat: 8g, Saturated Fat:1g, Total Carbs: 23g, Protein: 3g, Fiber: 4g, Sugar: 16g, Sodium: 83mg

Sea Salt Beet Chips with Hummus

Prep time: 5 minutes | Cook time: 25 minutes | Serves: 6

4 medium beets, rinse and sliced thin
1 teaspoon sea salt

2 tablespoons olive oil
Hummus, for serving

1. Preheat the air fryer to 380ºF (193ºC).
2. In a large bowl, toss the beets with sea salt and olive oil until well coated.
3. Put the beet slices into the air fryer and spread them out in a single layer.
4. Fry for 10 minutes. Stir, then fry for an additional 10 minutes. Stir again, then fry for a final 5 to 10 minutes, or until the chips reach the desired crispiness.
5. Serve with a favorite hummus.

PER SERVING
Calories: 63, Total Fat: 5g, Saturated Fat: 1g, Total Carbohydrates: 5g, Protein: 1g, Fiber: 2g, Sugar: 3g

Healthy Trail Mix

Prep time: 10 minutes | Cook time: 10 minutes | Makes 4 cups

1 tablespoon olive oil
1 tablespoon honey
1 teaspoon vanilla
½ teaspoon cardamom
½ teaspoon allspice
2 cups mixed, unsalted nuts

¼ cup unsalted pumpkin or sunflower seeds
½ cup dried apricots, diced or thin sliced
½ cup dried figs, diced or thinly sliced
Pinch salt

1. Combine the olive oil, honey, vanilla, cardamom, and allspice in a large sauté pan over medium heat. Stir to combine.
2. Add the nuts and seeds and stir well to coat. Let the nuts and seeds toast for about 10 minutes, stirring frequently.
3. Remove from the heat, and add the dried apricots and figs. Stir everything well and season with salt.
4. Store in an airtight container.

PER SERVING (½ cup)
Calories: 261, Total Fat: 18g, Total Carbohydrates: 23g, Protein: 6g, Fiber: 5g, Sugar: 12g, Sodium: 26mg

Curried Roasted Walnuts

Prep time: 5 minutes | Cook time: 15 minutes | Serves: 8 to 10

4 cups walnut halves
2 tablespoons extra-virgin olive oil
1 tablespoon mild curry

powder
1 teaspoon salt
¼ cup coconut sugar

1. Preheat the oven to 250ºF (121ºC). Line a baking sheet with aluminum foil.
2. In a large bowl, use clean hands to toss the walnuts with the olive oil to coat. Sprinkle with curry powder and salt and toss again.
3. Spread out the walnuts on the baking sheet and bake for 15 minutes. Remove from the oven and allow to cool just until warm to the touch, about 10 minutes.
4. Sprinkle the warm walnuts with the sugar and allow to cool to room temperature before storing in an airtight container.

PER SERVING
Calories: 306, Fat: 29.57g, Carbohydrates: 9.04g, Protein: 6.2g, Sugar: 4.12g, Fiber: 3.1g, Sodium: 292mg

Cucumber Cups with Bean Dip and Tomato

Prep time: 5 minutes | Cook time: 0 minutes | Serves: 2

1 (8-ounce / 227-g) medium cucumber (8 to 9 inches long)
½ cup hummus (any flavor) or white bean dip

4 or 5 cherry tomatoes, sliced in half
2 tablespoons fresh basil, minced

1. Slice the ends off the cucumber (about ½ inch from each side) and slice the cucumber into 1-inch pieces.
2. With a paring knife or a spoon, scoop most of the seeds from the inside of each cucumber piece to make a cup, being careful to not cut all the way through.
3. Fill each cucumber cup with about 1 tablespoon of hummus or bean dip.
4. Top each with a cherry tomato half and a sprinkle of fresh minced basil.

PER SERVING
Calories: 135, Total Fat: 6g, Total Carbohydrates: 16g, Protein: 6g, Fiber: 5g, Sugar: 4g, Sodium: 242mg

Couscous Stuffed Italian Breaded Shrimp

Prep time: 10 minutes | Cook time: 10 minutes | Serves: 2

1 cup vegetable stock
½ cup whole-wheat couscous
12 extra-large shrimp, peeled and deveined
1 egg, beaten
¼ cup Italian-seasoned breadcrumbs

1 tablespoon olive oil
2 sundried tomatoes, finely chopped
1 tablespoon prepared pesto sauce
Sea salt and freshly ground pepper, to taste

1. Bring stock to a boil and add the couscous.
2. Cover and remove from heat. Set aside for about 5 minutes. Coat the shrimp with the egg and dredge in the breadcrumbs.
3. In a large sauté pan, heat the olive oil and add the shrimp, cooking until just brown and crispy on all sides.
4. Remove the lid from the couscous, then stir in the sundried tomatoes and pesto.
5. Season with sea salt and freshly ground pepper.
6. To stuff the shrimp, slice the front of the shrimp open and spoon the couscous mixture inside.
7. Serve with leftover couscous on the side.

PER SERVING
Calories: 511, Fat: 13.59g, Carbohydrates: 27.34g, Protein: 68.76g, Sugar: 7.05g, Fiber: 5.2g, Sodium: 2181mg

Goat-Mascarpone Cheese Stuffed Bell Peppers

Prep time: 10 minutes | Cook time: 8 minutes | Serves: 8 to 10

20 to 25 mini sweet bell peppers, assortment of colors
1 tablespoon extra-virgin olive oil
4 ounces (113 g) Goat cheese, at room

temperature
4 ounces (113 g) Mascarpone cheese, at room temperature
1 tablespoon fresh chives, chopped
1 tablespoon lemon zest

1. Preheat the oven to 400°F (205°C).
2. Remove the stem, cap, and any seeds from the peppers. Put them into a bowl and toss to coat with the olive oil.
3. Put the peppers onto a baking sheet, bake for 8 minutes.
4. Remove the peppers from the oven and let cool completely.
5. In a medium bowl, add the Goat cheese, Mascarpone cheese, chives, and lemon zest. Stir to combine, then spoon mixture into a piping bag.
6. Fill each pepper to the top with the cheese mixture, using the piping bag.
7. Chill the peppers in the fridge for at least 30 minutes before serving.

PER SERVING
Calories: 141, Total Fat: 11g, Saturated Fat: 5g, Total Carbohydrates: 6g, Protein: 4g, Sugar: 3g, Fiber: 2g, Sodium: 73mg

Chocolate, Coconut, and Cranberry Granola Bars

Prep time: 10 minutes | Cook time: 15 minutes | Serves: 6

2 cups certified gluten-free quick oats
2 tablespoons sugar-free dark chocolate chunks
2 tablespoons unsweetened dried cranberries
3 tablespoons

unsweetened shredded coconut
½ cup raw honey
1 teaspoon ground cinnamon
⅛ teaspoon salt
2 tablespoons olive oil

1. Preheat the air fryer to 360°F (182°C). Line an 8-by-8-inch baking dish with parchment paper that comes up the side so you can lift it out after cooking.
2. In a large bowl, mix together all of the ingredients until well combined.
3. Press the oat mixture into the pan in an even layer.
4. Place the pan into the air fryer basket and bake for 15 minutes.
5. Remove the pan from the air fryer, and lift the granola cake out of the pan using the edges of the parchment paper.
6. Allow to cool for 5 minutes before slicing into 6 equal bars.
7. Serve immediately, or wrap in plastic wrap and store at room temperature for up to 1 week.

PER SERVING
Calories: 272, Total Fat: 10g, Saturated Fat: 4g, Total Carbohydrates: 44g, Protein: 5g, Fiber: 4g, Sugar: 25g

Savory Mediterranean Spiced Popcorn

Prep time: 10 minutes | Cook time: 2 minutes | Serves: 4 to 6

3 tablespoons extra-virgin olive oil
¼ teaspoon garlic powder
¼ teaspoon freshly ground black pepper
¼ teaspoon sea salt
⅛ teaspoon dried thyme
⅛ teaspoon dried oregano
12 cups plain popped popcorn

1. In a large sauté pan or skillet, heat the oil over medium heat, until shimmering, and then add the garlic powder, pepper, salt, thyme, and oregano until fragrant.
2. In a large bowl, drizzle the oil over the popcorn, toss, and serve.

PER SERVING
Calories: 183, Total Fat: 12g, Saturated Fat: 2g, Total Carbohydrates: 19g, Protein: 3g, Sugar: 0g, Fiber: 4g, Sodium: 146mg

Burrata Caprese Stack with Basil

Prep time: 10 minutes | Cook time: 0 minutes | Serves: 4

1 large organic tomato, preferably heirloom
½ teaspoon salt
¼ teaspoon freshly ground black pepper
1 (4-ounce/ 113-g) ball burrata cheese
8 fresh basil leaves, thinly sliced
2 tablespoons extra-virgin olive oil
1 tablespoon red wine or balsamic vinegar

1. Slice the tomato into 4 thick slices, removing any tough center core and sprinkle with salt and pepper. Place the tomatoes, seasoned-side up, on a plate.
2. On a separate rimmed plate, slice the burrata into 4 thick slices and place one slice on top of each tomato slice. Top each with one-quarter of the basil and pour any reserved burrata cream from the rimmed plate over top.
3. Drizzle with olive oil and vinegar and serve with a fork and knife.

PER SERVING (1 stack)
Calories: 153, Total Fat: 13g, Total Carbs: 2g, Net Carbs: 1g, Protein: 7g, Fiber: 1g, Sodium: 469mg

Seared Halloumi Cheese with Tomato

Prep time: 5 minutes | Cook time: 4 minutes | Serves: 2

3 ounces (85 g) Halloumi cheese, cut crosswise into 2 thinner, rectangular pieces
2 teaspoons prepared pesto sauce, plus additional for drizzling if desired
1 medium tomato, sliced

1. Heat a nonstick skillet over medium-high heat and place the slices of Halloumi in the hot pan. After about 2 minutes, check to see if the cheese is golden on the bottom. If it is, flip the slices, top each with 1 teaspoon of pesto, and cook for another 2 minutes, or until the second side is golden.
2. Serve with slices of tomato and a drizzle of pesto, if desired, on the side.

PER SERVING
Calories: 177, Total Fat: 14g, Total Carbohydrates: 4g, Protein: 10g, Fiber: 1g, Sugar: 3g, Sodium: 233mg

Salmon and Avocado Stuffed Cucumbers

Prep time: 10 minutes | Cook time: 0 minutes | Serves: 4

2 large cucumbers, peeled
1 (4-ounce/ 113-g) can red salmon
1 medium very ripe avocado, peeled, pitted, and mashed
1 tablespoon extra-virgin
olive oil
Zest and juice of 1 lime
3 tablespoons chopped fresh cilantro
½ teaspoon salt
¼ teaspoon freshly ground black pepper

1. Slice the cucumber into 1-inch-thick segments and using a spoon, scrape seeds out of center of each segment and stand up on a plate.
2. In a medium bowl, combine the salmon, avocado, olive oil, lime zest and juice, cilantro, salt, and pepper and mix until creamy.
3. Spoon the salmon mixture into the center of each cucumber segment and serve chilled.

PER SERVING
Calories: 159, Total Fat: 11g, Total Carbs: 8g, Net Carbs: 5g, Protein: 9g, Fiber: 3g, Sodium: 398mg

Paprika Chickpeas

Prep time: 5 minutes | Cook time: 15 minutes | Serves:4

1 (15-ounce / 425-g) can cooked chickpeas, drained and rinsed
1 tablespoon olive oil
¼ teaspoon salt
⅛ teaspoon chili powder
⅛ teaspoon garlic powder
⅛ teaspoon paprika

1. Preheat the air fryer to 380°F (193°C).
2. In a medium bowl, toss all of the ingredients together until the chickpeas are well coated.
3. Pour the chickpeas into the air fryer and spread them out in a single layer.
4. Roast for 15 minutes, stirring once halfway through the cook time.

PER SERVING
Calories: 109, Total Fat: 5g, Saturated Fat: 1g, Carbohydrates: 13g, Protein: 4g, Total Fiber: 4g, Sugar: 2g

Lemony Peanut Butter Hummus

Prep time: 10 minutes | Cook time: 0 minutes | Serves: 6

1 (15-ounce / 425-g) can chickpeas, drained, liquid reserved
3 tablespoons freshly squeezed lemon juice (from about 1 large lemon)
2 tablespoons peanut butter
3 tablespoons extra-virgin olive oil, divided
2 garlic cloves
¼ teaspoon kosher or sea salt (optional)
Raw veggies or whole-grain crackers, for serving (optional)

1. In the bowl of a food processor, combine the chickpeas and 2 tablespoons of the reserved chickpea liquid with the lemon juice, peanut butter, 2 tablespoons of oil, and the garlic. Process the mixture for 1 minute. Scrape down the sides of the bowl with a rubber spatula. Process for 1 more minute, or until smooth.
2. Put in a serving bowl, drizzle with the remaining 1 tablespoon of olive oil, sprinkle with the salt, if using, and serve with veggies or crackers, if desired.

PER SERVING
Calories: 125g, Total Fat: 6g, Saturated Fat: 1g, Total Carbs: 14g, Protein: 4g, Fiber: 3g, Sugar: 3g, Sodium: 369mg, Phosphorus: 57mg, Potassium: 85mg

Spicy Shrimp

Prep time: 5 minutes | Cook time: 4 minutes | Serves: 6

½ cup olive oil
5 cloves garlic, minced
1 teaspoon red pepper flakes
24 large shrimp, peeled
and deveined
Juice and zest from 1 lemon
Sea salt and freshly ground pepper, to taste

1. Heat the olive oil in a large skillet over medium-high heat. Add the garlic and red pepper flakes, and cook for 1 minute.
2. Add the shrimp and cook an additional 3 minutes, stirring frequently. Remove from the pan, and sprinkle with lemon juice, sea salt, and pepper.

PER SERVING
Calories: 186, Fat: 18.33g, Carbohydrates: 1.91g, Protein: 4.04g, Sugar: 0.25g, Fiber: 0.2g, Sodium: 159mg

Greek Yogurt Deviled Eggs with Parsley

Prep time: 10 minutes | Cook time: 15 minutes | Serves: 4

4 eggs
¼ cup nonfat plain Greek yogurt
1 teaspoon chopped fresh dill
⅛ teaspoon salt
⅛ teaspoon paprika
⅛ teaspoon garlic powder
Chopped fresh parsley, for garnish

1. Preheat the air fryer to 260°F (127°C).
2. Place the eggs in a single layer in the air fryer basket and cook for 15 minutes.
3. Quickly remove the eggs from the air fryer and place them into a cold water bath. Let the eggs cool in the water for 10 minutes before removing and peeling them.
4. After peeling the eggs, cut them in half.
5. Spoon the yolk into a small bowl. Add the yogurt, dill, salt, paprika, and garlic powder and mix until smooth.
6. Spoon or pipe the yolk mixture into the halved egg whites. Serve with a sprinkle of fresh parsley on top.

PER SERVING
Calories: 80, Total Fat: 5g, Saturated Fat: 2g, Total Carbohydrates: 1g, Protein: 8g, Fiber: 0g, Sugar: 1g

Mediterranean Nutty Fat Bombs

Prep time: 5 minutes | Cook time: 0 minutes | Makes 6 fat bombs

1 cup crumbled Goat cheese
4 tablespoons jarred pesto
12 pitted Kalamata olives, finely chopped
½ cup finely chopped walnuts
1 tablespoon chopped fresh rosemary

1. In a medium bowl, combine the Goat cheese, pesto, and olives and mix well using a fork. Place in the refrigerator for at least 4 hours to harden.
2. Using your hands, form the mixture into 6 balls, about ¾-inch diameter. The mixture will be sticky.
3. In a small bowl, place the walnuts and rosemary and roll the Goat cheese balls in the nut mixture to coat.
4. Store the fat bombs in the refrigerator for up to 1 week or in the freezer for up to 1 month.

PER SERVING (1 fat bomb)
Calories: 166, Total Fat: 15g, Total Carbs: 4g, Net Carbs: 3g, Protein: 5g, Fiber: 1g, Sodium: 337mg

Apples with Honey Walnuts Topping

Prep time: 10 minutes | Cook time: 12 minutes | Serves: 4

2 Granny Smith apples
¼ cup certified gluten-free rolled oats
2 tablespoons honey
½ teaspoon ground cinnamon
2 tablespoons chopped walnuts
Pinch salt
1 tablespoon olive oil

1. Preheat the air fryer to 380°F (193°C).
2. Core the apples and slice them in half.
3. In a medium bowl, mix together the oats, honey, cinnamon, walnuts, salt, and olive oil.
4. Scoop a quarter of the oat mixture onto the top of each half apple.
5. Place the apples in the air fryer basket, and roast for 12 to 15 minutes, or until the apples are fork-tender.

PER SERVING
Calories: 144, Total Fat: 6g, Saturated Fat: 1g, Total Carbohydrates: 22g, Protein: 1g, Fiber: 3g, Sugar: 17g

Turkish Spiced Mixed-Nuts

Prep time: 10 minutes | Cook time: 5 minutes | Serves: 4 to 6

1 tablespoon extra-virgin olive oil
1 cup mixed nuts (walnuts, almonds, cashews, peanuts)
2 tablespoons paprika
1 tablespoon dried mint
½ tablespoon ground cinnamon
½ tablespoon kosher salt
¼ tablespoon garlic powder
¼ teaspoon freshly ground black pepper
⅛ tablespoon ground cumin

1. In a small to medium saucepan, heat the oil on low heat.
2. Once the oil is warm, add the nuts, paprika, mint, cinnamon, salt, garlic powder, pepper, and cumin and stir continually until the spices are well incorporated with the nuts.

PER SERVING
Calories: 204, Total Fat: 18g, Saturated Fat: 2g, Total Carbohydrates: 10g, Protein: 6g, Sugar: 2g, Fiber: 4g, Sodium: 605mg

Stuffed Figs with Goat Cheese and Cinnamon

Prep time: 5 minutes | Cook time: 10 minutes | Serves: 4

8 fresh figs
2 ounces (57 g) Goat cheese
¼ teaspoon ground cinnamon
1 tablespoon honey, plus more for serving
1 tablespoon olive oil

1. Preheat the air fryer to 360°F (182°C).
2. Cut the stem off of each fig.
3. Cut an X into the top of each fig, cutting halfway down the fig. Leave the base intact.
4. In a small bowl, mix together the Goat cheese, cinnamon, and honey.
5. Spoon the Goat cheese mixture into the cavity of each fig.
6. Place the figs in a single layer in the air fryer basket. Drizzle the olive oil over top of the figs and roast for 10 minutes.
7. Serve with an additional drizzle of honey.

PER SERVING
Calories: 158, Total Fat: 7g, Saturated Fat: 3g, Total Carbohydrates: 24g, Protein: 3g, Fiber: 3g, Sugar: 21g

Air-Fried Popcorn with Garlic Salt

Prep time: 5 minutes | Cook time: 8 minutes | Serves: 2

2 tablespoons olive oil
¼ cup popcorn kernels
1 teaspoon garlic salt

1. Preheat the air fryer to 380°F (193°C).
2. Tear a square of aluminum foil the size of the bottom of the air fryer and place into the air fryer.
3. Drizzle olive oil over the top of the foil, and then pour in the popcorn kernels.
4. Roast for 8 to 10 minutes, or until the popcorn stops popping.
5. Transfer the popcorn to a large bowl and sprinkle with garlic salt before serving.

PER SERVING
Calories: 245, Total Fat: 15g, Saturated Fat: 2g, Total Carbohydrates: 25g, Protein: 4g, Fiber: 5g, Sugar: 0g

Honey-Glazed Rosemary Almonds

Prep time: 5 minutes | Cook time: 5 minutes | Serves: 6

1 cup raw, whole, shelled almonds
1 tablespoon minced fresh rosemary
¼ teaspoon kosher or sea salt
1 tablespoon honey
Nonstick cooking spray

1. In a large skillet over medium heat, combine the almonds, rosemary, and salt. Stir frequently for 1 minute.
2. Drizzle in the honey and cook for another 3 to 4 minutes, stirring frequently, until the almonds are coated and just starting to darken around the edges.
3. Remove from the heat. Using a spatula, spread the almonds onto a pan coated with nonstick cooking spray. Cool for 10 minutes or so. Break up the almonds before serving.

PER SERVING
Calories: 13g, Total Fat: 1g, Saturated Fat: 0g, Total Carbs: 3g, Protein: 1g, Fiber: 1g, Sugar: 3g, Sodium: 97mg

Orange-Marinated Olives

Prep time: 10 minutes | Cook time: 0 minutes | Makes 2 cups

2 cups mixed green olives with pits
¼ cup red wine vinegar
¼ cup extra-virgin olive oil
4 garlic cloves, finely minced
Zest and juice of 2 clementines or 1 large orange
1 teaspoon red pepper flakes
2 bay leaves
½ teaspoon ground cumin
½ teaspoon ground allspice

1. In a large glass bowl or jar, combine the olives, vinegar, oil, garlic, orange zest and juice, red pepper flakes, bay leaves, cumin, and allspice and mix well. Cover and refrigerate for at least 4 hours or up to a week to allow the olives to marinate, tossing again before serving.

PER SERVING (¼ cup)
Calories: 133, Total Fat: 14g, Total Carbs: 3g, Net Carbs: 1g, Protein: 1g, Fiber: 2g, Sodium: 501mg

Sage-Basil White Beans

Prep time: 5 minutes | Cook time: 15 minutes | Serves: 2

1 (15 ounce) can cooked white beans
2 tablespoons olive oil
1 teaspoon fresh sage, chopped
¼ teaspoon garlic powder
¼ teaspoon salt, divided
1 teaspoon chopped fresh basil

1. Preheat the air fryer to 380°F (193°C).
2. In a medium bowl, mix together the beans, olive oil, sage, garlic, ⅛ teaspoon salt, and basil.
3. Pour the white beans into the air fryer and spread them out in a single layer.
4. Bake for 10 minutes. Stir and continue cooking for an additional 5 to 9 minutes, or until they reach your preferred level of crispiness.
5. Toss with the remaining ⅛ teaspoon salt before serving.

PER SERVING
Calories: 308, Total Fat: 14g, Saturated Fat: 2g, Carbohydrates: 34g, Protein: 13g, Total Fiber: 9g, Sugar: 0g

Crunchy Kale Chips

Prep time: 5 minutes | Cook time: 10 minutes | Makes 4 cups chips

2 heads curly leaf kale
2 tablespoons olive oil

Sea salt, to taste

1. Tear the kale into bite-sized pieces.
2. Toss with the olive oil, and lay on a baking sheet in a single layer. Sprinkle with a pinch of sea salt.
3. Bake for 10 to 15 minutes until crispy. Serve or store in an airtight container.

PER SERVING (1 cup)
Calories: 64, Fat: 6.82g, Carbohydrates: 0.7g, Protein: 0.34g, Sugar: 0.18g, Fiber: 0.3g, Sodium: 585mg

Hot Spiced Roasted Cashews

Prep time: 5 minutes | Cook time: 10 minutes | Serves: 4

2 cups raw cashews
2 tablespoons olive oil
¼ teaspoon salt
¼ teaspoon chili powder

⅛ teaspoon garlic powder
⅛ teaspoon smoked paprika

1. Preheat the air fryer to 360ºF (182ºC).
2. In a large bowl, toss all of the ingredients together.
3. Pour the cashews into the air fryer basket and roast them for 5 minutes. Shake the basket, then cook for 5 minutes more.
4. Serve immediately.

PER SERVING
Calories: 476, Total Fat: 40g, Saturated Fat: 7g, Total Carbohydrates: 23g, Protein: 14g, Fiber: 3g, Sugar: 4g

Mediterranean-Style Trail Mix

Prep time: 10 minutes | Cook time: 0 minutes | Serves: 6

1 cup roughly chopped unsalted walnuts
½ cup roughly chopped salted almonds
½ cup shelled salted pistachios

½ cup roughly chopped apricots
½ cup roughly chopped dates
⅓ cup dried figs, sliced in half

1. In a large zip-top bag, combine the walnuts, almonds, pistachios, apricots, dates, and figs and mix well.

PER SERVING
Calories: 348, Total Fat: 24g, Saturated Fat: 2g, Total Carbohydrates: 33g, Protein: 9g, Sugar: 22g, Fiber: 7g, Sodium: 95mg

Air-Fried Sweet Potato Chips

Prep time: 5 minutes | Cook time: 13 minutes | Serves: 2

1 large sweet potato, sliced thin

⅛ teaspoon salt
2 tablespoons olive oil

1. Preheat the air fryer to 380ºF (193ºC).
2. In a small bowl, toss the sweet potatoes, salt, and olive oil together until the potatoes are well coated.
3. Put the sweet potato slices into the air fryer and spread them out in a single layer.
4. Fry for 10 minutes. Stir, then air fry for 3 to 5 minutes more, or until the chips reach the preferred level of crispiness.

PER SERVING
Calories: 175, Total Fat: 14g, Saturated Fat: 2g, Total Carbohydrates: 13g, Protein: 1g, Fiber: 2g, Sugar: 3g

Chapter 14 Desserts

Lemon Fool with Honey Drizzled

Prep time: 10 minutes | Cook time: 2 minutes | Serves: 4

1 cup 2% plain Greek yogurt
1 medium lemon
¼ cup cold water
1½ teaspoons cornstarch
3½ tablespoons honey,
divided
⅔ cup heavy (whipping) cream
Fresh fruit and mint leaves, for serving (optional)

1. Place a large glass bowl and the metal beaters from your electric mixer in the refrigerator to chill. Add the yogurt to a medium glass bowl, and place that bowl in the refrigerator to chill as well.
2. Using a Microplane or citrus zester, zest the lemon into a medium, microwave-safe bowl. Halve the lemon, and squeeze 1 tablespoon of lemon juice into the bowl. Add the water and cornstarch, and stir well. Whisk in 3 tablespoons of honey. Microwave the lemon mixture on high for 1 minute, stir and microwave for an additional 10 to 30 seconds, until the mixture is thick and bubbling.
3. Remove the bowl of yogurt from the refrigerator, and whisk in the warm lemon mixture. Place the yogurt back in the refrigerator.
4. Remove the large chilled bowl and the beaters from the refrigerator. Assemble your electric mixer with the chilled beaters. Pour the cream into the chilled bowl, and beat until soft peaks form—1 to 3 minutes, depending on the freshness of your cream.
5. Take the chilled yogurt mixture out of the refrigerator. Gently fold it into the whipped cream using a rubber scraper, lift and turn the mixture to prevent the cream from deflating. Chill until serving, at least 15 minutes but no longer than 1 hour.
6. To serve, spoon the lemon fool into four glasses or dessert dishes and drizzle with the remaining ½ tablespoon of honey. Top with fresh fruit and mint, if desired.

PER SERVING
Calories: 171g, Total Fat: 10g, Saturated Fat:6g, Total Carbs: 20g, Fiber: 0g, Protein: 3g, Sugar: 19g, Sodium: 37mg

Pomegranate and Quinoa Dark Chocolate Bark

Prep time: 5 minutes | Cook time: 13 minutes | Serves: 6

Nonstick cooking spray
½ cup uncooked tricolor or regular quinoa
½ teaspoon kosher or sea salt
8 ounces (227 g) dark chocolate or 1 cup dark chocolate chips
½ cup fresh pomegranate seeds

1. In a medium saucepan coated with nonstick cooking spray over medium heat, toast the uncooked quinoa for 2 to 3 minutes, stirring frequently. Do not let the quinoa burn. Remove the pan from the stove, and mix in the salt. Set aside 2 tablespoons of the toasted quinoa to use for the topping.
2. Break the chocolate into large pieces, and put it in a gallon-size zip-top plastic bag. Using a metal ladle or a meat pounder, pound the chocolate until broken into smaller pieces. (If using chocolate chips, you can skip this step.) Dump the chocolate out of the bag into a medium, microwave-safe bowl and heat for 1 minute on high in the microwave. Stir until the chocolate is completely melted. Mix the toasted quinoa (except the topping you set aside) into the melted chocolate.
3. Line a large, rimmed baking sheet with parchment paper. Pour the chocolate mixture onto the sheet and spread it evenly until the entire pan is covered. Sprinkle the remaining 2 tablespoons of quinoa and the pomegranate seeds on top. Using a spatula or the back of a spoon, press the quinoa and the pomegranate seeds into the chocolate.
4. Freeze the mixture for 10 to 15 minutes, or until set. Remove the bark from the freezer, and break it into about 2-inch jagged pieces. Store in a sealed container or zip-top plastic bag in the refrigerator until ready to serve.

PER SERVING
Calories: 268g, Total Fat: 12g, Saturated Fat: 4g, Total Carbs: 37g, Fiber: 3g, Protein: 4g, Sugar: 15g, Sodium: 360mg

Keto-Mediterranean Nut Butter Cup

Prep time: 10 minutes | Cook time: 0 minutes | Serves: 8

½ cup crunchy almond butter (no sugar added)
½ cup light fruity extra-virgin olive oil
¼ cup ground flaxseed
2 tablespoons unsweetened cocoa powder
1 teaspoon vanilla extract
1 teaspoon ground cinnamon (optional)
1 to 2 teaspoons sugar-free sweetener of choice (optional)

1. In a mixing bowl, combine the almond butter, olive oil, flaxseed, cocoa powder, vanilla, cinnamon (if using), and sweetener (if using) and stir well with a spatula to combine. Mixture will be a thick liquid.
2. Pour into 8 mini muffin liners and freeze until solid, at least 12 hours. Store in the freezer to maintain their shape.

PER SERVING (1 fat bomb)
Calories: 240, Total Fat: 24g, Total Carbs: 5g, Net Carbs: 3g, Fiber: 2g, Protein: 3g, Sodium: 3mg

Baked Lemon Cookies

Prep time: 10 minutes | Cook time: 10 minutes | Makes 12 cookies

Nonstick cooking spray
¾ cup granulated sugar
½ cup butter
1½ teaspoons vinegar
1 large egg
1 teaspoon grated lemon zest
1¾ cup flour
1 teaspoon baking powder
¼ teaspoon baking soda
¾ cup confectioners' sugar
¼ cup freshly squeezed lemon juice
1 teaspoon finely grated lemon zest

1. Preheat the oven to 350°F (180°C). Spray a baking sheet with cooking spray and set aside.
2. In a medium bowl, cream the sugar and butter. Next, stir in the vinegar, and then add the egg and lemon zest, and mix well. Sift the flour, baking powder, and baking soda into the bowl and mix until combined.
3. Spoon the mixture onto a prepared baking sheet in 12 equal heaps. Bake for 10 to 12 minutes. Be sure not to burn the bottoms.
4. While the cookies are baking, make the lemon glaze in a small bowl by mixing the sugar, lemon juice, and lemon zest together.
5. Remove the cookies from the oven and brush with lemon glaze.

PER SERVING
Calories: 233, Total Fat: 8g, Saturated Fat: 5g, Total Carbohydrates: 39g, Protein: 3g, Sugar: 26g, Fiber: 1g, Sodium: 132mg

Baklava with Syrup

Prep time: 10 minutes | Cook time: 30 minutes | Serves: 12

1½ cups finely chopped walnuts
1 teaspoon ground cinnamon
¼ teaspoon ground cardamom (optional)
1 cup water
½ cup sugar
½ cup honey
2 tablespoons freshly squeezed lemon juice
1 cup salted butter, melted
20 large sheets phyllo pastry dough, at room temperature

1. Preheat the oven to 350°F (180°C).
2. In a small bowl, gently mix the walnuts, cinnamon, and cardamom (if using) and set aside.
3. In a small pot, bring the water, sugar, honey, and lemon juice just to a boil. Remove from the heat.
4. Put the butter in a small bowl. Onto an ungreased 9-by-13-inch baking sheet, put 1 layer of phyllo dough and slowly brush with butter. Be careful not to tear the phyllo sheets as you butter them. Carefully layer 1 or 2 more phyllo sheets, brushing each with butter in the baking pan, and then layer ⅛ of the nut mix, layer 2 sheets and add another ⅛ of the nut mix, repeat with 2 sheets and nuts until you run out of nuts and dough, topping with the remaining phyllo dough sheets.
5. Slice 4 lines into the baklava lengthwise and make another 4 or 5 slices diagonally across the pan.
6. Put in the oven and cook for 30 to 40 minutes, or until golden brown.
7. Remove the baklava from the oven and immediately cover it with the syrup.

PER SERVING
Calories: 443, Total Fat: 27g, Saturated Fat: 11g, Total Carbohydrates: 47g, Protein: 6g, Sugar: 22g, Fiber: 3g, Sodium: 344mg

Mixed-Berries, Pecans and Oat Crumbles

Prep time: 5 minutes | Cook time: 30 minutes | Serves: 2

1½ cups frozen mixed berries, thawed
1 tablespoon butter, softened
1 tablespoon sugar
¼ cup pecans
¼ cup oats

1. Preheat the oven to 350°F (180°C) and set the rack to the middle position.
2. Divide the berries between 2 (8-ounce) ramekins
3. In a food processor, combine the butter, sugar, pecans, and oats, and pulse a few times, until the mixture resembles damp sand.
4. Divide the crumble topping over the berries.
5. Place the ramekins on a sheet pan and bake for 30 minutes, or until the top is golden and the berries are bubbling.

PER SERVING
Calories: 267, Total Fat: 17g, Total Carbohydrates: 27g, Fiber: 6g, Sugar: 13g, Protein: 4g, Sodium: 43mg

Panna Cotta with Blackberry

Prep time: 10 minutes | Cook time: 4 minutes | Serves: 2

¾ cup half-and-half, divided
1 teaspoon unflavored powdered gelatin
½ cup cream
3 tablespoons coconut sugar
1 teaspoon lemon zest
1 tablespoon freshly squeezed lemon juice
1 teaspoon lemon extract
½ cup fresh blackberries
Lemon peels to garnish (optional)

1. Place ¼ cup of half-and-half in a small bowl.
2. Sprinkle the gelatin powder evenly over the half-and-half and set it aside for 10 minutes to hydrate.
3. In a saucepan, combine the remaining ½ cup of half-and-half, the cream, sugar, lemon zest, lemon juice, and lemon extract. Heat the mixture over medium heat for 4 minutes, or until it's barely simmering—don't let it come to a full boil. Remove from the heat.
4. When the gelatin is hydrated (it will look like applesauce), add it into the warm cream mixture, whisking as the gelatin melts.
5. If there are any remaining clumps of gelatin, strain the liquid or remove the lumps with a spoon.
6. Pour the mixture into 2 dessert glasses or stemless wineglasses and refrigerate for at least 6 hours, or up to overnight.
7. Serve with the fresh berries and garnish with some strips of fresh lemon peel, if desired.

PER SERVING
Calories: 422, Total Fat: 33g, Total Carbohydrates: 28g, Protein: 6g, Fiber: 2g, Sugar: 21g, Sodium: 64mg

Cookies with Strawberry Preserves

Prep time: 15 minutes | Cook time: 12 minutes | Makes 3 dozen cookies

2 cups cornstarch
1½ cups all-purpose flour
2 teaspoons baking powder
1 teaspoon baking soda
1 cup cold butter, cut into 1-inch cubes
⅔ cup sugar
4 large egg yolks
2 tablespoons brandy
1 teaspoon vanilla extract
½ teaspoon salt
2 cups strawberry preserves
Confectioners' sugar, for sprinkling

1. In a bowl, combine the cornstarch, flour, baking powder, and baking soda and mix together. Using your hands or 2 forks, mix the butter and sugar just until combined, with small pieces of butter remaining.
2. Add the egg yolks, brandy, vanilla, and salt, stirring slowly until all ingredients are blended together. If you have a stand mixer, you can mix these ingredients together with the paddle attachment and then finish mixing by hand, but it is not required.
3. Wrap the dough in plastic wrap and place in a resealable plastic bag for at least 1 hour.
4. Preheat the oven to 350°F (180°C).
5. Roll the dough to ¼-inch thickness and cut, placing 12 cookies on a sheet. Bake the sheets one at a time on the top rack of the oven for 12 to 14 minutes.
6. Let the cookies cool completely and top with about 1 tablespoon of strawberry preserves.
7. Sprinkle with confectioners' sugar.

PER SERVING
Calories: 157, Total Fat: 6g, Saturated Fat: 3g, Total Carbohydrates: 26g, Protein: 1g, Sugar: 12g, Fiber: <1g, Sodium: 132mg

Summer Strawberry Panna Cotta

Prep time: 10 minutes | Cook time: 5 minutes | Serves: 4

2 tablespoons warm water	1 to 2 tablespoons sugar-free sweetener of choice (optional)
2 teaspoons gelatin powder	
2 cups heavy cream	1½ teaspoons pure vanilla extract
1 cup sliced strawberries, plus more for garnish	4 to 6 fresh mint leaves, for garnish (optional)

1. Pour the warm water into a small bowl. Sprinkle the gelatin over the water and stir well to dissolve. Allow the mixture to sit for 10 minutes.
2. In a blender or a large bowl, if using an immersion blender, combine the cream, strawberries, sweetener (if using), and vanilla. Blend until the mixture is smooth and the strawberries are well puréed.
3. Transfer the mixture to a saucepan and heat over medium-low heat until just below a simmer. Remove from the heat and cool for 5 minutes.
4. Whisking constantly, add in the gelatin mixture until smooth. Divide the custard between ramekins or small glass bowls, cover and refrigerate until set, 4 to 6 hours.
5. Serve chilled, garnishing with additional sliced strawberries or mint leaves (if using).

PER SERVING
Calories: 431, Total Fat: 44g, Total Carbs: 7g, Net Carbs: 6g, Fiber: 1g, Protein: 4g, Sodium: 49mg

Easy Blueberry Pomegranate Granita

Prep time: 5 minutes | Cook time: 6 minutes | Serves: 2

1 cup frozen wild blueberries	juice
	¼ cup coconut sugar
1 cup pomegranate or pomegranate blueberry	¼ cup water

1. Combine the frozen blueberries and pomegranate juice in a saucepan and bring to a boil. Reduce the heat and simmer for 5 minutes, or until the blueberries start to break down.
2. While the juice and berries are cooking, combine the sugar and water in a small microwave-safe bowl. Microwave for 60 seconds, or until it comes to a rolling boil. Stir to make sure all of the sugar is dissolved and set the syrup aside.
3. Combine the blueberry mixture and the sugar syrup in a blender and blend for 1 minute, or until the fruit is completely puréed.
4. Pour the mixture into an 8-by-8-inch baking pan or a similar-sized bowl. The liquid should come about ½ inch up the sides. Let the mixture cool for 30 minutes, and then put it into the freezer.
5. Every 30 minutes for the next 2 hours, scrape the granita with a fork to keep it from freezing solid.
6. Serve it after 2 hours, or store it in a covered container in the freezer.

PER SERVING
Calories: 214, Total Fat: 0g, Total Carbohydrates: 54g, Protein: 1g, Fiber: 2g, Sugar: 48g, Sodium: 15mg

Chilled Fruit Kebabs with Dark Chocolate

Prep time: 5 minutes | Cook time: 1 minute | Serves: 6

12 strawberries, hulled	24 blueberries
12 cherries, pitted	8 ounces (227 g) dark chocolate
24 seedless red or green grapes	

1. Line a large, rimmed baking sheet with parchment paper. On your work surface, lay out six 12-inch wooden skewers.
2. Thread the fruit onto the skewers, following this pattern: 1 strawberry, 1 cherry, 2 grapes, 2 blueberries, 1 strawberry, 1 cherry, 2 grapes, and 2 blueberries (or vary according to taste!). Place the kebabs on the prepared baking sheet.
3. In a medium, microwave-safe bowl, heat the chocolate in the microwave for 1 minute on high. Stir until the chocolate is completely melted.
4. Spoon the melted chocolate into a small plastic sandwich bag. Twist the bag closed right above the chocolate, and snip the corner of the bag off with scissors. Squeeze the bag to drizzle lines of chocolate over the kebabs.
5. Place the sheet in the freezer and chill for 20 minutes before serving.

PER SERVING
Calories: 297g, Total Fat: 17g, Saturated Fat: 9g, Total Carbs: 35g, Protein: 4g, Fiber: 6g, Sugar: 26g, Sodium: 12mg

Chocolate Chia Seeds Pudding

Prep time: 5 minutes | Cook time: 5 minutes | Serves: 4

2 cups heavy cream
¼ cup unsweetened cocoa powder
1 teaspoon almond extract or vanilla extract
½ or 1 teaspoon ground cinnamon
¼ teaspoon salt
½ cup chia seeds

1. In a saucepan, heat the heavy cream over medium-low heat to just below a simmer. Remove from the heat and allow to cool slightly.
2. In a blender or large bowl, if using an immersion blender, combine the warmed heavy cream, cocoa powder, almond extract, cinnamon, and salt and blend until the cocoa is well incorporated.
3. Stir in the chia seeds and let sit for 15 minutes.
4. Divide the mixture evenly between ramekins or small glass bowls and refrigerate at least 6 hours, or until set. Serve chilled.

PER SERVING
Calories: 561, Total Fat: 53g, Total Carbs: 19g, Net Carbs: 7g, Fiber: 12g, Protein: 8g, Sodium: 187mg

Baked Pears with Mascarpone Cheese

Prep time: 10 minutes | Cook time: 20 minutes | Serves: 2

2 ripe pears, peeled
1 tablespoon plus 2 teaspoons honey, divided
1 teaspoon vanilla, divided
¼ teaspoon ginger
¼ teaspoon ground coriander
¼ cup minced walnuts
¼ cup Mascarpone cheese
Pinch salt

1. Preheat the oven to 350ºF (180ºC) and set the rack to the middle position. Grease a small baking dish.
2. Cut the pears in half lengthwise. Using a spoon, scoop out the core from each piece. Place the pears with the cut side up in the baking dish.
3. Combine 1 tablespoon of honey, ½ teaspoon of vanilla, ginger, and coriander in a small bowl. Pour this mixture evenly over the pear halves.
4. Sprinkle walnuts over the pear halves.
5. Bake for 20 minutes, or until the pears are golden and you're able to pierce them easily with a knife.

6. While the pears are baking, mix the Mascarpone cheese with the remaining 2 teaspoons honey, ½ teaspoon of vanilla, and a pinch of salt. Stir well to combine.
7. Divide the Mascarpone among the warm pear halves and serve.

PER SERVING
Calories: 307, Total Fat: 16g, Total Carbohydrates: 43g, Fiber: 6g, Sugar: 31g, Protein: 4g, Sodium: 89mg

Pecan and Carrot Coconut Cake

Prep time: 10 minutes | Cook time: 45 minutes | Serves: 12

½ cup coconut oil, at room temperature, plus more for greasing the baking dish
2 teaspoons pure vanilla extract
¼ cup pure maple syrup
6 eggs
½ cup coconut flour
1 teaspoon baking powder
1 teaspoon baking soda
½ teaspoon ground nutmeg
1 teaspoon ground cinnamon
⅛ teaspoon sea salt
½ cup chopped pecans
3 cups finely grated carrots

1. Preheat the oven to 350ºF (180ºC). Grease a 13-by-9-inch baking dish with coconut oil.
2. Combine the vanilla extract, maple syrup, and ½ cup of coconut oil in a large bowl. Stir to mix well.
3. Break the eggs in the bowl and whisk to combine well. Set aside.
4. Combine the coconut flour, baking powder, baking soda, nutmeg, cinnamon, and salt in a separate bowl. Stir to mix well.
5. Make a well in the center of the flour mixture, then pour the egg mixture into the well. Stir to combine well.
6. Add the pecans and carrots to the bowl and toss to mix well. Pour the mixture in the single layer on the baking dish.
7. Bake in the preheated oven for 45 minutes or until puffed and the cake spring back when lightly press with your fingers.
8. Remove the cake from the oven. Allow to cool for at least 15 minutes, then serve.

PER SERVING
Calories: 255, Fat: 21.2g, Total Carbohydrates: 12.8g, Protein: 5.1g, Fiber: 2.0g, Sodium: 202mg

Fresh Fruit Kebabs with Honey Labneh

Prep time: 5 minutes | Cook time: 8 minutes | Serves: 2

⅔ cup prepared labneh, or, if making your own, ⅔ cup full-fat plain Greek yogurt
2 tablespoons honey
1 teaspoon vanilla extract

Pinch salt
3 cups fresh fruit cut into 2-inch chunks (pineapple, cantaloupe, nectarines, strawberries, plums, or mango)

1. If making your own labneh, place a colander over a bowl and line it with cheesecloth. Place the Greek yogurt in the cheesecloth and wrap it up. Put the bowl in the refrigerator and let sit for at least 12 to 24 hours, until it's thick like soft cheese.
2. Mix honey, vanilla, and salt into labneh. Stir well to combine and set it aside.
3. Heat the grill to medium (about 300°F) and oil the grill grate. Alternatively, you can cook these on the stovetop in a heavy grill pan (cast iron works well).
4. Thread the fruit onto skewers and grill for 4 minutes on each side, or until fruit is softened and has grill marks on each side.
5. Serve the fruit with labneh to dip.

PER SERVING
Calories: 292, Total Fat: 6g, Total Carbohydrates: 60g, Protein: 5g, Fiber: 4g, Sugar: 56g, Sodium: 131mg

Orange Almond Cupcakes

Prep time: 10 minutes | Cook time: 15 minutes | Makes 6 cupcakes

1 large egg
2 tablespoons powdered sugar-free sweetener (such as honey or monk fruit extract)
½ cup extra-virgin olive oil
1 teaspoon almond

extract
Zest of 1 orange
1 cup almond flour
¾ teaspoon baking powder
⅛ teaspoon salt
1 tablespoon freshly squeezed orange juice

1. Preheat the oven to 350°F (180°C). Place muffin liners into 6 cups of a muffin tin.
2. In a large bowl, whisk together the egg and powdered sweetener. Add the olive oil, almond extract, and orange zest and whisk to combine well.

3. In a small bowl, whisk together the almond flour, baking powder, and salt. Add to wet ingredients along with the orange juice and stir until just combined.
4. Divide the batter evenly into 6 muffin cups and bake until a toothpick inserted in the center of the cupcake comes out clean, 15 to 18 minutes.
5. Remove from the oven and cool for 5 minutes in the tin before transferring to a wire rack to cool completely.

PER SERVING
Calories: 211, Total Fat: 22g, Total Carbs: 2g, Net Carbs: 2g, Fiber: 0g, Protein: 3g, Sodium: 105mg

Ricotta Pumpkin Cheesecake

Prep time: 10 minutes | Cook time: 40 minutes | Serves: 10 to 12

1 cup almond flour
½ cup butter, melted
1 (14½-ounce / 411-g) can pumpkin purée
8 ounces (227 g) cream cheese, at room temperature
½ cup whole-milk Ricotta cheese

½ to ¾ cup sugar-free sweetener
4 large eggs
2 teaspoons vanilla extract
2 teaspoons pumpkin pie spice
Whipped cream, for garnish (optional)

1. Preheat the oven to 350°F (180°C). Line the bottom of a 9-inch springform pan with parchment paper.
2. In a small bowl, combine the almond flour and melted butter with a fork until well combined. Using your fingers, press the mixture into the bottom of the prepared pan.
3. In a large bowl, beat together the pumpkin purée, cream cheese, ricotta, and sweetener using an electric mixer on medium.
4. Add the eggs, one at a time, beating after each addition. Stir in the vanilla and pumpkin pie spice until just combined.
5. Pour the mixture over the crust and bake until set, 40 to 45 minutes.
6. Allow to cool to room temperature. Refrigerate for at least 6 hours before serving.
7. Serve chilled, garnishing with whipped cream, if desired.

PER SERVING
Calories: 242, Total Fat: 22g, Total Carbs: 5g, Net Carbs: 4g, Fiber: 1g, Protein: 7g, Sodium: 178mg

Fast Orange Olive Oil Mug Cakes

Prep time: 10 minutes | Cook time: 2 minutes | Serves: 2

6 tablespoons flour
2 tablespoons sugar
½ teaspoon baking powder
Pinch salt
1 teaspoon orange zest
1 egg
2 tablespoons olive oil

2 tablespoons freshly squeezed orange juice
2 tablespoons milk
½ teaspoon orange extract
½ teaspoon vanilla extract

1. In a small bowl, combine the flour, sugar, baking powder, salt, and orange zest.
2. In a separate bowl, whisk together the egg, olive oil, orange juice, milk, orange extract, and vanilla extract.
3. Pour the dry ingredients into the wet ingredients and stir to combine. The batter will be thick.
4. Divide the mixture into two small mugs that hold at least 6 ounces each, or one 12-ounce mug.
5. Microwave each mug separately. The small ones should take about 60 seconds, and one large mug should take about 90 seconds, but microwaves can vary. The cake will be done when it pulls away from the sides of the mug.

PER SERVING
Calories: 302, Total Fat: 17g, Total Carbohydrates: 33g, Fiber: 1g, Sugar: 14g, Protein: 6g, Sodium: 117mg

Nutty and Fruity Dark Chocolate Bark

Prep time: 5 minutes | Cook time: 2 minutes | Serves: 2

2 tablespoons chopped nuts (almonds, pecans, walnuts, hazelnuts, pistachios, or any combination of those)
3 ounces (85 g) good-

quality dark chocolate chips (about ⅔ cup)
¼ cup chopped dried fruit (apricots, blueberries, figs, prunes, or any combination of those)

1. Line a sheet pan with parchment paper.
2. Place the nuts in a skillet over medium-high heat and toast them for 60 seconds, or just until they're fragrant.
3. Place the chocolate in a microwave-safe glass bowl or measuring cup and microwave on high

for 1 minute. Stir the chocolate and allow any unmelted chips to warm and melt. If necessary, heat for another 20 to 30 seconds, but keep a close eye on it to make sure it doesn't burn.
4. Pour the chocolate onto the sheet pan. Sprinkle the dried fruit and nuts over the chocolate evenly and gently pat in so they stick.
5. Transfer the sheet pan to the refrigerator for at least 1 hour to let the chocolate harden.
6. When solid, break into pieces. Store any leftover chocolate in the refrigerator or freezer.

PER SERVING
Calories: 284, Total Fat: 16g, Total Carbohydrates: 39g, Fiber: 2g, Sugar: 31g, Protein: 4g, Sodium: 2mg

Olive Oil Almond Cake

Prep time: 10 minutes | Cook time: 12 minutes | Serves: 4

Olive oil cooking spray
1½ cups whole wheat flour, plus more for dusting
3 eggs
⅓ cup honey
½ cup olive oil
½ cup unsweetened

almond milk
½ teaspoon vanilla extract
½ teaspoon almond extract
1 teaspoon baking powder
½ teaspoon salt

1. Preheat the air fryer to 380°F (193°C). Lightly coat the interior of an 8-by-8-inch baking dish with olive oil cooking spray and a dusting of whole wheat flour. Knock out any excess flour.
2. In a large bowl, beat the eggs and honey until smooth.
3. Slowly mix in the olive oil, then the almond milk, and finally the vanilla and almond extracts until combined.
4. In a separate bowl, whisk together the flour, baking powder, and salt.
5. Slowly incorporate the dry ingredients into the wet ingredients with a rubber spatula until combined, making sure to scrape down the sides of the bowl as you mix.
6. Pour the batter into the prepared pan and place it in the air fryer. Bake for 12 to 15 minutes, or until a toothpick inserted in the center comes out clean.

PER SERVING
Calories: 546, Total Fat: 32g, Saturated Fat: 5g, Total Carbohydrates: 58g, Protein: 12g, Fiber: 4g, Sugar: 24g

Dark Chocolate and Avocado Mousse

Prep time: 5 minutes | Cook time: 5 minutes | Serves: 4 to 6

8 ounces (227 g) dark chocolate (60% cocoa or higher), chopped
¼ cup unsweetened coconut milk
2 tablespoons coconut oil
2 ripe avocados, deseeded
¼ cup raw honey
Sea salt, to taste

1. Put the chocolate in a saucepan. Pour in the coconut milk and add the coconut oil.
2. Cook for 3 minutes or until the chocolate and coconut oil melt. Stir constantly.
3. Put the avocado in a food processor, then drizzle with honey and melted chocolate. Pulse to combine until smooth.
4. Pour the mixture in a serving bowl, then sprinkle with salt. Refrigerate to chill for 30 minutes and serve.

PER SERVING
Calories: 654, Fat: 46.8g, Total Carbohydrates: 55.9g, Protein: 7.2g, Fiber: 9.0g, Sodium: 112mg

Quick Marzipan Fat Bomb

Prep time: 5 minutes | Cook time: 0 minutes | Serves: 8

1½ cup finely ground almond flour
½ to 1 cup powdered sugar-free sweetener of choice
2 teaspoons almond extract
½ cup light fruity extra-virgin olive oil or avocado oil

1. Add the almond flour and sweetener to a food processor and run until the mixture is very finely ground.
2. Add the almond extract and pulse until combined. With the processor running, stream in olive oil until the mixture starts to form a large ball. Turn off the food processor.
3. Using your hands, form the marzipan into eight (1-inch) diameter balls, pressing to hold the mixture together. Store in an airtight container in the refrigerator for up to 2 weeks.

PER SERVING (1 fat bomb)
Calories: 157, Total Fat: 17g, Total Carbs: 0g, Net Carbs: 0g, Fiber: 0g, Protein: 2g, Sodium: 0mg

Banana Crepe

Prep time: 10 minutes | Cook time: 10 minutes | Serves: 6

2 medium-sized bananas, mashed
1¼ cup milk
2 eggs
1½ cups rolled oats
1½ teaspoons baking powder
1 teaspoon vanilla extract
2 teaspoons coconut oil
1 tablespoon honey
¼ teaspoon salt
Non-fat cooking spray

1. Combine the ingredients in a blender and pulse until a completely smooth batter. Grease the inner pot with cooking spray. Spread 1 spoon batter at the bottom.
2. Cook for 2 minutes, on Sauté mode, flip the crepe and cook for another minute. Repeat the process with the remaining batter. Serve immediately.

PER SERVING
Calories: 194, Fat: 8.2g, Carbohydrates: 30.88g, Protein: 9.1g, Sugar: 10.9g, Fiber: 4.7g, Sodium: 156mg

Blueberry, Pecan, and Oat Crisp

Prep time: 10 minutes | Cook time: 20 minutes | Serves: 4

2 tablespoons coconut oil, melted, plus more for greasing
4 cups fresh blueberries
Juice of ½ lemon
2 teaspoons lemon zest
¼ cup maple syrup
1 cup gluten-free rolled oats
½ cup chopped pecans
½ teaspoon ground cinnamon
Sea salt, to taste

1. Preheat the oven to 350°F (180°C). Grease a baking sheet with coconut oil.
2. Combine the blueberries, lemon juice and zest, and maple syrup in a bowl. Stir to mix well, then spread the mixture on the baking sheet.
3. Combine the remaining ingredients in a small bowl. Stir to mix well. Pour the mixture over the blueberries mixture.
4. Bake in the preheated oven for 20 minutes or until the oats are golden brown.
5. Serve immediately with spoons.

PER SERVING
Calories: 496, Fat: 32.9g, Total Carbohydrates: 50.8g, Protein: 5.1g, Fiber: 7.0g, Sodium: 41mg

Grilled Honey Pineapple and Melon

Prep time: 5 minutes | Cook time: 7 minutes | Serves: 4

8 fresh pineapple rings, rind removed
8 watermelon triangles, with rind

1 tablespoon honey
½ teaspoon freshly ground black pepper

1. Preheat an outdoor grill or a grill pan over high heat.
2. Drizzle the fruit slices with honey and sprinkle one side of each piece with pepper. Grill for 5 minutes, turn, and grill for another 2 minutes. Serve.

PER SERVING
Calories: 81, Fat: 0.12g, Carbohydrates: 21.17g, Protein: 0.6g, Sugar: 19.41g, Fiber: 1g, Sodium: 1mg

Cool Vanilla Apple Tart

Prep time: 10 minutes | Cook time: 20 minutes | Serves: 6

2 pounds (907 g) apples, cubed
¼ cup coconut sugar
¼ cup breadcrumbs
2 teaspoons cinnamon, ground
3 tablespoons freshly

squeezed lemon juice
1 teaspoon vanilla sugar
¼ tablespoons oil
1 egg, beaten
¼ cup all-purpose flour
Pie dough

1. Combine breadcrumbs, vanilla sugar, granulated sugar, apples, and cinnamon, in a bowl. On a lightly floured surface, roll out the pie dough making 2 circle-shaped crusts.
2. Grease a baking sheet with cooking spray, and place one pie crust in it.
3. Spoon the apple mixture on top, and cover with the remaining crust. Seal by crimping edges and brush with beaten egg. Pour 1 cup of water in the instant pot and lay the trivet. Lower the baking sheet on the trivet. Seal the lid, and cook on High Pressure for 20 minutes. Do a quick release and serve chilled.

PER SERVING
Calories: 331, Fat: 12.22g, Carbohydrates: 53.38g, Protein: 4.21g, Sugar: 20.81g, Fiber: 4.9g, Sodium: 208mg

Fresh Apricot Dessert

Prep time: 5 minutes | Cook time: 10 minutes | Serves: 8

2 pounds (907 g) fresh apricots, rinsed, drained
1 pound (454 g) sugar
2 tablespoons lemon zest

1 teaspoon ground nutmeg
10 cups water

1. Add apricots, sugar, water, nutmeg, and lemon zest. Cook, stirring occasionally, until half of the water evaporates, on Sauté. Press Cancel, and transfer the apricots and the remaining liquid into glass jars. Let cool and close the lids. Refrigerate overnight before use.

PER SERVING
Calories: 317, Fat: 0.2g, Carbohydrates: 81.32g, Protein: 0.63g, Sugar: 78.1g, Fiber: 1.9g, Sodium: 12mg

Cherry Marble Cake

Prep time: 10 minutes | Cook time: 20 minutes | Serves: 6

1 cup flour
1½ teaspoons baking powder
1 tablespoon powdered honey
½ teaspoon salt

1 teaspoon cherry extract
3 tablespoons butter, softened
3 eggs
¼ cup cocoa powder
¼ cup heavy cream

1. Combine all dry ingredients, except cocoa in a bowl. Mix well to combine and add eggs, one at the time. Beat well with a dough hook attachment for one minute. Add sour cream, butter, and cherry extract.
2. Continue to beat for 3 more minutes. Divide the mixture in half and add cocoa powder in one-half of the mixture. Pour the light batter into a greased baking dish. Drizzle with cocoa dough to create a nice marble pattern.
3. Pour in one cup of water and insert the trivet. Lower the baking dish on top. Seal the lid and cook for 20 minutes on High Pressure. Release the pressure naturally, for about 10 minutes. Let it cool for a while and transfer to a serving plate.

PER SERVING
Calories: 230, Fat: 13.11g, Carbohydrates: 22.2g, Protein: 7.46g, Sugar: 3.55g, Fiber: 1.7g, Sodium: 295mg

Banana Chocolate Squares

Prep time: 5 minutes | Cook time: 15 minutes | Serves: 6

½ cup butter
3 bananas
2 tablespoons cocoa

powder
1½ cups water
Cooking spray, to grease

1. Place the bananas and almond butter in a bowl and mash finely with a fork. Add the cocoa powder and stir until well combined. Grease a baking dish that fits into the pressure cooker.
2. Pour the banana and almond butter into the dish. Pour the water in the pressure cooker and lower the trivet. Place the baking dish on top of the trivet and seal the lid. Select Pressure Cook for 15 minutes at High pressure. When it goes off, do a quick release. Let cool for a few minutes before cutting into squares.

PER SERVING
Calories: 192, Fat: 15.81g, Carbohydrates: 15.55g, Protein: 1.13g, Sugar: 7.26g, Fiber: 2.1g, Sodium: 124mg

Vanilla and Walnut Chocolate Cake

Prep time: 5 minutes | Cook time: 10 minutes | Serves: 8

3 standard cake crusts
½ cup vanilla pudding powder
¼ cup granulated sugar

4 cups milk
1 (10½-ounce / 297.7-g) box chocolate chips
¼ cup walnuts, minced

1. Combine vanilla powder, sugar and milk in the inner pot. Cook until the pudding thickens, stirring constantly, on Sauté. Remove from the steel pot.
2. Place one crust onto a springform pan. Pour half of the pudding and sprinkle with minced walnuts and chocolate chips. Cover with another crust and repeat the process. Finish with the final crust and wrap in foil.
3. Insert the trivet, pour in 1 cup of water, and place springform pan on top. Seal the lid and cook for 10 minutes on High Pressure. Do a quick release. Refrigerate overnight.

PER SERVING
Calories: 605, Fat: 32.74g, Carbohydrates: 67.83g, Protein: 10.65g, Sugar: 20.83g, Fiber: 2.1g, Sodium: 671mg

Sweet Cinnamon Pumpkin Pudding

Prep time: 10 minutes | Cook time: 10 minutes | Serves: 4

1 pound (454 g) pumpkin, peeled and chopped into bite-sized pieces
1 cup coconut sugar
½ cup cornstarch

4 cups apple juice, unsweetened
1 teaspoon cinnamon, ground
3 to 4 cloves

1. In a bowl, combine sugar and apple juice until sugar dissolves completely.
2. Pour the mixture into the pot and stir in cornstarch, cinnamon, cloves, and pumpkin. Seal the lid, and cook for 10 minutes on High Pressure. Do a quick release. Pour in the pudding into 4 serving bowls. Let cool to room temperature and refrigerate overnight.

PER SERVING
Calories: 928, Fat: 55.97g, Carbohydrates: 85.52g, Protein: 34.3g, Sugar: 49.81g, Fiber: 8.4g, Sodium: 33mg

Rice Pudding in Rose Water

Prep time: 5 minutes | Cook time: 45 minutes | Serves: 6

1¼ cups long-grain rice
5 cups whole milk
1 cup maple syrup

1 tablespoon rose water or orange blossom water
1 teaspoon cinnamon

1. Rinse the rice under cold water for 30 seconds.
2. Put the rice, milk, and maple syrup in a large pot. Bring to a gentle boil while continually stirring.
3. Turn the heat down to low and let simmer for 40 to 45 minutes, stirring every 3 to 4 minutes so that the rice does not stick to the bottom of the pot.
4. Add the rose water at the end and simmer for 5 minutes.
5. Divide the pudding into 6 bowls. Sprinkle the top with cinnamon. Cool for at least 1 hour before serving. Store in the fridge.

PER SERVING
Calories: 394, Total Fat: 7g, Saturated Fat: 4g, Total Carbohydrates: 75g, Protein: 9g, Sugar: 43g, Fiber: 1g, Sodium: 102mg

Pressure Cooked Apples

Prep time: 5 minutes | Cook time: 3 minutes | Serves: 2

2 apples, peeled and cut into wedges
½ cup lemon juice
½ teaspoon cinnamon
1 tablespoon butter
1 cup water

1. Combine lemon juice and water in the pressure cooker. Place the apple wedges in the steaming basket and lower the basket into the cooker. Seal the lid, select the Pressure Cook for 3 minutes at High.
2. Release the pressure quickly. Open the lid and remove the steaming basket. Transfer the apple wedges to a bowl. Drizzle with almond butter and sprinkle with cinnamon.

PER SERVING
Calories: 161, Fat: 6.22g, Carbohydrates: 29.87g, Protein: 0.77g, Sugar: 20.47g, Fiber: 4.9g, Sodium: 51mg

Apple Crisp with Oat Topping

Prep time: 10 minutes | Cook time: 10 minutes | Serves: 5

For the Topping:
½ cup oat flour
½ cup old-fashioned rolled oats
½ cup coconut sugar
¼ cup olive oil
For the Filling:
5 apples, peeled, cored, and halved
2 tablespoons arrowroot powder
½ cup water
1 teaspoon ground cinnamon
¼ teaspoon ground nutmeg
½ teaspoon vanilla paste

1. In a bowl, combine sugar, oat flour, rolled oats, and olive oil to form coarse crumbs. Ladle the apples into the instant pot. Mix water with arrowroot powder in a bowl. Stir in salt, nutmeg, cinnamon, and vanilla.
2. Toss in the apples to coat. Apply oat topping to the apples. Seal the lid and cook on High Pressure for 10 minutes. Release the pressure naturally for 5 minutes, then release the remaining Pressure quickly.

PER SERVING
Calories: 309, Fat: 12.77g, Carbohydrates: 51.52g, Protein: 3.66g, Sugar: 28.98g, Fiber: 6.9g, Sodium: 5mg

Cream Cheese-Vanilla Bites

Prep time: 10 minutes | Cook time: 45 minutes | Makes 24 bites

1 (12-ounce / 340-g) box butter cake mix
½ cup butter, melted
3 large eggs, divided
1 cup maple syrup
1 (8-ounce / 227-g) cream cheese
1 teaspoon vanilla extract

1. Preheat the oven to 350°F (180°C).
2. To make the first layer, in a medium bowl, blend the cake mix, butter, and 1 egg. Then, pour the mixture into the prepared pan.
3. In a separate bowl, to make layer 2, mix together maple syrup, cream cheese, the remaining 2 eggs, and vanilla and pour this gently over the first layer. Bake for 45 to 50 minutes and allow to cool.
4. Cut the cake into 24 small squares.

PER SERVING
Calories: 160, Total Fat: 8g, Saturated Fat: 5g, Total Carbohydrates: 20g, Protein: 2g, Sugar: 15g, Fiber: 0g, Sodium: 156mg

Poached Pears in Red Wine

Prep time: 10 minutes | Cook time: 2 hours | Serves: 6

6 pears, peeled, cored, and halved
1 (750 ml) bottle red wine
1 cup granulated sugar
1 teaspoon vanilla
1 cinnamon stick
2 star anise
1 cup whipping cream
1 tablespoon confectioners' sugar

1. Place pear halves in the slow cooker.
2. Add the wine to the slow cooker.
3. Stir the sugar into the slow cooker, trying to keep the pear halves undisturbed.
4. Add the vanilla, cinnamon stick, and star anise to the slow cooker.
5. Cover and cook on low for 5 hours or on high for 2 hours.
6. About 10 minutes before the cooking time has elapsed, whip the cream with the confectioners' sugar.
7. Serve the pears warm in bowls with a dollop of sweetened whipped cream.

PER SERVING
Calories: 254, Fat: 2.6g, Carbohydrates: 35.9g, Protein: 1.05g, Sugar: 29.39g, Fiber: 1.8g, Sodium: 3mg

Summer Mix-Berries Granita

¼ cup coconut sugar
1 cup fresh strawberries
1 cup fresh raspberries

1 cup fresh blackberries
1 teaspoon freshly squeezed lemon juice

1. In a small saucepan, bring 1 cup water to a boil over high heat. Add the sugar and stir well until dissolved.
2. Remove the pan from the heat, add the berries and lemon juice, and cool to room temperature. Once cooled, place the fruit in a blender or food processor and blend on high until smooth.
3. Pour the puree into a shallow glass baking dish and place in the freezer for 1 hour. Stir with a fork and freeze for 30 minutes, then repeat.
4. To serve, use an ice cream scoop to portion the granita into dessert dishes.

PER SERVING
Calories: 153, Fat: 0.28g, Carbohydrates: 38.82g, Protein: 1.62g, Sugar: 33.35g, Fiber: 5g, Sodium: 4mg

Flourless Brownies with Balsamic Raspberry Sauce

For the Raspberry Sauce:
¼ cup good-quality balsamic vinegar
1 cup frozen raspberries
For the Brownie:
½ cup black beans with no added salt, rinsed
1 large egg
1 tablespoon olive oil

½ teaspoon vanilla extract
4 tablespoons unsweetened cocoa powder
¼ cup sugar
¼ teaspoon baking powder
Pinch salt
¼ cup dark chocolate chips

Make the Raspberry Sauce
1. Combine the balsamic vinegar and raspberries in a saucepan and bring the mixture to a boil. Reduce the heat to medium and let the sauce simmer for 15 minutes, or until reduced to ½ cup. If desired, strain the seeds and set the sauce aside until the brownie is ready.

Make the Brownie
1. Preheat the oven to 350°F (180°C) and set the rack to the middle position. Grease two 8-ounce ramekins and place them on a baking sheet.
2. In a food processor, combine the black beans, egg, olive oil, and vanilla. Purée the mixture for 1 to 2 minutes, or until it's smooth and the beans are completely broken down. Scrape down the sides of the bowl a few times to make sure everything is well-incorporated.
3. Add the cocoa powder, sugar, baking powder, and salt and purée again to combine the dry ingredients, scraping down the sides of the bowl as needed.
4. Stir the chocolate chips into the batter by hand. Reserve a few if you like, to sprinkle over the top of the brownies when they come out of the oven.
5. Pour the brownies into the prepared ramekins and bake for 15 minutes, or until firm. The center will look slightly undercooked. If you prefer a firmer brownie, leave it in the oven for another 5 minutes, or until a toothpick inserted in the middle comes out clean.
6. Remove the brownies from the oven. If desired, sprinkle any remaining chocolate chips over the top and let them melt into the warm brownies.
7. Let the brownies cool for a few minutes and top with warm raspberry sauce to serve.

PER SERVING
Calories: 510, Total Fat: 16g, Total Carbohydrates: 88g, Fiber: 14g, Sugar: 64g, Protein: 10g, Sodium: 124mg

Mascarpone and Fig Jam on Baguette

Prep time: 5 minutes | Cook time: 5 minutes | Serves: 6 to 8

1 long French baguette
4 tablespoons salted butter, melted
1 (8-ounce) tub Mascarpone cheese
1 (12-ounce / 340-g) jar fig jam or preserves

1. Preheat the oven to 350ºF (180ºC).
2. Slice the bread into ¼-inch-thick slices.
3. Arrange the sliced bread on a baking sheet and brush each slice with the melted butter.
4. Put the baking sheet in the oven and toast the bread for 5 to 7 minutes, just until golden brown.
5. Let the bread cool slightly. Spread about a teaspoon or so of the Mascarpone cheese on each piece of bread.
6. Top with a teaspoon or so of the jam. Serve immediately.

PER SERVING
Calories: 445, Total Fat: 24g, Saturated Fat: 12g, Total Carbohydrates: 48g, Protein: 3g, Sugar: 24g, Fiber: 5g, Sodium: 314mg

Chocolate Hummus with Caramel

Prep time: 10 minutes | Cook time: 1 minute | Serves: 2

For the Caramel
2 tablespoons coconut oil
1 tablespoon maple syrup
1 tablespoon almond butter
Pinch salt
For the Hummus
½ cup chickpeas, drained and rinsed
2 tablespoons unsweetened cocoa powder
1 tablespoon maple syrup, plus more to taste
2 tablespoons almond milk, or more as needed, to thin
Pinch salt
2 tablespoons pecans

Make the Caramel
1. To make the caramel, put the coconut oil in a small microwave-safe bowl. If it's solid, microwave it for about 15 seconds to melt it.
2. Stir in the maple syrup, almond butter, and salt.
3. Place the caramel in the refrigerator for 5 to 10 minutes to thicken.
Make the Hummus
1. In a food processor, combine the chickpeas, cocoa powder, maple syrup, almond milk, and pinch of salt, and process until smooth. Scrape down the sides to make sure everything is incorporated.
2. If the hummus seems too thick, add another tablespoon of almond milk.
3. Add the pecans and pulse 6 times to roughly chop them.
4. Transfer the hummus to a serving bowl and when the caramel is thickened, swirl it into the hummus. Gently fold it in, but don't mix it in completely.
5. Serve with fresh fruit or pretzels.

PER SERVING
Calories: 321, Total Fat: 22g, Total Carbohydrates: 30g, Protein: 7g, Fiber: 6g, Sugar: 15g, Sodium: 100mg

Apple Pockets Bake

Prep time: 10 minutes | Cook time: 15 minutes | Serves: 6

1 organic puff pastry, rolled out, at room temperature
1 Gala apple, peeled and sliced
¼ cup sugar
⅛ teaspoon ground cinnamon
⅛ teaspoon ground cardamom
Nonstick cooking spray
Honey, for topping

1. Preheat the oven to 350°F (180°C).
2. Cut the pastry dough into 4 even discs. Peel and slice the apple. In a small bowl, toss the slices with sugar, cinnamon, and cardamom.
3. Spray a muffin tin very well with nonstick cooking spray. Be sure to spray only the muffin holders you plan to use.
4. Once sprayed, line the bottom of the muffin tin with the dough and place 1 or 2 broken apple slices on top. Fold the remaining dough over the apple and drizzle with honey.
5. Bake for 15 minutes or until brown and bubbly.

PER SERVING
Calories: 250, Total Fat: 15g, Saturated Fat: 2g, Total Carbohydrates: 30g, Protein: 3g, Sugar: 9g, Fiber: 1g, Sodium: 98mg

Avocados Chocolate Pudding

Prep time: 10 minutes | Cook time: 0 minutes | Serves: 4

2 ripe avocados, halved and pitted
¼ cup unsweetened cocoa powder
¼ cup heavy whipping cream, plus more if needed
2 teaspoons vanilla extract
1 to 2 teaspoons liquid honey or monk fruit extract (optional)
½ teaspoon ground cinnamon (optional)
¼ teaspoon salt
Whipped cream, for serving (optional)

1. Using a spoon, scoop out the ripe avocado into a blender or large bowl, if using an immersion blender. Mash well with a fork.
2. Add the cocoa powder, heavy whipping cream, vanilla, sweetener (if using), cinnamon (if using), and salt. Blend well until smooth and creamy, adding additional cream, 1 tablespoon at a time, if the mixture is too thick.
3. Cover and refrigerate for at least 1 hour before serving. Serve chilled with additional whipped cream, if desired.

PER SERVING
Calories: 230, Total Fat: 22g, Total Carbs: 10g, Net Carbs: 4g, Fiber: 6g, Protein: 3g, Sodium: 163mg

Almond Butter Cookies

Prep time: 5 minutes | Cook time: 5 minutes | Serves: 4 to 6

½ cup sugar
8 tablespoons room temperature salted butter
1 large egg
1½ cups all-purpose flour
1 cup ground almonds or almond flour

1. Preheat the oven to 375°F (190°C).
2. Using a mixer, cream together the sugar and butter.
3. Add the egg and mix until combined.
4. Alternately add the flour and ground almonds, ½ cup at a time, while the mixer is on slow.
5. Once everything is combined, line a baking sheet with parchment paper. Drop a tablespoon of dough on the baking sheet, keeping the cookies at least 2 inches apart.
6. Put the baking sheet in the oven and bake just until the cookies start to turn brown around the edges, about 5 to 7 minutes.

PER SERVING
Calories: 604, Total Fat: 36g, Saturated Fat: 16g, Total Carbohydrates: 63g, Protein: 11g, Sugar: 26g, Fiber: 4g, Sodium: 181mg

Sesame Seeds Salted Buttery Cookies

Prep time: 5 minutes | Cook time: 5 minutes | Serves: 14 to 16

1 cup sesame seeds, hulled
1 cup maple syrup
8 tablespoons salted butter, softened
2 large eggs
1¼ cups flour

1. Preheat the oven to 350°F (180°C). Toast the sesame seeds on a baking sheet for 3 minutes. Set aside and let cool.
2. Using a mixer, cream together the maple syrup and butter.
3. Add the eggs one at a time until well-blended.
4. Add the flour and toasted sesame seeds and mix until well-blended.
5. Drop spoonfuls of cookie dough onto a baking sheet and form them into round balls, about 1-inch in diameter, similar to a walnut.
6. Put in the oven and bake for 5 to 7 minutes or until golden brown.
7. Let the cookies cool and enjoy.

PER SERVING
Calories: 218, Total Fat: 12g, Saturated Fat: 5g, Total Carbohydrates: 25g, Protein: 4g, Sugar: 14g, Fiber: 2g, Sodium: 58mg

Chapter 15 Sauce, Spices and Salad Dressing

Zhoug Sauce

Prep time: 10 minutes | Cook time: 1 minute | Makes ½ cup

6 tablespoons extra-virgin olive oil
½ teaspoon ground coriander
¼ teaspoon ground cumin
¼ teaspoon ground cardamom
¼ teaspoon salt

Pinch ground cloves
¾ cup fresh cilantro leaves
½ cup fresh parsley leaves
2 green Thai chiles, stemmed and chopped
2 garlic cloves, minced

1. Microwave oil, coriander, cumin, cardamom, salt, and cloves in covered bowl until fragrant, about 30 seconds, let cool to room temperature.
2. Pulse oil-spice mixture, cilantro, parsley, chiles, and garlic in food processor until coarse paste forms, about 15 pulses, scraping down sides of bowl as needed. (Green Zhoug can be refrigerated for up to 4 days.)

PER SERVING (½ cup)
Calories: 751, Fat: 81.81g, Carbohydrates: 6.97g, Protein: 1.91g, Sugar: 0.89g, Fiber: 2.6g, Sodium: 614mg

Pearl Onion Dip

Prep time: 10 minutes | Cook time: 12 minutes | Serves: 4

2 cups peeled pearl onions
3 garlic cloves
3 tablespoons olive oil, divided
½ teaspoon salt
1 cup nonfat plain Greek yogurt

1 tablespoon lemon juice
¼ teaspoon black pepper
⅛ teaspoon red pepper flakes
Pita chips, vegetables, or toasted bread for serving (optional)

1. Preheat the air fryer to 360°F (182°C).
2. In a large bowl, combine the pearl onions and garlic with 2 tablespoons of the olive oil until the onions are well coated.
3. Pour the garlic-and-onion mixture into the air fryer basket and roast for 12 minutes.

4. Transfer the garlic and onions to a food processor. Pulse the vegetables several times, until the onions are minced but still have some chunks.
5. In a large bowl, combine the garlic and onions and the remaining 1 tablespoon of olive oil, along with the salt, yogurt, lemon juice, black pepper, and red pepper flakes.
6. Cover and chill for 1 hour before serving with pita chips, vegetables, or toasted bread.

PER SERVING
Calories: 150, Fat: 10.1g, Total Carbohydrates: 7.8g, Protein: 7.2g, Fiber: 1.3g, Sodium: 3mg

Classic Tzatziki Sauce

Prep time: 10 minutes | Cook time: 0 minutes | Serves: 2

1 medium cucumber, peeled, seeded and diced
½ teaspoon salt, divided, plus more
½ cup plain, unsweetened, full-fat Greek yogurt
½ lemon, juiced

1 tablespoon chopped fresh parsley
½ teaspoon dried minced garlic
½ teaspoon dried dill
Freshly ground black pepper, to taste

1. Put the cucumber in a colander. Sprinkle with ¼ teaspoon of salt and toss. Let the cucumber rest at room temperature in the colander for 30 minutes.
2. Rinse the cucumber in cool water and place in a single layer on several layers of paper towels to remove the excess liquid.
3. In a food processer, pulse the cucumber to chop finely and drain off any extra fluid.
4. Pour the cucumber into a mixing bowl and add the yogurt, lemon juice, parsley, garlic, dill, and the remaining ¼ teaspoon of salt. Season with salt and pepper to taste and whisk the ingredients together. Refrigerate in an airtight container.

PER SERVING
Calories: 77, Fat: 2.9g, Total Carbohydrates: 6.2g, Protein: 6.1g, Fiber: 1.2g, Sodium: 607mg

Green Jalapeño Sauce

Prep time: 10 minutes | Cook time: 2 minutes | Serves: 4

4 ounces (113 g) green jalapeno peppers, chopped
1 green bell pepper, chopped
2 garlic cloves, crushed
½ cup white vinegar
1 tablespoon apple cider vinegar
1 teaspoon sea salt
4 tablespoons water

1. Add all ingredients to the instant pot. Seal the lid and cook on High Pressure for 2 minutes. When done, release the steam naturally, for about 5 minutes.
2. Transfer to a blender, pulse until combined and store in jars.

PER SERVING
Calories: 22, Fat: 0.13g, Carbohydrates: 3.72g, Protein: 0.58g, Sugar: 1.89g, Fiber: 1g, Sodium: 585mg

Romesco Sauce

Prep time: 10 minutes | Cook time: 0 minutes | Serves: 10

1 (12-ounce / 340-g) jar roasted red peppers, drained
1 (14½-ounce / 411-g) can diced tomatoes, undrained
½ cup dry-roasted almonds
2 garlic cloves
2 teaspoons red wine vinegar
1 teaspoon smoked paprika or ½ teaspoon cayenne pepper
¼ teaspoon kosher or sea salt
¼ teaspoon freshly ground black pepper
¼ cup extra-virgin olive oil
⅔ cup torn, day-old bread or toast
Assortment of sliced raw vegetables such as carrots, celery, cucumber, green beans, and bell peppers, for serving

1. In a high-powered blender or food processor, combine the roasted peppers, tomatoes and their juices, almonds, garlic, vinegar, smoked paprika, salt, and pepper.
2. Begin puréeing the ingredients on medium speed, and slowly drizzle in the oil with the blender running. Continue to purée until the dip is thoroughly mixed.
3. Add the bread and purée.
4. Serve with raw vegetables for dipping, or store in a jar with a lid for up to one week in the refrigerator.

PER SERVING
Calories: 96, Fat: 6.8g, Total Carbohydrates: 8.1g, Protein: 3.2g, Fiber: 3.2g, Sodium: 2mg

Spanakopita Dip

Prep time: 15 minutes | Cook time: 14 minutes | Serves: 2

Olive oil cooking spray
3 tablespoons olive oil, divided
2 tablespoons minced white onion
2 garlic cloves, minced
4 cups fresh spinach
4 ounces (113 g) cream cheese, softened
4 ounces (113 g) Feta cheese, divided
Zest of 1 lemon
¼ teaspoon ground nutmeg
1 teaspoon dried dill
½ teaspoon salt
Pita chips, carrot sticks, or sliced bread for serving (optional)

1. Preheat the air fryer to 360°F (182°C). Coat the inside of a 6-inch ramekin or baking dish with olive oil cooking spray.
2. In a large skillet over medium heat, heat 1 tablespoon of the olive oil. Add the onion, then cook for 1 minute.
3. Add in the garlic and cook, stirring for 1 minute more.
4. Reduce the heat to low and mix in the spinach and water. Let this cook for 2 to 3 minutes, or until the spinach has wilted. Remove the skillet from the heat.
5. In a medium bowl, combine the cream cheese, 2 ounces of the Feta, and the remaining 2 tablespoons of olive oil, along with the lemon zest, nutmeg, dill, and salt. Mix until just combined.
6. Add the vegetables to the cheese base and stir until combined.
7. Pour the dip mixture into the prepared ramekin and top with the remaining 2 ounces of Feta cheese.
8. Place the dip into the air fryer basket and cook for 10 minutes, or until heated through and bubbling.
9. Serve with pita chips, carrot sticks, or sliced bread.

PER SERVING
Calories: 550, Fat: 51.8g, Total Carbohydrates: 9.1g, Protein: 14.2g, Fiber: 2.3g, Sodium: 113mg

Rasel Hanout Spice Mix

Prep time: 10 minutes | Cook time: 2 minutes | Makes ½ cup

16 cardamom pods
4 teaspoons coriander seeds
4 teaspoons cumin seeds
2 teaspoons anise seeds
½ teaspoon allspice berries
¼ teaspoon black peppercorns
4 teaspoons ground ginger
2 teaspoons ground nutmeg
2 teaspoons ground dried Aleppo pepper
2 teaspoons ground cinnamon

1. Toast cardamom, coriander, cumin, anise, allspice, and peppercorns in small skillet over medium heat until fragrant, shaking skillet occasionally to prevent scorching, about 2 minutes. Let cool to room temperature.
2. Transfer toasted spices, ginger, nutmeg, Aleppo, and cinnamon to spice grinder and process to fine powder. (Ras el hanout can be stored at room temperature in airtight container for up to 1 year.)

PER SERVING (½ cup)
Calories: 216, Fat: 7.13g, Carbohydrates: 41.58g, Protein: 7.83g, Sugar: 5.32g, Fiber: 15.2g, Sodium: 30mg

Marinara Sauce

Prep time: 10 minutes | Cook time: 36 minutes | Makes 8 cups

1 small onion, diced
1 small red bell pepper, stemmed, seeded and chopped
2 tablespoons plus ¼ cup extra-virgin olive oil, divided
2 tablespoons butter
4 to 6 garlic cloves, minced
1 teaspoon salt, divided
½ teaspoon freshly
ground black pepper
2 (32-ounce / 907.2-g) cans crushed tomatoes (with basil, if possible), with their juices
½ cup thinly sliced basil leaves, divided
2 tablespoons chopped fresh rosemary
1 to 2 teaspoons crushed red pepper flakes (optional)

1. In a food processor, combine the onion and bell pepper and blend until very finely minced.
2. In a large skillet, heat 2 tablespoons olive oil and the butter over medium heat. Add the minced onion, and red pepper and sauté until just

starting to get tender, about 5 minutes.
3. Add the garlic, salt, and pepper and sauté until fragrant, another 1 to 2 minutes.
4. Reduce the heat to low and add the tomatoes and their juices, remaining ¼ cup olive oil, ¼ cup basil, rosemary, and red pepper flakes (if using). Stir to combine, then bring to a simmer and cover. Cook over low heat for 30 to 60 minutes to allow the flavors to blend.
5. Add remaining ¼ cup chopped fresh basil after removing from heat, stirring to combine.

PER SERVING (1 cup)
Calories: 265, Fat: 19.9g, Total Carbohydrates: 18.7g, Protein: 4.1g, Fiber: 5.1g, Sodium: 693mg

Dukkah Spice

Prep time: 10 minutes | Cook time: 40 minutes | Makes 2 cups

1 (15-ounce / 425-g) can chickpeas, rinsed
1 teaspoon extra-virgin olive oil
½ cup shelled pistachios, toasted
⅓ cup black sesame seeds, toasted
2½ tablespoons coriander seeds, toasted
1 tablespoon cumin seeds, toasted
2 teaspoons fennel seeds, toasted
1½ teaspoons pepper
1¼ teaspoons salt

1. Adjust oven rack to middle position and heat oven to 400°F (205°C). Pat chickpeas dry with paper towels and toss with oil. Spread chickpeas into single layer in rimmed baking sheet and roast until browned and crisp, 40 to 45 minutes, stirring every 5 to 10 minutes, let cool completely.
2. Process chickpeas in food processor until coarsely ground, about 10 seconds, transfer to medium bowl. Pulse pistachios and sesame seeds in now-empty food processor until coarsely ground, about 15 pulses, transfer to bowl with chickpeas. Process coriander, cumin, and fennel seeds in again-empty food processor until finely ground, 2 to 3 minutes, transfer to bowl with chickpeas. Add pepper and salt and whisk until mixture is well combined. (Dukkah can be refrigerated for up to 1 month.)

PER SERVING (1 cup)
Calories: 774, Fat: 52.58g, Carbohydrates: 60.84g, Protein: 27.86g, Sugar: 7.82g, Fiber: 26.4g, Sodium: 1799mg

Herbes de Provence Blend

Prep time: 5 minutes | Cook time: 0 minutes | Makes ½ cup

2 tablespoons dried thyme
2 tablespoons dried marjoram

2 tablespoons dried rosemary
2 teaspoons fennel seeds, toasted

1. Combine all ingredients in bowl. (Herbes de Provence can be stored at room temperature in airtight container for up to 1 year.)

PER SERVING (½ cup)
Calories: 32, Fat: 1.11g, Carbohydrates: 6.03g, Protein: 1.44g, Sugar: 0.14g, Fiber: 4.1g, Sodium: 7mg

Cilantro Yogurt Sauce

Prep time: 5 minutes | Cook time: 0 minutes | Makes 1 cup

1 cup plain yogurt
2 tablespoons minced fresh cilantro
2 tablespoons minced

fresh mint
1 garlic clove, minced
Salt and pepper, to taste

1. Whisk yogurt, cilantro, mint, and garlic together in bowl until combined. Season with salt and pepper to taste. Let sit until flavors meld, about 30 minutes. (Sauce can be refrigerated for up to 2 days.)

PER SERVING (1 cup)
Calories: 165, Fat: 8.15g, Carbohydrates: 14.91g, Protein: 9.35g, Sugar: 11.48g, Fiber: 1.5g, Sodium: 118mg

Fresh Herb Butter

Prep time: 5 minutes | Cook time: 0 minutes | Makes ½ cup

½ cup butter, at room temperature
1 garlic clove, finely minced
2 teaspoons finely

chopped fresh rosemary
1 teaspoon finely chopped fresh oregano
½ teaspoon salt

1. In a food processor, combine the butter, garlic, rosemary, oregano, and salt and pulse until the mixture is well combined, smooth, and creamy, scraping down the sides as necessary. Alternatively, you can whip the ingredients together with an electric mixer.

2. Using a spatula, scrape the butter mixture into a small bowl or glass container and cover. Store in the refrigerator for up to 1 month.

PER SERVING (1 tablespoons)
Calories: 103, Fat: 12.4g, Total Carbohydrates: 0g, Protein: 0g, Fiber: 0g, Sodium: 227mg

Tahini-Greek Yogurt Sauce

Prep time: 5 minutes | Cook time: 0 minutes | Makes 1 cup

⅓ cup tahini
⅓ cup plain Greek yogurt
¼ cup water
3 tablespoons lemon

juice
1 garlic clove, minced
Salt and pepper, to taste

1. Whisk tahini, yogurt, water, lemon juice, garlic, and ¾ teaspoon salt together in bowl until combined. Season with salt and pepper to taste. Let sit until flavors meld, about 30 minutes. (Sauce can be refrigerated for up to 4 days.)

PER SERVING (1 cup)
Calories: 1492, Fat: 129.49g, Carbohydrates: 61.3g, Protein: 47.02g, Sugar: 7.22g, Fiber: 23.4g, Sodium: 470mg

Minty Lemon-Yogurt Sauce

Prep time: 5 minutes | Cook time: 0 minutes | Makes 1 cup

1 cup plain yogurt
1 tablespoon minced fresh mint
1 teaspoon grated lemon

zest plus 2 tablespoons juice
1 garlic clove, minced
Salt and pepper, to taste

1. Whisk yogurt, mint, lemon zest and juice, and garlic together in bowl until combined. Season with salt and pepper to taste. Let sit until flavors meld, about 30 minutes. (Sauce can be refrigerated for up to 2 days.)

PER SERVING (1 cup)
Calories: 163, Fat: 8.11g, Carbohydrates: 14.71g, Protein: 9.14g, Sugar: 11.59g, Fiber: 1g, Sodium: 115mg

Basic Tahini Sauce

Prep time: 5 minutes | Cook time: 0 minutes | Makes 1¼ cups

½ cup tahini
½ cup water
¼ cup lemon juice

2 garlic cloves, minced
Salt and pepper, to taste

1. Whisk tahini, water, lemon juice, and garlic together in bowl until combined. Season with salt and pepper to taste. Let sit until flavors meld, about 30 minutes. (Sauce can be refrigerated for up to 4 days.)

PER SERVING (¼ cup)
Calories: 151, Fat: 12.97g, Carbohydrates: 7.22g, Protein: 4.33g, Sugar: 1.08g, Fiber: 2.5g, Sodium: 63mg

Simple Lemon-Tahini Dressing

Prep time: 5 minutes | Cook time: 0 minutes | Serves: 8 to 10

½ cup tahini
¼ cup freshly squeezed lemon juice
¼ cup extra-virgin olive oil

1 garlic clove, finely minced or ½ teaspoon garlic powder
2 teaspoons salt

1. In a glass mason jar with a lid, combine the tahini, lemon juice, olive oil, garlic, and salt. Cover and shake well until combined and creamy. Store in the refrigerator for up to 2 weeks.

PER SERVING (2 tablespoons)
Calories: 121, Fat: 12.1g, Total Carbohydrates: 3.1g, Protein: 2.4, Fiber: 1.2g, Sodium: 479mg

Cucumber-Dill Yogurt Sauce

Prep time: 10 minutes | Cook time: 0 minutes | Makes 2½ cups

1 cup plain Greek yogurt
2 tablespoons extra-virgin olive oil
2 tablespoons minced fresh dill

1 garlic clove, minced
1 cucumber, peeled, halved lengthwise, seeded, and shredded
Salt and pepper, to taste

1. Whisk yogurt, oil, dill, and garlic together in medium bowl until combined. Stir in cucumber and season with salt and pepper to taste. (Sauce can be refrigerated for up to 1 day.)

PER SERVING (½ cup)
Calories: 97, Fat: 7.46g, Carbohydrates: 6.42g, Protein: 2.6g, Sugar: 3.3g, Fiber: 1g, Sodium: 25mg

Basic Vinaigrette

Prep time: 5 minutes | Cook time: 0 minutes | Makes ¼ cup

1 tablespoon wine vinegar
1½ teaspoons minced shallot
½ teaspoon low fat yogurt
½ teaspoon Dijon

mustard
⅛ teaspoon salt
Pinch pepper
3 tablespoons extra-virgin olive oil

1. Whisk vinegar, shallot, low fat yogurt, mustard, salt, and pepper together in bowl until smooth. Whisking constantly, slowly drizzle in oil until emulsified. (Vinaigrette can be refrigerated for up to 2 weeks.)

PER SERVING (¼ cup)
Calories: 384, Fat: 40.72g, Carbohydrates: 5.03g, Protein: 1.2g, Sugar: 2.69g, Fiber: 0.9g, Sodium: 345mg

Lemony Vinaigrette

Prep time: 10 minutes | Cook time: 0 minutes | Makes ¼ cup

¼ teaspoon grated lemon zest
1 tablespoon juice
½ teaspoon low fat yogurt
½ teaspoon Dijon mustard

⅛ teaspoon salt
Pinch pepper
Pinch sugar
3 tablespoons extra-virgin olive oil

1. Whisk lemon zest and juice, low fat yogurt, mustard, salt, pepper, and sugar together in bowl until smooth. Whisking constantly, slowly drizzle in oil until emulsified. (Vinaigrette can be refrigerated for up to 2 weeks.)

PER SERVING (¼ cup)
Calories: 385, Fat: 40.72g, Carbohydrates: 6.33g, Protein: 0.5g, Sugar: 4.4g, Fiber: 0.7g, Sodium: 342mg

Za'atar Spice

Prep time: 5 minutes | Cook time: 0 minutes | Makes ½ cup

½ cup dried thyme, ground
2 tablespoons sesame seeds, toasted
1½ tablespoons ground sumac

1. Combine all ingredients in bowl. (Za'atar can be stored at room temperature in airtight container for up to 1 year.)

PER SERVING (½ cup)
Calories: 175, Fat: 13.93g, Carbohydrates: 11.75g, Protein: 4.95g, Sugar: 0.39g, Fiber: 6.7g, Sodium: 11mg

Red Wine Vinaigrette

Prep time: 10 minutes | Cook time: 0 minutes | Serves: 2

¼ cup plus 2 tablespoons extra-virgin olive oil
2 tablespoons red wine vinegar
1 tablespoon apple cider vinegar
2 teaspoons honey
2 teaspoons Dijon mustard
½ teaspoon minced garlic
⅛ teaspoon kosher salt
⅛ teaspoon freshly ground black pepper

1. In a jar, combine the olive oil, vinegars, honey, mustard, garlic, salt, and pepper and shake well.

PER SERVING
Calories: 386, Fat: 40.8g, Total Carbohydrates: 5.8g, Protein: 0.9g, Fiber: 0g, Sodium: 198mg

Dijon Balsamic Vinaigrette

Prep time: 10 minutes | Cook time: 0 minutes | Makes ¼ cup

1 tablespoon balsamic vinegar
2 teaspoons Dijon mustard
1½ teaspoons minced shallot
½ teaspoon low fat yogurt
½ teaspoon minced fresh thyme
⅛ teaspoon salt
Pinch pepper
3 tablespoons extra-virgin olive oil

1. Whisk vinegar, mustard, shallot, low fat yogurt, thyme, salt, and pepper together in bowl until smooth. Whisking constantly, slowly drizzle in oil until emulsified. (Vinaigrette can be refrigerated for up to 2 weeks.)

PER SERVING (¼ cup)
Calories: 388, Fat: 40.96g, Carbohydrates: 5.46g, Protein: 0.91g, Sugar: 2.87g, Fiber: 1.1g, Sodium: 428mg

Tahini-Lemon Salad Dressing

Prep time: 10 minutes | Cook time: 0 minutes | Makes ½ cup

2½ tablespoons lemon juice
2 tablespoons tahini
1 tablespoon water
1 garlic clove, minced
½ teaspoon salt
⅛ teaspoon pepper
¼ cup extra-virgin olive oil

1. Whisk lemon juice, tahini, water, garlic, salt, and pepper together in bowl until smooth. Whisking constantly, slowly drizzle in oil until emulsified. (Dressing can be refrigerated for up to 1 week.)

PER SERVING (½ cup)
Calories: 670, Fat: 70.25g, Carbohydrates: 10.23g, Protein: 5.47g, Sugar: 1.14g, Fiber: 3.1g, Sodium: 1200mg

Walnut Oil Vinaigrette

Prep time: 10 minutes | Cook time: 0 minutes | Makes ¼ cup

1 tablespoon wine vinegar
1½ teaspoons minced shallot
½ teaspoon low fat yogurt
½ teaspoon Dijon mustard
⅛ teaspoon salt
Pinch pepper
1½ tablespoons roasted walnut oil
1½ tablespoons extra-virgin olive oil

1. Whisk vinegar, shallot, low fat yogurt, mustard, salt, and pepper together in bowl until smooth. Whisking constantly, slowly drizzle in oils until emulsified. (Vinaigrette can be refrigerated for up to 2 weeks.)

PER SERVING (¼ cup)
Calories: 373, Fat: 40.9g, Carbohydrates: 2.24g, Protein: 0.54g, Sugar: 0.41g, Fiber: 0.8g, Sodium: 342mg

Apple Cider Dressing

2 tablespoons apple cider vinegar	Salt, to taste
1/3 lemon, juiced	Freshly ground black pepper, to taste
1/3 lemon, zested	

1. In a jar, combine the vinegar, lemon juice, and zest. Season with salt and pepper, cover, and shake well.

PER SERVING
Calories: 2, Fat: 0g, Total Carbohydrates: 0.8g, Protein: 0.4g, Fiber: 0.4g, Sodium: 1mg

Herb Olive Oil

1/2 cup extra-virgin olive oil	rosemary leaves
1 teaspoon dried basil	2 teaspoons dried oregano
1 teaspoon dried parsley	1/8 teaspoon salt
1 teaspoon fresh	

1. Pour the oil into a small bowl and stir in the basil, parsley, rosemary, oregano, and salt while whisking the oil with a fork.

PER SERVING
Calories: 486, Fat: 53.8g, Total Carbohydrates: 2.3g, Protein: 1.2g, Fiber: 1.4g, Sodium: 78mg

Oregano Cucumber Dressing

1 1/2 cups plain, unsweetened, full-fat Greek yogurt	1 tablespoon dried, minced garlic
1 cucumber, seeded and peeled	1/2 tablespoon dried dill
1/2 lemon, juiced and zested	2 teaspoons dried oregano
	Salt, to taste

1. In a food processor, combine the yogurt, cucumber, lemon juice, garlic, dill, oregano, and a pinch of salt and process until smooth. Adjust the seasonings as needed and transfer to a serving bowl.

PER SERVING
Calories: 209, Fat: 10.3g, Total Carbohydrates: 14.1g, Protein: 17.8g, Fiber: 2.2g, Sodium: 69mg

Apple Cider Yogurt Dressing

1 cup plain, unsweetened, full-fat Greek yogurt	1 tablespoon chopped fresh oregano
1/2 cup extra-virgin olive oil	1/2 teaspoon dried parsley
	1/2 teaspoon kosher salt
1 tablespoon apple cider vinegar	1/4 teaspoon garlic powder
1/2 lemon, juiced	1/4 teaspoon freshly ground black pepper

1. In a large bowl, combine the yogurt, olive oil, vinegar, lemon juice, oregano, parsley, salt, garlic powder, and pepper and whisk well.

PER SERVING
Calories: 402, Fat: 40.4g, Total Carbohydrates: 3.8g, Protein: 7.9g, Fiber: 0.8g, Sodium: 417mg

Herby Vinaigrette

1 tablespoon wine vinegar	marjoram, or oregano
1 tablespoon minced fresh parsley or chives	1/2 teaspoon low fat yogurt
1 1/2 teaspoons minced shallot	1/2 teaspoon Dijon mustard
1/2 teaspoon minced fresh thyme, tarragon,	1/8 teaspoon salt
	Pinch pepper
	3 tablespoons extra-virgin olive oil

1. Whisk vinegar, parsley, shallot, thyme, low fat yogurt, mustard, salt, and pepper together in bowl until smooth. Whisking constantly, slowly drizzle in oil until emulsified.
2. Serve this vinaigrette immediately.

PER SERVING (1/4 cup)
Calories: 373, Fat: 40.73g, Carbohydrates: 2.47g, Protein: 0.66g, Sugar: 0.47g, Fiber: 0.9g, Sodium: 342mg

Harissa Paste

Prep time: 10 minutes | Cook time: 0 minutes | Makes ½ cup

6 tablespoons extra-virgin olive oil
6 garlic cloves, minced
2 tablespoons paprika
1 tablespoon ground coriander
1 tablespoon ground dried Aleppo pepper
1 teaspoon ground cumin
¾ teaspoon caraway seeds
½ teaspoon salt

1. Combine all ingredients in bowl and microwave until bubbling and very fragrant, about 1 minute, stirring halfway through microwaving, let cool to room temperature. (Harissa can be refrigerated for up to 4 days.)

PER SERVING (½ cup)
Calories: 813, Fat: 83.64g, Carbohydrates: 19.31g, Protein: 4.68g, Sugar: 3.95g, Fiber: 6.7g, Sodium: 1184mg

Napoli Sauce

Prep time: 10 minutes | Cook time: 30 minutes | Serves: 4

1 pound (454 g) mushrooms
2 cups canned tomatoes, diced
1 carrot, chopped
1 onion, chopped
1 celery stick, chopped
1 tablespoon olive oil
1 teaspoon salt
½ teaspoon paprika
1 teaspoon fish sauce
1 cup water

1. Heat olive oil on Sauté. Stir-fry carrot, onion, celery, and paprika, for 5 minutes. Add all remaining ingredients, except for the tomatoes, and cook for 5-6 more minutes, until the meat is slightly browned. Seal the lid.
2. Cook on High Pressure for 20 minutes. When done, release the steam naturally, for about 10 minutes. Hit Sauté, and cook for 7-8 minutes, to thicken the sauce.

PER SERVING
Calories: 402, Fat: 4.79g, Carbohydrates: 93.36g, Protein: 12.26g, Sugar: 6.78g, Fiber: 15.3g, Sodium: 751mg

Orange Garlic Dressing

Prep time: 10 minutes | Cook time: 0 minutes | Serves: 2

¼ cup extra-virgin olive oil
2 tablespoons freshly squeezed orange juice
1 orange, zested
1 teaspoon garlic powder
¾ teaspoon za'atar
seasoning
½ teaspoon salt
¼ teaspoon Dijon mustard
Freshly ground black pepper, to taste

1. In a jar, combine the olive oil, orange juice and zest, garlic powder, za'atar, salt, and mustard. Season with pepper and shake vigorously until completely mixed.

PER SERVING
Calories: 283, Fat: 27.2g, Total Carbohydrates: 11.1g, Protein: 0.9g, Fiber: 2.2g, Sodium: 597mg

Garlicky Rosemary Infused Olive Oil

Prep time: 5 minutes | Cook time: 30 minutes | Makes 1 cup

1 cup extra-virgin olive oil
4 large garlic cloves, smashed
4 (4- to 5-inch) sprigs rosemary

1. In a medium skillet, heat the olive oil, garlic, and rosemary sprigs over low heat. Cook until fragrant and garlic is very tender, 30 to 45 minutes, stirring occasionally. Don't let the oil get too hot or the garlic will burn and become bitter.
2. Remove from the heat and allow to cool slightly. Remove the garlic and rosemary with a slotted spoon and pour the oil into a glass container. Allow to cool completely before covering. Store covered at room temperature for up to 3 months.

PER SERVING (2 tablespoons)
Calories: 241, Fat: 26.8g, Total Carbohydrates: 1.1g, Protein: 0g, Fiber: 0g, Sodium: 1mg

Creamy Lemon Yogurt Dressing

Prep time: 5 minutes | Cook time: 0 minutes | Serves: 2

1 cup plain, unsweetened, full-fat Greek yogurt
1 large lemon, zested and juiced
½ teaspoon dried oregano
½ teaspoon dried parsley
1½ teaspoons garlic salt
Freshly ground black pepper, to taste

1. In a medium bowl, whisk the yogurt, lemon juice and zest, oregano, parsley, and garlic salt. Season with pepper. Pour over the salad of your choice.

PER SERVING
Calories: 133, Fat: 5.8g, Total Carbohydrates: 10.3g, Protein: 11.2g, Fiber: 1.2g, Sodium: 193mg

Aïoli

Prep time: 10 minutes | Cook time: 0 minutes | Makes 1¼ cups

2 large egg yolks
2 teaspoons Dijon mustard
2 teaspoons lemon juice
1 garlic clove, minced
¾ cup vegetable oil
1 tablespoon water
Salt and pepper, to taste
¼ cup extra-virgin olive oil

1. Process egg yolks, mustard, lemon juice, and garlic in food processor until combined, about 10 seconds. With processor running, slowly drizzle in vegetable oil, about 1 minute. Transfer mixture to medium bowl and whisk in water, ½ teaspoon salt, and ¼ teaspoon pepper. Whisking constantly, slowly drizzle in olive oil until emulsified. (Aïoli can be refrigerated for up to 4 days.)

PER SERVING (¼ cup)
Calories: 403, Fat: 45.39g, Carbohydrates: 0.99g, Protein: 1.25g, Sugar: 0.12g, Fiber: 0.2g, Sodium: 26mg

Appendix 1 Measurement Conversion Chart

Volume Equivalents (Dry)

US STANDARD	METRIC (APPROXIMATE)
1/8 teaspoon	0.5 mL
1/4 teaspoon	1 mL
1/2 teaspoon	2 mL
3/4 teaspoon	4 mL
1 teaspoon	5 mL
1 tablespoon	15 mL
1/4 cup	59 mL
1/2 cup	118 mL
3/4 cup	177 mL
1 cup	235 mL
2 cups	475 mL
3 cups	700 mL
4 cups	1 L

Temperatures Equivalents

FAHRENHEIT (F)	CELSIUS(C) (APPROXIMATE)
225 °F	107 °C
250 °F	120 °C
275 °F	135 °C
300 °F	150 °C
325 °F	160 °C
350 °F	180 °C
375 °F	190 °C
400 °F	205 °C
425 °F	220 °C
450 °F	235 °C
475 °F	245 °C
500 °F	260 °C

Volume Equivalents (Liquid)

US STANDARD	US STANDARD (OUNCES)	METRIC (APPROXIMATE)
2 tablespoons	1 fl.oz.	30 mL
1/4 cup	2 fl.oz.	60 mL
1/2 cup	4 fl.oz.	120 mL
1 cup	8 fl.oz.	240 mL
1 1/2 cup	12 fl.oz.	355 mL
2 cups or 1 pint	16 fl.oz.	475 mL
4 cups or 1 quart	32 fl.oz.	1 L
1 gallon	128 fl.oz.	4 L

Weight Equivalents

US STANDARD	METRIC (APPROXIMATE)
1 ounce	28 g
2 ounces	57 g
5 ounces	142 g
10 ounces	284 g
15 ounces	425 g
16 ounces (1 pound)	455 g
1.5 pounds	680 g
2 pounds	907 g

Appendix 2: Recipes Index

References and Citations:

1. Laure Schnabel, MD, MSc; Emmanuelle Kesse-Guyot, PhD; Benjamin Allès, PhD. Association Between Ultra Processed Food Consumption and Risk of Mortality Among Middle-aged Adults in France. February 11, 2019; JAMA Intern Med. 2016;176(8):1124-1132. doi:10.1001/jamainternmed.2016.2410

2. Centers for Disease Control and Prevention. Underlying Cause of Death, 1999–2018. CDC WONDER Online Database. Atlanta, GA: Centers for Disease Control and Prevention; 2018. Accessed March 12, 2020.

Available online: https://www.cdc.gov/heartdisease/facts.htm

3. Georgoulis M, Kontogianni MD, Yiannakouris N. Mediterranean Diet and Diabetes: Prevention and Treatment. Nutrients. 2014; 6(4):1406-1423.

Available online: https://doi.org/10.3390/nu6041406

Printed in Great Britain
by Amazon